ORDER AND CONFLICT
IN CONTEMPORARY
CAPITALISM

Edited by
JOHN H. GOLDTHORPE

Sponsored by the Joint Committee on Western
Europe of the American Council of Learned Societies and the Social Science Research Council

CLARENDON PRESS · OXFORD

Oxford University Press, Walton Street, Oxford OX2 6DP
Oxford New York Toronto
Delhi Bombay Calcutta Madras Karachi
Petaling Jaya Singapore Hong Kong Tokyo
Nairobi Dar es Salaam Cape Town
Melbourne Auckland
and associated companies in
Berlin Ibadan

Oxford is a trade mark of Oxford University Press

Published in the United States
by Oxford University Press, New York

First published 1984 in hardback and paperback
Paperback reprinted 1985, 1988

British Library Cataloguing in Publication Data
Order and conflict in contemporary capitalism.
1. Europe—Economic policy 2. Europe—Politics
and government—1945– I. Goldthorpe, John H.
330.94   HC240
ISBN 0–19–878007–9

Library of Congress Cataloging in Publication Data
Order and conflict in contemporary capitalism.
Bibliography: p.
Includes index.
1. Europe—Economic conditions—1945– —Congresses.
2. Europe—Politics and government—1945– —Congresses.
3. Corporate state—Europe—Congresses. 4. Industrial
relations—Europe—Congresses. I. Goldthorpe, John H.
HC240.0'675 1984   330.94'055   84–19081
ISBN 0–19–878007–9

Printed in Great Britain by
Billing & Sons Ltd
Worcester

Contents

Contributors

RUNE ÅBERG
> Professor of Sociology, University of Umeå, Sweden

DAVID R. CAMERON
> Associate Professor of Political Science, Yale University, USA.

GÖSTA ESPING-ANDERSEN
> Associate Professor of Sociology, Harvard University,
> Cambridge, Mass., USA.

JOHN H. GOLDTHORPE
> Official Fellow, Nuffield College, Oxford, UK.

ROBERT O. KEOHANE
> Professor of Politics, Brandeis University, Waltham, Mass., USA

WALTER KORPI
> Professor of Social Policy, Swedish Institute for Social Research
> and Department of Sociology, University of Stockholm, Sweden

PETER LANGE
> Associate Professor of Political Science, Duke University,
> Durham, North Carolina, USA.

GERHARD LEHMBRUCH
> Professor of Political Science, University of Konstanz,
> West Germany

CHARLES S. MAIER
> Professor of History, Harvard University, Cambridge,
> Mass., USA.

MARINO REGINI
> Associate Professor of Sociology, University of Milan, Italy

FRITZ W. SCHARPF
> Professor and Research Fellow, International Institute of
> Management, Wissenschaftszentrum, Berlin

KERRY SCHOTT

Lecturer in Economics, Department of Political Economy, University College London, UK.

DON S. SCHWERIN

Comptroller, Schwerin Farms Inc. and Schwerin Concaves Inc., Walla Walla, Washington, USA.

WOLFGANG STREECK

Research Fellow, International Institute of Management, Wissenschaftszentrum, Berlin

Preface

The papers presented in this collection are the work of a study group established under the auspices of the Joint Committee on Western Europe of the Social Science Research Council and The American Council of Learned Societies. With the support of the Social Science Research Council, members of the study group were able to meet on two occasions: first, at Nuffield College, Oxford, in January 1982, and secondly at the Studienhaus Wiesneck, Buchenbach bei Freiburg, in May 1983. I would like to record the gratitude felt by all members of the group to the Social Science Research Council for making these seminars possible, and in particular to the Staff Associates who were directly responsible for their organization—in both cases, it should be said, under the most adverse meteorological conditions. Robert A. Gates encouraged us through temperatures of −20° centigrade at Oxford; and Sophie Sa through five days of continuous rain and the attendant hazards of floods and landslides in the Black Forest.

I would also like to add my personal thanks to Dr Gates for his enthusiasm and support when the idea of the study group was first mooted; to the successive chairmen of the Joint Committee, Charles Maier and Philippe Schmitter, for their most helpful cooperation; and to Nikiforos Diamandouros of the Social Science Research Council for his unfailing assistance over the last six months with the flow of miscellaneous problems which inevitably accompanies the editing of a collection of this kind. I have also been sustained in my editorial duties by my family, by my secretary, Audrey Skeats, and by Monica Dowley, who undertook with great efficiency the daunting task of compiling the Bibliography.

J. H. G.

Abbreviations used in text

AFL-CIO	American Federation of Labour-Congress of Industrial Organisations
ASVG	Allgemeine Sozialversicherungsgesetz
	(the Austrian social insurance law)
BDA	Bundesvereinigung der Deutschen Arbeitgeberverbände
	(the Central Federation of West German Employers' Associations)
BIS	Bank for International Settlements
CDU	Christlich Demokratische Union
	(the West German Christian Democratic Party)
CGIL	Confederazione Generale Italiana del Lavoro
	(the Italian Trade Union Confederation, with close links with the
	Communist Party)
CGT	Confédération Générale du Travail
	(the French Trade Union Confederation, with close links with the
	Communist Party)
CISL	Confederazione Italiana Sindacati Lavoratori
	(the Italian Trade Union Confederation, with links with the
	Christian Democratic Party)
CSU	Christlich-Soziale Union
	(the Bavarian Christian Democratic Party—a sister-party to the CDU)
DAG	Deutsche Angestelltengewerkschaft
	(the West German Salaried Employees Union)
DB	Deutscher Beamtenbund
	(the West German Association of Civil Service Officials)
DGB	Deutscher Gerwerkschaftsbund
	(the West German Trade Union Confederation)
DIW	Deutsches Institut für Wirtschaftsforschung
	(the West German Institute for Economic Research)
DM	Deutsche Mark
EEC	The European Economic Community
FDP	Freie Demokratische Partei
	(the West German Free Democratic Party)
GATT	General Agreement on Tariffs and Trade
GDP	Gross Domestic Product
GNP	Gross National Product
IEA	International Energy Agency
LDC	Less developed country
LO	Landsorganisasjonen i Norge
	(the Norwegian Trade Union Confederation) or
	Landsorganisationen i Sverige
	(the Swedish Trade Union Confederation)

NAF	Norsk Arbeidsgiverforening (the Norwegian Employers Association)
NIC	Newly industrialized country
NOU	Norges Offentlige Utredninger (Norwegian governmental reports)
OECD	Organisation for Economic Cooperation and Development
ÖGB	Österreichischer Gewerkschaftsbund (the Austrian Trade Union Confederation)
OPEC	Organisation of Petroleum Exporting Countries
ÖVP	Österreichische Volkspartei (the Austrian Peoples Party)
PCF	Parti Communiste Français (the French Communist Party)
PCI	Partito Comunista Italiano (the Italian Communist Party)
SACO	Sveriges Akademikers Centralorganisation (the Swedish Confederation of Professional Associations)
SAF	Svenska Arbetsgivareföreningen (the Swedish Employers Association)
SAP	Socialdemokratiska Arbetarepartiet (the Swedish Social Democratic Party)
SOU	Statens Offentliga Utredningar (Swedish governmental reports)
SPD	Sozialdemokratische Partei Deutschlands (the West German Social Democratic Party)
SPÖ	Sozialistische Partei Österreichs (the Austrian Socialist Party)
TCO	Tjänstemännens Centralorganisationen (the Swedish Salaried Employees Confederation)
TUC	Trades Union Congress
VVD	Volkspartij voor Vrijheid en Democratie (the Dutch Peoples Party for Freedom and Democracy)
WIFO	Österreichisches Institut für Wirtschaftsforschung (the Austrian Institute for Economic Research)

Note: Billion is used throughout this book to mean a thousand millions and not a million millions, as was the old European usage.

Introduction

JOHN H. GOLDTHORPE

It is no accident that over the last ten to fifteen years the study of 'political economy' has enjoyed a remarkable revival. To be sure, very different understandings are apparent of what the concerns of political economy might be. It is indicative of the appeal of the term that various attempts should have been made at its intellectual appropriation: for example, so as to have it relate specifically to Marxist analyses of contemporary capitalism or, in contrast, to efforts to extend the application of quite conventional economic theory to political behaviour. However, the powerful renewal of interest in 'political economy' is due primarily to the fact that it has been able to provide—at a time when this was manifestly needed—a rather general rubric under which may be examined, in freedom from orthodoxies of any kind, the effects on the performance of modern economies of the political systems with which they are enmeshed and, in turn, of the larger social structures and processes which comprehend economy and polity alike.

In the mid-1960s such an area of inquiry could scarcely have been regarded as one of the first importance, at least within the Western world. After almost two decades of sustained economic growth, at high levels of capacity utilization and with no more than modest inflation, it appeared that the problems of managing modern capitalist economies had been reduced to ones of a largely technical kind—still capable, perhaps, of exciting party squabbles but in truth raising no fundamental political issues. Thus, in this context, it was in no way surprising that the idea of political economy should have appeared as more or less archaic— that is, as one which harked back to the pre-history of the modern scientific economics which was now validating itself via the new and impressive standards of economic management that were being displayed. Keynes's vision of economics becoming as much a matter of technique as dentistry—and, presumably, carrying no greater political significance—was, it seemed, at least on the way to realization. However, within a relatively short period of time, all this was changed.

First of all, and most importantly, a marked falling-off occurred in the performance of Western economies. Growth rates declined and, still more disturbingly, a tendency emerged for the general price level and the unemployment level to rise simultaneously. In other words, the business cycle proved not to be obsolete after all and, further, it appeared that inflation and recession could now be complementary rather than alternative expressions of economic disorder. Symptomatically, a new economic indicator came into use: the 'discomfort index', which is the sum of the rate of inflation and the rate of unemployment. Averaged over seven major OECD countries, this index stood at around 5.5 percentage points for the decade 1959–69 but, by 1974–5, had risen to 17 percentage points (OECD, 1977).

Secondly, this termination of what could now best be seen as the 'long boom' of the post-war years carried grave consequences for economics. If it is too much to say that it precipitated a 'crisis in economics', what is certain is that it threw macroeconomics at least into a state of confusion, breaking the broad consensus that had developed from the 1940s on, with the fusion of Keynesian and classical theory in the 'neo-classical synthesis', and producing a diversity of contending schools. The coexistence of rising inflation and rising unemployment was the crucial difficulty. In the 1960s, following on the 'discovery' of the Phillips curve, which purported to show a close relationship between the rate of change in money wages and the proportion of the labour force out of work, it appeared possible to 'endogenize' the determination of these variables to the economic system. Thus, demand-management policy would in itself be able to provide the means of arriving at some acceptable trade-off between inflation and unemployment—a conclusion which was attractive not only politically but also as indicating the self-sufficiency of economic analysis as the basis for economic policy-making. However, with the effective breakdown of the Phillips-curve relationship by the early 1970s, such a trade-off strategy was clearly no longer available; and moreover the problem of how to account for, and handle, the new phenomenon of 'stagflation' forced economists into confronting an awkward dilemma.

To the extent that they introduced *ad hoc* such notions as 'a growing downward rigidity of prices' or 'a secular increase in the natural rate of unemployment'—let alone ones of 'growing worker militancy' or 'codes of good behaviour enforced by social pressures' (cf., for example, Hicks, 1974; Scott, 1978; Solow, 1979)—they were in effect accepting that the reigning paradigms of economic analysis were in themselves inadequate to the task before them. But if, on the other hand, they sought to preserve the intellectual autarky of economics and to reaffirm the basic validity of conventional analyses, then, it seemed, they had to build into their explanations very large 'residual categories' (see further, Goldthorpe, 1978). Current economic difficulties had to be substantially attributed either to 'error' or 'ignorance' on the part of major economic actors, notably politicians and governments, or in effect to mere historical accident: in the words of the McCracken Committee (OECD, 1977: 14), to 'an unusual bunching of unfortunate disturbances unlikely to be repeated on the same scale'—such as the Vietnam war and its financing, the collapse of fixed exchange rates, the sudden oil and food price increases of the early 1970s etc. But, whichever option was followed, the way was laid open for the political scientists and the sociologists to move in: that is, either, so to speak, at the economists' own invitation or alternatively by taking up the factors consigned by the economists to their residual categories and showing that these became amenable to more systematic understanding if approached from a different analytical standpoint.

Thirdly, as the 1970s progressed, it became evident that, apart from the overall decline in standards of performance, there was one other feature of the new economic era succeeding the long boom which further served to promote a revival of political economy. If a number of different economic indicators were examined—for example, ones relating to growth, inflation, employment and unemployment—then Western nations displayed far more *variation* from one to another than had been generally the case during the post-war years, so that no unidimensional ranking of their performance could very usefully be made. That is to say, nations appeared to be responding to the new and more difficult conditions that they faced in contrasting ways. And in attempts to account for this wider variance, attention was then increasingly drawn to cross-national differences in economic and also in governmental institutions—the significance of which for economic performance had tended to be played down by commentators in the 1960s (cf. Shonfield, 1965: 65–7); and further to differences in national political cultures and ideologies and their social structural bases, in so far as these could be seen to bear on 'policy repertoires' (cf. Scharpf, 1981 and this volume) and their chances of successful implementation. To seek to discuss what was happening in Western nations (accidents apart) merely in terms of whether, in the light of highly generalized economic analyses, governments and other economic actors could be said to be following 'correct' policies came to appear as unacceptably jejune.

The new political economy, one could say, has developed two areas of concern, closely related to each other, which are reflected in the title of this volume. On the one hand, there has been a concern with the social and political sources of *order* within the modern capitalist world; and on the other, with the economic implications of social and political *conflict*. Underlying conventional economic analysis, there is usually to be discovered one or other of two assumptions: either that capitalist market economies have an inherent propensity towards stability—and are disequilibrated only by misguided meddling or external 'shocks'; or that they are in fact capable of being stabilized by means of technically-skilled management based on analysis of the kind in question.[1] The contrasting view, characteristic of the new political economy, is that capitalist market economies are inherently unstable; or, to be rather more precise, that they tend to exert a constant destabilizing effect on the societies within which they operate, so that their own efficient functioning is thereby threatened and can continue only to the extent that this destabilizing effect is offset and contained by quite 'exogenous' institutional arrangements. Thus, from this latter standpoint, the attempt is made to go beyond the representation of current inflationary or stagflationary problems—or likewise of those of productivity or capital formation—as being merely, and thus in the end rather unintelligibly, the outcome of 'bad economics', human folly or historical misfortune. Rather, the aim is to understand these problems as being generated—quite intelligibly if not usually intentionally—as the divisions and conflicts between groups and classes (and their organizations, movements and parties) which are inseparable from the working of a capitalist economy find their historical expression. And correspondingly, then, what is seen as crucial to the more satisfactory performance of such economies, including their capacity to respond to adverse external conditions, is some form of relatively durable—if never permanent—settlement or 'historical compromise' between these contending elements; one, that is, which allows institutional recognition to be given to a prevailing balance-of-power situation, so that the conflicts which are still implicit in it can be mediated and channelled in ways that do not seriously impede economic efficiency and may even perhaps enhance it.

All the authors represented in this volume had previously made contributions of relevance to these concerns with order and conflict within western European nations, although in ways that clearly reflected distinctive disciplinary pre-occupations and socio-political interests. The seminars for which the papers here collected were first drafted were in fact deliberately constituted so as to bring together individuals whose work had to some extent, and rather intriguingly, converged from different starting points. It was not so much the purpose of the seminars to advance this convergence as to explore its nature and limits; and, as will be evident to the reader, it remains far from complete. However, in consequence of the exchanges which were begun in the seminars, and which have been continued through personal meetings in other contexts and through correspondence, the papers as they have emerged in their final form display a rather complex network of interconnections—a more complex one, it might be added, than could be entirely captured by explicit cross-referencing, without undue disruption of the text. The relationships thus established are often ones of a supportive or complementary kind, so that certain themes recur to an extent which, in viewing the volume as a whole, the contributors themselves may find somewhat surprising. And where perspectives, arguments and judgements still do differ, a greater awareness of intellectual engagement has now been created and, it is hoped, is communicated to the reader.

While it is certainly gratifying to an editor to find a high degree of connectedness among the papers that he is charged with assembling, a problem of presentation is thus created in that there is no obvious sequence in which the papers should be ordered: whichever ones are placed towards the front might, it seems, be more profitably read after those which come later. The sequence that I have imposed can lay claim to some degree of logicality, but it should be understood that it is not one which every reader will find it most useful to follow.

The collection begins with three papers of a wide-ranging kind. In the first of these, Keohane starts from a question which, as he points out, must be seen as prior to any consideration of differences in economic performance among Western European nations: namely, what are the common external challenges—that is, challenges deriving from the world political economy—to which these nations have to respond? Keohane's paper is thus of significance as a counter to the charge sometimes made against exponents of the new political economy that, in their preoccupation with questions of order and conflict within nation states, they neglect the international aspects of current problems. But still more important is the fact that Keohane, in marked contrast to the McCracken Committee—of whose report he was a trenchant critic (Keohane, 1978)—refuses to discuss changes in international economic relations at the level, so to speak, of mere happenstance. Rather, the main objective of his paper is to establish, first, that in the post-war period Western nations benefitted considerably from a 'settlement' within the world political economy which was produced largely under US hegemony and could be described, following Ruggie (1982), as one of 'embedded liberalism'; and secondly, that these nations must now be seen as facing serious economic difficulties which stem from the progressive break-up of this settlement—not as the result of historical accidents but rather of developments, such as the shift of economic activity from 'centre' to 'periphery', which the settlement itself has promoted. A further question raised in Keohane's paper which is of interest in its own right and also because it relates to the central concerns of several later contributions is that of whether the international order of 'embedded liberalism' has been biased against social democracy. The answer offered is that it has not—provided that social-democratic regimes have been able to draw on organizational and institutional resouces facilitating cooperation with, and between, capital and labour, which allow them to pursue their goals of full employment and redistribution without unduly undermining productive and market efficiency.

In this way, the portentous theme of 'corporatism' is introduced, and is taken up at length in the next two papers. Maier proposes a distinction between corporatist and pluralist arrangements within the field of industrial relations which would be accepted by most later contributors and which turns essentially on whether the state plays in some way a co-ordinating role in negotiations between employers and labour or merely a supervisory one. Maier's main aim is then to examine across a broad historical canvas the range of conditions that may favour corporatist institutional developments. Two rather different kinds of conditions emerge as being of particular interest. First, Maier notes an association between corporatist tendencies and situations of recognized national emergency or, more generally, of vulnerability, whether political or economic. An awareness of such vulnerability is conducive to a muting of social conflict, or at all events it creates what Maier nicely terms 'a diffidence at hegemony' and a readiness to seek ways of expressing conflict that will not further threaten national political or economic viability. Secondly, Maier makes an observation on the connection between social democracy and corporatism which links with Keohane's but which, in its emphasis on chronological phasing, is distinctively that of a historian. Those nations in which social-democratic regimes have been most able to sustain and benefit from corporatist arrangements, Maier points out, have been ones—mainly northern and central European—where the industrial and political wings of labour movements advanced more or less *pari passu*, rather than ones where union development dominated party development, as in Britain, or party development ran ahead of union organization, as in France.

The third paper in the opening trio, that by Lehmbruch, also starts from a conceptual distinction on which several subsequent papers draw: that between corporatist arrangements as they may operate within a particular industry or sector and such arrangements as they may operate trans-sectorally, so as to concert the policies and strategies of major economic interests and of government within the context of the *Gesamtwirtschaft*. As Lehmbruch notes, sectoral corporatism has a rather long history: it is corporatism directed towards trans-sectoral concertation that is the relatively new phenomenon. Substantively, Lehmbruch's prime concern is then with the way in which in 'strong' corporatist countries—that is, those where concertation has become most securely established—this development has been supported by rather distinctive patterns of the institutionalization of both intra- and inter-organizational relationships. Supportive linkages between political parties and economic interest organizations must, in Lehmbruch's view, be understood as a particularly important feature of corporatist 'networks'. Thus, the interpretation that he would offer of the association between social-democratic government and 'strong' corporatism would be that this is part of the legacy of the northern and central European tradition of reformist Marxism: one in which—in contrast with both French syndicalism and British labourism—a unified working-class movement aims to concentrate its activity in the political rather than the industrial arena, so as to be able to pursue in a solidaristic fashion distinctively *class*, rather than merely sectional interests.[2]

With this argument, Lehmbruch broaches an issue which is central to the next four papers in the collection. That is, the issue of whether the participation of trade unions in corporatist arrangements, usually entailing some form of wage restraint, can be an effective means of upholding and advancing the interests of their members; or whether such participation must rather imply a sell-out or class 'betrayal' on the part of union leaders and an attempt by them to dupe or coerce their rank-and-file into accepting 'restraint' which serves only the interests of capital.

The papers by Schott and Lange are both attempts to address this issue theoretically. Schott adopts the classic strategy of the economist by setting up a much simplified but rigorously specified model of a complex reality, and then seeking insights into this reality from the results which the model generates. The result which bears most directly on the issue posed is one which well illustrates the value of her approach in that it also suggests an underlying rationale for certain well-known empirical findings. It emerges from Schott's model that one should not presume any positive association between working-class strength and industrial militancy. A strong working class may quite rationally underutilize its labour-market power at any one time, because it can have confidence that it will later be able to extract from capital an adequately compensating return for its restraint—whereas a weak working class, lacking such confidence, may rationally decide to get what it can when it can (cf. Korpi & Shalev, 1980, on comparative strike rates; and Cameron, this volume). A further notable implication of Schott's model, in regard to corporatist developments, is that when the stage of a necessary restructuring of the economy is reached, a strong working class can make this process more difficult for capital than a weak one, but that only a strong working class is likely to receive overtures from capital concerning the terms on which the restructuring is to be carried out *or* is likely to be interested (by the same logic as before) in negotiations on this matter.

Lange focuses on the question of whether it could in any circumstances be rational for workers themselves—as distinct from their unions—to agree to wage regulation. The most cogent argument against such a possibility is that which treats a proposal for wage regulation as creating a 'prisoner's dilemma' situation. Even if all workers would gain from regulation, any workers actually consenting to it risk losing out through others attempting to 'free-ride' to the point at which regulation collapses: hence, the rational strategy must be one of non-cooperation. However, Lange points out that if this game-theoretic approach is to be followed, it would be more realistic to think of wage regulation as involving not simply a 'one-off', but rather an *iterated* game; and he goes on to show that, under assumptions appropriate to the iterated game, it *is* possible to envisage situations in which regulation could come about through workers acting in an entirely rational, self-interested way. The crucial requirements are, first, collective identities that reach beyond immediate bargaining units and, secondly, extended time-horizons. The further question then of course arises, and is treated at some length, of how likely these requirements are to be met. At the end of his analysis, Lange is in no doubt that consensually-based wage regulation is highly contingent, often fragile, and by no means equally available at all times and places. None the less, it remains the case that it cannot be precluded *a priori* and that the conditions conducive to it can be specified: hence, it is an objective towards which policy may be legitimately directed.

Following on from the contributions of Schott and Lange, but in a more empirical mode, come those of Regini and Cameron. Regini's study of corporatist 'episodes' in Italy and Britain in the 1970s is presented in the context of a critique of earlier analyses in which corporatist arrangements are seen either as a functional response to the 'needs' of the state or as the result of a 'design' which is conceived and imposed by the state. As against such unilluminating accounts, Regini argues that corporatism—in the sense of attempts at concertation in national economic policy-making—should rather be seen as emerging only contingently, out of a convergence of the interests and strategies of the several actors involved. From the standpoint of the unions, conditions *can* clearly arise in which it will be to the advantage of their members as a whole that they should engage in the political bargaining and 'exchange' which concertation implies: for example, when more is to be gained from bargaining with government than with employers, or when unrestrained labour-market action would be merely counter-productive within a desperately weak national economy. An involvement in concertative policy-making will, Regini recognizes, always carry with it the threat of a 'crisis of representation' and union movements will vary in their capacity for coping with such a threat. In this respect, however, density levels and organizational features may be of less direct importance—as Lange's analysis would suggest—than ideological resources for forming and upholding collective identities: in particular, identities of a class rather than a sectional character. The Italian unions in fact revealed a considerable capacity for sustaining support for their strategy of political exchange in the period of *soldiarietà nazionale*, and the strategy was chiefly undermined by the failure to 'deliver' on the part of government and the public administration. But in the British case the Social Contract broke down because in the end the unions were unable to control the crisis of representation and the costs that it imposed upon them.

Cameron, for his part, faces up to the issue of *cui bono?* directly. Since Western nations have responded in evidently diverse ways to mounting economic problems from the 1960s on, a good opportunity arises for asking whether this variance can in any part be attributed to governments of—or including—parties of the Left acting in ways that favour working-class interests; and, relatedly, whether the corporatist arrangements often associated with such governments do reflect a shift in the balance of class power towards labour rather than simply a growing need for control over labour. Using data for a wide range of OECD countries, Cameron shows a marked pattern of covariance in economic performance which tends to divide nations into two main blocs: those in which labour quiescence, as indicated by low strike rates and only modest shifts in the rate of change of earnings, goes together with relatively stable prices and high levels of employment, and those in which labour militancy goes together with relatively large increases in prices and high levels of unemployment. Further analysis then reveals that the former, more 'successful' pattern has some association with Left government, but a clearly stronger one with a measure of the organizational strength of labour—which correlates closely with indices of corporatism. Thus, the crucial issue becomes that of whether the connection indicated between corporatism and labour quiescence works in labour's interest or not. Cameron finds no evidence that under corporatism labour loses out on factor shares and, if anything, the 'social wage' is higher. But from the standpoint of the working class as a whole, the major advantage must be reckoned as the preservation of high levels of employment, even if some groups within the working class are denied gains that militancy could have brought.

The remaining five papers in the collection—my own concluding piece aside—have in common a focus on the political economies of those nations in which, over recent decades, corporatist institutions have been of greatest importance.[3] However, their concerns are by no means limited to these institutions *per se*. Rather, when taken together, these papers provide a valuable complement, and to some extent a corrective, to the existing literature in bringing out, on the one hand, the wider contexts within which corporatist institutions operate—and at the same time the range of variation therein—and, on the other hand, the ways in which 'strong' corporatist nations do and do not differ in their economic strategies and performance from those in which corporatist tendencies have been less developed.

From this standpoint, the paper by Esping-Andersen and Korpi is of particular significance in qualifying the commonly held view that nations in which a sustained effort has been made to base political economy on 'social partnership' are in some way distinctively consensual ones. Esping-Andersen and Korpi view social policy as an area in which crucial issues must necessarily arise over the role of markets and of politics in determining distributive processes; and they show that even in the seemingly peaceable societies of Scandinavia and post-war Austria and West Germany, the making of social policy has continuously involved fierce conflicts between different groups and classes. Moreover, there is no evidence of a 'logic of industrialism' forcing a convergent pattern on the eventual policy outcomes. On the contrary, in consequence of different constellations of political forces, cross-national variation seems to be widening, and to be likely to widen still further, in the degree to which wage-earners are 'decommodified' and the boundaries of social citizenship are expanded. Also of great importance is the way in which Esping-Andersen and Korpi bring out from their case studies the close linkages that exist between social and economic policies; and indeed, as they remark, it is an objective of social democracy that they should in effect be fused. But, as they then further recognize, it is in this respect that the most fundamental conflicts of all may be expected—as is indeed already signalled in the Swedish case with the struggle to establish 'wage-earner funds' as a necessary complement both to the solidaristic wages policy and to the commitment to a social right to work.

This same theme of the interconnectedness of social and economic policies is then taken up by Åberg in his contribution. To the extent that economic activity becomes politically regulated in the pursuit of social objectives, Åberg observes, questions are likely to be raised regarding both efficiency and legitimacy. However, what he seeks primarily to show, so far as the operation of labour markets is concerned, is that there should be no presumption—of the kind that liberal economists are wont to make—that efficiency must necessarily be undermined by attempts at centralized wage regulation. From comparisons between the Swedish and the US labour markets in the recent past, Åberg finds that although wage differentials have widened in the US whereas in Sweden they have been narrowed as an express goal of wage policy, there is little difference between the two countries in the degree to which control has been exercised over the growth of wages (though via quite different mechanisms) and it is the US labour market that has moved more towards disequilibrium. Åberg suggests, therefore, that wage differentials may be less important to labour-market efficiency than has often been supposed; and that, especially in advanced welfare states, such efficiency may in fact be better secured by intervention—in particular, by 'active' labour-market policies on the Swedish pattern. Legitimacy presents a more serious problem: the pursuit of egalitarian goals through centralized wage regulation, and especially when growth rates are low, must draw heavily on class solidarity. However, it is relevant here to point out, as Åberg does, that the alternative to such regulation is not the free labour market of the economics textbooks, but rather one with either a fragmented pluralist or a dualist structure. And it could scarcely be suggested that problems of either legitimacy or efficiency are thus avoided.

In Schwerin's paper, the examination of the implications of 'social-democratic planning' for economic efficiency is continued and enlarged. The central empirical issue that Schwerin raises is that of the economic consequences of 'historical compromises'. As earlier noted, such compromises have been typically regarded by exponents of the new political economy as a means whereby some requisite degree of order may be brought into modern capitalist societies. But, Schwerin points out, as regards subsequent developments a range of different scenarios has been elaborated. Thus, for example, as against the idea that such compromises may provide a basis for the successful evolution of social-democratic planning, one can set the claim (cf. Olson, 1982) that the degree of organization of interests that is characteristically involved will lead rather to the path of 'pluralist decline'. If growth is taken as the indicator of economic performance, then, Schwerin shows, this latter argument must be reckoned as at best 'not proven'. However, for countries where social democrats have regularly held power, another scenario has been presented: that of 'socialist exploitation', in which profits are eroded, labour costs rise rapidly with government as the wage-leader, and private investment is 'crowded out' by the financing of a large public-sector deficit. Taking the Nordic countries as a 'best-case test' of the plausibility of this scenario, Schwerin arrives at generally negative results. What rather appears significant is the fact that in regard to profits, wages, investment etc., the Nordic countries *are not* distinctive among those of the Western world— despite their commitment to collective consumption, high employment and distributive equality.

A corollary of Schwerin's conclusion here is of course that in their patterns of economic performance, the Nordic countries vary a good deal among them- selves; and such variation within the larger bloc of countries which have usually been thought of as having relatively well developed corporatist institutions is then the starting point of Scharpf's contribution. The general argument that Scharpf advances is that this variation cannot be entirely accounted for insti- tutionally, nor yet by what may be seen as more fundamental differences in power relations between classes: one must also bring into the analysis cross- national differences in 'policy repertoires' and in the compatibility of these with both the institutions through which they must be implemented and the econ- omic conditions that actually prevail. Scharpf develops this argument with reference to full-employment strategies in Sweden, Austria and West Germany. A comparison between the first two nations brings out the importance of choice of strategy. In Sweden an ambitious attempt has been made to resist external economic pressures by translating only modest growth into increased public sector employment, for the most part financed 'solidaristically' through high personal taxation. In Austria the more orthodox approach has been followed of seeking to avoid unemployment by the vigorous promotion of growth. A comparison between Austria and West Germany then serves to show how similar strategies can produce different outcomes within different institutional contexts. In both countries, relatively successful strategies of wage restraint were pursued during the 1970s; but while Austria took advantage of this to maintain high levels of employment, West Germany failed to do so. Monetary policy was inadequately co-ordinated with incomes policy, largely because of a lack of trust and communication between the unions and the Bundesbank.

Finally in this series of papers, Streeck takes up directly the question which is touched upon in several previous contributions of how well corporatist institutions are likely to fare under the harsh economic conditions of the present day and foreseeable future. It is easy to be misled here, Streeck argues, by supposing, as many commentators have done, that corporatist institutions function essentially to regulate wages, and that it is therefore employers rather than workers who benefit from them. For this is to neglect not only the opportunities afforded to unions to influence macroeconomic and social policy, but further the major advantages that unions obtain from the centralized bargaining and agreements which are an integral feature of corporatist industrial relations systems. This point is best appreciated by considering what, conversely, would be gained by employers—especially in present economic conditions—if they could break free of the comprehensive and uniform regulation of employment relationships which such systems impose. It is, then, Streeck suggests, from the actions of employers rather than of unions that the main threat to corporatist institutions is now to be expected. In the West German case, the degree of legal backing given to such institutions means that it is difficult for employers to make any direct escape from their constraints. But, on the other hand, an employer strategy aimed at bringing workers increasingly into enterprise-level 'alliances' is favoured not only by the prevailing state of the labour market but further by the existence of Works Councils, which can serve as a most effective vehicle of *Betriebsegoismus*. Moreover, such a strategy, if successful, will not only undermine corporatism but further, by fragmenting the working class and destroying its solidarity, will pose a major threat to West German unions at least as organizations whose aim is to formulate and pursue class interests rather than merely to 'service' pre-given sectional ones.

My own paper, with which the collection ends, is not in any way intended to provide a synthesis of the positions and arguments that are contained in the contributions that precede it. In so far as it has a distinctive purpose as a concluding paper, it is rather to bring out the relevance that these contributions have for the debate, now in train for over two decades, on the direction of the broad developmental tendencies that may be discerned within modern industrial societies. In an early intervention in this debate (Goldthorpe, 1962), I pointed to various difficulties, empirical and theoretical, in the thesis that the developmental paths on which these societies were set were ones convergent on 'pluralistic industrialism'. At that time, I focused my criticism on the claim entailed by this convergence thesis—and pressed by its liberal exponents—that the societies of the Soviet bloc would prove politically unstable, as the exigencies of the 'logic of industrialism' forced pluralism upon them. Subsequently, I have become increasingly convinced not only that such a claim is indeed quite misconceived, but further that in Western societies the continued development of pluralism in the post-war period, far from being prompted by the requirements of industrialism, has rather been a source of severe problems for industrialism in its capitalist mode.

The central argument of my paper is, then, that new developmental tendencies are now apparent within Western European nations, the origins of which also lie in the post-war period, but which represent in fact differing—and indeed quite *divergent*—responses to the incompatibilities that have emerged between integral features of liberal pluralist societies and the successful performance of capitalist economies. In their advanced form, such societies in various ways promote the extensive and effective organization of economic interests—with labour gaining in particular in its capacity to engage in distributional conflict. But all such organization is essentially organization against market forces, on the operation of which the efficiency of capitalist economies, even when 'mixed' and 'managed', must still ultimately depend. Thus, I suggest, corporatist tendencies can be understood as a response in which governments attempt to cope with intensifying problems of inflation and stagflation by bringing the major economic actors, and most crucially organized labour, into processes of policy formation and implementation. In other words, institutional and ultimately political substitutes are sought for market mechanisms, in order to aggregate and concert different interests and to render their pursuit consistent with policy goals. However, if the development of corporatist institutions can in this way be seen as embodying an 'inclusionary' strategy in regard to labour, tendencies are also widely evident in the direction of what I would refer to as economic dualism, which imply rather an 'exclusionary' response: that is, the creation of a sizable work-force whose members are in one way or another marginal to the key institutions of the plural society and who therefore lack effective organization and the resources to achieve it. To the extent, then, that areas of the economy are developed within which market forces can operate with considerable freedom, the rigidities that prevail elsewhere may be offset.

Since both corporatist and dualist tendencies entail significant departures from the model of 'pluralistic industrialism', their emergence, as I seek to show at some length, seriously undermines the liberal theories of industrial society in which this model plays a crucial role. However, in re-reading my co-authors' contributions in their finished form, I have been made aware that there is one point in my paper which is, in comparison, insufficiently pursued and which should here be returned to if this Introduction at least is not to be left unbalanced: namely, that most mainstream Marxist analyses of recent developments in the political economies of Western European nations now also appear to be seriously inadequate, and in particular in their treatment of corporatist institutions. As should already be clear, the view that such institutions can be understood as the latest or 'highest' form of the social control of labour under capitalism is repeatedly challenged, whether directly or indirectly, in the papers in this collection. But it would seem important that the several different arguments here involved and the full extent of the misjudgments that they reveal in Marxist analyses should be somewhat more systematically set out.

First, strong theoretical arguments can be advanced to the effect that, under various conditions, workers can quite rationally under-utilize their labour-market power; and this would seem more likely to be the case the *stronger* their organization. Thus, it should not be supposed *a priori* that union participation in corporatist arrangements, requiring wage regulation, must in some way or other be imposed by leaderships on their rank and file. Moreover, the implication that labour-market militancy need not be the most effective mode of working-class action finds support in empirical results which indicate that labour-market restraint in conjunction with corporatist participation brings distinct advantages for labour, above all in the preservation of high levels of employment. Secondly, the political bargaining in which unions engage via corporatist arrangements is far more evidently action oriented towards specifically *class* interests than is 'free' collective bargaining of a conventional kind (no matter how militant) in which sectional—that is, enterprise, occupational or industrial—interests are typically involved and often dominant. A strategy of political bargaining depends on class solidarity—even 'consumes' it—but, where successful, can in turn powerfully reinforce it.[4] Thirdly, although it may appear that all that can be obtained through such solidaristic action is what Scharpf calls, in reference to Sweden, 'socialism in one class', the participation of organized labour in corporatist arrangements can in fact be shown to have its own logic, the thrust of which is clearly radical: most obviously, as the Swedish case can equally well illustrate, in regard to social policy and the control of investment. As I do observe in my paper, while corporatist institutions can be seen as providing a context of order for modern capitalist economies, it is one within which basic class conflicts may still be carried on and may indeed in certain respects be promoted rather than suppressed.

The final argument is that in Western Europe at the present day, it would be difficult to find instances in which it could be plausibly held that corporatist institutions are being sustained in the interests of capital—for example, by right-wing governments and representatives of employers; but easy to find ones in which the latter have either openly rejected corporatism, in the sense of concertation, or are seeking in one way or another to undermine it. Contrary to what is suggested by the implicit functionalism of most Marxist analyses—but as I believe my discussion of dualism serves to illustrate—other versions of capitalist order can be created, and ones which are for more congenial to its supporters essentially because they structure conflict on lines which run through classes rather than between them.

Notes

1. Again, the *locus classicus* is the McCracken Report, which was produced by a group of distinguished economists from OECD countries and which sought explicitly to defend the view that the economic problems that had emerged in these countries since the early 1970s could be 'largely . . . understood in terms of conventional economic analysis' and that what essentially was needed to overcome them was 'better use of existing instruments of economic policy and better functioning and management of existing market mechanisms'. (OECD, 1977: 14.)

2. One respect in which a difference did remain among some participants in the seminars was in their readiness to use the term 'corporatism' (or 'neo-corporatism') to refer to institutional arrangements for 'trans-sectoral concertation' in Lehmbruch's sense. Thus, for example, Korpi would be evidently unwilling to accept the designation of Sweden as a corporatist country (1983, ch.2, and note also the comments made on this matter in Regini's paper). However, it seems to me important to recognize here (i) that Lehmbruch's character-ization of 'corporatism as concertation' is not open to the cogent criticisms that Korpi directs against earlier accounts; (ii) that nothing would stand in the way of Lehmbruch's accepting Korpi's own hypothesis (1983: 20) that 'tripartite "neo-corporatist" institutional arrangements largely reflect the compromises and settlements generated by the decreasing differences in the distribution of power resources between wage-earners and representatives of capital and allied groups'; and (iii) that Lehmbruch would most certainly underwrite Korpi's claim that such 'societal bargaining of the tripartite type that was developed in some countries of Western Europe in the post-war period clearly differs from traditional corporatist arrangements'. I have therefore to conclude that what really does explain the reluctance to use the word 'corporatism' is simply that, as Korpi notes, it is one 'which many have found it hard to swallow'; and that while this is then an eminently understand-able objection, it is still—at least to a good Popperian—a quite trivial one.

3. This bias is a deliberately chosen one, and I am quite unmoved by the criticism that the countries in question—with of course the considerable exception of West Germany—are only small ones. I know of no reason for supposing that what one can learn about the political economy of capitalism from the study of particular national cases is correlated with size of population or GNP. What would in principle have been highly desirable would have been to incorporate into the collection papers dealing with the 'Thatcher experiment' in Britain and the 'Mitterrand experiment' in France, which, as it is, are only referred to *en passant*. But when the work of the study group began, these experiments were still in their infancy, and it is, in my view, still too early for any very serious assessment of them to be made.

4. It is of great interest to note how closely the analyses of the papers in this collection connect in this respect with recent attempts at the rethinking of the Marxist theory of class which, though sure to be rejected by the faithful, are of a refreshingly rigorous kind. Several contributors refer to the work of Przeworski and Wallerstein (1982); and one may here further signal Elster's major study (1984, ch. 6 esp.), in which is developed the striking idea that class consciousness may be understood as the ability of a class to overcome the free-rider problem in realizing class interests.

1

The World Political Economy and the Crisis of Embedded Liberalism

ROBERT O. KEOHANE

Introduction

The political economies of modern Western European states do not exist in isolation, but within a context established by the international system. In pursuing policies designed to facilitate economic growth and social cohesion, governments react not just to the interests and power of domestic groups, but to constraints and incentives provided by the world political economy.

These international conditions affect each country differently: each economy occupies a particular location in the international division of labour, and changes in the environment (for example, increasing competitiveness of exports in a particular sector from newly industrializing countries) will affect each one in a distinctive way. This is most obvious with respect to oil: Britain and Norway, alone among Western European countries, are net exporters. In other sectors there are also differences in the sensitivity of different countries to external events: for instance, the effects of cheap Third World textile and clothing exports on a given European country will depend not only on the size of its textile and clothing industry, but also on whether it competes directly with such products or, as in the case of Switzerland, uses them as inputs in the production of high-quality final products (Katzenstein, 1984).

Much of this volume seeks to explain the substantial differences among European countries in economic policy and performance during the 1970s. For this purpose it is important to understand their somewhat different locations in the world economy. This chapter, however, seeks to identify the international forces impinging on Western Europe as a whole, to establish a context for the comparison and evaluation of national policies. My argument is that these common forces are significant enough that they must be taken into account in any analysis of the European political economies, and the evolution of the welfare state, during the 1970s and 1980s (Katzenstein ed. 1978; Gourevitch 1978).

Without an analysis of common patterns, comparative political-economic studies can be quite misleading. Analysts focusing on the domestic politics and economics of one or a few countries may ascribe patterns of behaviour and outcomes to distinctively national causes, without recognizing the degree to which common forces affecting a range of countries operate powerfully in each. Consider the example of inflation. One could have investigated inflation in the 1970s by considering it as a separate phenomenon in Britain, France, Germany,

Holland, and Sweden, and by searching for its causes within each country. In each case, domestic forces could have been located that contributed to rapid increases in prices. But this would have missed a key point: that inflation was a world-wide phenomenon, which no country could singlehandedly resist. After understanding this, the analyst of domestic German policy would not seek to explain high rates of inflation simply on the basis of those policies, but would rather seek to solve the puzzle of why German inflation was so *low*, relative to the inflation rates of most other industrial countries (Keohane, 1985).

An international-level analysis such as the one offered in this paper is therefore neither an alternative to studying domestic politics, nor a mere supplement to it—an afterthought in which 'the international dimension' is introduced. On the contrary, it is a *precondition* for effective comparative analysis. Without a conception of the common external problems, pressures, and challenges facing European political economies in the 1970s and 1980s, we lack an analytical basis for identifying the role played by domestic interests and pressures in the various countries. Understanding the constraints imposed by the world political economy allows us to distinguish effects of common international forces from those of distinctive national ones.

My purpose in this paper is to locate the European economies in a changing world political economy, by analysing how changes in the world political economy during the last two decades have affected European societies and conditioned their policy reactions. I will emphasize constraints that the international political economy of modern capitalism places on domestic policy choices, and how these constraints may be changing.

My principal theme has to do with liberalism, or what I call, following John Ruggie, 'embedded liberalism'. I inquire about the preconditions for its emergence after the Second World War; the political biases that it may embody; and the sources of reactions against it that became apparent during the 1970s. My working assumption is that liberalism was acceptable in Europe for such an unprecedentedly long time largely because of the extended period of prosperity, associated with liberal policies, that lasted until the early 1970s. Conversely, in the absence of a strong ideological commitment to liberalism, economic adversity can be expected to lead to increased protectionism, as it did after the crises of 1873 and 1931. Thus my examination of the preconditions for, and reactions to, liberalism rests in part on an analysis of the international sources of economic growth. This involves a comparison between conditions in the 1950s and 1960s, which facilitated both liberalism and extensive systems of social welfare; and those of the 1970s, which sharpened conflicts between the maintenance of liberalism and the continued expansion of the welfare state.

I begin by indicating how conditions in the world political economy and American policy during the 1950s and early 1960s facilitated European economic growth and reduced the severity of dilemmas facing European governments seeking to combine capitalism, increased openness with respect to the world economy, and social welfare. Ironically, it was American hegemony that provided the basis for the development and expansion of the European welfare state.

The second section of the paper then considers the argument made by both Marxists and conservatives that international liberalism is biased in favour of conservative governments favouring capital, and against socialist or social-democratic regimes supported by labour. This claim has considerable force, although it suffers from failing to take into account different strategies that can be followed by social-democratic regimes, and different sets of institutions and policy networks that affect the feasibility of one strategy or another. Some of these strategies, as the contributions to this volume by Cameron and Scharpf indicate, have been much more effective than others. Thus the 'bias against social democracy', allegedly inherent in international capitalism, can be reinterpreted as a bias against those forms of social democracy that do not sufficiently take account of the constraints of the market.

The third section of this paper directs our attention to some international forces that have helped to undermine liberalism (either through worsening the economic situation of Western Europe or otherwise) during the 1970s and early 1980s. I distinguish three sets of changes. First, features of the world economy that had been transmitting prosperity from one country to another began to transmit inflation and recession. The forces generating prosperity, inflation or recession can be regarded as in the first instance internal, endogenous to one society or another (although such developments in each country are surely influenced by observations of events elsewhere). Yet in an open world political economy their effects spread out beyond borders. Even if the international 'transmission belts' did not change greatly, their impact was altered as they began to carry the virus of economic failure rather than the vaccine of success from one economy to another. The costs of interdependence became increasingly severe. A second change had more direct negative effects on the real incomes of Europeans: the terms of trade deteriorated after 1973, largely as a result of huge increases in oil prices. This negative shift in the terms of trade, compounded by indirect effects on aggregate demand, seems to have made liberalism more diffi-cult to maintain, since it worsened the European economic situation. Finally, Europe was affected by the expansion of capitalism to the periphery, especially East Asia and Latin America, as reflected in the increases in exports of manu-factured goods by less developed countries, especially the newly industrializing countries, to Europe over the last two decades. Although the direct economic effects of these exports may have been positive for Europe (as neo-classical economists claim), they seem to have provided a catalyst for intensified protec-tionism.

In the conclusion, I ask about the stability of a liberal world order. Liberalism can be regarded as a self-reinforcing system, in which declines in trade barriers both foster prosperity and weaken the inefficient sectors pressing for protection, thus creating political conditions for further liberalization. According to this perspective, disturbances and setbacks should be considered unpredictable 'shocks', as the McCracken Report (OECD, 1977) suggested. But liberalism can also be viewed as beset by contradictions, containing the seeds of its own destruction so that its very success undermines it. In so far as the latter is the case, the current problems of liberalism have their sources in the inherent dynamics of an open capitalist world political economy.

Embedded Liberalism and American Hegemony

Goldthorpe has suggested that an analysis of contemporary economic failure and social conflict in the advanced industrialized countries should begin with an understanding of the political bargains that provided a basis for the successful growth of their economies, and the expansion of their welfare states, during the 1950s and 1960s. Thus he writes (Memorandum to the Study Group):

If the current problems of western capitalist economies are to be seen as grounded in institutional and other social changes [as opposed to the McCracken Report view emphasizing exogenous shocks], then it would appear only logical to see the success of these economies in the post-war years as being likewise grounded in some form of social order or 'settlement': that is, one which could provide for conditions favourable to a higher level of economic performance than now prevails. Thus, the need is indicated to understand the nature of this post-war order, as it applied both internationally and—in differing versions—within western industrial societies, as a precondition for understanding the nature of its subsequent breakdown and, in turn, the possibilities for further collapse or for reconstruction or transcendance.

In my view, this settlement is well characterized by Ruggie's felicitous phrase, 'embedded liberalism' (Ruggie, 1982). To understand what this concept means, it is useful to think of the political-economic choices faced by governments as falling along two dimensions:

(i) *The extensiveness of the welfare state:* that is, the extent to which the state reallocates resources to individuals, firms, and groups, as compared to the allocations that would be made by markets;.

(ii) *The degree of liberalism or protectionism* in foreign trade and international monetary policy.

These two dimensions can provide the basis for a simple illustration, as shown in Figure 1.1. In the top left of the diagram is found the classic *laissez-faire* state, characterized by market allocations and liberal foreign economic policies. This state neither reallocates income internally nor stands as a shield between world markets and the domestic economy. On the opposite end of the main diagonal is the ideal type of socialism, or closed welfare-state national capitalism, in which the state is both intimately involved in the domestic economy, and social welfare arrangements, and interposes itself between that economy and world markets.

The lower-left hand box of the diagram represents the location of a state pursuing *laissez-faire* policies at home but mercantilist ones abroad. I label this the 'self-help' state. The most important example of this pattern is probably

ROLE OF THE STATE

		laissez-faire	interventionist
POLICIES TOWARD WORLD ECONOMY	liberal	classic liberalism	embedded liberalism
	protectionist/ mercantilist	self-help	socialism or closed national capitalism

FIG. 1.1. *The two dimensions of embedded liberalism*

provided by the United States in the period between the Civil War and the Great Depression, culminating in the high Smoot-Hawley Tariff of 1930, enacted by a Congress and acquiesced in by an administration hostile to the development of an extensive welfare state at home. One still observes nostalgic tendencies in this direction on the part of some Americans, but the United States has not really fitted this category since the New Deal.

In combining liberalism in foreign economic relations and activist, welfare-oriented policies at home, European societies after the Second World War pursued policies that were diametrically opposed to the self-help model. These constitute what has previously been described as 'embedded liberalism'. Liberalism was 'embedded' in the acceptance of an extensive role for the state, both in the steering of the economy and in assuring a decent life to citizens. Internationally, the form of liberalism agreed to after World War II had to be consistent with the welfare state rather than in conflict with it (Ruggie, 1982). Thus the constraints imposed on national economic policies by the classical gold standard were relaxed, and the pursuit of 'free trade' replaced by the goal of non-discrimination. Furthermore, the goal of price stability was sacrificed, when this seemed necessary to maintain an open international economy (Hirsch, 1978).

Embedded liberalism did not develop automatically after World War II. And it certainly was not the product of purely domestic political bargains or settlements. On the contrary, the United States devoted a great deal of thought, and huge resources, to ensuring this outcome.

Part of the American effort was ideological. The United States propagated the view that the maintenance of capitalism and the welfare state could be rendered compatible by what Maier (1978) has called the 'politics of productivity'. Cooperation among classes would ensure rising real wages and increasing opportunities, as well as extensive social welfare benefits, to the mass of the population. Liberalism, policies of macroeconomic management, and a limited form of welfare state would reinforce one another rather than be in conflict. Liberal trade would bring economic benefits through the international division of labour.

Yet the ideological appeal of the 'politics of productivity' was not sufficient to persuade Europeans to support an open capitalist system based on non-discriminatory trade. Liberalism was not deeply rooted in continental Europe, and even Britain had turned in the 1930s to protectionism, in the form of the Ottawa System of Imperial Preference. The United States self-consciously set out to create a liberal system in Germany, and sought to promote the victory of pro-capitalist coalitions in Italy and France. Furthermore, it provided both positive and negative incentives for European countries to adopt liberal external policies and to renounce what Block (1977) has called 'national capitalism'.

The groundwork for this American policy was laid during and after World War II, in successful US attempts to gain political control over the two most crucial areas of the world economy: finance and energy. Before the Bretton Woods conference of 1944, the United States apparently sought to 'fine-tune' British power, keeping Britain strong enough to be able to adopt liberal trade and payments policies after the war, but too weak to be in a position to re-nounce American credits and follow an independent economic strategy (Kolko, 1968). At the conference itself, and later in negotiations on a loan to Britain, the United States pursued its interests as the only large creditor country in the world economy, and the chief international banking centre (Gardner, 1956; Block, 1977). At the same time, the United States sought to establish its control over Middle Eastern oil, whether through an agreement with Britain, which proved abortive or, successfully, through the rupture of the Red Line Agreement and the re-enforcement of exclusive control over Saudi oil by American companies (Keohane, 1984).

Finding its initial attempts quickly to construct a liberal world capitalist economy thwarted by the difficulties of reconstruction and the political influence of labour and the Left in Europe, the United States shifted its policies in 1947 without abandoning its basic objective: it provided massive financing through the Marshall Plan, and accepted trade and payments liberalization by stages rather than all at once. As Hirsch and Doyle comment (1977: 31), 'such a policy was then possible because of the fundamental characteristic of the international political economy of the time: United States leadership on the basis of only qualified hegemony'. The United States was not strong enough to achieve its objectives exactly as it preferred; but it was sufficiently powerful to be able to find routes to achieve its goals, even if these were neither entirely direct, nor those originally preferred by the policy-makers themselves.

During the 1950s and 1960s the United States continued to pursue policies that reinforced embedded liberalism in Europe. It supported an international monetary regime of pegged exchange rates, in which it acted as the Nth country, keeping its currency tied to gold at a fixed price and allowing others to maintain exchange rates that enabled their exports to be competitive on world markets. In conjunction with the now-liberal European governments, the United States pressed for trade liberalization in a series of negotiations, culminating in the successful conclusion of the Kennedy Round, at least in so far as trade in manufactured goods was concerned, in 1967. American policy also sought, in the face of greater European reluctance, to secure most-favoured-nation treatment for

Japan: between 1951 and the mid-1960s the United States pressed European governments first to admit Japan to the GATT, then to end discrimination against Japanese exports, which many of them had continued to maintain even after Japan became a Contracting Party of GATT in 1955. Yet even as it pressed for trade liberalization, the United States accepted the barriers erected by the Common Market, and its initial protests against the highly protective Common Agricultural Policy of the European Community—which itself had a major welfare component—were muted. American policy accepted the 'embeddedness' of European liberalism in the welfare state.

By the mid-1960s it appeared that the prophets of productivity had been correct in their praise of liberalism. The development of a common market within Europe and the reduction, on the whole, of trade barriers between Europe and other industrialized areas of the world (particularly North America) had led to efficiencies resulting from economies of scale. Liberalization also increased competition within European economies, presumably resulting in positive dynamic effects. The combination of selective state interventionism and international openness seemed to have assured steady capitalist economic growth. Different countries could achieve this benign result by different combinations of demand management and export-led growth (Shonfield, 1965).

Europe also benefited from a peculiar sort of 'invisible hand', in the form of improving terms of trade for Europe with other countries, particularly the raw materials-producing areas of the Third World. This was the counterpart to the worsening terms of trade faced by the Third World producers themselves. Such a trend was most striking in the case of oil. Prices of oil, which were around $3.00 a barrel shortly after the war, fell to $1.80 during the 1950s and remained quite stable in nominal terms until 1971. Since manufactured exports from the advanced industrialized countries were subject to inflation (albeit moderate compared to the 1970s) during this time, the real cost of oil fell between 1950 and 1971 (Maull, 1980: 211). Even after the rise in posted oil prices in 1971 from $1.80 to $3.00 per barrel, world prices of oil between 1963 and 1972 only rose at the same rate as for manufactures during that same period (IMF, 1982, Table 9: 150). The favourable trends in terms of trade that characterized the period between 1950 and 1971 provided resources that could be used by Western European governments both to enhance the benefits provided by the welfare state and to increase investment and growth. In effect, transfer payments from the primary-producing countries to the industrialized ones made it easier for the latter to satisfy the demands arising from groups within their societies.

Thus European economies in the 1950s and 1960s benefited both from liberalization of the world economy and from improving terms of trade, particularly with respect to oil. The prosperity to which these trends contributed financed the expanding European welfare states that emerged during this period and that continued to grow during the 1970s. Yet neither liberalization on a world scale (as opposed to within the six-nation European Community) nor the improving terms of trade were principally the result of European actions. On the contrary, both were highly dependent on the hegemonic leadership of the United States. American policy fostered liberal trade among the advanced industrialized countries: one could even say that the policies of the Truman administration were designed to 'force Europe to be free'. US domination of the Middle East, and the willingness of the United States to use American oil reserves, in a crisis, to support Europe (as in 1956–7), kept oil prices low. The European welfare state was built on foundations provided by American hegemony.

The Political Bias of Liberalism

Both Marxist and neo-classical writers have recently contended that liberal capitalism exerts pressure against social-democratic solutions to economic problems in advanced industrialized countries. For the purposes of evaluating this argument, liberal capitalism can be defined as a world system embodying arrangements for the production and exchange of goods in which three conditions are met: (i) property rights to productive resources are vested principally in private individuals and corporations; (ii) production for profit takes place predominantly with wage labour, to be sold on a market; and (iii) privately controlled capital and goods are able to move relatively freely across national boundaries. The hypothesis to be explored in this section is that liberal capitalism, thus defined, generates a systematic bias against social-democratic solutions to economic problems in advanced industrial countries. In so far as this hypothesis is correct, liberalism in Europe both constrained the Left from going as far as it would have liked to ensure welfare through public policy, and gave the Left (or at least its more radical elements) incentives to break out of the strait-jacket of liberalism, particularly when general economic conditions worsened.

The contention that international liberalism contains a bias against labour, and thus against social democracy and the extensive welfare state, has been employed by prominent Marxist writers. For instance, Hymer (1972) argued that openness in the world political economy favours capitalists *vis-à-vis* labour, since it leads capital to coalesce, but fragments labour. Capitalists benefit politically from openness because capital is more mobile than labour and because they have superior access to information. In an open system, new investment can move abroad, and even established firms can relocate. Goods produced abroad can be exported back to home markets. Block, who also stresses the role of capital exports, argues that 'the openness of an economy provides a means to combat the demands of the working class for higher wages and for economic and social reforms' (1977: 3).

Conservatives make a remarkably similar argument, albeit with different language and opposite normative implications. Thus the McCracken Report (OECD, 1977: 136–7) contends that the scope for social-democratic economic policies is limited by economic interdependence:

Some governments may have underrated the consequence[s] of international interdependence and overrated their scope for independent action. With the improvement in international communications there are increasing signs of an international 'demonstration effect' which, coupled with the greater mobility of skilled labour, may lead to a capital flight and a brain drain from countries pursuing equality strenuously with an inadequate growth rate, while in others failure to do enough about inequality creates political unrest.

This argument develops, in different phrases, the essential Marxian claim that liberal capitalism benefits capital over labour and constrains governments from pursuing social-democratic policies much beyond the modal world level. In the first place, as explained further below, the transnationalization of financial flows, as capital movements become ever easier and cheaper, is likely to make it difficult for any country long to maintain a rate of profit significantly below the norm for the advanced countries, without suffering capital flight and loss of private investment. A sort of Gresham's Law may operate in which policies that reinforce the position of capital drive out policies that reduce its dominance and distribute wealth more equally. Secondly, as capital becomes more mobile, labour in the industrialized countries comes more directly into competition with labour in the less developed countries, particularly the 'newly industrializing countries'. Immobile labour employed in manufacturing industry becomes particularly vulnerable to competition from much cheaper labour in places such as South Korea, Mexico, or Taiwan. Thus measures that increase the real wage of labour in the advanced industrialized countries, either through pay increases or increases in welfare payments borne in whole or part by employers, will increase the incentives for firms to relocate production abroad. In a liberal world economy, the price, in terms of employment, paid by labour in return for increasing its real wage, will tend to rise, as the mobility of capital, technology, and managerial expertise increases. This development corresponds, at the international level, to the development of economic dualism, in which migrant labour plays an important role, at the level of European (or American) society.

The conservative economists draw the conclusion from these international constraints not that international interdependence is harmful (which might imply that protectionist policies would be in order), but that national social welfare objectives should be trimmed. Acceptance of international liberalism reinforces the need for what I have elsewhere called the neo-orthodox conception of a 'disciplinary state' (Keohane, 1978).

Both Marxist and neo-classical political economists argue, implicitly or explicitly, that international openness improves the bargaining position of investors *vis-à-vis* governments and other groups in society. In a closed economy, governments interested in promoting private investment need only ensure that expected rates of profits from productive investment, discounted for risk, are higher than those to be gained from holding financial instruments or engaging in speculation, and higher than the rewards anticipated from consumption. For an open economy with capital mobility, however, investment at home must also bring profits higher than those anticipated from investment abroad. If the prospective marginal rate of profit at home falls below expected returns abroad, one can expect an investment outflow and a slowing down of economic activity at home, relative to activity abroad. As a result, the minimum ordinary rate of profit that the government must allow to be generated at home in order to avoid capital outflow and a lack of investment, will be determined not simply by convention, domestic interest rates, and the willingness of investors to defer consumption, but by the marginal world rate of profit. Thus the internationaliz- ation of capital flows—the ease with which financial capital can be transferred across national boundaries—makes it more difficult for any country to institute measures that change the distribution of income against capital and in favour of labour, if this implies a marginal rate of profit significantly below that for the world as a whole. Unless the government has the ability to withstand the short- term costs (as well as potential long-term efficiency costs) of closing off its economy from the world economy, it must keep profit rates from falling too far below the world standard. At the same time, the 'exit' possibilities that capitalists have available are likely to increase the efficacy of their attempts at 'voice'—their ability to influence policy through the political process at home (Hirschman, 1970).

Once an open capitalist world system has been established, it may create a bias in favour of pro-capitalist, and against socialist-leaning, governments. When Thatcher or Reagan induces a recession through tight monetary policies, as part of a strategy to control inflation through reducing the rate of wage increases, the pound or dollar appreciates and funds flow into the country. This may be in- convenient for a country seeking to control its money supply or expand exports; but it does not lead to a loss of confidence in the government, and expands rather than contracts the resources at its disposal. No help needs to be sought from other governments as a result. When Mitterand tries to stimulate demand and to nationalize selected industries, by contrast, the franc declines, France's foreign reserves are jeopardized, and assistance may be needed from the IMF or selected governments of wealthy countries. Socialist and social-democratic governments are thus induced to maintain openness. The experience of Britain's Labour party during the 1960s and 1970s illustrates the dilemma. In the face of international economic problems, reflected in payments deficits, Labour sought to resolve the contradictions it faced by abandoning socialism, and even some elements of its plans for social democracy, in the interests of maintaining busi- ness confidence (Panitch, 1976). This process culminated in the decision of James Callaghan's Labour Government, in 1976, to sign a Letter of Intent to secure an IMF loan (Bernstein, 1983).

This argument implies that an open capitalist world financial system tends to reinforce itself. When pro-capitalist governments are in power, they have strong incentives to promote openness, not only for the sake of efficiency and gains from trade, but to reinforce the power of capital *vis-à-vis* labour. They also find that reinforcing economic openness helps their own political fortunes, since the web of interdependence thus created makes it more difficult for subsequent left-wing governments to achieve their purposes. When socialist and social-democratic governments come into power, they soon find that to avoid runs on their currencies, and financial crises, they need to gain the confidence of the business 'community', and that this may require that they abandon some of their more socialist objectives.

This argument is oversimplified and potentially misleading because it ignores variations in strategies followed by social-democratic governments, and in the policy institutions and networks that those governments can use. Indeed, the contrast between the substantial success of social democracy in both Scandinavia and Austria, on the one hand, and the difficulties encountered by attempts to move to the Left in Britain and France, on the other, suggests that variations in national strategies are important determinants of success or failure. From the standpoint of the Marxist/neo-classical argument about the bias of liberal capitalism, these variations are puzzling.

The answer to this conundrum may lie in the institutions of trans-sectoral concertation (cf. Lehmbruch, this volume) involving both labour and business, that some European countries have developed: that is, in 'corporatism'. Indeed, it may be helpful to think of the problem in terms of two ideal-typical forms of social democracy. Type A is typical of large countries such as Britain and France. It is characterized by only sporadic control of government by socialist parties; by policies of socialist governments that seek rapidly to shift the distribution of rewards from private capital to labour; and by a lack of domestic corporatist institutions permitting trans-sectoral concertation. Type B, by contrast, which is most closely exemplified by Austria and Sweden, is typical of small, open economies that need to export to survive: it is characterized by continuous left-wing rule over a long period of time, on the basis of strong union movements; by policies designed to maintain employment and improve equity in ways consistent with market incentives; and by corporatist institutions linking the state with leaders of both business and labour.

This distinction could help us to reformulate the Marxist/neo-classical argument. International capitalism does seem to exert a bias against Type A social democracy. Capital flight, or the threat thereof, typically leads to pressures on social-democratic governments in these countries to move toward the Right. That is, international capitalism *reinforces* the pressures exerted by the market against anti-capitalist policies in open, non-corporatist economies. Yet no such bias seems to exist against Type B social democracy. Capital flight does not seem to have been a serious problem for these countries during the 1970s; Sweden, for example, has maintained capital controls. Indeed, international capital markets *financed* Austrian and Swedish balance of payments deficits, permitting either an investment-led boom, as in Austria, or extensive job-training programmes, as in Sweden (Scharpf, this volume).

The McCracken Report suggested the existence of a 'narrow path to growth' for the advanced industrialized countries after the first oil shock. This analysis, by contrast, indicates that there may be a 'narrow path to social democracy'. Strategies for social democracy that exploit the market are more effective than those based on the assumption that market pressures can be ignored or over-ridden by the exercise of state power.

It is not clear whether small countries have an inherent advantage in designing appropriate strategies that reconcile social democracy with world capitalism. The Marxist/neo-classical argument seems to imply that small states should have more difficulty in coping with the pressures of world capitalism than large ones, because they are more open and because they have less power over the 'rules of the game'—the international arrangements, such as those agreed to at Bretton Woods, that define the terms under which a given country can link itself to the world political economy. Furthermore, in bilateral relationships where both sides are involved with equal intensity, small states might be expected to be more constrained by the policies of larger ones than vice versa (Hirschman, 1945). Yet Cameron (1978) has shown that it is precisely the small European countries that have the largest state budgets, in proportion to their size: far from simply succumbing to the pressures of the world political economy, they seem to try, actively, to provide a buffer between the world political economy and their citizens. Perhaps this is a result of the fact that as citizens of small countries their social democrats were acutely aware of the need to make social democracy consistent with export competitiveness. They therefore were willing to design domestic institutions and policy networks that facilitated mutual adjustment between labour and management (Katzenstein, 1984).

In so far as a bias exists against Type A social democracy, socialist movements in such countries will have incentives to consider radical moves toward state intervention to sever key links with the world economy. Cutting oneself off from world capitalism may seem to be the only effective way of regaining autonomy, even if the economic costs are recognized as being enormous. As the international conditions fostering prosperity were undermined during the 1970s, such arguments regained some of their appeal. It is not surprising that the sympathy for measures such as these was greater on the British and French Left—especially in certain elements of the British Labour party and the French Socialists—than on the Right, or in countries which had developed effective strategies of social-democratic corporatism.

International Forces Undermining Embedded Liberalism

Embedded liberalism is now under pressure in Europe. Protectionism and state interventionism in the economy have increased in the last decade, and tendencies toward socialism, or national capitalism, are more evident than they have been since the 1940s. The question is not whether there is a 'new protectionism', but what it represents, and why the previous trend toward increasing liberalism has been reversed. From the neo-classical liberal standpoint protectionism is an atavistic reaction by groups that refuse to adjust to the efficiency-creating pressures of competition. For instance, Olson (1982) regards protectionism as the result of the political influence of narrowly-based, self-serving 'distributional coalitions', and Baldwin (1982), and in more extreme form Brock and Magee (1978), following the same long line of analysis, see it as an economically perverse outcome of the competition of groups in the political market-place. Conversely, from the standpoint of Polanyi (1944) and his followers, protection-ism could be regarded as an effort at self-defence by 'society', against the rampages of the market-place.

Polanyi's notion of action by 'society' is vague and could be regarded as a mystification of more concrete political processes. The neo-classical analysis of the political economy of protectionism, on the other hand, naïvely incorporates the political theory of pluralism: policy outcomes are simply the result of group and sectoral pressures; the state is a virtual cipher without a political stance or ideology of its own. As a basis for description and partial explanation, pluralism is a useful notion, but it begs issues of the role and structure of the state, the sources of group interests, and the role of ideology. In this section of the present paper, I will not consider the potential sources of protectionism within European societies but rather focus on features of the *international* political economy that seem to have had negative effects on the ability of these societies to attain economic growth and to manage social conflicts. These characteristics of the world system may have intensified pressures throughout Europe for protection-ism. As indicated in the introduction, I will consider three forces: (i) the trans-mission of prosperity, inflation and recession; (ii) the deterioration of the terms of trade; and (iii) the expansion of capitalism to the periphery.

From Transmission of Prosperity to Transmission of Stagflation

The construction of an increasingly open world economy in the 1950s and 1960s meant that economic growth in one country contributed to growth elsewhere. Demand for imports in prosperous economies created demand for exports in others, increasing incomes and the demand for imports in the latter. Until the late 1960s, this beneficent pattern of exchange took place in a world economy with pegged exchange rates and great confidence in the dollar as the key currency, yet with persistent United States payments deficits that helped to maintain world liquidity. America was the chief supporter of an international financial regime that facilitated non-inflationary economic growth.

In the 1970s, international transmission mechanisms had less benign effects. From 1966 onward the United States pursued an inflationary fiscal policy associated with the war in Vietnam, and in 1971 the United States ceased to support pegged exchange rates and formally cut the linkage between the dollar and gold. The international monetary system, which continued to be highly integrated despite the changes it went through during the next few years, then carried inflation from country to country. This occurred, although by different means and perhaps to a lesser extent, under flexible as well as fixed exchange rates (Salant, 1977). Particularly during the period of greatest uncertainty about the exchange rate regime, between August 1971 and March 1973, national monetary policies in the major OECD countries were highly inflationary, perhaps partly as a result of the absence of incentives from the international regime to follow more stringent policies (Keohane, 1985).

In the 1970s the rules governing both exchange rates and oil prices were much less clear, and less constraining of national policy, than they had been during the Bretton Woods era. The changes in oil prices reflected a decline in American and European control over the terms of exchange; in money, they reflected an attempt by the United States to free itself from the burdens of the Bretton Woods regime. In both cases, the result was that the structure of authority became more decentralized. Neither a well-defined set of rules, nor a hegemonic power (in conjunction with its large corporations and its allies) determined outcomes (Keohane, 1984).

From this decentralized authority structure emerged a pattern of relations that is similar to what Hirschman (1981) has described in another context as a 'political tug-of-war'. In such a situation, organizations or groups can determine the prices for their own products (that is, they have market power), but there is no central authority capable of establishing a consistent set of non-inflationary prices for all goods. Each group would prefer stable prices if it could also be assured of its desired share of the social product; but since it cannot accomplish this on its own, it demands more, in nominal terms, in the hope of gaining, or at least not losing, in real terms. In this model, inflation is explained 'in terms of social conflict between groups each aspiring to a greater share of the social product', and by the absence of an effective government that can authoritatively allocate shares of that social product.

Such an inflationary tug-of-war seems to have taken place between the major oil-importing countries and OPEC in the years immediately following the major price increases of 1973-4. The *nominal* price of oil had an effective floor under it, since OPEC feared the consequences of initiating a downward spiral. But the *real* price of oil could be reduced either by increases in the prices of goods sold to OPEC countries, or by declines in the value of the dollar, either of which could be facilitated by inflation in the United States. This does not mean that the United States deliberately fostered inflation to reduce the real price of oil, but it does suggest that concern about oil prices and terms of trade reduced the incentives to deal decisively with inflation. To some extent, inflation was a face-saving device by which the demands of producers for high prices could be reconciled with the desire of consumers for lower prices.

Inflationary American macroeconomic policies in 1977-8 meant that European countries paid lower prices for imported oil, since the price of oil was denominated in depreciating dollars. Yet American policy also transmitted less welcome effects to Europe. Having been unsuccessful at persuading Germany and Japan to reflate more rapidly in early 1977, the United States sought to put pressure on them by letting the dollar depreciate, therefore making German and Japanese exports less competitive against those of the United States. This led eventually to an agreement at the Bonn summit, in July 1978, by which Germany and Japan were to stimulate their economies in return for phased decontrol of US oil prices and a tightening of American monetary policy. Unfortunately for these governments, the Bonn summit did not lead to a resumption of the virtuous circle of non-inflationary growth: in the fall of 1978, the dollar came under severe pressure, requiring extensive exchange market intervention, and in early 1979 the effects of the Iranian Revolution began to lead to a new escalation of oil prices.

Since the tightening of American monetary policy that took place in the fall of 1979, and particularly since the Reagan administration took office, another vicious circle of international transmission has contributed to the difficulties faced by European governments. High American interest rates have led European governments and central banks to increase their interest rates, for fear of foreign exchange crises resulting from capital flight. The consequence, of course, is that American monetarism has been imitated even by governments that do not sympathize either with its economic logic or its political biases. This is not to say, of course, that these governments had no choices: they could have sought to reflate their economies regardless of American policy. But then they would have encountered difficulties similar to those experienced by the socialist government in France since 1981: foreign exchange crises and losses of reserves, as capital fled the country for areas where real rates of return (nominal interest rates adjusted for inflation and expectations of exchange rate movements) were higher. Faced with such dilemmas, governments that are unable to sustain strategies to counteract, or even take advantage of, international constraints are under severe pressure to return to orthodoxy.

Viewed politically, the point is that the pressures transmitted by the international monetary system are not merely the results of impersonal market forces but reflect the policies of political coalitions in major countries, particularly the United States. When these policies shift, the effects are transmitted quickly throughout the system.

Thus international transmission of economic forces has had a different impact since 1971 from that of the two previous decades. Often the shift to flexible exchange rates is cited as a major source of these changes, although flexible rates are really more symptoms of disorder than cause. If national fiscal and monetary policies diverge sharply in a highly interdependent world economy but politically fragmented world system, fixed exchange rates will be impossible to sustain for long. In some respects, flexible rates may enable governments to control the effects of international disturbances more effectively—for instance, a low-inflation country can counteract the effects of inflation emanating from other countries by letting its own currency appreciate. Nevertheless, even if flexible rates are unavoidable, and have certain advantages, they do complicate the task of economic management by introducing another unpredictable variable into the managers' calculations.

The key issue, in my view, is not so much how economic effects are transmitted internationally, but what is being transmitted. Is it helpful or harmful to the recipient? The 1950s and early 1960s seem to have been characterized largely by 'virtuous circles', in which non-inflationary growth in one area reinforced non-inflationary growth in another. In the last decade and a half, transmission has been characterized by 'vicious circles', in which inflation and recession, perhaps generated originally within one society as a result of a combination of economic and political forces partly endogenous to it, are carried to others. International interdependence remains, but its consequences for social conflict and economic management are different.

The Deterioration of the Terms of Trade

All significant changes in the world economy have uneven effects on various countries, groups, or sectors. Furthermore, those countries, groups and sectors adversely affected by changes have differential abilities to force the costs of adjustment to change on to others. Power is, by one measure, the ability not to have to adjust to change.

Governments, of course, have to allocate the costs of adjustment among their citizens, and in particular, between capital and labour. If they are powerful in the world system, this internal adjustment may be facilitated by their ability to force foreigners to bear some of those costs. Conversely, if they are weak (or become weaker from a formerly strong situation), their internal adjustments may be rendered more difficult by adverse shifts imposed on them by others.

During the 1950s, the industrialized countries, including Europe, benefitted substantially from improving terms of trade between manufactured goods, which they exported, and primary products, of which they were net importers: these terms of trade improved by about 25 per cent (from the standpoint of exporters of manufactured goods) between 1950 and 1963 (OECD, 1977, Chart 9: 61). During the next decade (1963–72), these terms of trade were essentially stable, continuing to improve slightly in favour of manufactures: the industrialized countries' terms of trade improved by about 3 per cent. Between 1973 and 1982, however, the terms of trade for these countries worsened by about 20 per cent. This dramatic shift, caused largely by the huge oil price increases of that period, reflected the inability of the industrialized countries to force the costs of adjustment to higher oil prices entirely on to others: indeed, during that decade, taken as a whole, the terms of trade of the non-oil developing countries were almost stable, deteriorating only after 1977, while the terms of trade of the oil producers improved sharply (IMF, 1982, Table 9: 150).

Since the deterioration in the terms of trade was essentially a result of the huge oil price rises in 1973–4 and 1979–80, we need to look somewhat more closely at the effects of those price increases on the economies of the industrial-ized countries. The first set of price rises led to an increased import bill for the OECD countries of $65,000,000,000 dollars, equivalent to about 1½ per cent of their collective GNP (OECD, 1977: 67). The second price spiral led to increased import costs of about $150,000,000,000, equivalent to about 2 per cent of

OECD GNP (BIS, 1981: 40; Ostry, *et al.*, 1982: 37). In addition to these terms of trade effects, the oil shocks reduced aggregate demand. In 1980 the OECD countries lost about 3 per cent of GNP as a result of the oil price increases of the previous year; in 1981 the loss was about 4 per cent (Ostry, *et al.*, 1982: 38).

Oil price increases therefore both made the industrialized countries poorer and directly reduced their levels of economic activity. But the price rises also, of course, had an inflationary effect in the short run. In an effort to counter inflation, governments contracted their monetary and fiscal policies (OECD, 1977: 70). This led to a further reduction in real income in these societies, which was particularly pronounced after the second oil shock. The consequent reduction in GNP was about one-fourth of one per cent in 1980 and almost 2 per cent in 1981 (Ostry *et al.*, 1982: 38). Thus the combined loss of output from the second oil shock amounted to about 5 per cent of Gross Domestic Product (GDP) in 1980 and nearly 8 per cent in 1981 for a two-year total of over $1,000,000,000,000 (IEA, 1982: 63-4).

The immediate effects on worker-consumers in the OECD countries were cushioned by the fact that the distribution of income in 1974-5 shifted quite sharply from capital to labour, and from investment to consumption, throughout the area. Labour's share of total domestic factor income rose between 1970-3 and 1974-7 from about 69 per cent to about 72 per cent in Germany, from 64 to almost 70 per cent in France, and from 76 to 80 per cent in the United Kingdom (BIS, 1981: 41). This had temporarily positive effects on consumption but very negative effects on private investment, with serious consequences for subsequent unemployment (BIS, 1981: 44). After the second oil shock, in contrast, changes in labour's share of income, and in the balance between consumption and investment, were much less marked (BIS, 1981: 42; 1982: 30). Although European societies responded to the first oil shock by trying to cushion their citizens against it, they were not able to repeat this performance. The reaction to the second oil shock, especially in Britain and the United States (in the latter, even before Reagan took office), was to follow tight monetary policies in an attempt to force the costs of adjustment on to the present population, rather than to impose it, through inflation and low investment, on the future. As we have seen, this policy was transmitted, through international markets, to other countries, even where their governments had different preferences or different theories about how the world looked.

The crucial point about this is a familiar one. Governments have to allocate costs among their people, between classes and sectors. Much of political analysis is about how this is done: 'who gets what, when, how?' in Lasswell's phrase. But domestic allocations depend on the allocations resulting from political struggle at the international level. Weak countries have to bear the burdens of adjustment to change: they cannot impose them on others. Unless they are being subsidized by rich allies or politically naïve bankers, their governments must allocate costly adjustments among their people—inevitably leading to discontent—or else let them be inflicted through the market (for instance, in the form of inflation). Between the 1960s and the 1980s the willingness of the United States to maintain a stable international monetary system declined. Furthermore, its ability, in conjunction with selected European governments and major oil firms, to control petroleum prices virtually disappeared. As a result, the dependence of European governments on other countries increased. The higher petroleum prices that accompanied this loss of control reduced the ability of Europeans as well as people in other oil-importing areas to purchase manufactured goods: real incomes had to fall. The corollary of this process, thrusting adjustment costs on to Europe, was that domestic allocational dilemmas were sharpened, and the task of social conflict management made more difficult.

The Rise of Exports from Less Developed Countries

During the last two decades, less developed countries (LDCs), and in particular the eight principal newly industrializing countries (NICs) of Asia and Latin America (Hong Kong, Singapore, South Korea, and Taiwan—the 'gang of four—in East Asia, India in South Asia, Argentina, Brazil, and Mexico in Latin America) have experienced rates of economic growth much above those in Europe and North America (IMF, 1982, Appendix B, Tables 1 and 2: 143-4; Bradford, 1982b: 175-6). This growth has been led by exports. Manufactured exports from LDCs rose annually by 16.2 per cent between 1960 and 1976, a rate higher than the rate of export growth for industrialized countries (14.1 per cent) or for all trade commodities (13.7 per cent) (Stein, 1981: 36). The pace of LDC expansion was, at least at first, not seriously retarded by the oil crisis: largely as a result of the rapid growth of NIC exports, imports to both the EEC and the United States from non-OPEC developing countries increased threefold between 1973 and 1978 (Belassa, 1980, Table 1). Although LDC exports accounted for less than 10 per cent of the world market for manufactured goods in 1976, in sectors such as clothing and footwear they had increased by that time to over 30 per cent of the market; and in the more technologically advanced sector of electrical machinery they increased from less than 1 per cent in 1963 to 12 per cent in 1977 (OECD, 1979, Table 5: 24). This relative growth continued even in the recession: in 1981-2, the volume of industrial country exports remained roughly constant, but the exports of non-oil LDCs rose by about 7 per cent; and preliminary figures for 1983 indicated that LDC exports continued to do relatively better than those of the industrial countries (IMF, 1983: 179, 181; *IMF Survey*, 5 March, 1984: 65, 71).

Questions about the implications of this export growth for employment in the advanced industrialized countries have been raised with increasing urgency in recent years. Hager, for instance, has claimed that 'the supply of industrial labour of the Third World will approach, for practical purposes, the infinite', and that 'there is no natural equilibrium solution possible even in theory' (Hager, 1982: 421; 420). Yet OECD economists and others point out that exports from the advanced industrialized countries to the non-oil developing countries have increased almost as fast as imports in percentage terms; since exports to the

LDCs of manufactured goods exceeded imports by almost a three to one ratio in 1973, the result was that the positive trade balance of the advanced countries with the LDCs, in manufactured goods, increased from $25,000,000,000 dollars in 1973 to almost $70,000,000,000 dollars in 1979 (Bradford, 1982b: 178).

These changes suggest that rapid adjustment to change has been taking place in the world trade system since 1973. Branson has documented this for the United States; whether similar patterns characterize Western European adaptation is not yet clear. Between 1973 and 1978 the United States trade surpluses in capital goods, chemicals, and agricultural products almost doubled, to approximately $26,000,000,000, $7,000,000,000 and $13,000,000,000, respectively. During the same period of time, its trade deficits in consumer goods and automotive products also doubled, to about $18,000,000,000 in the former category and $10,000,000,000 in the latter. Branson infers that this reflects clear patterns of comparative advantage (1980, Table 3.19: 220).

The dominant view among economists is that this pattern of adjustment is good for the advanced industrialized countries as well as for the newly industrializing countries: both parties benefit, in Ricardian fashion, from trade and the associated investment (Belassa, 1980; Bradford, 1982b; Bhagwati, 1982). The conclusion of one analyst reflects the dominant neo-classical wisdom: 'there seems little doubt that it is to the advantage of developed countries to absorb more LDC exports and to adjust their economies accordingly' (Stein, 1981: 57). Thus the increasing economic interdependence between advanced countries and the newly industrializing countries is seen as a triumph of liberalism, only somewhat tarnished by economically irrational, politically inspired protectionism.

Yet if adjustment is a reality, so is protectionism. This has been evident both in the United States and Western Europe, but Europe has shown stronger tendencies to act in a protectionist manner, and considerably greater willingness to deviate from the rhetoric of liberal trade. In textiles, the EEC has taken the lead in tightening up the provisions of the Multi-Fiber Agreement, and in steel and shipbuilding it has also intervened to protect old industries (Turner et al. eds., 1982; Verreydt & Waelbroeck, 1982). Individual European countries have gone further, particularly in areas such as automobiles and consumer electronics. The major target of European ire was Japan, but as Turner points out, 'some of the NICs began to be sucked into such trade disputes' (Turner et al. eds., 1982: 138).

European resistance to Japanese and LDC imports is taking place at levels of import penetration below those already attained by these exporters in the US market. Less than 16 per cent of EEC imports (excluding intra-EEC trade) were accounted for in 1978 by the LDCs, while the corresponding figure for the United States was almost 22 per cent. Even as a percentage of GDP, American imports from the LDCs were almost a third higher than Europe's. Perhaps partly as a consequence, the rate of growth of LDC imports into the EEC between 1973 and 1978 was lower than into the US market (Belassa, 1980, Table 3).

It is not surprising that resistance to imports should increase during times of economic stress. Workers facing unemployment are strongly motivated to use political action to preserve their jobs. If firms 'satisfice', seeking to maintain customary levels of profits, many of them will redouble their lobbying efforts in a downturn as actual profits and earnings fall below these thresholds. Even if firms and workers act as maximizers, they may intensify their efforts to secure protection during depressions. In such a period, their gains are less likely to be competed away by new entrants, since rates of return even after protection may still be too low to justify new investment within the area enclosed by the trade barriers (McKeown, 1982).

Imports into advanced countries from less industrialized ones can also be expected to stir up more opposition than imports from other advanced economies. Both tentative theoretical models and experience suggest that liberalization of trade is most likely where neither country has a strong comparative advantage in the industry and the products of different firms within the industry are highly differentiated, since under these conditions firms in *both* countries can benefit from liberalization (Krugman, 1982). Where advantages are all on one side, however, one finds what Bhagwati calls the 'growing dominance of external products' scenario, leading to protectionist demands both from entrepreneurs (especially if cheap migrant labour is not available) and from labour (Bhagwati, 1982; 177-9). In so far as protectionism results from political pressures by affected groups, therefore, one can expect it to be particularly intense against imports from LDCs, especially the well-organized NICs, with their tendency to focus suddenly on one sector or another for massive import penetration.

The findings of the literature on the political economy of protectionism are ironic, if not paradoxical. Since Europe and the United States benefit economically from LDC exports, one might expect the changing international division of labour to reinforce embedded liberalism. However, the conjunction of surplus capacity and unemployment (the results overwhelmingly of other factors) with rapid increases in NIC exports makes the NICs obvious scapegoats for advocates of protection. Wages in the NICs are low, and many of these countries have highly repressive governments; so the charge of 'unfairness' is easier to make than it is with respect to the Japanese.

Thus the significance of the newly industrializing countries for European liberalism may be more indirect than direct. The NICs serve as catalysts for action to scuttle non-discriminatory patterns of trade. Mercantilists can play down the importance of exports by the advanced countries to the NICs, arguing that these will only temporarily increase in response to gains by the less developed, lower-cost trading partners. Hager, for instance, characterizes Europe as 'a high cost area with decentralized real-capital formation, and hence intrinsically on the defensive. Under free trade conditions, any of the low-cost producers can decide to produce anything for the European market, constrained only by other outside competitors' (1982: 423). He thus conjures up the extraordinary spectacle of the NICs having comparative advantages over Europe in *everything*.

From the protectionist standpoint, the existence of the welfare state makes international liberalism even more intolerable. Hager comments as follows (1982: 424):

With unemployment approaching 10 per cent, the full-employment-of-factors assumption of free trade welfare economics looks threadbare. The welfare state adds a twist to the classical story by insisting that the idled factor labour be paid nearly in full, as if it were still producing. The cheap shirt is thus paid for several times: once at the counter, then again in unemployment benefits for the idled workers. Secondary losses involve input industries (although in the short term their exports rise): machinery, fibres, chemicals for dyeing and finishing products.

Western Europe seems more likely than the United States to follow protectionist policies during this decade. Ideological beliefs in liberalism are weaker in Europe than across the Atlantic, European industry is less dynamic technologically, and governments have more instruments available for intervention in the economy. 'Industrial policy' is therefore more attractive to many European governments, especially that of France, than it is to the United States. As Woolcock notes (1982: 236) 'there are no specific trade-related adjustment policies in Western Europe. With extensive structural-policy instruments of both a selective and a non-selective nature, there is little need to introduce new policy instruments.'

Protectionism coupled with industrial policy is not inevitable. European protectionism would conflict with the fact that the huge debts of many less developed countries can only be serviced if those countries can continue to increase their exports. For this reason, as well as its own political-security concerns with countries such as Mexico, South Korea, and Taiwan, the United States is likely to resist pressures for extensive protection. Since not all European governments are as enthusiastic about industrial policy as the French, pressures against protectionism are likely to be strong.

Neo-classical economists have long held that a well-functioning liberal world economy provides opportunities for the poor and weak. Despite the denial of this argument by dependency theorists, the developments of the last decade in the world political economy strongly support it. The rise of the NICs was itself a consequence of liberalism. Yet the result is not the further increase in economic openness envisioned by liberals: on the contrary, the suddenness of the process, characteristic of capitalist uneven development, forces adjustment costs on to groups that are weak economically but relatively strong politically. Polanyi's metaphor captures the effects, if not the nature of the process: 'society protects itself' against the ravages of the market. Or, to use the phrases of the literature on the political economy of protectionism, groups threatened by change lobby for protection in order to create rents for themselves. The policy connotations are different but the results are the same: unless its effects are cushioned by deliberate policy, the success of liberalism, even embedded liberalism, tends to destroy the conditions for its existence.

Even within the parameters of liberal assumptions about the best long-run path of the political economy, therefore, proponents of adjustment assistance, subsidies, and other forms of support for threatened industries and workers can make a strong case. Their argument is strengthened if these measures appear, in the medium to long run, to facilitate adjustment and maintain the conditions for liberalism. From this perspective, a reduction in the rate of increase in economic interdependence could be seen as a precondition for avoiding the demise of embedded liberalism in Western Europe.

Conclusions

Behind the variety of international forces impinging on Europe from the world political economy, two closely related patterns of change seem to be crucial: the rise and erosion of American hegemony and the expansion of capitalism on a world scale. As we have seen, American dominance, and the willingness of the United States to use its resources to build a liberal international political economy, were crucial elements in the post-war triumph of embedded liberalism in Europe. Conversely, the adverse shifts in terms of trade and the transmission of economic distress that characterized the 1970s were aggravated, if not caused, bý a decline in the ability and willingness of the United States to manage the world economy for its own benefit and that of its allies. Even when it would have been possible for the United States to continue managing the world political economy, to do so in a way that benefited Europe would have required more costly adjustments by the United States than it cared to make (Calleo, 1982).

As American authority over the world capitalist system was eroding in the 1970s, the system itself continued to expand. The earlier expansion of the 1940s and 1950s, incorporating Europe into the Americano-centric world political economy, contributed to European economic growth and to the gradual expansion of the welfare state, even if it contained a bias against rapid increases that went beyond the modal pattern of the time. The incorporation of Japan into the system as an advanced country during the 1960s and 1970s was received with less enthusiasm in Europe, since it imposed adjustment costs on their economic and political institutions and threatened the European position at or near the top of the international division of labour. Yet throughout this period, the political bias of liberalism benefited interests, groups, and political élites that were favourable to maintaining internationally oriented capitalism.

In conjunction with the economic crises of the 1970s (which had a variety of sources), the later rise of exports of manufactured goods from the newly industrializing countries, coupled with an increasing Japanese challenge, began to generate a powerful counter-reaction. Increasing state interventionism, designed at first to cushion societies from some of the adverse effects of interdependence, threatened to overwhelm liberalism itself. The problem was not the failure of capitalism but, in Schumpeterian fashion, its success. Uneven development again took place in the 1970s, as in the 1950s—but this time the most rapid rates of growth were in East Asia rather than Europe. Not surprisingly, the reactions of Europeans to this turn of events were quite different from their response to the Marshall Plan.

Against this background it is hard to regard the problems of the world political economy in the 1970s as exogenous, unpredictable shocks, as argued in the McCracken Report. Admittedly, not all of these events seem inevitable, and misguided American policies on both oil and monetary relations had a great deal to do with the subsequent crises (Keohane, 1984, 1985). Nevertheless, there is an inherent logic to the decline of hegemonic powers in a capitalist system, since their technological and organizational advantages are inherently subject to diffusion to the periphery, driven by the incentives of profit and power (Gilpin, 1981). Equally fundamental to the hegemon's position is the relationship between power and adjustment. As we have seen, power is in part the ability not to have to adjust to change. Adjustment is a 'political bad': people do not like to have to change their habits, especially if the results are psychologically and financially distressing. Voters tend to punish politicians who seek to force adjustments on to them. Yet adjustment is an 'economic good': neo-classical economists never tire of singing its praises as the principal engine of growth. The economy that does not adjust does not grow (Blackhurst *et al.*, 1977).

Hegemonic powers can avoid adjustment longer than others, precisely because they are powerful. Yet this ability to evade the necessity to make unpleasant changes can itself contribute to long-term decay. If weaker states adjust more readily than strong ones (not necessarily because they are more farsighted but because they have less choice), their economies will become more efficient, and they will become stronger. Japan's rapid adjustment to the 1973–74 oil shock, compared to that of the United States, is a case in point. No law prescribes that hegemonic powers will necessarily decline at any given time, but they are subject to the temptation to take the easy path. Their power gives them enough rope with which to hang themselves.

Even more than the decline of hegemony, the expansion of capitalism is the result of endogenous factors: unconstrained by state power, capitalism continuously reaches out not only for new markets and sources of raw materials, as in the past, but for new areas in which production for export can profitably take place. As new manufacturing centres enter the world system, the international division of labour becomes more extensive and interdependence grows rapidly. Yet the *political* economy of capitalism follows a more contorted path. Political reactions arise against what may seem, on efficiency grounds, to be a beneficial process. Europe, and to some extent the United States, are now going through such a reaction.

At the heart of this problem is a fundamental tension, or contradiction, in the international political economy of modern capitalism. International capitalism keeps expanding to the periphery, but depends on interventionist, self-interested states in the centre for its maintenance and support (Gilpin, 1975). Embedded liberalism is endangered because its peculiar combination of state interventionism and international openness rested on conditions—American political dominance and the pre-eminent position of Europe in the international division of labour—that can no longer be maintained, and that indeed were undermined by the success of liberalism itself. Major adjustments must now take place: to a new form of embedded liberalism that accepts the expansion of capitalism away from Europe, uncontrolled by the United States; or toward greater self-reliance and protectionism for Western Europe, perhaps in conjunction with selected areas of the Third World. Domestic political pressures point toward protectionism, yet its economic costs, and the threat it poses to transatlantic political relations, are well appreciated in Europe as well as in the United States. One plausible compromise would incorporate elements of both cooperation and protection. 'Cooperative protectionism' could limit political friction through the use of multilateral agreements, while cushioning the costs of rapid economic change (Keohane, 1984: 189-90). Such a strategy could easily degenerate to a discordant and stringent protectionism if too many concessions were made to obsolescent industries and interest groups seeking to prevent, rather than merely to delay, painful adjustments to change. Yet it offers the promise of reconciling the realities of international political and economic interdependence with demands for protection at home. Europe may have to choose, not between liberalism and protectionism in stark forms, but between defensive and discordant, or adjustment-oriented and cooperative, variants of protectionism. Its future will be affected — one is tempted to say, determined — by its reaction to this fateful choice.

Acknowledgements

I am grateful for comments on earlier versions of this paper to Professors Judith Goldstein, Peter J. Katzenstein, Craig Murphy and Harold Wilensky, and to members of the SSRC Study Group, particularly John Goldthorpe.

2

Preconditions for Corporatism

CHARLES S. MAIER

Introduction

In a century of world wars, political murder, and mass exterminations, wage negotiation certainly seems an undramatic human interaction. Why should a historian be intrigued by the process? For a start, wages and salaries have grown to comprise about two-thirds or higher of the national income of modern societies. Periods in which that ratio has increased rapidly are usually associated with significant price inflation. Behind today's wage bargaining, moreover, stands more than a century's evolution of labour organization: a development that once seemed to bring Western society to the brink of social revolution. Seen in this light, the history of wage settlements must be understood as the routinization of potential civil war into cumbersome negotiation, the transcending of Armageddon through political economy—a theme that Mill or Martineau might have relished and one that the post-Victorian mind might also find significant. Certainly it is one whose importance looms when the structures of settlement threaten to break down.

Wage settlements can be reached in many ways. They can rest on the exhaustion that follows acrimonious conflict, including strikes or lock-outs. They can be dictated 'from above' if public authorities possess the requisite force. They can derive from quick agreement as to what the labour market justifies, which may range from a degree of unemployment that impels labour to reluctant concessions to a boom market that motivates management to offer quick and generous pay increases. As wage negotiation has grown more centralized, moreover, the determination of the pay packet has usually come to represent only part of the stake involved in an implicit negotiation over the broader social role of labour. A wage negotiation in which the overall influence of labour and business is tacitly at stake is especially characteristic of what can be termed here 'consensual' wage determination. By consensual wage determination we mean collective bargaining among spokesmen for employers and for workers in which pay settlements emerge out of a set of considerations broader than normal market forces alone might sanction.

Consensual wage determination can rest upon a simple political exchange (Pizzorno, 1978b) in which, for example, union leaders seek enhanced power or status in return for delivering some degree of wage restraint. Or, in inflationary circumstances, employer and employee representatives can agree to wage increases that can be passed on to consumers by means of subsequent price rises. Such bargains are struck for narrow group advantage. However, consensual wage regulation can also respond to criteria of a broader public interest, transcending the short-term profits or pay increases that a given labour market might allow.

This paper focuses above all on the historical background of that sort of consensual wage regulation which seeks to incorporate broad social goals of economic welfare. To a degree, all peaceable settlements must do this. As theorists from Schumpeter (1943) and Polanyi (1944) to Goldthorpe (1978) and Hirsch (1976: ch. III) have pointed out, the capitalist market rests upon a normative consensus of non-market assumptions. Consensual wage bargaining means that the actors pull their economic punches to safeguard the normative foundation. But some national patterns of wage determination build this sort of restraint into the negotiating process itself, and these are of interest here. Obviously each party in consensual wage negotiations insists that its own objectives also represent the public interest. A major part of consensual wage bargaining involves establishing which economic objectives (investment, growth, employment, environmental protection) are indeed social priorities. Still, where consensual wage negotiations succeed, some mix of targets usually commands assent as a national objective. Can we, then, discern common historical patterns in those societies where spokesmen for labour and employers openly accept public-interest objectives of economic stability, export performance, investment and growth as well as their narrower wage or profit targets? Likewise, can we discover why certain time periods—cutting across all societies—have proved more conducive to consensual wage regulation than others?

The historian's temptation is to be dazzled by the complexity and uniqueness of each case and thus to fall into a sort of cultural reductionism: for example, the Dutch could rely upon their prior religious communities and general tradition of *Verzuiling*; the Austrians have learned to partition all offices and public enclaves; the Germans are orderly and inflation-averse. But any useful historical account must go beyond such national-character argumentation, not because it is not 'true' at some level, but because it forecloses so many other lines of analysis that should first be tested.

Since there is a large literature on 'corporatism', 'pluralism', consensual wage regulation and the like, a few brief definitions may help to keep distinct the historical phenomena under consideration. By corporatism in this essay—in partial contrast to my less specific usage in earlier work (Maier, 1975)—I refer to a broad concertation between employer and employee representatives across industries, which is usually established and sometimes continually supervised under state auspices (cf. Lehmbruch, this volume). Corporatism suggests a co-ordination of national negotiations in which state agencies endow major private economic associations with quasi-public authority. This can be used to arrive at binding commitments with the force of legislation and to discipline members. Pluralism is used here to refer to a pattern of collective bargaining where spokesmen for major groups of employers and of workers negotiate, but state supervision is confined to the elaboration of procedural guidelines such as guarantees for unions to speak for labour (cf. Pizzorno, 1980; Cessari, 1983). The distinction is not a hard and fast one, however. Societies often combine elements of both ideal types and they can move between situations of more or less continuing state intervention, as during wartime. This essay thus tends to consider both sorts of arrangements. Sometimes, moreover, it is convenient to label as 'corporatist' not an actual system as such, but the tendency of development: the evolutionary terminus of activist welfare states with highly developed peak associations. (For other efforts to put precision into usage see Schmitter, 1974, 1977; Panitch, 1977a.) In this sense, as a sort of political-economy horizon, corporatism a decade ago seemed to lie ahead for most Western societies. Even though the economic difficulties since the 1970s have revealed its vulnerability, we can still use the concept of corporatism to suggest the trajectory of consensual wage determination. In this essay at least, we shall employ the term as much for its aura as its actuality.

The Corporatist Imperative before the Second World War

Although theorists of 'corporatism' tend to focus on national experiences since 1945, that perspective is too short. Even if we concentrate only on efforts at consensual wage regulation (and exclude other aspects of interest mediation and private government through organized interests), historical understanding requires that we go back at least to the era of the First World War. It was clear by the late nineteenth century, if not before, that the emergence of mass labour movements meant a political as well as an economic challenge. Spokesmen for industrial capital might insist that the social and legal framework of a free labour market would provide sufficient vent for working-class aspirations. But traditionalists on the Right, whether statesmen such as Bismarck, or Catholic corporatist writers, had long recognized that the liberal market worked to fragment communities and to incite revolutionary ideologies. Likewise bourgeois progressives recognized the collective aspirations and power of labour as a class and sought to channel working-class demands into moderate and gradualist programmes.

The aspirations of organized labour did not consist of economic demands alone. To be sure, higher wages, shorter hours, and safety demands might dominate trade-union programmes. But, more fundamental, the very categories of liberal individualist representation seemed inadequate in the light of a 'collectivist' challenge. A keen awareness of group claims to representational legitimacy underlay particular issues. Legal theorists and political writers from the turn of the century on recognized, for instance, that the liberal civil codes on the Continent, or the anti-monopoly legislation in the US and its common-law equivalent in Britain, were inadequate to guide developments under way. Legislators had to provide *ad hoc* amendments to the framework of civil law or to the enshrined concepts of free contract, whether to deal with such issues as liability for industrial accidents or to set limits on dangerous employment. The laboriously constructed legal codes of the eighteenth and nineteenth century, or the whole Anglo-American thrust of judicial de-regulation of the same era, now met with a cascade of amendments. If to some observers this was a cause for alarm, others called for a more systematic overhaul. Whether guild socialists or functionalist liberals, authoritarian nationalists or conservatives, many jurists and political writers announced the obsolescence of liberal individualism. Modern society was tending towards corporatist associations, they declared, and the trend should be encouraged (see further Maier, 1981).

Public regulation of labour relations constituted the major project for those who advocated (or those who resisted) adoption of collectivist or corporatist approaches. The Left tended to press for recognition of collective bargaining. The Right likewise sought a collective framework for negotiating with labour. The Right, however, argued that the appropriate representational framework should be the firm, or all the firms in a given economic sector, not the working class as a whole. Some envisaged formal corporatist structures grouping labour with management by sector. None the less, until the First World War, debate over collective negotiations focused less on theoretical corporatist schemes than upon the role of unions or, in the parliamentary arena, on the role of socialist parties. Business and union spokesmen argued also about substantive controversies, such as the length of the working day or the conditions of labour or the right to strike. Only after 1905 did their agenda become far more political, as working-class parties introduced issues of colonialism, militarism and international relations, and universal suffrage into their demands. Not that these issues had not earlier constituted part of long-term working-class programmes. But by 1905, activists took them up as immediate objectives as well. Still, as of 1914, labour leaders often resisted imposing political objectives on strikes and unions. Consequently, until the First World War the question of how to construct a suitable post-individualist institutional framework—that is, short of socialism itself—remained somewhat marginal. Professional associations of clerks, teachers, bureaucrats, and the like might pursue corporate advantages, but did not elaborate any corporatist social organization.

The great economic exertions caused by the First World War and the subsequent post-war years of upheaval moved such projects, however, to centre stage. Without tracing the political events of the inter-war period in any detail, we can cite the emerging patterns of national wage-bargaining institutions that distinguished the era from 1914–1918 through to the Great Depression. Given the fragile post-war economic performance and the growth of unions and social democracy, the corporatist accommodation of labour, whether along authoritarian or democratic lines, seemed almost inevitable. Nevertheless, real corporatist institutions made only limited or ephemeral gains in most societies. What determined the differential degrees of progress that were chalked up?

Most of the European societies had made significant strides toward national labour regulation during the war. The unprecedented needs for war production and the consequent desire to minimize labour unrest at a time when intense demands were being placed on workers led each society to think about meeting labour grievances. At the same time, the authority now granted to ministries of munitions to negotiate war contracts provided an instrumentality for instituting new corporatist arrangements by private-law contracts without explicit national legislation. Wartime milestones included, therefore, such no-strike pledges as the Treasury Agreement of May 1915 in Britain, or the 'internal' factory committees that were created to air labour grievances in France, Italy, and Germany. Labour leaders entered into clear compacts of 'political exchange', in which they traded their capacity to deliver working-class co-operation for enhanced influence at governmental levels, whether through consultative arrangements or even cabinet office. Even in wartime Germany, where effective political authority passed to the military leadership, the Generals' demands for wartime output were so great that they were impelled to institute grievance committees and consultation far beyond what employers wished to concede. In France, the Ministry of Armaments under Louis Loucheur used its extensive contract authority to institute workers' factory committees that French entrepreneurs certainly distrusted. And not only entrepreneurs. Old-style trade-union leaders also feared the rival channels that such committees formed wherever they were established. (Feldman, 1966, 1970; Middlemas, 1979: 68–151; Oualid and Picquenard, 1928; Einaudi, 1933; Hardach, 1977: 176–96; Procacci, 1983.)

Wartime concessions were clearly exceptional. They outlined a corporatist order but did not assure its continuity. By and large, the institutions started during World War I did not prove enduring unless they were renegotiated afterwards. Usually this renegotiation required a new source of pressure: if no longer the state's need for continuous production, then the revolutionary threat of an aroused working class. Perhaps the clearest example was that of the Stinnes-Legien Agreement in Germany, where, foreseeing the revolution that was about to break over a discredited regime, percipient industrial leaders negotiated a private contractual arrangement with the leadership of the social-democratic trade unions. This provided for the institution of the eight-hour day and of a continuing consultative framework, the *Zentralarbeitsgemeinschaft*, which grouped trade unionists and industrial spokesmen until the great inflation finally destroyed the collaboration in early 1924. The arrangements negotiated by private social partners in mid-November were thereupon decreed as public legislation by the new revolutionary regime.

A resurgent Left imposed similar concessions throughout the advanced societies in the years to come. In the United States, the New Deal's National Recovery Administration of 1933 encouraged an extensive fabric of publicly superintended 'code' negotiations among business and trade associations. These were complemented by recognition of collective bargaining. But the NRA corporatist structure remained a patchy one. Its restrictions on output and its cartelistic approach aroused intense opposition even among reform adherents. Few lamented its being struck down by the Supreme Court in 1935. When collective bargaining was then resurrected by the 1937 Wagner Act, it was installed under different auspices; less as a corporatist enfolding of organized labour than as an effort to give unions the organizational power they would need to stand up against industrial employers. The Wagner Act envisaged pluralism, one might summarize, but not the continuing substantive co-ordination that usually is implicit in the notion of corporatism. (Hawley, 1966.)

An officially sanctioned pluralism also characterized the recognition of collective bargaining wrested by French unions at the outset of the 1936 Popular Front. Under the impact of the Left's electoral victory and the anxiety of the massive sit-down strikes, the French employers' association agreed to a list of demands in negotiations supervised by the new premier, Léon Blum, including the forty-hour week, two-week paid vacations, and the recognition of the unions. In the French case the state intervened to speed a collective private-law agreement, but provided little continuing institutionalization of co-operation (Lorwin, 1954: ch. v; Lefranc, 1967, 1969).

The Swedish Saltsjöbaden agreement of 1938 (following upon employer recognition of union rights to organize in December 1906 and the regulation of association by law in 1936) provides a final inter-war example of supervised pluralism, but one instituted with greater time for reflection on the part of employers. This 'framework agreement' was consented to after five years of Social Democratic administration had already demonstrated that the rule of the Left was not incompatible with capitalist development, and indeed might inaugurate a vigorous economic performance in the prevailing conditions of world depression. Moreover, Swedish labour spokesmen powerfully inclined toward private corporatist compromises to regulate the labour market. Discussions were stimulated in 1935, once Norway instituted a 'Basic Agreement' and the Nothin Report at home emphasized the value of a voluntary capital-labour compact, building upon the centralization of union power. Saltsjöbaden provided for the orderly continuation of a responsible collaboration, and, as a result, was less politically vulnerable to erosion or conservative rejection (Johnston, 1962: 124-9, 163-5, 168-75; Korpi, 1978: 210 ff.).

Each of these major developments depended upon a determined union movement being able to bring decisive power to bear. In the German and French cases, however, the power was potentially revolutionary: employers submitted for fear of a more radical expropriation were they to resist. In the Swedish instance the power rested upon the electoral strength of the affiliated Social Democratic party (SAP), although the gradualist approach of the latter worked as much to reassure industrialists as to frighten them. In each of these cases, trade-union federations mobilized sources of political power to win economic concessions. In each case, too, trade-union leaders also secured their own influence against radical pressures from within their movements. They brought home new concessions, but in return imposed a commitment upon the rank-and-file to live within the new compact. (For the tension this discipline can cause see Sabel, 1981.)

Finally, each of the political coalitions that superintended the new compact could seek its own short-term gains. The left-wing governments that supervised these major social treaties might in some cases, such as Sweden, diminish opposition among the business classes. On the other hand, in the case of Germany and France, many industrialists felt humiliated. They nursed their resentments and hoped for revenge. Perhaps more effectively, social-democratic governments could exploit the social compacts to contain the pressure of left-wing dissidents. The inter-war framework agreements thus helped social democracy to carry out some of its more ambiguous ambitions of securing tangible labour gains and participation in progressive, but capitalist coalitions.

Yet social democrats, unionists, and industrial leaders were not alone in seeking out these arrangements. Authoritarian political regimes also required a corporatist assurance, just as wartime governments had needed it. Indeed rightist politicians could utilize the corporative beginnings undertaken under more reformist auspices. The extensive provisions for labour courts and arbitration under Weimar, for instance, initially represented a Social Democratic achievement. By the end of the 1920s, however, conservative and proto-Nazi forces were exploiting the same provisions for collective responsibility to limit workers' right to strike and to assign liability for work-days lost to employees. Whichever political side enjoyed the momentary upper hand might exploit legalized corporatist tendencies. Corporatist representation could serve labour and social democracy, but it could also provide a device to control and undermine labour gains.

Consider the divergent approaches taken by Primo de Rivera in Spain, and Mussolini in Italy. Primo's 1923 dictatorship did not allow for liberal representation, but he cultivated connections with the Spanish Socialist party and trade union confederation, which, under Largo Caballero, fully acquiesced in this de facto collaboration (Ben Ami, 1983). Mussolini, however, took power within a society more advanced than Spain even if its industrial development was unevenly distributed. The bitter conflicts over wartime intervention and post-war aspirations, the industrial mobilization that had been achieved no matter how imperfectly, meant that no rightist project could rely on reinstatement of a traditionalist authoritarianism. Nor would a fascist leadership drawn from syndicalist and ex-socialist, as well as rightist elements, have consented to simple reaction. Mussolini was thus impelled to grope for an appropriate format for dealing with an organized and militant labour movement. His successive answers began with brute terrorism, then moved on to the Fascist party's own counter-organization of labour. Fascist-sponsored syndicates were to be granted collective representation—indeed this representation was to be imposed upon industrialist leaders who disliked even fascist unions. But despite a Charter of Labour and a system of labour courts supposedly designed to resolve workers' grievances, control was subordinated to the regime's political leadership. Although in the years from 1922 to 1929 the new fascist unions and then 'corporations' periodically threatened to assume an independence of action, Mussolini subordinated them at critical points. Still, Italian fascism demonstrated that the hallmark of modern dictatorship had precisely to consist of its corporatist co-ordination of collective social forces, including that of the working class (Lyttelton, 1973: chs. 9, 12, 13; Jocteau, 1978).

This was also the lesson of Nazi Germany, which by its labour legislation of February 1934 instituted a comprehensive Labour Front designed to speak for the working class as a whole within the regime. In Germany, as in fascist Italy, this encompassing organization was also designed to suppress the crystallization points for a potentially independent working-class representation within the factory. Italian fascist factory 'trustees', (*fiduciari di fabbrica*) and the National Socialist Factory Organization both grouped together adherents of the respective ruling parties, but they also were led by spokesmen who thought they had a genuine mission to represent labour in their new regimes. These illusions were to be quashed by the more monolithic national labour groupings. Just as social-democratic or trade-union leaders in the democratic states sometimes utilized social compacts to restrain militant challenges from below, so the leaders of the official labour fronts froze out dissident fascists and Nazis (Mason, 1977: ch. III; Mai, 1973: 573–613).

What relevance, might it be asked, did the authoritarian labour corporations (one can also include the Vichy federation under René Belin) have for the background of democratic consensual wage regulations? Primarily, they illustrated that, given the emergence of industrial societies, regimes of any ilk have felt the need for a collective disposition of labour issues. After industrialization, and—just as critical—after the mass political mobilization that followed universal male suffrage and the world war, authoritarian and democratic national political economies alike perceived the imperative for dealing with collective interests in the market-place as well as in government agencies. For the dictatorial regimes this collective approach arose from the desire to replace earlier pluralist contenders, such as free trade unions and parties. It also arose, in the Italian case at least, from the perceived need for economic and social modernization, which in turn seemed to require calling collective interlocutors into being. Modernization was a corporate task and no longer an individualist possibility.

None the less, if different sorts of regimes responded to the corporatist imperative, not every individual society responded. Pre-eminently in Great Britain (a big and interesting exception, to be sure), the institutions of organized pluralism or corporatism remained largely undeveloped. Certainly there were interesting collaborative ventures, such as the Mond–Turner talks or the various projects sketched by the young Harold Macmillan. But, by and large, British collectivist needs could be met within the more traditionalist cadres of Parliament and given trade unions. One important reason for this was that at no point in inter-war Britain, apart from flamboyant episodes in 1919 and 1926, did labour pose a serious collective threat. Employers felt no need for corporatist concessions. Another reason lay in the deep distrust that most British trade unionists also felt in any system that limited their traditional adversarial role. Had there been a more serious breakdown of the inter-war economy, instead of the dispiriting but non-catastrophic performance it registered, or had there been more unrest, then corporatism might have come more openly to Britain. In so far as consensual wage regulation existed, it existed because market conditions precluded more labour aggressiveness. In so far as corporatism existed, it found its roots in a traditionalist mode of 'collectivist' solidarity that Beer (1967) and others have well described: a concern by labour leaders to preserve the autonomy of their working-class communities as much as to negotiate encompassing political bargains.

Between the wars, then, corporatist institutions remained rather *ad hoc* responses. In some societies they represented an achievement of the Left, won under exceptional conditions and thus vulnerable to reversal; in others, such as Sweden, the result of a mature conviction of the need for harmonious shared power; in the new fascist regimes, the way ostensibly to reconcile total control with the need to find working-class interlocutors. Finally in Britain and, to a degree, in the United States and other democracies, corporatism involved a mode of bargaining that was still unfamiliar outside wartime, unwished for by many labour leaders who sought to preserve community and organization as much as to influence policy, and unnecessary if business leaders could avert, or recover from economic catastrophe. Thus the inter-war period brought approaches towards corporatism but no uniformity of outcome.

The Conditions of Post-war Outcomes, 1944–1968

If from the vantage point of the 1970s we had surveyed the strength of consensual wage determination in different societies, the correlation with inter-war experiments would have been partial at best. As reviewed above, many of the inter-war experiments depended upon political successes that were now rolled back, whether through the defeat of fascism or the erosion of popular-front coalitions in the democracies. The shattering experiences of the Second World War, the persecution of labour movements, the Resistance, and post-war labour schism, also contributed to the recombination of elements. National societies drew upon historical legacies but in new ways. Instead of merely narrating these vicissitudes from country to country, it makes more sense to establish the patterns of wage regulation and then seek reasons for these patterns. The development will be surveyed as of the end of the 1960s, for the quarter century from the Liberation to the new labour militancy of the late 1960s and to the simultaneous onset of prolonged inflation comprises a historical epoch with its own logic of development. Once we have established the pattern of development for that now closed and historical period, we can turn to the still open events of the past decade and a half.

From the late 1960s or early 1970s, one might label as strongly consensual the wage determination systems in Scandinavia, West Germany, Austria, Switzerland, and the Netherlands. In Scandinavia framework agreements still governed the prevailing wage settlements, although the play allowed for local plant amendment (wage drift) was a necessary complement. By and large, settlements were achieved on the basis of forecasts as to what increases were possible without endangering export performance. The dual sector economic models developed by the Scandinavians—the Swedish 'EFO' Model (Edgren *et al.*, 1973) and the similar Norwegian one proposed by Aukrust (1977)—provided a rationale for moderating wage increases in the protected service sector to those allowable in the traded-goods sector. In West Germany trade unions observed significant wage restraint throughout the 1950s and much of the 1960s and then entered a formal 'Concerted Action' framework in 1966 in which they bargained within the range of targets that officials announced would not endanger growth and stability. In Austria unions negotiated with similar restraint within a society where Catholics and Socialists had worked out a general sharing of positions and influence. Dutch workers accepted a tripartite bargaining framework with binding settlements until 1964 as a legacy of Occupation measures. In one way or another these countries wove labour representation into collaborative structures that established overall growth and stability parameters which union spokesmen then felt compelled to observe. Only when unexpected surges of profits seemed to make labour's restraint one-sided did these arrangements collapse. Except for the Dutch case at mid-decade, this did not come to pass until the onset of inflation and the tidal wash of dollars and exchange-rate difficulties at the end of the 1960s.

It can hardly be surprising that measures of consensual wage determination have been found to correlate with those of 'neo-' or 'societal' corporatism: the degree of labour-union centralization and the absence of open conflict, after all, are indices for both (cf. Schmitter, 1981; Lehmbruch, 1977 and this volume). Of the societies distinguished by high degrees of corporatism, Austria and the Netherlands have often been identified as 'consociational' democracies (Lijphart, 1968; Daalder, 1966; Engelmann, 1966), where long-standing confessional or ethnic cleavages have forced a parcelization of office and influence. The Dutch referred to their 'pillarization'; the Austrians to their 'camps'. West Germany, Sweden, Norway, and Denmark, were less consociational, but working-class parties remained such durable political participants in local, if not always national institutions, that it was understood that no policies could fundamentally seek to negate their influence. Moreover, workers and employers in the Federal Republic and the Scandinavian countries (along with the Netherlands) perceived their economies as vulnerable, subject to the buffets of the international market. Approximately half their GNP consisted of goods and services traded across their national frontiers.

In contrast to these patterns of consensual negotiation France and Italy revealed a more conflictual pattern. Major sectors of the labour movement were grouped in unions affiliated with a Communist party that was excluded from sharing in national power. And as non-communist unions showed increased vitality during the 1960s, they did so often by demonstrating that they could remain as militant as the Communist federations.

Britain and the United States, finally, tended to display behaviour different from either the corporatist or the Latin (i.e. the Franco-Italian) pattern. Their labour relations remained fragmented and conflictual. In Britain, Labour party policy might formally rest on union representation and depend upon the unions' electoral mobilization, but the party was rarely in a position to impose a particular labour-market behaviour upon its affiliated unions. In the United States, the Democratic party enjoyed labour sympathies (with exceptions in the 1950s and 1970s), but no formal connections. None the less, even in Britain and the United States, consensual wage agreements or even corporatist arrangements could be instituted under conditions perceived of as demanding extraordinary discipline. The TUC had accepted a wage freeze under the Labour Government during 1948-9; it would also enter into wage-policy agreements— in the form of the 'Social Contract'—during the Callaghan government after 1974 (Thomson, 1981: 30 ff.). Similarly, American labour reluctantly accepted wage controls from 1971 through 1973 (Goodwin, 1975). But these remained *ad hoc* arrangements that usually generated labour restiveness from their outset. On the whole, no formal structures of consensual negotiation or corporatist bargaining prevailed. (Which is not to say that there were not functional substitutes: until persistent inflation undermined the system, American labour tended to accept wage rises keyed to productivity gains. An implicit social compact adjourned any labour effort to slice a larger share of the pie so long as the pie remained growing.)

In seeking to account for these different outcomes we find that one striking variable is that cited by Goldthorpe in this volume: 'the fact that the countries in which [corporatist] tendencies have been most sustained are ones in which social-democratic parties have played a dominant role in government is readily intelligible: union movements will be more prepared to enter into political bargaining, and will have greater confidence of eventual gains from it, where they possess close ideological as well as organizational ties with the ruling party'. Still, as Goldthorpe's summary also notes, West German and Dutch unions have joined in participatory mechanisms even when socialists have not been dominant, and in Britain they have remained distrustful even when the Labour party has been in power.

Certainly the strong presence of reformist social democracy is a major encouragement to corporatist participation in consensual regulation. As Goldthorpe and others argue, one reason is the possibility of 'political exchange' to win elaboration of social-welfare or full-employment policies. Moreover, the existence of a powerful social-democratic movement should in the course of things accompany the development of corporatist tendencies. Social democracy itself testifies to acceptance of an ideology and comportment that views state and market as already woven together. Social democracy was built upon the premise of continuing bargaining between class actors for political and social gains. Hence, it is only natural that corporatist structures should emerge easily in countries with strong social-democratic traditions. Still, not every labour movement in a country with strong labour political representation need adopt corporatist behaviour, as the case of Britain suggests, and consensual wage regulation among producer groups can be maintained even when social democracy is relatively weak, as in the Netherlands. In the case of Holland, however, the German occupiers themselves organized the initial labour-management pact. Although it might have been tainted by this early sponsorship, in fact during the period of post-war austerity the co-operation seemed worth preserving, and it took less strenuous commitment to keep it in being than it would have taken to organize it voluntarily in the first place (Windmuller, 1957). Founding conditions are different from maintenance conditions.

Let us review the founding conditions for the cases of strongly consensual wage determination. The situation of the Netherlands has already been mentioned. Belgium shared a similar experience. Aware of the economic burdens that German occupation would bequeath—not least a potential hyperinflation—the Belgian government in exile helped institute a social compact upon its return from London. This included a currency reform that hit bank accounts, froze wages and prices, and promised welfare advances. Socialists and Liberals had co-operated in exile; post-war agreement on wage controls represented a prolongation of the felt need to co-operate. Belgian Communists went along with this general compact until 1947, when the sharpening cold war and the restiveness of their workers led them to break with the government, ostensibly over opposition to coal price increases. But until that point wage restraint formed part of a broadly perceived effort to share the burdens of austerity equitably. Nor did Flemish-Walloon antagonism directly affect the social compact; it fed into the chronic political dispute over the fate of King Leopold III rather than the socio-economic divergence of Flanders and Wallonia that subsequent Flemish economic development and French decline has aggravated. In sum, even without the consociational pillars of the Netherlands, the felt imperatives of post-war economic reconstruction and political conciliation contributed to an initial pattern of labour co-operation (Lorwin, 1966: 165–9).

The same could be claimed for the Scandinavian countries that emerged from occupation, Denmark and Norway. Norway maintained compulsory arbitration until 1952, but thereafter depended upon a delicate balance of economic and political forces to preserve social equilibrium into the 1960s (Rokkan, 1966). In contrast to her German-occupied neighbours, Sweden had already inaugurated consensual wage regulation before the war. Precarious neutrality and the generally shattered European economy of the early post-war years only continued the inducement to routinize wage bargaining. Sweden thus remained the primary case in which an inter-war framework agreement carried over into the post-war period—a continuity made possible by the fact that Sweden remained neutral and prosperous. What remained motivating in each of these cases, I believe, was a clear sense of potential economic *vulnerability*. Small countries, highly developed, clearly had to create and maintain the conditions for export viability at a time when the level of economic demand throughout Europe was much reduced. At the same time, the presence of strong social-democratic parties, their legitimacy enhanced by earlier repression in the occupied countries, meant that any bargain to secure wage restraint could not be one-sided. Institutions that promised equity even as they asked for restraint had to be invented. Part of the larger framework included elaboration of the institutions of the welfare state; part included implicit commitments to full employment (cf. Katzenstein, 1983, 1984).

For Scandinavia, Belgium, and the Netherlands we can best infer perceived vulnerability from the share of GNP passing through imports and exports. For West Germany and Austria a different vulnerability was also involved. Their labour forces had just emerged from National Socialist repression and their working-class movements remembered that when they had been momentarily strong they had not been able to achieve durable preponderance. Indeed their very strength had helped evoke a violent counter-reaction. The *grandes journées* of inter-war German and Austrian labour history were days of painful defeat: the Prussian *Staatsstreich* of 20 July 1932, the Nazi coming to power of 30 January 1933, and the suppression of the Viennese Socialists on 12 February 1934, to cite just some. Inter-war history demonstrated that consolidation of partial economic influence might be more realistic than the dream of moving toward the magic 51 per cent that would supposedly sanction the transition to a full socialism. Hilferding's analyses were over-optimistic as a theory of socialism, but as a strategy for modifying capitalism they were still promising.

Moreover, post-war constraints on social transformation were considerable. The Austrian and German economies remained under Allied supervision. If it had been the sole factor, the memory of repression might possibly have led to a demand for retribution and a more uninhibited flexing of union muscles. But economic destruction and the continuing feeling that their countries would be subject to reparation and dismantling precluded any nurturing of old wounds. The unification of the labour movement in West Germany, moreover, made it necessary to find a common programme for Catholics and Socialists. In the early years of the Occupation and the Federal Republic, labour militancy expressed itself in the campaign for codetermination and economic democracy. Once the German trade unions had achieved the degree of workers' participation that the political circumstances of 1949–51 permitted, they did not convert further militancy into a wage struggle. Instead they effectively used their energies to rebuild the organizations shattered in the Third Reich. Throughout the 1950s union leaders stressed labour's commitment to reconstruction even at the cost of seeing the wage share of national income decline. To be sure, post-war legislation did not make it easy to use the strike in wage disputes since elaborate voting procedures hedged any legal walk-out. None the less the record of restraint probably went beyond whatever formal impediments were placed in the way of strikes. German labour wagered on growth and recovery even at the cost of wage shares, and probably (if Britain be viewed as the alternative case) won their wager. And while by the early 1960s clear signs of restiveness troubled the labour scene, unions were still prepared to enter a formal negotiation framework during the period of the Great Coalition after 1966. In fact, the Concerted Action was more an expression of an internalized union restraint than an effective institution for achieving it. It even helped secure union observance of monetarist targets, which in many other countries would have been simply unacceptable economics for labour (Riemer, 1982: 61).

Austrian labour likewise demonstrated a commitment to consensual wage determination; indeed, it proved an even more resilient one when the troubled 1970s arrived. In Austria, too, labour's own perception of historical vulnerability conditioned the collaboration. In the light of the inter-war civil conflict between a Catholic Right that became quasi-fascist and a strong social-democratic Left, how was such harmony established? Between the wars it appeared that the tension between 'red' and 'black' was so unmediated by other forces that no peaceful community might be established among German Austrians. That inter-war conflict culminated in the forcible suppression of the Socialists in 1934 and the installation of an Austro-fascist state in the four years before *Anschluss*. How then did Austria become a model of labour collaboration after the war?

Again, some of the answer lay in the fact that the memory of violence and democratic failure induced restraint on both sides. For the Austrian Catholics (as for the Right elsewhere in Europe) a fascist recourse was just simply excluded after the excesses of 1933 to 1945. But there was no scope either for a radical left, given the four-power occupation. Co-operation seemed essential in the limited ambit left to domestic politics. Once the State Treaty restored sovereignty in 1955, co-operation seemed all the more necessary in the light of a fragile nationality. Austrians effectively partitioned the welfare state (Shell, 1962: 64-8, 172-9). They enjoyed a certain bonus in the massive state sector, which now inherited the German-built infrastructure in hydroelectric power and steel. Disposition of this new industrial capacity was suspended during the four-power occupation, but it offered the foundation of an ample state sector after 1955. *Cuius regio eius religio* was applied to local government, control of the massive nationalized sector, welfare agencies, and political office; and in this comprehensive application of *Proporz*, wage determination naturally fell into a pattern of compromise settlement. Thus the very polarization of Austrian politics that had made the inter-war decades so bitter encouraged a co-operative approach once the international environment changed from that of an encroaching fascism to confidence in growth and democracy.

So far we have suggested that institutions for consensual wage bargaining—efforts, say, at proto-corporatism—arose under conditions of exceptional vulnerability. For West Germany and Austria vulnerability included political precariousness: the labour movement's own memories of historical repression and its caution in reclaiming a national role, its very diffidence at hegemony. Industrial leaders also had reason to be cautious. Out of the reciprocal diffidence consensus emerged. Pulling their punches lest they recapitulate earlier errors, German and Austrian labour operated in polities where all actors had to tread gingerly. For the small countries of Scandinavia, Belgium, and the Netherlands, vulnerability had a pronounced economic component. But industrial leaders there too might demonstrate conciliation lest they provoke a radical *épuration* that would expropriate many of their number for wartime collaboration.

We can, however, also learn about the conditions for corporatist arrangements from studying the countries where they did not take root. In France and Italy the labour movements pursued a distinctive strategy, relying on their affiliation with a powerful Communist party that was represented within government until 1947 and was in opposition thereafter. Up to 1946 Communist leaders themselves stressed labour co-operation and wage restraint in the effort to demonstrate their respectability as coalition partners. Thereafter pressures from the rank-and-file forced the leadership to become less 'productivist' and more demanding (see further Horowitz, 1963; Lefranc, 1969; Turone, 1973; Lange *et al.*, 1982).

Why, though, did the period of tripartite governmental coalitions with Communist participation not lead to institutionalized frameworks for centralized labour-management negotiation? Certainly the fact that the labour unions in France and Italy had established united confederations at the time of Liberation should have abetted such an effort. Even if the Left's political parties were not to fuse, labour movements merged as part of the joint Resistance effort. They would divide again during 1947-8, but made no effort during the years of labour unity to establish corporatist institutions with employers, and for several reasons. Labour unity probably contributed a sense of strength that made formal restraint seem unnecessary: the working class—so Communists and Socialists felt—might not claim exclusive rule, but it possessed a virtual social hegemony that arose out of the armed resistance. This confidence contrasted with the tone of the labour groups which re-formed in the smaller countries or even in Germany and Austria. Moreover, French and Italian labour claimed a historical legitimacy, based on their contribution to the mass resistance movements, whereas industrial leaders were badly compromised by association with the Vichy or Italian fascist regimes.

Neither in France nor in Italy, moreover, were governments initially prepared to move resolutely against inflation. In part, labour resistance itself made monetary reform difficult, but business spokesmen also mounted opposition. Had the post-Liberation governments attempted serious stabilization, demanding sacrifices among all classes (the Belgian model), they might have enlisted labour cooperation. In situations where the state just continued to finance a deficit, there was less incentive to enter into long-term compacts. Instead labour either accepted politically-conditioned Communist appeals for restraint or, by 1946-7, felt it had to wrest what wage increases might best protect it against chronic price rises. By this date, however, cold war trade-union schisms and the impact of the Marshall Plan had helped to undermine labour militancy. Any working-class foundation for social hegemony had been dissipated. Industrial leaders now felt themselves ready to assume a stance of confrontation. Labour, in effect, missed the moment to establish reciprocal consensual institutions in France and Italy.

But there were longer term structural reasons beyond the legacy of wartime resistance and the legitimation of Communist parties that it provided. To understand the role of these other factors we should consider the contrast with Britain, where similar outcomes resulted for different reasons. In Great Britain, as well as in France and Italy, consensual wage determination and corporatist institutions proved feeble. British unions also stood aloof from corporatist arrangements. Consent to the wage freeze of 1948 was reluctant and short-lived, extracted because of the grave difficulties faced by a Labour government. As most commentators stress, British trade unionism remained decentralized and craft-oriented under the umbrella of the TUC. Taken together, British unions covered a far larger percentage of the working class than either French or Italian unions; but it was difficult for the TUC to enter into binding agreements on behalf of its fragmented constituents, whereas the French CGT or Italian CGIL might ultimately serve as a more creditable interlocutor. These different conditions brought two different sorts of impediment to the development of corporatist institutions. The British lacked a powerful central voice for labour, although labour was widely organized. The French and Italian unions had powerful central federations, but only in rare moments of radical upheaval, such as the end of the world wars or in 1936 or in 1968-9, did the federation leaders speak for an imposing mass of workers.

There were, however, further factors at work in the British case to contribute to a weakly corporatist outcome. The British Labour party had not inherited a corporatist legacy. It was willing to impose 'austerity' on its constituency in return for policies that assured full employment and a universality of welfare benefits. It envisaged a community of citizens with entitlements, not a society of bilateral contracts. Its strategy required changing society as a whole, not focusing on the labour market. After all, the formative period for British Labour, as it emerged in 1945, had been the 1930s (cf. Pimlott, 1977). This decade had nurtured the Morrison-Durbin-Attlee corps of planners as well as reducing the party to its electoral core of the distressed working class in the areas of high unemployment. Labour did not emerge as a governing party having to worry about the problem of reining in the inflationary militancy of its workers. They were already hobbled by unemployment before the war and committed by the coalition during the years after 1940. Nor did British Labour ever have to make overtures to a more conservative countryside vote as in Scandinavia, since few farmers remained. The pull of cross-cutting interests did not influence the party.

The reasons for different British and continental outcomes can also be understood by considering the different phasing of trade-union achievements and political-party victories. British trade unions had wrested collective bargaining from their employers ever since the nineteenth century, whereas French unions made their breakthrough in 1936 and Italian unions had achieved only fragile and reversible bargaining status in the aftermath of the First World War. (To be sure, what mattered for the French and Italian unions was less their long-term numerical weakness than their momentary *élan* in the wake of the wartime resistance.) Indeed, British trade-union success had preceded the formation of a labour party. The impulse to form the party sprang in part from union legal setbacks before 1906, and the new party was formally to rest on its union affiliates. In France and Italy, however, the respective socialist parties achieved political maturity *before* the national union movements chalked up national victories for collective bargaining. Unions sometimes kept their distance from the party (the syndicalist model) and sometimes they engaged in significant local organizational victories or battles against employers. But their efforts to extract national bargaining arrangements tended to follow in the wake of political party mobilization and/or electoral success. The primacy of the party was a result of the later industrialization of the Latin countries: decisive political transformations which helped precipitate out parties preceded the development of the mining, heavy industry, and transport sectors that provided the unions with militancy and power.

The British and Franco-Italian patterns thus both contrasted with the northern European and German evolution of social democracy, where unions and parties kept approximate pace with one another. But it was precisely the latter synchronization that most abetted long-term consensual or corporatist outcomes in the post-war generation. Development out of phase—whether a labour party that followed the establishment of collective bargaining, or unions that made their decisive breakthroughs as a consequence of prior political advance—did not yield the same fertile terrain for corporatism. Corporatist or consensual arrangements meant the bridging of the market and political arenas, and this was easiest where working-class representation developed in both at an equal pace.

Finally one might cite even longer-term legacies. German and Austrian corporatism could link up with the collaborative structures of the old monarchies, their elected social-insurance boards, their paternalist ministries, and even the dim legacy of a state cameralism. In Sweden, government through royal commission was a venerable recourse. The corporatist societies enjoyed, to use that imprecise concept, 'strong states'. Of course, from most points of view, so did France. But so-called strong states could relate in different ways to the organizational patterns of their respective societies (cf. Hall, 1984: 21-43). Corporatist tendencies did not emerge where strong states confronted fragmented and conflictual economic and cultural forces (the French case), but where they could work with disciplined and cohesive associations. The strong states of German-speaking Europe or perhaps Scandinavia were strong precisely because they worked congruently with the forces of civil society. The strength of the French state rested more on its splintering of civil society.

The recourse to consensual wage determination or to corporatism reflected, therefore, in its formative post-war period a particular combination of strength and weakness. The strength consisted of the close relation between cohesive union movements and strong social-democratic parties. The weakness consisted in exposure to the discipline of the international market or in the historically grounded fear of political polarization and reaction. The perception of vulnerability suggested renouncing too exclusive a vision of working-class power. Political use of the labour market seemed an appropriate strategy. That choice differed from the wager of British Labour on paying for Marshallian entitlements at home in part through the residues of Empire. It also differed from the Franco-Italian Communist vision that saw post-war politics as a continuation of wartime resistance by other means. Together the interaction of strength and vulnerability created the incentive to buffer and swaddle an industrial relations system that had proved so disruptive earlier.

Corporatist Restructuring in the Era of Inflation

The analysis above attempts to suggest under what circumstances corporatist or consensual wage determination could take root in the early post-war period. But that period underwent significant stress and transformation from the late 1960s, as Western societies saw a period of labour militancy and then prolonged inflation. How did these developments from the late 1960s modify the institutional outcomes of the two post-war decades?

Long-term inflationary pressures made corporatist arrangements more beckoning and more fragile. They tempted governments to seek labour collaboration more urgently, but rendered it ever more precarious. The upshot was a series of formalized labour compacts: Nixon's Phases II and III (Phase I was merely a decreed freeze); Callaghan's Mark I, II, and III; Sweden's Haga I and Haga II. Such ephemeral agreements littered the labour-market landscape between 1971 and 1979. However, it would be misleading to think of all of them as constituting equally durable corporatist frameworks. In the Swedish case they might emerge as adaptations of a long consensual tradition. In the Anglo-American case, however, they comprised more an effort at *ad hoc* importation. They did not last long enough to lead to the centralization of wage bargaining that would have been required to entrench a consensual system. Perhaps they could be best characterized as a sort of pseudo-corporatism. Labour unions in both the UK and US left these experiments behind, however, swearing never to get entangled again (Thomson, 1981; Weber & Mitchell, 1978).

Instead of focusing on these fragile social compacts, it is more fruitful to look at subtler transformations that reveal some of the implicit bargains which underlay consensual wage determination. Inflation at the end of the 1960s, and even more after the OPEC oil price rises from 1973-4, corresponded with a slowdown in the remarkable growth that characterized the European economy after 1948. Having to deal with the consequences of faltering growth and later with outright decline in national incomes necessarily placed a heavy burden on consensual wage determination. To maintain corporatist institutions took less energy and commitment than to erect them, so long as anticipated growth provided continued dividends that could be distributed among the social partners. But after a decade and a half or more of relative wage restraint and heavy capital formation, European labour sought more immediate gains for consumption. The Dutch framework, as noted, broke down with major wage demands in 1964; by the end of the 1960s German unions had abandoned their traditional restraint, and in the Latin countries workers remobilized with spectacular militancy. Although, as Cameron suggests (this volume), social democratic parties might offer labour more social consumption in return for wage restraint, ultimately either social consumption or a higher wages bill had to cut into profit and investment. The virtuous circle of wage restraint, investment, and growth slipped into a vicious circle of lagging investment, slower growth, and a more intensive conflict over income shares (cf. Sachs, 1979, 1983).

There were other seismic pressures that weakened the basis for labour restraint. By the late 1960s unions faced potential generational conflict as the stalwarts of post-war labour collaboration passed from the scene. The disciplinary rigour of the cold war lost its force in an era of *détente*. The massive exodus from agriculture in the Latin countries, the expansion of education, the advent of television, accessible automobiles, and vacations, all contributed to a major cultural shift in which the balance between present consumption and renunciation for future benefits probably shifted toward the present.

More immediately, the late 1960s undermined several of the implicit decision rules that had facilitated consensual wage determination. Consensus was easier when objective circumstances and indicators seemed to dictate the parameters of settlements. The Concerted Action after 1966 relied on the forecasts of the 'Wise Men' to suggest the rational bounds of wage and price movements; but even without such an explicit framework, there were equivalents elsewhere. Much of the breakdown of decision rules was attributable to the changing role of the United States. A major factor facilitating the establishment of consensual systems was the plausible (though hardly necessary) notion that wages and profits should be keyed to productivity advances. Productivity played more than a technical role. It was the American principle for helping to organize the post-war Western political economy (Maier, 1978). American unions accepted productivity guidelines; and most labour spokesmen who participated in wage bargaining accepted a productivity indexed standard for pay advances. They relied on growth rather than redistribution to secure larger primary income streams, allocating mild redistributive tasks to the welfare state. Sweden became a partial exception, for its solidaristic wages policy imposed the growth potential of the traded-goods sector on domestic service producers as well. Even in Sweden, however, balance-of-payments constraints provided a decision rule until the 1970s.

The onset of inflation, however, weakened these decision rules. In the initial stages of Vietnam War finance, American dollars, now formally overvalued by the nominal exchange values, poured into Europe. Forced to accept them,

European Central Banks could not but inflate their own money supplies and in effect share in the burden of financing the American deficit. This placed countries such as Sweden and West Germany in difficult situations. So long as they postponed revaluation, they could not resist importing inflation. But should they revalue their own currencies upward to dampen the inflationary impulse emanating from Washington, then their own exports and balance of payments must suffer. From the late 1960s, as more and more American dollars sloshed around Europe, through the oil crisis, the European countries embarked on a series of currency adjustments. These, however, often proved destabilizing (cf. Keohane, this volume and 1985).

It was not coincidental that these difficulties shook the consensual and non-consensual economies differentially. They had to deal with similar challenges but in a different sequence. Wages exploded first in the Latin countries. France faced a major wage offensive in 1968-9; but, finding it necessary to concede major wage increases to newly militant unions, the French economic authorities sought to compensate for the inflationary thrust by quick devaluation. The Italians were less adroit and lost control of prices and wages (Gigliobianco & Salvati, 1980). The countries with consensual systems, however, tended to face an opposite order of events. Their social discipline had been designed primarily to strengthen their balance of payments position which they always saw as critical. Consequently, they tended to be the countries that had to face dilemmas of revaluation, not devaluation. And revaluation was hard to control. In Germany in 1970, in Sweden in 1974, revaluations led to overshooting and sudden surges in industrial profits. The result was to compel union leaders to ask for compensatory, and more than compensatory wage increases in the year after. A system that had been designed to move price and wage movements toward equilibrium in fact moved them further and further away. American abandonment of the gold standard between 1971 and 1973 only increased volatility (cf. OECD, 1977).

It would be misleading to attribute the strains of consensual bargaining only to American-originated inflationary pressures. OPEC's price increases and subsequent inflation further strained consensual wage determination as unions and industry faced infringements on real income. Still, from the late 1960s on, the earlier guidelines no longer guided. In effect, United States policy itself abandoned the 'productivity' keyed criteria by means of which it had helped to reconstruct Western economies, discipline labour movements, encourage private investment, and organize a non-Communist coalition of countries.

The result was to stimulate frantic efforts to provide new incentives for labour, to enlarge codetermination privileges, as in Germany, to contemplate real-wage insurance through tax rebates, and similar measures. Policy-makers indulged in a sort of compactomania that only indicated the underlying erosion of real consensual motives. Countries, moreover, that went into the decade of stagflation in 1973 with formally similar institutions for consensual bargaining experienced different outcomes: Austria, for instance, could keep a good record in terms of wage restraint; Norway's arrangements preserved less discipline (Flanagan *et al.*, 1983: 38). Not that all corporatist frameworks collapsed, but the rhetoric and the façades of corporatism became more extensive than the real move toward consensual bargaining. This was certainly true in Britain during the 1970s and perhaps in the US as well. Recent authors such as Middlemas (1979: (430–63), Thomson (1981) and Crouch (1977) might all dissent from this assessment. But the fragmentation of coherent public authority over economic and social policy should not be mistaken for the purposeful delegation of power to non-state actors. On the other hand, where formal corporatist institutions had been largely absent, economic stagnation as well as the search by Communist parties for some form of public power led to a latent coalition that opened up more corporatist possibilities than formal social compacts. None the less, the inability to advance beyond this implicit consensus and to dismantle the trade unions' economic power (expressed, for instance in the Italian *scala mobile*) limited development. Indeed, by 1980, what seemed to remain as the only convincing recourse for renewed stabilization was the old-fashioned 'stabilization crisis' with extensive unemployment. But the unemployment of the early 1980s derived from a structural crisis as well as a cyclical one. It coincided with the long-term difficulties of the heavy industry with whose development Europe's classic union federations and socialist parties had emerged. Perhaps it also signalled a long-term transformation of these working-class organizations themselves.

It is inappropriate to peer into the future. But it might be asked whether the earlier thrust toward consensual wage determination did not represent the 'highest stage' of the social-democratic, 'welfarist' political economy that was adumbrated as early as the First World War and instituted after the Second. The weakening of consensual systems means that if bargained corporatism were to be reconstructed, far more public tutelage might have to be involved. The choices of the mid-1980s appear different from those at the outset of the post-war period that inaugurated the partial triumphs of corporatism. If reliance on a reinvigorated market works, as it may for the moment, then consensual bargaining could be modestly re-established or may not even be needed. But if in future crises or in the course of industrial restructuring market forces seem to falter, then probably the mix of institutions that re-emerges will be more explicitly political than before—more responsible to voting publics or to state bureaucracies and less to the specific economic groups that these institutions embrace.

3

Concertation and the Structure of Corporatist Networks

GERHARD LEHMBRUCH

Introduction

The political structure of a number of advanced capitalist economies, according to widely held—but often vague—hypotheses, is characterized by the emergence of 'corporatism' or 'neo-corporatism'. Speculation that there might here be evidence of a secular trend, reflecting functional prerequisites of advanced capitalism, was for a time influential. However, there would probably now be wide agreement that the phenomena described under the label of 'corporatism' are contingent. The failure of several corporatist experiments and the abrupt return in countries such as Britain to governmental strategies based not on co-operation with economic interest organizations but rather on their 'exclusion' (cf. Goldthorpe, this volume) and relying essentially on co-ordination through markets, has made it clear that the 'century of corporatism' by no means represents a secular trend in modern political economies. Two decades ago, Shonfield (1965: 65) asserted that, notwithstanding the varying institutional patterns of economic policy-making in the countries of Western Europe and North America, 'there is a certain uniformity in the texture of these societies. In terms of what they do, rather than of what they say about it, and even more markedly in terms of the pattern of their behaviour over a period of years, the similarities are striking.' Today, this apparent convergence can no longer be taken for granted. As European economies have lost their competitive advantage on world markets and face the problems of adapting their industries to this new situation, governments are confronted with strategic options that are conspicuously divergent. Correspondingly, social scientists have shifted their attention towards the conditions which influence the choices that are made among different strategies. These choices, it has been argued, are largely constrained by the institutional structures of politics and markets (Scharpf, this volume; Zysman, 1983).

The following essay is based on the assumption that the inter-organizational networks of interest representation which stabilize collective action are an important element in such institutional constraints. It aims at a systematic analysis of the elementary institutional structures of corporatist politics, and of the variations which contribute to shaping the differing strategies pursued by governments in managing the economy.

Sectoral Corporatism and Concertation

The discussion of patterns of interest representation in relation to the choice of political strategies suffers from the lack of any generally accepted understanding of the concept of 'corporatism'. In the literature, 'corporatism' has a broad range of connotations, and—as pointed out elsewhere—there are different schools of conceptualization (Lehmbruch, 1982). In particular, three analytically distinct developments have been labelled as 'corporatism':

(i) the development and strengthening of centralized interest organizations—or 'peak' associations—which possess a representational monopoly;

(ii) the granting to these associations of privileged access to government, and the growth of—more or less institutionalized—linkages between public administration and such interest organizations;

(iii) the 'social partnership' of organized labour and business aimed at regulating conflicts between these groups, in co-ordination with government policy (usually in the form of 'tripartism').

I have earlier argued (1982) that, since these different developments are interrelated, they should be integrated into a pluridimensional concept of corporatism. This should permit a ranking of countries for the purpose of cross-national comparison and for the investigation of empirical regularities. In this essay, some tentative interpretations will be presented of the results of comparative empirical research in which such a conceptualization has been employed. These results relate primarily to organizational centralization, to the institutionalization of corporatism, and to linkages with the party system. First, however, an attempt at conceptual demarcation is required in order to avoid some current misunderstandings.

In historical perspective, the significance and meaning of 'corporatism' has obviously been subject to change; this is underlined by the increasing use of the prefix 'neo-'. Much attention has been given to the opposition of 'state' and 'societal' (or 'authoritarian' and 'liberal') corporatism which was often set up in the early days of the 'debate on corporatism' in the social science literature (Schmitter, 1974, 1977; Lehmbruch, 1977, 1979a). At that time the distinction had some heuristic value. But it soon became clear that the political, economic, and cultural constellations to which these polar constructs referred were so heterogeneous that in most cases they could not usefully be located as points on a historical continuum. Hence, they are of limited use as the basis of an empirical typology, and in some respects even misleading.[1] Historically, the new European corporatism is more usefully related to developments in the nineteenth century which antedate the 'state' corporatist experiments of the inter-war years (cf. Maier, 1981; Nocken, 1981). And these developments one can capture with the aid of a different typological distinction: namely, that between 'sectoral corporatism', on the one hand, and 'corporatist concertation', on the other.

By 'sectoral corporatism', I understand a corporatist representation of interests—in the sense of Schmitter's definition (1974)—that is limited to specific sectors of the economy. Sectoral organizations are centralized and enjoy representational monopoly. Moreover, the granting to such organizations of privileged access to government may result in strong institutional linkages with government. Sectoral corporatism, in this sense, is a relatively old phenomenon. In many parts of Europe it can be traced back at least to the restoration of 'chambers' and 'guilds' (*Innungen*) in the later decades of the nineteenth century, following earlier liberal interludes of free associational activities, and went together with a return to protectionism and neo-mercantilism.

Agriculture provides an obvious example. In countries such as Germany, the pluralist competition of different agricultural organizations gradually gave way to a representational monopoly on the part of peak associations. This trend towards concentration was often assisted by government (on the French case, see Keeler, 1981), and was associated with decisive organizational participation in the formation and implementation of sectoral policies. It also tended to go along with a specific selectivity in the representation of members' interests, so that, for example, the policies jointly produced by government and organized agriculture might favour large producers rather than small family farms. Although, as noted, the developments in question date back to the protectionism of the late nineteenth century, they have been reinforced by the spread of interventionist agricultural policies since the depression of the 1930s. Government intervention, that is, has remained oriented towards sectoral objectives and has been of a 'clientelist' nature—aimed at defending the relative position of agriculture in distributional conflict with the industrial sector. This sectoral and clientelist approach remains in fact dominant in the agricultural policy of the EEC—the latter being thus an interesting case of sectoral corporatism on a supranational level.[2] It is evident that sectoral interests may even succeed in colonizing segments of the administration so as to form a 'robbers' coalition' at the expense of other groups or of more 'encompassing' considerations of national economic and social policy.

'Corporatist concertation' is distinguished from sectoral corporatism by two essential features:

(i) it involves not just a single organized interest with privileged access to government but rather a plurality of organizations usually representing antagonistic interests; and

(ii) these organizations manage their conflicts and co-ordinate their action with that of government expressly in regard to the systemic (*gesamtwirtschaftliche*) requirements of the national economy.

This pattern of co-ordination among major economic interest groups emerged during the First World War and its immediate aftermath, when organized business and labour co-operated with governments in the war economy and demobilization (see, for example, on the German *Zentralarbeitsgemeinschaft*, Feldman,

1981). It then re-emerged in some countries during the economic crisis of the 1930s—for example, in Sweden and Switzerland—and spread to many others during and after the Second World War. Often such co-operation broke down again in the late 1940s and early 1950s, as in Britain, the US, and West Germany, but there were still some remarkable exceptions; most notably, the establishment of corporatist institutions in the Netherlands, the growth of Austria's 'social partnership' from the mid-1950s, and developments in the Scandinavian countries.

This survival of tripartite co-operation, it may be noted, was related—at least in some instances—to the re-emergence of an idea that had already surfaced in the context of German tripartism at the end of the First World War. At that time, Walter Rathenau, the organizer of the war economy, and his associate Wichard von Moellendorf, developed the vision of a planned economy administered by technocrats in co-ordination with corporate interests. This idea of a planning system, supported by consensus-building between organized interests, then reappeared after the Second World War, most explicitly in Jean Monnet's design for an *économie concertée*.

However, over recent decades, the most important instances of corporatist concertation as here defined have undoubtedly resulted from attempts by governments to conduct incomes policies with the co-operation of the major interest organizations concerned. If, as Panitch argues (1977a), such corporatist incomes policies tend to be highly unstable, it is precisely because of the inter- and intra-organizational strains that often go along with the concertation of antagonistic interests. Sectoral corporatism, in comparison, tends to be much more stable because of the greater degree of convergence of the interests involved.

The distinction between 'corporatist concertation' and 'sectoral corporatism' is then crucial for an understanding of the changing importance of interest organizations in recent political economy; but so also is an understanding of their developmental relationship. Sectoral corporatism dates back to the late nineteenth century, while concertation is a more recent phenomenon. But the success of concertation presupposes a strong capacity for intra-organizational co-ordination and a high degree of representational monopoly at the level of sectoral interests. Concertation is, moreover, facilitated by institutional linkages between the state and interest organizations of the kind that emerge in sectoral corporatism. Although such linkages do not *per se* lead to concertation as here defined, they favour its development.[3]

The turning-point comes when government intervention is no longer limited to mere sectoral protectionism. Thus, with the adoption of Keynesian policies of economic management, intervention takes the form of deliberate attempts at co-ordinating macroeconomic parameters. But the classical instruments of Keynesianism—such as demand management through fiscal policy—are still aimed only at exerting an indirect influence on the behaviour of economic actors. When such indirect controls were eventually found to be inadequate, governments became increasingly aware that macroeconomic parameters were also influenced by large interest organizations and might therefore be more effectively manipulated with their support. At this stage, then, the patterns of organization prepared under sectoral corporatism (and outlined in Schmitter's definition) take on a new functional significance. With the introduction of a strategy of macroeconomic co-ordination, interest organizations tend to become involved if (i) they have already established organizational linkages with government and administration, and (ii) their organizational structures are such as to permit an effective implementation of 'concerted' policies.

Tripartism and Concertation

The typical pattern of corporatist concertation involves government with organized business and labour. In some cases, as will be noted below, the formal role of government may appear relatively small—as, for example, with Austrian or Swedish wage policies. Although other organized groups, such as ones representing agriculture, are sometimes also included, in most cases, 'tripartite' relations form the core element of concertation.

However, 'tripartism' is not simply equivalent to 'concertation' (or to 'social partnership'). Specialized tripartite advisory commissions or boards, with administrative functions, may define their goals in terms of sectoral considerations or of a quite specific range of issues—as, for example, in social policy. These are, then, instances of sectoral corporatism. But they do differ from clientelistic relationships (as in agricultural policy) by serving to regulate conflicts of interest. And when such conflicts gain 'systemic' relevance for essential functions of government and the national economy, it may happen that sectoral corporatism turns into concertation; and such an enlargement of functions is then likely to be accompanied by institutional growth.

A remarkable illustration of this process is provided by recent developments in West German health policy. (At the same time this example shows that concertation may be extended to redistributive conflicts in fields other than industrial relations.) In German social policy 'paritary' administration by the 'social partners' has traditionally been important. The objective is to manage conflicts of interest arising from the introduction of social policy schemes, especially those financed partly by employer and partly by employee contributions, and considerations relevant to the overarching objectives of national economic policy have not been involved. There may even have been tendencies towards the formation of 'robbers' coalitions' at the expense of other parties or of the taxpayer.

However, the recent cost explosion in public health obviously had major consequences in West Germany, as elsewhere, for public finances and the national economy. Rising obligatory contributions to health insurance were not only a serious cost factor for business but, moreover, the scope for raising income taxes without provoking protest was dangerously narrowed. This situation led in 1977 to an attempt at 'concerted action in the health sector' (Wiesenthal, 1981; Billerbeck, 1982). This involved representatives of the federal government, the public health insurance schemes (*Gesetzliche Krankenversicherung*), various medical and dental associations (the *Kassenärztliche Vereinigungen*, in which membership is necessary in order to practise in the public health insurance system), the pharmaceuticals industry, the pharmacists, the employers, and the trade unions. All these interests are periodically brought into negotiations over the aggregate increase in health expenditures. In this development, previously established bipartite and tripartite sectoral bodies serve as the basis for a new system of corporatist concertation within which considerations of public finance and national economic policy are paramount. Thus, in a complex game of mutual compensations, medical associations come under some obligation to practice 'wage restraint', just as labour unions do in incomes-policy bargaining; and in turn, they too have to cope with problems of rank-and-file compliance.

A Classification of OECD Countries

The conceptual distinction that has been developed between 'sectoral' and 'concerted' corporatism permits some refinement of the measures of corporatism that have so far been employed in cross-national research. The favourite method has been to rank-order nations in terms of variables such as the degree of centralization and representational monopoly of labour and employer organizations.[4] However, in principle, these variables measure only the *sectoral* organization of interests. Of course, as was pointed out above, successful concertation will be strongly favoured by the existence of centralized and monopolistic interest organizations, and hence a correlation between them is to be expected. But from the existence of centralization and representational monopoly, the emergence of concertation cannot be inferred *a priori*. The latter should therefore be measured separately.

   Since tripartism is the dominant pattern of corporatist arrangements, a useful indicator for ordering OECD countries according to the degree of corporatism that they display is the nature of trade-union participation in public policy formation. On this basis, a cumulative scale can be established, the range of which extends from 'pluralism' to 'strong corporatism'.[5] *Pluralism* is characterized by the predominance of 'pressure-group' politics and the lobbying of government agencies and parliament by fragmented and competing interest groups, and by a low degree of effective participation by unions in policymaking. The second class of the scale, *weak corporatism*, is distinguished by the institutionalized participation of organized labour in the formation and implementation of policies only within certain limited sectors of policy or by its participation only in specific stages of the policy process—for example, consultation *or* implementation. With both 'pluralism' and 'weak corporatism' alike, the 'scope of collective bargaining' is restricted.[6] Bargaining on a nation-wide or industry level is not very important, and therefore concerted incomes policies are difficult to implement. *Medium corporatism*, the third class of the scale, is characterized by sectoral union participation similar to that of 'weak corporatism' but the scope of collective bargaining is in this case broader and attempts at concerted incomes policies have temporarily met with some success. The fourth class, *strong corporatism*, is then characterized by the effective participation of labour unions (and organized business) in policy formation and implementation across those interdependent policy areas that are of central importance for the management of the economy. Thus, in 'strong corporatist' countries, the concertation of major economic interests is an important and relatively durable feature. In Table 3.1 an allocation of OECD countries to the classes of the scale is attempted.[7]

TABLE 3.1. *A cumulative scale of corporatism*

(I)	Pluralism United States, Canada, Australia, New Zealand;
(II)	Weak corporatism United Kingdom, Italy;
(III)	Medium corporatism Ireland, Belgium, West Germany, Denmark, Finland, Switzerland (borderline case);
(IV)	Strong corporatism Austria, Sweden, Norway, the Netherlands; Not covered by the scale are cases of
(V)	'Concertation without labour' Japan, France.

Corporatist Concertation as 'Generalized Exchange'

Corporatist concertation may originate within the specific policy fields, for example, in incomes policies. But it gains momentum and stability where it covers a broader policy domain. In part, this may come about through processes of social learning and diffusion within a political culture. In the case of West German health policy, previous 'concerted action' over incomes policy served as a model of political management via inter-organizational co-ordination.

But the extension of concertation across policy fields is probably not only the result of a transfer of experience. At the same time, it appears to derive from an immanent logic of concerted policy-making. As I have argued elsewhere (Lehmbruch, 1979b; 304 ff.), a genetic theory of corporatist concertation can be based upon 'rational actor' assumptions. The leaders of interest organizations opt for a corporatist strategy on the basis of an exchange calculus (cf. in this volume Lange and Regini). Here I will explore some of the implications of this argument for the diffusion of concertation within a given country.

To understand the characteristic dynamics of a corporatist exchange calculus, let us focus on organized labour and begin by examining the inherent logic of the West German 'concerted action' over incomes policy as it was devised in 1967 by the Social Democratic Minister of Economics, Karl Schiller. In this case, voluntary wage restraint was implicitly interpreted in terms of exchange—that is, in terms of compensation for restraint—but without the unions negotiating any specific quid pro quo with government or organized business. The guiding idea was the macroeconomic interdependence of wages, profits, investment, and employment.[8] The process of concertation essentially consisted in the actors involved informing each other of their responses to the 'orientation data' furnished by the government and clarifying their assumptions and expectations. Schiller hoped that the 'social partners' would thus arrive at a consensus about the appropriate policies to follow under the given market conditions. Wage restraint could in this way be traded for high and stable employment as a result of a shared insight into the logic of market processes rather than as the result of a barter transaction. But this approach proved unsuccessful in practice. Experience taught labour leaders to mistrust expectations arrived at via concertation. The predictions derived from the underlying model often proved unrealistic, and the wave of wildcat strikes in the late 1960s and early 1970s also served to undermine confidence in the possibility of concertation of this 'rationalistic' kind.

One way of trying to strengthen the stability of expectations in an exchange calculus is to introduce explicit barter transactions. This is in effect what happened in the 'social contracts' of the 1970s. Package deals, tying wage restraint to agreements on transfer payments and tax policy, were struck in a number of countries (Armingeon, 1983; Flanagan et al., 1983). One idea behind this approach was that a sort of 'deficiency guarantee' should be given by government in order to compensate for uncertainty. But incomes policies of the kind in question still largely failed because, once again, assumptions and expectations concerning important parameters of policy turned out to be fallacious.

However, the stability of corporatist concertation can be further increased where concertation is not limited to incomes policy but extends, in particular, to labour-market and employment policy. Austria is in this respect a significant case. Here, wage restraint by unions has been the permanent and visible core element of concertation (Lang, 1978; Flanagan et al., 1983). But Austrian unions have refrained from striking bargains of the 'social contract' type which make wage restraint conditional upon specified compensations.[9] Underlying this policy there has been, rather, the expectation that, thanks to the strong influence of the 'social partners' on practically all aspects of economic and social policy, the national economy would be managed with the long-term interests of union members appropriately in view. Wage restraint would thus pay off even without agreed quid pro quos. In terms of an exchange calculus, one could here speak of 'generalized exchange', as distinct from barter transactions.[10]

The policy-mix devised in Sweden during the late 1950s and known as the Rehn model—an attempt to foster industrial change through a 'solidaristic' wages policy, and an 'active' labour-market policy to promote the requisite mobility of labour (cf. Martin, 1979)–is another example of 'generalized exchange' across policy sectors. Even if in retrospect its success is controversial, it illustrates the immanent logic characteristic of concertation. The rationale behind the Rehn model was, first, that instead of inflation being fought through an incomes policy, the active labour-market policy would help to overcome the bottlenecks in labour supply that generated wage-push; and secondly, that the solidaristic wages policy would squeeze out marginal firms and thus lead to a reallocation of production factors which would increase productivity and growth. The long-term gains for labour were supposed to compensate for the sacrifices which this policy-mix might, in the short run, demand from some groups of workers. It should be evident that this type of inter-organizational exchange cannot be based on unstable and shifting coalitions but, rather, demands durable, institutionalized relationships between government and the organizations involved.

The Institutionalization of Concertation

The institutional patterns of fully developed, corporatist concertation are far from being uniform. To discover some underlying regularities, two dimensions should be distinguished: first, a vertical dimension, which relates to the pattern of participation of individual peak associations in policy-making and implementation, and the corresponding integration of lower organizational levels into corporatist arrangements; and, second, a horizontal dimension which relates to the pattern of concertation between different peak associations and government. This distinction leads to an important generalization. It is typically the case that under 'strong' corporatism vertical participation and integration tend to be highly formalized, while in the majority of cases horizontal relationships are comparatively informal.

The institutionalization of 'vertical' participation is an important aspect of sectoral corporatism. It is, therefore, found in 'medium' as well as 'strong' corporatist countries. Two devices are of particular importance: the obligatory consultation of interest organizations over government bills (*Begutachtung, remiss*), and their representation on advisory and administrative committees or *Beiräte*. It is difficult to establish comparative cross-national measures of the relative importance of these devices, but a list of countries where they have been judged important, not by isolated authors but in a relatively large body of research, can be provided.[11] It includes the 'strong' corporatist countries– Austria, Sweden, Norway and the Netherlands–together with Denmark, Finland and Switzerland. It cannot be entirely excluded that some other important cases have been overlooked but the trend is quite apparent: the formalized vertical participation of peak associations is correlated with concertation.

The vertical integration into corporatist arrangements of lower organizational levels has two main aspects: intra-organizational mechanisms favouring cohesion and compliance, and institutional constraints preventing disintegration. According to a widely held hypothesis, centralized organizational structures are an essential prerequisite for corporatist concertation (cf. Headey, 1970; Schmitter, 1974). Indicators available for cross-national comparison tend to support this hypothesis. None the less, in the light of more detailed studies (Armingeon, 1983), it has to be qualified. The optimum structure is, apparently, not rigid hierarchical centralization but rather one which provides for some limited autonomy for lower organizational levels while giving sufficient authority to the peak association to co-ordinate their activities effectively. It is true that in countries such as Austria, Sweden, and Norway, collective bargaining is quite strongly co-ordinated by trade-union confederations. But this does not mean that industrial unions do not retain any autonomy. In Austria, wage negotiations are still conducted at the industry level, even if the industrial unions need the approval of the central organization. In Sweden, central negotiations (until they were suspended in 1983) did not lead to contracts in a legal sense but to 'recommendations', and industrial unions might opt out. In Norway, the union federations have sometimes chosen to decentralize the bargaining process. All these may then be seen as devices for combining central co-ordination with some autonomy at lower levels. Rigid hierarchical centralization would be less effective in obtaining vertical integration because of the higher probability of intra-organizational tensions.

The vertical integration of lower organizational levels can be further supported by an institutional framework which limits their range of activities. There is no uniform tendency in the 'strong' corporatist countries but, in some cases, legal restrictions on the representation of labour at the enterprise or shop level are of importance. In Austria and Germany such restrictions are referred to as the *Verrechtlichung* ('juridification') of labour relations. A framework of legal rules circumscribes the functions of the *Betriebsräte* (Work Councils) and the admissible forms of industrial conflict. One consequence of this is that unions may be better able to cope with intra-organizational tensions in the form of rank-and-file protest than under conditions of immunity from law and that labour representatives at the shop level are prevented from effectively challenging the prerogatives of the leadership. The 'juridification' of industrial relations in Austria and Germany is admittedly a special case, which has to be explained in terms of the highly legalistic political culture of these countries. But it serves as a clear example of the high degree of formalization of vertical relationships which is characteristic of corporatism.

In sharp contrast, the horizontal dimension of corporatist concertation tends to remain informal. In particular, the arrangements through which peak associations meet with government in order to co-ordinate their policies have for the most part been so conceived as to keep formalization to a minimum. In Norway, the attempt in the early 1950s to establish a Board of Economic Co-ordination was a failure since 'the partners felt that such a formal body made them hostages of the government and committed them to policies they could not defend within their constituent organizations' (Rokkan, 1966: 108). The 'Contact Committee', established in 1962, was portrayed, rather, as an informal 'bargaining table' around which information could be exchanged, but with no authority to determine policy (cf. also Olsen, 1983: 177 ff.). Likewise, in Sweden, the locus of concertation until the mid-1960s was informal yearly meetings at the summer residence of the Prime Minister ('Harpsund Democracy'). In both countries, such summit meetings have from the later 1960s been superseded or complemented by other arrangements but these also retain a low degree of formality.[12] Thus the Swedish 'Economic Planning Council', instituted in 1962, includes members of government, some high civil servants and economists, and—in a majority— representatives of the peak associations. It has however been described as 'merely a deliberating body. There are no decisions taken, hence no minutes, and no public accountability for its activity . . . It is a meeting place, forum for discussions, and information center' (Elvander, 1972a: 204). And yet more discreet has been the co-ordination of wage policies in Sweden through entirely informal contacts between government and union and business leaders during annual wage negotiations.

A similar pattern of institutionalization is found in Austria (Marin, 1982, 1983). Again the vertical participation of individual associations is highly formalized—involving compulsory membership in the 'chambers' established as organizations of public law. Given Austria's legalistic political culture, an over-arching 'economic parliament' might then appear to be the logical culmination of these elaborate constructions. And, indeed, some influential legal scholars of conservative views have strongly advocated such a 'constitutionalization' of the *Verbändestaat* ('associational state'). However, the Joint Committee for Wages and Prices (*Paritätische Kommission*) and related bodies (for details, see Lehmbruch, 1979a: 158 ff.) have only a *de facto* existence and no legal basis or powers: 'The Parity Commission cannot be reached: there is no fixed location or address or only meeting place, no telephone number, no stationery, no special or unchanging personnel' (Marin, 1981: 29). Correspondingly, the control of wage policy is characterized by 'indeterminacy'. As in the Swedish case, there is no formal incomes policy nor even guide-lines (which would be open to possible challenge by rank-and-file activists). Legally, free collective bargaining prevails and wage restraint is the result of entirely informal and voluntary co-ordination. Marin (1981: 33) describes the Austrian system as a 'pyramid of institutionalization', with a 'highly formalized institutional infrastructure' supporting the 'trapeze act of top organizational leaders to negotiate and co-operate without explicit norms, written contracts and other securities'.

What is particularly notable about this 'weak' institutionalization of corporatism at the top is the sharp contrast it offers with the characteristically 'strong' institutionalization of parliamentary representation. This contrast points to a specific logic of corporate, as opposed to individual, representation. The function of electoral and parliamentary institutions is the aggregation of highly heterogeneous, individual acts of political choice. These institutions must, therefore, be able to cope directly with the problems of maintaining stability, predictability and responsiveness in representation. On the other hand, corporate representation presupposes a high degree of prior, intra-organizational aggregation: its stability and predictability rest upon the internal cohesion of relatively centralized associations. And in the maintenance of such cohesion, a rigid formalization of the procedures of inter-organizational coordination could prove to be counterproductive.

The differences between the logics of corporate and individual representation were overlooked by those theorists of the late nineteenth and early twentieth century who produced blueprints for the institutionalization of corporatist systems. One of their favourite ideas was that of an 'economic parliament' where interest organizations could be represented and thus formally participate in legislation. In some cases—such as Weimar Germany, France and Italy—this idea was realized through the creation of 'Economic and Social Councils'. However, the political importance of these bodies remained for the most part limited, and sometimes (as in Weimar Germany) they were totally ineffective.

But there is one exception to the general argument being advanced: the case of the Netherlands. After the Second World War, the Dutch Social-Economic Council was established as the centrepiece of a system of institutions which also included the state arbitrators for industrial conflicts (abolished in 1970) and the 'Foundation of Labour'—a private body, set up by the peak organizations of business and labour, (Estor, 1965), which has remained an important element in the system. Thus, in its overall character Dutch corporatism must be reckoned as clearly more formalized than that of Norway, Sweden or Austria.

This deviant character of the Dutch case results from specific historical circumstances. Whereas in Austria, traditional corporatist blueprints were discredited by the 'Austro-fascist' regime established by Dollfuss (1934–8), in the Netherlands, nineteenth-century corporatist ideas remained strong enough to have an influence on the institutionalization of the modern system (Estor, 1965: 33 ff.). Until the 1960s, this system functioned quite smoothly but was then subject to increasing strains. Strong tendencies towards *entzuiling* ('de-pillarization') and rank-and-file unrest created considerable intra-organizational strains and unsettled the established 'politics of accommodation' (Lijphart, 1975). Although similar difficulties arose elsewhere in the early 1970s, no other 'strong' corporatist country experienced the same degree of disruption as the Netherlands, and it is plausible that the situation there was aggravated by the degree of formalization of its concertative institutions. However, this does not mean that the Dutch system lacked stabilizing mechanisms. In particular, institutional constraints helped vertical integration in a way similar to 'juridification' in the Austrian case. During the 1970s, wage restraint tended to be imposed by government, after consultation and informal agreement with unions and employers (Armingeon, 1983). This procedure meant that labour leaders, having no formal responsibility for the wages policy, were able to preserve the cohesion of their organizations and at the same time still to remain within the system of consultation and cooperation. Strong institutionalization thus served to prevent, or at least to slow, the breakdown of corporatist structures.

Corporatist Policy Formation and Political Parties

Repeatedly the argument has been advanced that 'parties . . . and the parliamentary arena in which they function are of reduced importance in corporatist societies' (Harrison, 1980: 185). This is held to be so because, in Crozier's words, there are strong 'barriers between different subsystems which tend to close up and operate in isolation' (Crozier, 1977: 11, cited in Harrison, 1980: 186). How far such contentions are based on systematic observation or on speculation is often difficult to assess. Complaints about a 'decline of parliament' have a long tradition, but it has been demonstrated that the reality of the supposedly 'golden age' of parliaments was a good deal different from what such complaints would imply (see, in particular, Butt, 1969). The actual empirical evidence concerning the impact of corporatist arrangements on parliaments and party systems is—to say the least—ambiguous.

An early experiment in the concertation of organized business and labour, the German *Zentralarbeitsgemeinschaft*, which was earlier mentioned in this respect, is instructive. Feldman, in his careful research on this case, has argued that 'basically, the ideology of the ZAG was that of voluntaristic collaboration and agreement arrived at autonomously on the basis of consultation and discussion and then accepted by the government and parliament because those directly involved had made up their minds' (1981: 178). But, as Feldman goes on to note, neither parliament nor the administration were 'eliminated as a vital element in the regulation of society and economy'. He points to 'two sets of insurmountable difficulties': first, the intra-organizational tensions provoked by inter-organizational bargaining; and second, 'the limited capacity for consensus building between interest groups that makes a corporatist arrangement insufficient as a substitute for parliamentary government through parties' (181).

What holds true for the polarized party system of the Weimar Republic will do so *a fortiori* for one of a more consolidated kind. Its capacity to generate power resources will not normally be equalled by a body representing capital and labour at the national level. Co-operation between capital and labour may sometimes succeed in particular industries where it is based on shared interests in inter-sectoral conflicts. But, at the national level, the essentially antagonistic character of the relationship between capital and labour must prevent the development of the stable, autonomous power-base that would be required if a corporatist 'subsystem', were to be able to match the legitimate power resources that are mobilized through electoral and parliamentary channels.

The advantage that the party system holds can be further illustrated by more recent instances where attempts at corporatist consensus-building have failed because of resistance within the party system and the parliamentary arena. In an earlier article (Lehmbruch, 1977), I argued that incomes policy had become a central domain of corporatist concertation because of the inevitable difficulties of building consensus on wage restraint within the party system. That argument has now to be qualified in view of more recent developments in incomes policy. As pointed out above, a rational justification of earlier agreements on wage restraint could be sought in terms of exchange processes consistent with the logic of post-Keynesian macroeconomics: if cost-push inflation caused by excessive wage demands were avoided, then both real wages and employment would benefit. Under the 'stagflationary' conditions of the 1970s, the possibility of such 'built-in' compensations for wage restraint was increasingly questioned, and one consequence, as noted, was the adoption of the 'social contract' strategy: that is, the inclusion of wage restraint in 'package deals' which also comprised agreements on non-wage elements of income, in particular, on taxes and transfer payments. However, this implied decision-making on issues traditionally falling within the jurisdiction of parliamentary institutions and involving their budgetary and legislative privileges. Thus, as Armingeon (1983) has made clear, social-contract policies were in fact often conditional upon the securing of sufficient consensus within the party system.

Characteristically, such policy formation involved complex sequences of bargaining. In the Scandinavian countries, for example, the 'social contract' did not have the form of a single document assented to by all the relevant parties but rather that of a bundle of separate—although connected—agreements, including the legislative measures that were part of the package deal. In some instances, governments gave undertakings to the 'social partners' that they would mobilize the necessary majorities in parliament; and in others, party leaders in parliament themselves participated in the preparatory negotiations (Armingeon, 1983; Schwerin, 1980a).

The outcome of parliamentary processes might thus be largely anticipated, and especially where governments possessed large and disciplined parliamentary majorities. But this is not always the case, and there are several instances of package deals that failed because of the refusal of parliaments to 'ratify' their involvement in them. In Finland, in 1973, the introduction of an incomes policy was linked to a free-trade agreement with the EEC, and since no majority was obtained for the latter, the incomes policy also failed. In Denmark, in 1979, the labour unions made wage restraint conditional upon the introduction of their plans for economic democracy or, in other words, for 'collective capital formation' through investment funds financed by employers' contributions and controlled by labour. As this proposal was not accepted by parliament, the unions lost their interest in the package deal. In Sweden, because of the parliamentary stalemate from 1973 to 1976 (when the bourgeois parties had the same number of seats as the Left) decisions on tax policy, intended to provide compensation for wage restraint, had to be negotiated between the Social Democratic government and the opposition parties in conferences held at Haga Castle (Nedelmann & Meier, 1977). As elections approached, consensus could no longer be maintained and the arrangement broke down.

To summarize, the examination of corporatist incomes policies in the 1970s does not support the hypothesis that essential functions of parliamentary institutions were taken over by a 'parallel' subsystem of policy formation. It may of course be true that in specific issue areas, the making of public policy owed more to corporatist than to parliamentary processes. But this does not warrant the conclusion that in the absence of corporatist structures, parliament and the party system would have been in greater control of these issues. The growth of governmental functions which characterizes the interventionist welfare state has led to a relative decline in the influence of parliamentary institutions, which reflects their failure to develop adequate instruments for controlling interventionist activities. This tendency, however, clearly antedates the emergence of modern corporatism, and there is little empirical evidence for supposing that corporatism has further contributed to it. On the contrary, the core functions of parliamentary institutions can still impose definite constraints on the autonomy of corporatist concertation.

There is one case that seems to contradict the above argument: namely, the history of labour and cartel legislation in Austria, which I have discussed elsewhere (Lehmbruch, 1977). Indeed, in this case, parliament did largely limit itself to 'ratifying' bills that had been worked out through direct negotiations among the interest organizations concerned. Such *de facto* delegation of legislative power to interest organizations presupposes a close and mutual penetration of party and interest organizations which—as I shall show in the following section— is typical of Austria.

The Network of Parties and Interest Organizations

I have argued earlier (1977) that the emergence of corporatist 'networks' in areas such as incomes policy aids political parties in the task of building consensus on issues where the competitive character of the party system would have counter-productive effects. In other words, neo-corporatism serves to smooth out the 'political business cycle'. Conversely, though, corporatist concertation depends for its effectiveness on support from the party system and on co-ordination with it. Corporatism has grown strong where such support and co-ordination have been facilitated by close, and often traditional, linkages between parties and organized interests. The structural basis of concertation is a network of interconnected organizations, comprising the economic peak associations, government, the public administration, and the parties in parliament—or at least the dominant, majority party. Interconnections can be established through such 'junction points' as joint committees or, more durably, through overlapping memberships, in particular at the leadership level. 'Interlocking directorates' (cf. Fennema & Schijf, 1978–9) provide a close analogy.[13]

In describing corporatist networks, it is again helpful to distinguish a horizontal and a vertical dimension. Horizontal interconnections—in particular, between organized labour, business and government—have already been discussed, and it has been shown that the 'junction points' tend to have a quite informal character. But the vertical dimension is often neglected. A central feature of it is a political structure characterized by ideologically-based alliances between parties and organized interests, which come together to form political 'camps' (*Lager*).[14] In other words, such camps comprise organizations which typically have overlapping memberships and interlocking leaderships,[15] and which often extend also into segments of the public administration as the result of party patronage.

One peculiarity of this kind of network, found in most of the 'strong' or 'medium' corporatist countries, is a difference in the degree of inter-organizational density[16] within the two major camps. Vertical interlocks are more important between socialist parties and trade unions than they are between bourgeois (Conservative or Liberal) parties and business associations. In Sweden, for example, the blue-collar union federation (LO) and the Social Democratic party have extensive interlocks between their national leaderships.[17] Traditionally, the LO president is a member of parliament, and so too usually are the presidents of some of the more important industrial unions. At regional and local level, 'cooperation is so intimate and the amount of overlapping membership is so great that it is sometimes impossible to distinguish trade unions and political elements' (Elvander, 1974: 61 ff.). The white-collar unions are politically 'neutral', but this only means that they have ties (including interlocking leadership positions) with different parties—for example, with the Liberal and Center parties as well as with the Social Democrats. The situation is somewhat different in the case of organized business. The employer and industrial associations also have interlocks with political parties; but while many union leaders who sit in parliament are considered as spokesmen for their organizations, the business leaders in parliament are not so regarded (Elvander, 1972a).[18]

This asymmetry can be traced back to the strong vertical integration of traditional continental European labour movements (and, in Scandinavia, of peasant movements). In comparison, the bourgeois camp has generally been characterized by a stronger functional differentiation of political parties and interest organizations, and an additional factor of importance in many countries is the existence of several different bourgeois parties (Lipset & Rokkan, 1967: 32 ff.). In consequence, business associations tend to be less closely tied into the corporatist network than trade unions, and it should thus be easier for them to withdraw from it. One may also hypothesize that the stability of a corporatist network increases with both the density and the symmetry of its interconnections.

The Austrian case is highly illustrative in all these respects. First, interlocks are found at the highest levels of the organizational hierarchy. The president of the trade-union confederation is, at the same time, president of the first chamber of parliament (the *Nationalrat*), and the presidents of several industrial unions are usually found in important ministerial positions (Pelinka, 1980). The president of the Federal Chamber of Business ranks high among Conservative members of parliament. In parliamentary committees, moreover, the number of members who hold office in interest organizations is such that in cases of extra-parliamentary legislative bargaining of the kind earlier described, the difference between the two roles becomes rather tenuous. Again, experts from the peak associations are increasingly drawn into committee deliberations. The point may be made that there is no need for an 'economic parliament' in Austria simply because the *Nationalrat* itself fulfils this function.

Moreover, in Austria the corporatist network is relatively symmetrical because of the firm inclusion of organized business in the conservative camp. The Federal Chamber of Business is closely interlocked with the Business League, which, together with the Farmers' League and the Workers' and Employees' League, are constituent elements of the conservative *Österreichische Volkspartei* (ÖVP).

In addition, the two political camps themselves interlock in a complex pattern. This structure developed under the 'black-red' coalition government of Conservatives and Socialists between 1945 and 1966. During much of that time, all important decisions were made in a 'coalition committee' consisting of approximately five leaders from each of the two parties. Among these were the leaders of organized labour, business, and agriculture. The establishment, in 1957, of the Joint Commission on Prices and Wages (Lehmbruch, 1979a) led to a functional differentiation within the network, and in the early 1960s the role of the Joint Commission increased further while the coalition committee lost its importance. After the break-up of the coalition, the network linking the parties and the 'social partners' continued to function, and was sometimes referred to as a *Bereichskoalition* (coalition within an issue-area). Still to the present day, the ÖVP regards itself as forming part of the 'social partner' network although, since 1970, it has been in opposition. On the other hand, it may be noted, the small Liberal party remains excluded from this network, even though in 1983 it became a coalition partner of the ruling Socialists and received the portfolio of commerce.

This distinctive pattern of the corporatist network in Austria rests on the close parallelism of parties and interest organizations. Historically, the linkages forming the two political camps originated in the ideologically segmented—or 'pillarized'—structure of the older Austrian political culture. But since 1945, the former strict separation of the camps has given way to some remarkable cross-connections. For example, the Austrian Federation of Trade Unions and the Chambers of Labour are dominated by the Socialists, but have a Conservative minority representation. On the other hand, a representative of a Socialist organization, the Free Business Association, is co-opted on to the governing body of the—predominantly Conservative—Federal Chamber of Business (Lehmbruch, 1977; Pelinka, 1980; Marin, 1983).

While the symmetrical structure of the corporatist network in Austria can be traced back to the ideological segmentation of the late nineteenth and early twentieth centuries, the asymmetry of the network found in other corporatist

countries must be seen as part of the organizational heritage of labour movements of a certain type (cf. Lehmbruch, 1983). Under the influence of Marxist
theory in its social-democratic variant, these movements saw themselves as acting
in the interests of an encompassing working class, and the development of the
corporatism of the present day cannot in fact be adequately understood without
reference to this emphasis on class, as distinct from narrower sectional interests.
This becomes the more evident when it is recognized that two other ideological
and organizational traditions of blue-collar workers in Europe have remained
refractory to the establishment of corporatist networks.

One is exemplified by the British trade union movement, in which the identification of distinctively class interests was never strong enough to lead to the
organizational concentration that is found in Sweden, Norway, or Austria. Moreover, while many Labour MPs are union-sponsored, the cumulation of leadership
functions is avoided (Minkin, 1974). To co-ordinate the policies of the TUC and
the Labour party, a special Liaison Committee has been established, but that this
had in fact to be done indicates that organizational linkages between the unions
and the party are generally much looser than in Scandinavia and Central Europe.

The other tradition that militates against corporatist linkages is revolutionary
syndicalism as may be exemplified by the case of France. As a heritage of the
syndicalist distrust of parliamentary socialism, the cumulation of union and
party (or parliamentary) functions continues to be avoided even by unionists
who have ideological affinities with the Socialist party. The widespread assumption of a strong association between a Socialist presence in government and the
emergence of effective corporatism has thus to be qualified. To be sure, the
strategic design of Mitterrand bears a strong resemblance to that of other,
relatively successful Socialist governments which have followed the corporatist
path. But the cultural heritage of the French labour movement presents here a
serious obstacle, and it is not unreasonable to expect that French experiments in
corporatism may face similar problems to those of British Labour governments
in the 1960s and 1970s, especially during the period of the Social Contract.[19]

Finally, it may be noted that linkages between interest organizations and
parties under corporatism appear to be related to characteristic trends within the
party system. Issues that come under the 'jurisdiction' of the corporatist network tend to be depoliticized, in the sense that parties no longer compete on
these issues with opposing policy platforms. Corporatist consensus-building in
economic and social policy is not compatible with party conflict in these same
areas. Conservative opposition parties, for example, cannot credibly oppose
policies that have been negotiated with organized business.

It has been observed that such neutralization of party competition is further
encouraged by the increasing importance of experts in corporatist systems (cf.
Lehmbruch, 1977). For example, this tendency has been seen as particularly
marked in Norway (Kvavik, 1976; Flanagan et al., 1983); and Austria has been
labelled 'technocorporatist' (Marin, 1982). But to associate the idea of techno-
cracy with corporatist concertation is misleading. Expert advisory bodies play an

important role in corporatist countries; but, in contrast with the Council of Economic Advisors in the United States or the West German *Sachverständigenrat*, their members are nominated by—if not recruited from—the 'social partners', and thus participate in the building of consensus among conflicting interests (Lehmbruch, 1984). This implies, among other things, that the range of policy alternatives that they can consider is more restricted than that which would be available to 'free-floating' technocrats. For example, allowing unemployment to rise as a means of restraining wages could not easily be envisaged by a corporatist advisory body.

However, even if the neutralization of party competition is to some extent fostered and legitimated by the intervention of experts, what essentially is presupposed is a given and stable balance of political power. Thus, in such corporatist countries as Austria, Sweden, and Norway the real significance of the strength of socialist parties is that it has been an important condition for the establishment of a 'historical compromise' based on the acceptance of private control over investments[20] and 'solidaristic' redistribution through parliamentary channels—or the payment of a 'political wage'.[21] In some cases, where Communist parties are strong, these too have been co-opted into reformist coalitions supporting a corporatist network. Thus, in Finland an incomes-policy package deal first became possible in 1966 on the basis of a 'popular front' which included the reformist wing of the Communists.

Furthermore, 'consociational' coalitions embracing Social Democrats and Christian parties (with a reformist wing) may also contribute to a stable balance of power which is then capable of supporting a corporatist network. In this respect the Netherlands is the most conspicuous example. However, the salient feature of recent political developments in this country is, of course, the decay of traditional alliances. The polarization of the party system, following, in particular, the ascendance of the aggressively 'free-market' Liberal party (VVD), has eroded the power basis of corporatist concertation. As was earlier noted, the institutional framework may still prevent organized labour from turning to highly militant strategies. But the Dutch case serves to reinforce the conclusion that stable corporatist relationships are not compatible with polarized party politics.

Acknowledgements

The research project on which this essay is based has been conducted with the aid of a grant from the Stiftung Volkswagenwerk. I have profited from discussions with my collaborators on the project at Konstanz: Klaus Armingeon, Roland Czada, Walter Dittrich, Johannes Misslbeck and Erwin Zimmermann. I have further benefited from a fellowship at the Woodrow Wilson International Center for Scholars, Washington D.C., in 1981-2. John Goldthorpe and Edgar Grande have been helpful in revising the text.

Notes

1. The parallelism of 'state' and 'societal' corporatism in Schmitter's original formulation implied that 'societal corporatism' could be distinguished from 'pluralist' interest intermediation by, among other things, *de facto* compulsory membership of organizations and their hierarchical structures. In the subsequent literature this has sometimes led to an élitist interpretation of modern corporatism in the tradition of Michels' concept of 'oligarchy'. One empirical objection would be that 'societal' (informal) equivalents of compulsory membership—in particular, the 'closed shop' or 'union shop'—are not systematically correlated with centralized organization and representational monopoly.

2. A further illustration is provided by the politics of organized medicine in many advanced capitalist societies. The American Medical Association offers a well-known case of clientelist privileges being granted to a quasi-monopolistic body (McConnell, 1966), in a way that largely conforms to Schmitter's definition of corporatist interest intermediation. And here again, as in the making of agricultural policy, the co-operation of government and private interests is oriented towards sectoral objectives rather than goals on the level of the national economy viewed as a whole (*Gesamtwirtschaft*).

3. This relationship explains why the operational definition developed below results in a rank-ordering of countries quite similar to that of Schmitter (1981). But it remains important to make the analytical distinction.

4. See, in particular, Schmitter (1981: 294). Wilensky (1976) combines an index of trade-union centralization (adapted from Headey, 1970) with an index of governmental centralization. But the latter variable is of contestable validity, and the weight given to it distorts the scores for France and Italy.

5. This scale is a modified version of one developed by Czada (1983). I have divided Czada's class of 'sectoral participation' with the aid of Cameron's index of 'scope of collective bargaining'. On my different classification of France and Japan see below, note 7.

6. This measure is taken from Cameron's index (this volume). All countries with a score of 0.8 or more are classified as 'medium corporatist' (if not placed in the class of 'strong corporatist'). West Germany is included here because Cameron's score (0.6) overrates the formal decentralization of the German system of collective bargaining. In practice, the largest industrial unions (in particular, the metal workers) act as national 'wage leaders', and the other unions in general follow the pattern they set. Moreover, the regional decentralization of bargaining in the metal industry is entirely dictated by tactical and legal considerations, and the regional negotiations are *de facto* centralized. On the other hand, the score for Ireland (1.0) may be judged too high since the centralized collective bargaining system established in 1960 was abandoned in 1981.

7. On the basis of different indicators, Schmidt (1982a; 1982b) arrives at a similar classification. His ordering differs for the Netherlands (because of incomes policies there that formally had a mandatory character), for Switzerland (due to adjustment on the basis of subjective judgement), and for France and Japan. Schmitter's index (cf. note 3) is strongly correlated with our scale. The importance of his organizational variables for the degree of concertation is thus evident. Our classification is based on long-term observation of the countries included: Spain, Portugal and Greece have therefore been omitted because it seems premature to assess the patterns that have developed after the breakdown of dictatorship.

Switzerland is a borderline case in the classification in several respects. *Inter alia*, the relative influence of organized labour is clearly weaker than in other corporatist countries (cf. Kriesi, 1982).

The allocation of the Netherlands is based on the observation of patterns from 1945 to the late 1970s. It must be left open whether recent strains indicate a definitive breakdown of concertation.

In France (where, ironically, the term *concertation* was invented), *planification* has been largely dominated by co-operation between the governmental bureaucracy and big business (Cohen, 1969). This special case must be attributed to the weakness of organized labour (Schain, 1980). The accession to power of the Socialists has been accompanied by trends towards corporatist arrangements, but it must be left open whether these will be sustained. On Japan as a further case of 'concertation without labour', see Pempel and Tsunekawa (1979).

8. In the terminology of German economists, this is the perspective of *Kreislauftheorie*.

9. An isolated exception was a tax-wage exchange with a Conservative government in 1967.

10. The distinction between 'barter' and 'generalized exchange' is derived from Parsons (1959).

11. The importance of these devices has been stressed for Austria (Karisch, 1965: 119 ff.; Pütz, 1966: 60 ff., 316 ff., 412 ff., 531 ff.; Klose, 1970: 68 ff.); for the Scandinavian countries (Olsen, 1983: 166 ff., with many further references); specifically for Norway (Kvavik, 1974: 102 ff.), Denmark (Johansen & Kristensen, 1978) and Finland (Anekar & Helander, 1983); and for Switzerland (Meynaud, 1963: 276 ff.).

12. The Norwegian 'Technical Reporting Committee on the Income Settlement', established in the 1960s, has a highly 'technocratic' character, on account of the important role which experts—apart from representatives of government and the peak organizations—play in its deliberations (cf. Flanagan *et al.*, 1983).

13. In a pioneering study of Switzerland, Kriesi (1980, 1982) has demonstrated that such relationships may fruitfully be explored with the aid of sociometric network analysis and related methods.

14. In Almond's terminology, 'subsystem autonomy' is limited. I have pointed out elsewhere that research on corporatism leads to a different evaluation of this limitation than Almond's analysis would suggest (Lehmbruch, 1983).

15. In all 'strong' corporatist countries, the cumulation of leadership functions is an important mechanism in the linking of interest organizations with parties and parliaments. This holds true for Sweden (Rustow, 1955; Elvander, 1972a); for Norway (Olsen, 1983) and for the Netherlands (Lijphart, 1975).

16. The density of an inter-organizational network 'refers to the extensiveness of ties between elements' (Aldrich & Whetten, 1981: 398).

17. This is more important than overlapping rank-and-file membership. In Sweden, collective affiliation of local labour unions to the socialist party accounted for 73 per cent of the party membership in 1974. But in the elections of 1976, more than one quarter of LO members voted for bourgeois parties, often without being aware that they were collectively affiliated to the socialist party (Elvander, 1979).

18. In Norway, the situation is very similar to that found in Sweden. But since no strong and autonomous white-collar unions exist, the homogeneity of the union-socialist camp is greater (cf. Martin, 1974).

19. But it should be kept in mind that—as Zysman (1983) has pointed out—the instruments for a concertation of government and big business are much more developed in the French than in the British case. Such instruments, in particular those permitting a selective credit policy, appear also to favour tripartite corporatist policies.

20. It must be noted that in Austria the fact that most large industries and the banking sector are nationalized appears as a further important element in the compromise. Medium and small businesses continue to be financially assisted by a 'watering can' system of investment subsidies (Misslbeck, 1983). Nationalization was in 1946 part of a package deal of the Conservatives with the Socialists—the other part being the legal establishment of the compulsory chambers of business.

21. The traditional Austro-Marxist metaphor for this compromise was the 'equilibrium of class forces'. This equilibrium concept may be fraught with ambiguity, but, fundamentally, the underlying analysis is not unlike Korpi's analysis of 'welfare capitalism' as a historical compromise (Korpi, 1978; 1983). The hypothesis that such a compromise is a condition of the stability of corporatist networks appears more plausible than the prediction of an eventual 'transition from capitalism to socialism' (e.g. Stephens, 1979).

4

Investment, Order and Conflict in a Simple Dynamic Model of Capitalism

KERRY SCHOTT

Introduction

Current economic problems of slow growth, unemployment and inflation are dismally persistent and widespread. Discussing this phenomenon in the late 1970s, the McCracken Report (OECD, 1977) largely blamed the situation on an unfortunate and unusual bunching of exogenous disturbances. While oil and commodity price movements, along with changes in the international monetary system, have certainly not been without economic influence, one might be rather sceptical of an explanation that is largely based on historical accident. The McCracken Report may give some explanation for the start of our economic problems in the early 1970s but it hardly seems adequate to understand the persistence of these difficulties.

One particular shortcoming in this Report is the lack of attention it paid to social conflict and economic order. In particular it can be argued that the working class in developed countries has increased in strength over this century and that the increase in the relative power of this class has profound implications for economic management (Korpi, 1983; Schott, 1984). The developed countries of Western Europe are now in a social and economic position which is unique in their history, and it may be this particular conjuncture of events that is making economic recovery so difficult to achieve.

The increase in working-class strength has implications for economic behaviour that have already been noted elsewhere. Even in the United States, where the working class is less powerful than in many other developed countries, Sachs (1980) has shown that money wages are now very sticky in a downward direction. In all severe recessions in the US since the Second World War there has not been a fall in money wages and this is a comparatively new development. Before 1945 economic downturns were typically accompanied by falling money wages and Sachs suggests that one reason for the recent stickiness in money wages is the increased strength of labour. Over this century, in all developed countries, the percentage of workers unionized has steadily increased. Furthermore, the degree of political influence that workers exert has also risen with the introduction of universal suffrage and a related increase in the support for social-democratic and left-of-centre political parties. Labour has generally become more forceful and articulate in its claim over resources. A similar line of argument appears in the political science literature where writers, such as Crozier *et al.* (1975) have suggested that the increased size of the public sector is a result of increased demands made upon government. The agenda of state concerns has grown historically and demands upon government have been sufficiently strong to cause public sector expansion as the attempt was made to meet them.

Now this increased strength on the part of the working class obviously has implications for the distribution of resources in developed countries and for the maintenance of the capitalist economic order. We are no longer in the eighteenth century when Adam Smith's factory labourers had little economic or political clout. But neither have we entered a situation where the interests of workers and capitalists are so irreconcilable that order has broken down. The inherent instability of capitalism that Marx claimed has, as yet, turned out to be a false prediction. Capitalism, in its now democratic form, has been rather long-lived and orderly.

Marxist economists have explained this persistence of the capitalist order by reference to state activity. The government intervenes in various ways, they suggest, in order to maintain capitalism, and this intervention has been successful. This theme runs through the Marxist literature on the state but strangely enough little attention has been paid to the increasing power resources at labour's disposal and to the problem of why, in the presence of this relative increase in working-class strength, order has prevailed.[1]

In this paper I intend to explore the question of the conditions under which labour quiescence appears to be rational, and thus of when we might expect to observe a minimum of conflict in capitalist society. The only conflict examined is that over the distribution of resources between capital and labour; and I will particularly focus upon this distribution of resources around a crisis point where new investment and growth are stagnant. This emphasis is pertinent given the present low growth and investment slowdown in developed countries. Due attention will be paid to the strength of workers in pressing their claims over resources and to what this implies for economic management and order.

Most economic work on social conflict has focused on wage bargaining, labour-market behaviour, and inflation, and I will not attend to these issues here. However, in line with economics methodology, I work with a model which highlights certain issues and completely ignores many others. The simple dynamic model of capitalism that is posited emphasizes that in capitalism it is private entrepreneurs who make investment decisions. Workers may forgo current consumption, and save, with a view to increasing investment and output and in due course their own future consumption. But the decision to invest rests entirely with the capitalists who will only do so when *their* expected returns are sufficient. Keynesian demand is entirely absent in this model, and increased consumption does not encourage investment through any increase in demand. Indeed increased consumption simply makes less resources available for investment; in this sense the model is essentially neo-classical.

My analytical point of departure is the dynamic model of capitalism first explored by Lancaster (1973). This is taken as a framework for discussion and it is not intended to imply that the model really represents capitalism; it is far too simplistic. However, this caricature of capitalism does highlight several important issues and suggests various strategies on the part of workers, capitalists, and the state that may emerge at particular junctures. The dynamic Lancaster model is different from the recurring static model of Przeworski and Wallerstein (1982a) which treats worker and capitalist strategies independently of time. The advantage of using a dynamic approach is that we can focus on the returns to investment over time and their interactions with the decisions of capitalists and workers, given their relative power positions in society. In this way, the analysis here presented complements Przeworski and Wallerstein's static model and the strategies they derive from it. The use of simplistic models, both in their paper and here, enables several issues to be studied in detail and this is their great advantage. The disadvantage is that this procedure necessarily rules out many other factors. None the less, the conclusions reached remain of interest.

The approach adopted suggests that there are periods in capitalism where order is quite likely to prevail; but that there are also periods where conflict is likely to emerge. These periods are determined by both the position of the economy and the strength of the working class. Furthermore, in these different situations we are likely to see different strategies adopted by workers, capitalists, and the state.

In the next section the simple dynamic model of capitalism is introduced. The presentation is rather technical and will be difficult for non-mathematical readers, so an attempt is made in the third section of the paper to explain the ideas involved in a more accessible way. Readers who are willing to take results on trust could simply skim the formal presentation and pick up the threads of the paper again in this third section. Lancaster did not pursue the implications for order and conflict that can be drawn from his model; but in the present case such implications are of evident interest and are therefore taken up in the final section of the paper. Despite the similarity of the overall economic problems now facing developed countries, different nations are in different positions within the capitalist dynamic. As a consequence, the strategies of different groups may vary cross-nationally, and the emergence of different policies and institutions to deal with them should be of little surprise. Many of the implications of the model that will be considered tie in with discussions and arguments already conducted in the political science and sociology literature, and these links will be noted where most relevant.

The Simple Dynamic Model of Capitalism

We begin by assuming that capitalist society is composed of only two groups of people, capitalists and workers. The capitalists have complete control over investment decisions but workers are sufficiently strong to insist upon some proportionate claim over resources, which they then consume. Basically, capitalists decide whether or not to invest the resources that they control. On the other hand, workers decide whether to immediately consume the resources they control or alternatively whether to leave some of these resources aside for investment. The reason why workers might choose to leave some of the resources they control aside for investment purposes is that this investment causes growth and creates the possibility of more consumption later. At this point in the discussion we treat public and private goods as if they were the same and continue with the assumption that capitalists alone make the investment decisions.

The objective of the workers is to maximize their total (undiscounted) consumption over a fixed-time horizon and the objective of the capitalists is also to maximize their (undiscounted) consumption over the same time-horizon.[2] There is just one sector in this caricatured economy which produces output using a particular, single investment technology. Output can either be consumed or invested and the capital stock is assumed to have zero depreciation.

If u_1 is the proportion of total resources devoted to worker consumption,

$$c \leqslant u_1 \leqslant b \qquad b > c; 0 < b, c < 1$$

u_2 is the proportion of the remainder devoted to investment,

$$0 \leqslant u_2 \leqslant 1$$

k is capital stock
q is total output
and a is the fixed output/capital ratio,

we can depict our capitalist economy by

Total output	$q_t = ak_t$	(4.1)
Worker consumption	$C_w = ak_t u_{1t}$	(4.2)
Capitalist consumption	$C_c = ak_t (1 - u_{1t})(1 - u_{2t})$	(4.3)
Investment	$I = ak_t (1 - u_{1t}) u_{2t}.$	(4.4)

The total of workers' consumption up to the end horizon T, is

$$J_1 = \int_0^T ak_t u_{1t} dt \qquad (4.5)$$

and the total of capitalists' consumption up to the end horizon T is,

$$J_2 = \int_0^T ak (1 - u_{1t})(1 - u_{2t}) dt. \qquad (4.6)$$

Thus, in this model, the problem for the workers is to maximize J_1 (equation 4.5) by choosing u_{1t}, the proportion of resources they consume in any time period. In considering their choice of u_{1t}, which lies between some lower and upper limit, the workers must consider the contribution of investment to their later consumption. If they consume less now, thus leaving more resources available for investment, they can consume more later if, and only if, the capitalists undertake the investment. This possibility is depicted in equation (4.5).

On the other hand the capitalists are attempting to maximize J_2 (equation 4.6) which gives their total consumption over the period. The capitalists choose u_{2t}, the proportion of resources that are invested in each time period, in order to maximize their consumption. However, like the workers, they also know that if they invest now, rather than consume, they will have more to consume later.[3]

The solution to this problem is found by solving a simple differential game which gives the path of u_{1t} and u_{2t} over time. In other words, the model gives us a solution that tells us what choice workers will make about the proportion of resources they consume over time; and what choice capitalists will make about the proportion of resources they will invest over time. Both these choices, by workers and by capitalists, depend on what the other does.

Formally, the solution is of two separate maximizing problems, one for workers and the other for capitalists. Each problem is in a form that allows Pontryagin's (1964) maximum principle to be applied, and I begin with the workers. Their problem is to choose u_1 so as to maximize,

$$J_1 = \int_0^T aku_1 \, dt$$

subject to

$$\dot{k} = ak \, (1 - u_1)u_2$$

$$c \leqslant u_1 \leqslant b$$

and some anticipated choice of u_2 by the capitalists. The workers' Hamiltonian is,

$$H_1 = aku_1 + y_1 \, ak \, (1 - u_1)u_2 \tag{4.7}$$

where y_1 is the costate variable associated with k, the capital stock. This must satisfy,

$$y_1 = - \delta H1/\delta k = -\{u_1 + y_1 \, (1 - u_1)u_2\}a. \tag{4.8}$$

Here y_1 represents the value *to workers* of a marginal increase in investment. Since workers do not look beyond some time horizon T, the marginal value of investment at this point T is zero, so $y_1 \, (T) = 0$. From the maximum principle, the optimal path for u_1, given some anticipated u_2, is

$$u_1 = c \quad \text{whenever } y_1 u_2 > 1$$

and

$$u_1 = b \quad \text{whenever } y_1 u_2 < 1.$$

Note that u_1, the workers' choice of the proportion of resources to consume, depends on y_1, the value of investment *to workers*, and u_2, the anticipated proportion of resources that will be invested.

For the capitalists the problem is to choose u_2, the proportion of resources to invest for some anticipated u_1. Thus they maximize,

$$J_2 = \int_0^T ak(1 - u_1)(1 - u_2)\, dt$$

subject to

$$\dot{k} = ak(1 - u_1)u_2$$

$$0 \leqslant u_2 \leqslant 1$$

and the anticipated choice of u_1. The capitalists' Hamiltonian is,

$$H_2 = ak(1 - u_1)(1 - u_2) + y_2\, ak(1 - u_1)u_2. \tag{4.9}$$

The costate variable y_2 is different from that in the workers' problem because it represents the marginal value of investment *to the capitalists* rather than to the workers. Following similar reasoning to before,

$$y_2 = -\delta H_2/\delta k = -\left\{1 + (y_2 - 1)u_2\right\}(1 - u_1)a. \tag{4.10}$$

Since the capitalists also do not look beyond some time horizon T, $y_2(T) = 0$ and the capitalists' Hamiltonian is linear in u_2 with coefficient $ak(1 - u_1)(y_2 - 1)$. Now $(1 - u_1)$ is always positive so the capitalist solution is,

$$u_2 = 0 \text{ when } y_2 < 1$$
$$u_2 = 1 \text{ when } y_2 > 1.$$

Combining the two solutions we can see that there are four potential combinations of u_1 and u_2 to consider. These are,

    I. $u_1 = c, u_2 = 0$ when $y_1 u_2 > 1, y_2 < 1$
    II. $u_1 = b, u_2 = 0$ when $y_1 u_2 < 1, y_2 < 1$
    III. $u_1 = c, u_2 = 1$ when $y_1 u_2 > 1, y_2 > 1$
    IV. $u_1 = b, u_2 = 1$ when $y_1 u_2 < 1, y_2 > 1$.

Now combination I can never be possible since if $u_2 = 0, y_1 u_2 > 1$ is incompatible. This leaves three combinations to consider, and in problems of this type it is usual to begin at the end. There is an end boundary condition $y_2(T) = 0$, and y_2, the return on investment to capitalists, must be a continuous function of time. Thus at the end we must have $y_2 < 1$ and also for some period, say t^* to T, before the end. In this final phase of the capitalist dynamic we therefore must have combination II ($u_1 = b, u_2 = 0$) because $y_2 < 1$ in this phase. Furthermore we know that this final phase, which begins at t^*, must begin at the point where $y_2 = 1$ and since y_1 and y_2 are both declining linearly during the final phase we can compute t^* as,

$$t^* = T - \frac{1}{a(1 - b)}. \tag{4.11}$$

Hence, provided $T > 1/a(1 - b)$ the capitalist system enters its final dynamic phase at t^*. After this point in time the return on investment to capitalists is not sufficient to induce them to invest at all and from t^* to T all resources are consumed by both the workers and the capitalists. The workers take proportion b of these resources, from t^* to T, and the capitalists consume the remainder $(1-b)$. This maximum proportionate amount that the workers can consume is b and in this problem b is entirely determined by workers' strength or their effective claim over resources.

Now the way in which this final phase is interesting is that in a sense it denotes the death of the capitalist dynamic based on a particular investment technology. After t^*, the crisis point, there is no accumulation, and resources cease to grow. Between t^* and the end point T there is no growth and no new investment and resources are simply consumed. Hence, the final phase of this capitalist dynamic is reached at a crisis point t^* where accumulation ceases. After t^* the system theoretically continues to the end point T but over this final period the economy ceases to grow and resources are simply consumed.

The period prior to t^* can now be examined, and it is clearly going to be characterized by either combination III or combination IV. In both these combinations y_2, the marginal value of investment to capitalists, is greater than unity and there will be accumulation. However, in combination III the workers choose to consume their minimal proportion of resources, c, and in combination IV they choose to consume the maximum proportion of resources they can get, b. Since in both combinations III and IV we have $u_2 = 1$ we must have $y_1 > 1$ in combination III and $y_1 < 1$ in combination IV. This means that if the return on investment to workers, y_1, is greater than unity, they will choose their minimal consumption plan, c, and leave some resources aside for investment. When $y_1 > 1$ it is worthwhile for workers to put resources aside for investment so they can consume more later (combination III). On the other hand, if $y_1 < 1$ the return on investment *to workers* is not sufficient to induce them to forgo any consumption now and they will take b, the maximum of resources they can get. In this case, combination IV, there is no rational reason for them to leave resources aside for investment since they will get insufficient return on their forgone consumption.

Returning to the final phase, between t^* and T, note that $y_1(T) = 0$ and that y_1 declines linearly at a rate of ab during this period. At t^* the value of y_1 must therefore be

$$y_1(t^*) = ab(T - t^*) = b/1 - b \qquad (4.12)$$

from equation (4.11). Hence, if $b > \frac{1}{2}$, so that workers are sufficiently strong to claim over 50 per cent of resources, the phase before the final phase must be combination III. Here $y_1 = b/1 - b \; > 1$ and workers choose c, their minimal plan. The reason they do this is because they can consume proportionately more later when investment ceases. The return to workers on investment is high enough to warrant them setting aside resources for capitalist investment and subsequent growth.

Thus if we examine the dynamic of this simple capitalist system around the crisis point, t^*, we have a situation like that shown in Figure 4.1. In the period from $\bar{t}$ to t^* we have accumulation in progress and after t^*, to T, we have no accumulation.

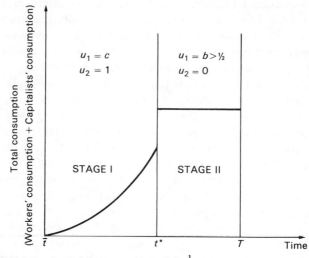

FIG. 4.1. *The path of total consumption:* $b > \frac{1}{2}$

This solution, depicted in Figure 4.1, is for the case where workers are sufficiently powerful to claim over 50 per cent of resources if they wish to ($b > \frac{1}{2}$). Between $\bar{t}$ and t^*, before the crisis point, workers' consumption goes up each time period at a rate of $cak(t)$. The capital stock grows exponentially during this period at a rate of $a(1 - c)$. Income goes up exponentially at similar rates and at the end of the period income has grown to

$$y(t^*) = a\bar{y}\,e^{a(1 - c)t^*} \qquad \qquad \text{for } b > \frac{1}{2}$$

where $\bar{y}$ is income at $\bar{t}$, the beginning of this period.

This basic result, shown in Figure 4.1, is for the case where $b > \frac{1}{2}$; workers could press for claims on resources that were in excess of 50 per cent of the total. Initially, however, in Stage 1 workers are quiescent and do not press these claims. They settle for some lower proportion, c, of resources and leave some current consumption aside for investment purposes. Once new investment halts, ($u_2 = 0$) in Stage 2, they do press their maximum claim and they then consume b of resources. The reason why new investment stops in Stage 2 is that the rate of return on this investment to capitalists (y_2) is no longer sufficient to warrant investment by them. Investment does not stop because of workers' strength and claims on resources; it ceases because it is no longer viable.

When workers are not sufficiently powerful to press for claims on resources that are in excess of 50 per cent, the result is different. In this case $b < \frac{1}{2}$ and the combination before the final phase is combination IV. In this phase

$$y_1 = \frac{b}{1 - b} < 1$$

and workers have no inducement to set aside resources for investment. The return on investment to workers is not sufficient for them to restrain their immediate consumption plans and they consume all they can get. However, in this phase the return on investment to capitalists (y_2) is still adequate to call forth new investment and we have a situation where workers are consuming maximally and capitalists are investing.

But instead of being a 'bang-bang' solution in two stages, the solution when $b < \frac{1}{2}$ is in three stages. The mathematics behind this result is similar to that pursued before, so for the sake of brevity I will simply spell out the result. Before combination IV the system begins with combination III as above. Workers begin by leaving some resources aside for investment because the rate of return on this investment for the workers (y_1) is sufficient to encourage savings. At some point t^*, however, this return on investment to workers falls and they revert to combination IV. Hence when workers can claim only less than 50 per cent of resources the solution is that depicted in Figure 4.2. It has three stages.

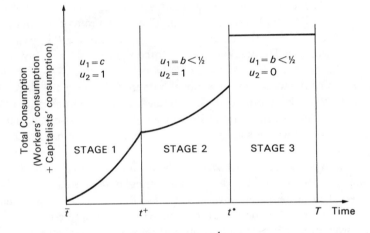

FIG. 4.2. *The path of total consumption:* $b < \frac{1}{2}$

Between $\bar{t}$ and t^+ in stage 1, workers' consumption goes up each time period at a rate of $cak(t)$ and the capital stock and income grow exponentially at a rate of $a(1-c)$. In stage 2, between t^+ and t^*, growth continues to occur but at a lesser exponential rate of $a(1-b)$. In this second phase the workers are pressing their consumption claims and their proportion of resources consumed rises from c to b. The final stage, stage 3, is similar to before. New investment has stopped, growth ceases, and output is simply divided between capitalists and workers, with workers taking the maximum they can get.

A Non-Technical Recapitulation

This formal dynamic model, despite its mathematical difficulty, can be intuitively understood fairly easily. We posit a society composed of capitalists and workers where each group is trying to maximize its own consumption or its share of available resources over time. Because the society is capitalist, the private entrepreneurs are the group who make the investment decisions, and they do so on the basis of the expected return of this investment to them. When this return is adequate they decide to invest and when their return is not adequate they cease their new investment activity. Thus the capitalists' decision is basically whether or not to invest and they make this decision on the basis of *their* expected returns.

The workers in this capitalist scenario have no control over investment. They are aiming to maximize their consumption or their share of total resources, but this does not necessarily imply that they will always consume all the resources that they can. Sometimes workers may forgo current consumption, or save, and leave these resources aside for investment. They choose to do this because the added investment will generate more output and hence more consumption for them in the future. But the dilemma for the workers is that if they choose not to consume all they can, there is no guarantee that the capitalists will actually invest their (the workers') forgone consumption. If the rate of return on investment is sufficiently low, the capitalists will simply consume the resources left aside by the workers. The workers cannot force the capitalists to invest if they choose not to.

The power of the workers in this model is defined simply as the share of total resources they could consume if they wished. This potential proportion of resources that the workers could claim was set at b and we assumed that $b < 1$. In other words, our workers are not so strong that they command a claim over all resources.

When the workers decide to save and leave some resources aside for investment they are doing so with a view to consuming more in the future. They give up some of their current claim over resources so that these can be invested. This lowers the proportion of resources that the workers initially consume, and we set this lower proportion at c. This proportion is more than zero but it is less than b, the maximum claim that the workers could make if they wished.

Now in this capitalist world there is just one investment technology but it yields a different rate of return to workers and to capitalists. For the workers the return on investment (y_1) depends on the share of output that they can eventually command and how effective the investment is in generating a growth in output. At some point (T) the value of investment to workers has declined to zero, though the value of investment to workers is initially larger and positive. For the capitalists the return on investment (y_2) depends on the share of output that they can command and also on how effective the investment is in generating a growth in output. At some point (T) the value of investment to capitalists on this particular technology has declined to zero, though initially it is larger and positive. Since the capitalists control investment, they decide what proportion of the resources they command to devote to investment. They can for instance invest all the resources under their control or at the other extreme invest none of them. In the latter case, the capitalists are simply assumed to consume resources and undertake no new investment. The economy is then stagnant with no growth.

Now in a static world with no investment it is obvious that workers would simply go for all the resources they could get and capitalists would do likewise. In this static and stagnant position the workers would get b of the resources, where b is determined by their power, and capitalists would claim $(1 - b)$ being the only other group. In such a static world the conflict between workers and capitalists is quite stark and simple. What one group gets, the other does not.

In a dynamic, but still very simple world, the position is less straightforward since it is sometimes quite rational for workers to save and thus leave aside resources for investment. This enhances their future consumption; sacrifice now entails more consumption later. When both groups make their decision simultaneously with an aim to maximizing their share of resources for consumption over time, we found there were two solutions, and these depended on the power of the working class.

The first solution is depicted in Figure 4.1 in the previous section. Here the working class is relatively powerful and can claim over 50 per cent of total resources $(b > \frac{1}{2})$. When this is the case the capitalist dynamic goes through two phases. It begins with stage 1 when a particular investment technology is introduced. In this stage the return on this investment to both capitalists and workers is high. Workers decide to forgo some consumption to increase the investment allocation and they consume only c of the resources. They could claim $b > c$ of resources but during this stage they do not do so since the extra output produced by the additional investment can be at least partly consumed by them later. At the same time, in this first stage, the return on investment to capitalists is also high and they decide to invest all the resources they can command. Since the workers are consuming c of resources this means that the capitalists invest $(1 - c)$ of the total. The economy grows exponentially.

But, because the return on this investment technology is falling over time, we eventually reach a position where the return on investment to the capitalists is not sufficient to induce them to invest. At this stage they cease any new investment and simply consume. Since investment stagnates, there is no reason why workers should forgo any consumption and in stage 2 they consume all they can. Thus in stage 2 the workers and capitalists divide the output of a stagnant economy between them simply on the basis of their power position. The workers take b share and the capitalists take $(1 - b)$.

If workers are not so powerful the solution is different. This scenario, where workers can only command a maximum of resources that is less than 50 per cent, $(b < \frac{1}{2})$, is depicted in Figure 4.2 in the previous section. The introduction of the investment technology is shown in stage 1, and this is similar to the position in stage 1 just discussed above. Workers forgo consumption and consume only c of resources $(c < b)$ and more resources are invested. The return on investment to capitalists is sufficient for them to invest all the resources they can and they invest $(1 - c)$ of the total. The end stage is also similar to that when workers are more powerful. The return on investment to capitalists has fallen and is not sufficient to encourage new investment. The workers do not forgo consumption and they take all they can $(b < \frac{1}{2})$ and the capitalists, having halted their new investment, simply consume $(1 - b)$. This is stage 3 in Figure 4.2.

But in this case of the less powerful workers, there is also an intermediate phase, stage 2. In this middle stage of the dynamic the return on investment to the workers is not sufficient for them to decide to forgo consumption. Their potential share of future output is less than a half and they judge that there is no point in any further sacrificing of current claims. They thus consume $b > c$ of resources. However, the capitalist return on investment is still sufficient to make new investment worthwhile and the capitalists invest all the resources they can. Thus in this middle phase, stage 2', the workers are consuming b of resources and the capitalists are investing the remainder $(1 - b)$ of the total.

Now these two solutions, shown in Figures 4.1 and 4.2, clearly imply some interesting behaviour on the part of the two groups in our caricature of capitalist society. It is to this that we now turn, and we will focus on the circumstances in which both order and conflict are likely to appear. The behaviour of the model around the crisis point (t^*) is also pertinent since it is at this point that investment and growth stagnate, and this may be of some relevance to the present economic difficulties facing the developed countries.

The Implications for Conflict and Order

Consensus and Militancy

One obvious result that emerges from the previous two sections is that workers will sometimes agree, quite rationally, not to press for all the resources they could potentially command. When this occurs the workers may appear to be quiescent, and the capitalist system may seem quite orderly. Furthermore, this quiescence is forthcoming without any intervention by the state being necessary. We noted earlier that Marxists have explained order and working-class quiescence by invoking the role of the state; but the model suggests that a class consensus could prevail without any such state involvement.

However, it is also clear that this position of consensus is not stable in the sense that it will necessarily go on for ever. Workers' agreement or quiescence is contingent upon there being a sufficient return *to workers* on investment, and this seems intuitively sensible. Should this return not be forthcoming, it is clear that workers would revert to their maximum consumption claim immediately, and militancy on their part would be expected in making this claim. So in those countries, or historic periods, where workers perceive that their return on forgone consumption is high there will be consensus. On the other hand, where the workers' return on saving (or forgone consumption) is low we would expect militancy as workers press for their maximum claim over resources. This result also seems intuitively sensible, and in line with the familiar *ad hoc* argument that an expanding economy is likely to be less conflict-ridden than a stagnating economy.

But whether or not there will be consensus or conflict does not just depend on investment activity. It also depends on working-class strength in relation to the power of capitalists. When workers are so powerful that they can potentially claim over 50 per cent of resources they will be quiescent until new investment ceases. This is the scenario depicted in Figure 4.1. So long as new investment occurs, the relatively strong workers will save or forgo consumption; but once new investment halts they will exercise their maximum claim and in all likelihood they will exhibit militancy in doing so.

But if the workers are less powerful, and can claim only less than 50 per cent of resources, the situation is somewhat different. This is the scenario depicted in Figure 4.2. In this case, the workers are initially quiescent and forgo consumption because the return on investment to them is sufficient. But this return is falling over time and at some point, before new investment ceases, the workers will exercise their maximum claim over resources and become militant. The relatively weaker working class will be militant for a period even when there is new investment because the decreased return on this investment to them is not sufficient to encourage quiescence. And of course this militancy will continue when new investment halts altogether.

These conclusions might at first glance suggest that, paradoxically, a stronger working class is in the interest of capitalism. The stronger working class is quiescent until new investment halts, while a relatively weak working class is militant even before the cessation of accumulation. But in fact it is not the case that a stronger working class is more in the interests of the capitalists, as closer examination reveals. In the stages before the investment crisis, before t^*, it is obvious that investment and output growth will be higher in those countries where proportionately less of resources are consumed. In nations where investment is high as a percentage of resources, the relative economic situation at this crisis point will be more favourable in the sense that national income will have grown faster and to a higher relative level. And this crisis point for capitalism will be more slowly reached the lower is working-class strength as represented by their maximum claim over resources. In equation (4.11), in section 2, t^* is closer to T, the ultimate end-point, the smaller is b, or working-class strength. The weaker the working class, the longer it takes to reach a position where new investment stops. This of course is hardly surprising since the return on investment to capitalists is higher when their share of output is greater and we would expect capitalism to be more sustainable if proportionately more resources were available for accumulation. Thus, when the working class is strong ($b > \frac{1}{2}$) there is consensus when there is new investment but the point at which this new investment ceases comes earlier; and, at this point, conflict is liable to emerge.

Restructuring

Now the model has assumed one particular investment technology. In reality, once the crisis point, t^*, is reached, and accumulation ceases, there would not of course be an acceptance of economic stagnation. If capitalism is to be sustained, what would necessarily happen would be restructuring and capitalists would search for a new investment technology that would give then a suitable return on their investment. At some point after the crisis point, t^*, we would expect a shift in the capitalist dynamic back to its beginning phase. A new investment technology would imply a different y_1 and y_2—different returns on investment to workers and capitalists; and, with restructuring, the new returns on invest-ment would be greater than unity. The system would begin its dynamic again with a different technology.

Restructuring in this sense involves the replacement of an old investment technology with a new one. The return on the original investment technology has fallen, perhaps due to other capitalist nations adopting it and providing competition. But, for whatever reason, once this investment is no longer viable, some new technology must be introduced if the capitalist system is not to stagnate. It is also clear that restructuring is likely to pose several problems. The resources for the new investment technology are unlikely to be sought until the crisis point is reached; before this time the existing investment technology is yielding adequate returns. However, after the crisis point, workers will be expecting to get their maximum claim on resources and this will limit the resources available for new investment. Other things being equal, it is obvious that restructuring will be easier the lower is working-class strength and thus the weaker their claim over resources.

Strategies

In the context of the simple dynamic model of capitalism that has been devel-oped, it is instructive to examine the conflict, and the possible strategies, of both workers and capitalists in the general vicinity of the crisis point. Just before this crisis point the return on investment to capitalists has almost fallen to the level where accumulation in the existing investment technology ceases. The economy is approaching stagnation. At the crisis point and beyond there is total stag-nation; no new investment and no growth. As a rough approximation, for argument's sake, we might consider that the developed countries have been somewhere close to this crisis point for some time. Some nations may not have stagnated completely but their investment and growth rates will be faltering; other nations may be at or beyond the crisis point where the economy is stagnant.

Now in all cases under the model it is clearly in the best interests of capitalists, if they wish to sustain capitalism, to try and keep working class strength (b) as low as possible. At the same time it is always in workers' best interests, if they wish to maximize their consumption, to increase their strength. This conflict is basic in this simple world, and implies strategies on the part of each class to achieve these conflicting ends.

However, in this same world other less obvious conflicts and potential strategies are also apparent. First, in countries where the workers are strong, so that $b > \frac{1}{2}$, and we are approaching stagnation, we would expect to see capitalists attempting to persuade workers that the return on investment *to workers* is high. If this capitalist strategy is successful, workers will agree to set aside resources for investment. However there are problems attached to this strategy for the capitalists since, once stagnation occurs, the workers will demand their returns on past abstinence. This will make capitalist restructuring plans more difficult as in stagnation the capitalist command over resources will be constrained. At this point we might expect capitalists to point out the necessity of restructuring and to argue that if the workers assist, by freeing resources for investment, the workers will ultimately gain returns from this investment. This amounts to offering the workers an indefinitely postponed splurge, since if the workers continually agree to minimal consumption they will never see the rewards from it. Basically, restructuring will be more difficult and more conflict-ridden where workers are strong.

Nevertheless, around the point of stagnation we would expect to observe considerable friendly persuasive dialogue on the part of capitalists with workers if, and only if, the working class is strong. If the working class is not so strong ($b < \frac{1}{2}$) it will be already aiming for maximum consumption plans (see Figure 4.2) and will be less amenable to friendly discourse about the gains on investment to workers as a group. Workers are so relatively weak that they never expect to reap these gains, so friendly dialogue will get nowhere. We might therefore argue that it is no surprise that neo-corporatism, with the state acting as a mediator between capitalists and workers, and the state itself seeking to sustain the system, should only arise in countries where the workers are strong and where they perceive high returns on investment. If the workers are not strong there is no point in trying to get an agreement to curtail worker consumption since the workers would not agree to it. Furthermore, the need for this type of agreement, to curtail consumption, is more pressing as stagnation is approached. Co-operation may not just be a feature when workers' strength is high and their perceived returns on investment are high; it is more necessary as stagnation occurs. This position is one also explored by Lange (this volume) in some detail.

It is also of interest to consider the situation just beyond the stagnation point, t^*. It can be shown (Lancaster, 1973) that for some time period beyond this point the return on investment to workers ($y_1 > 1$) is sufficient for them to curtail their consumption if they are strong ($b > \frac{1}{2}$). But capitalists have stopped investment because the return on investment to capitalists is insufficient ($y_2 < 1$), and as a consequence the workers consume maximally. There is no investment. If at this juncture a state had the aim of maximizing social welfare, defined as maximizing total consumption, investment would continue until the workers' return on investment had fallen to $y_1 < 1$. This happens at some point beyond t^*, and before T. Thus, once the economy has got to t^*, workers in such a social welfare state would continue to leave resources aside for investment if such investment would occur. Capitalists will not carry it out however ($y_2 < 1$) and, if this social welfare solution is to hold, one solution would be for the state to do the investment itself. The social value of investment is above the capitalists' value of investment immediately beyond t^*, so there is a potential consensus here between workers and the state.

There is a clear link between this strategic argument and the 'power resources' approach of Korpi (1983). He has argued that a strong working class will be less likely than a weaker one to seek to maximize its gains in the labour market and more likely to engage in political bargaining with capitalists and the state. The basic problem inherent in this bargaining strategy is, however, clearly apparent in the model presented. The workers will bargain but they want more investment; and if the capitalists will not invest then the state must.

There are shades of such a response in the recent Social Democratic legislation in Sweden to establish 'wage-earner funds', through which investment will become more socialized and more under the control of workers. Such a move can be thought of as shifting the point of economic stagnation, and no new investment, further into the future; but it is hardly a capitalist solution and will obviously be opposed by capitalists. It could be a peaceful road to socialism but the opposition to the Swedish legislation was entirely predictable (cf. Esping-Andersen & Korpi, this volume). Capitalists lose control over investment decisions, or at least some part of them, and this is a clear threat to their position.

Also, this socialization of investment, while perfectly rational, only delays the day when restructuring becomes necessary. It is not a stable solution unless a new investment technology is introduced. Further growth ultimately depends on this restructuring; and, if investment is socialized, the state is now in the position of having to restructure investment at some point in order to achieve this growth. This means that continuing workers' agreement is needed to put aside resources for the restructuring and that the state must be capable of managing this process. However, and more generally, on the basis of this argument we might expect the pressure for restructuring to be more urgent in those countries where the state does little investment and where investment is less socialized.

It is also remarkable that on the basis of our simple model we would not necessarily expect similar strategies to emerge in all countries. The strategy that does logically suggest itself depends both on the strength of the workers *and* on the economic position of the country in question in its capitalist economic dynamic. The end-of-convergence thesis that Goldthorpe argues in this volume, and the emergence in some cases of dualist tendencies rather than corporatist ones, are linked with the simple story spelled out here. As working-class strength and the economic position of nations vary, so too will the strategies adopted by the major economic actors.

Finally, it should be noted that in this paper I have not considered any differences between public and private consumption. There is of course a difference in reality, and the strength of the workers in making demands for these two kinds of consumption may well differ. In some countries workers may be strong in their demands for private consumption but have little strength in their demands over public consumption. In this case the relative proportion of goods consumed from the public and private sectors will reflect this relative strength as well as consumer preferences. Furthermore, the perceived impact by the workers of these different consumption demands on investment behaviour will matter a great deal. If workers perceive, correctly or not, that public goods consumption does not crowd out either private investment or public investment, then there is no reason why they should restrain their demands for public goods. They will simply consume as many public goods as their strength can get them; there is no reason to abstain since investment behaviour is not perceived to be influenced. On the other hand, if the state or the capitalists can persuade the workers that public consumption crowds out investment, then the workers may choose a minimal demand level for public goods. Again, this persuasion is likely to be more successful if the working class is strong and can therefore expect to get more returns on its present abstinence later.

Notes

1. Marxist economic theories of the state are reviewed by Jessop (1977). The work of Korpi (1983) is an exceptional study from a Marxist perspective which does examine the implications of the increased power resources at workers' disposal.

2. The assumption that there is no discounting can be relaxed without any loss of generality, though the timing of the switch points will change.

3. The assumption that capitalists seek to maximize their consumption may seem an unrealistic view of the basics of capitalist behaviour. It might be more reasonable to consider this capitalist consumption-maximization as an attempt by capitalists to maximize their available resources over time, given their strength and that of the workers. In this sense the maximum resources that the capitalists aim to get may not necessarily be consumed by them; it could, for example, be invested abroad. But in any case the capitalists *are* aiming to maximize the resources they can get, given their relative power position. These resources may then be invested in the country in question, or they may not be.

5

Unions, Workers and Wage Regulation: The Rational Bases of Consent

PETER LANGE

Introduction: Unions, Workers and Wage Regulation

If wage regulation is an essential part of a 'politics of the virtuous circle' (Castles 1978)[1], the weakest link of the chain of causation is generally considered to be the workers whose wages are to be regulated. Whatever the systemic benefits of regulated wages, the primary point of instability and breakdown is at the micro-level: in the unwillingness of workers to sacrifice potential short-term individual wage gains in the name of a potential 'public interest' or a possible medium-term benefit for workers generally.

Two basic approaches, both of which assume a fundamental opposition between the interests of workers (treated individually or collectively) and wage regulation, can be identified. The first is the Marxist or neo-Marxist approach which stresses class conflict and the fundamentally zero-sum character of the relationship between workers and capital. Workers can be expected to resist wage regulation because the underlying logic of such a policy is to support capital and capitalism and to shift a portion of the product which workers could extract for themselves into the hands of employers. Even if wage regulation improves the lot of workers for a period of time, it can be expected to lead to internal struggles within the unions, which will undermine their willingness to support regulated wages. Thus, sooner or later, the underlying logic of class conflict under capitalism will either doom wage regulation policies to collapse or require increasing coercion for their enforcement (Panitch, 1977a, 1981; Sabel, 1981).

The second approach is rooted in an entirely different tradition, that of individual rational choice (see Schwerin, 1980a, for an application). Here, there is no assumption that wage regulation could not, in principle, produce real benefits for workers individually and for the working class as a whole (and for capitalists and capital): quite the contrary. The theory takes on particular power and fascination because such benefits from regulation are assumed to be theoretically possible, but unlikely to be produced in practice since it is not 'rational' for individual workers to contribute to their production. The wily free-rider is on the prowl, seeking to assure that he does as well as he can, and no worse than he must, and knowing that his little 'theft' will be of no consequence to others (Olson, 1965). Again the implication is clear: co-operation will have to be assured by coercion or by the provision of private goods which make it worthwhile for the individual worker not to free-ride; otherwise the policy of wage regulation will return to something more closely resembling wage determination under the market.

Both of these approaches produce seemingly firmly-rooted pessimism—or, in the case of the Marxists, one should perhaps say, optimism—about the prospects for wage regulation. Yet, it is worthwhile asking whether the theories which underlie them can withstand close scrutiny, for they have important implications for the linkages between industrial and class relations, economic performance, and democratic values in the advanced industrial democracies.

A recent study by Przeworski and Wallerstein (1982a) casts considerable doubt on the empirical utility of the Marxist or neo-Marxist stance in regard to wage regulation. Using a game-theoretic and abstractly deductive approach to the analysis of labour-capital relations in advanced capitalist democracies, these authors demonstrate that, *under certain conditions*, there is nothing collectively irrational in class compromise for the working class.[2] Bilateral compromise and restraint between capital and labour (each treated as a collective entity) can produce medium-term outcomes for both sides which are superior to those which would result from more militant class strategies. It does not necessarily follow that workers (treated as a collective actor) will restrain their wage militancy. This depends on 'the wages they expect in the future if the compromise holds and the risk that the compromise will not hold' (219), both of which, in turn, are in considerable part a function of rationally-behaving capital. None the less, there is no reason to assume that wage-regulation arrangements reflect false consciousness on the part of workers (when they accept them) or a betrayal of class interests on the part of the workers' organizations (235–7).

Przeworski and Wallerstein demonstrate, then, that union restraint of wage militancy can produce a public good for labour; but, they leave open the question of whether *workers* can be expected to contribute to its production, even when capital is willing to play. They explicitly recognize this problem by noting that (221):

workers as well as capitalists are placed by a compromise into a prisoner's dilemma, in which each participant may find it preferable not to pay the costs of the compromise even if such a compromise is collectively optimal for the class.

For reasons of presentational economy and elegance, however, they forgo any detailed analysis of the likelihood that sufficient co-operation within the working class can be achieved. Having disposed of the view that workers necessarily lose from wage regulation, they leave us with the possibility that it may still not be 'rational' for workers to co-operate in order to gain from it.

This is, of course, precisely what those who have applied the 'logic of collective action' (Olson, 1965) to the issue of wage regulation have been arguing (e.g. Schwerin, 1980a). Under most conditions, workers will not believe that their individual contribution to the provision of the public goods claimed to result from wage regulation (for example, lower inflation, improved international competitiveness of the national economy, recovery from a negative balance of payments) will make any difference to the probability of these goods being obtained. Thus, the temptation exists to cheat by not regulating one's own wage, while at the same time drawing on the public goods resulting from the wage regulation of others.

Of course, workers do not generally bargain individually, but in most industrial relations systems there is a practical—if not always formally established—opportunity for small groups of workers to bargain for higher wages at the plant or firm levels. For any particular group of workers,[3] it is then 'only rational' to get the best wage it can. If the group maximizes, and enough other workers (behaving 'irrationally') regulate, it will yield nothing of its potential short-term wage *and* gain from the public goods achieved through wage restraint on the part of others. If it maximizes, and others, behaving 'rationally' also do, it will not get to share in the public goods that would have resulted from joint regulation, but it will have maximized its own short-term wage *and* it will have avoided the worst possible outcome: that it regulates its wage and all others maximize theirs. Moreover, it may be held that where wage-regulation is attempted, the rewards to labour of a strategy of co-operation, if it were chosen, would not be immediate but rather deferred; and their realization would be heavily dependent on the behaviour of capital and the state—behaviour which is only partially a function of the strategy chosen by labour (Przeworski & Wallerstein, 1982a).

But is all this really valid? Historical experience and research findings would indicate that it is worthwhile looking further before accepting the conclusion that the potential gains for workers and society which wage regulation might provide cannot be realized with workers' rationally-based consent and co-operation. Wage regulation *has* occurred in the advanced industrial democracies, sometimes for extended periods of time and with at least partial success (Lange & Garrett, 1983). Furthermore, there is evidence that it has been achieved in union movements in which workers have had significant opportunities to influence both contracts and union policy with regard to wages (Lange, 1984).[4] This would, therefore, suggest that workers' effective acceptance of regulated wages may be a more contingent outcome than the 'logic of collective action' would lead us to expect.

Theory also prompts caution. The 'model' of decision-making of the logic of collective action is a very simple one. It is based on an extremely narrow understanding of 'rational' behaviour and of the time-horizon of decisions. In fact, when the wage-regulation problem is explored with the analytical tools of the Prisoner's Dilemma game *played repeatedly over time*, a more complex analysis of the strategies of workers becomes possible. This analysis, in turn, suggests that workers'—and not just union—consent to and co-operation with wage regulation is more contingent, more rational and more likely than previous studies (including that of Przeworski and Wallerstein) would suggest.

Wage Regulation and the Prisoner's Dilemma

Taylor (1976) and Hardin (1971, 1982), among others, have pointed out that the situation captured by the logic of collective action is analogous to a multi-player Prisoner's Dilemma (PD) game. That this is formally the case requires too lengthy and complex an analysis to develop here. For heuristic purposes, however, let us imagine an industrial relations system in which wages are centrally set through a single, annual, national contract binding on all workers, but in which there are effective (if unsanctioned) possibilities for exceeding the nationally set wage-norms through plant-level bargaining. We can then think of a game being played between any group of workers and all other workers in which, when wage regulation is proposed, the group of workers has two strategies: co-operation (C), in which it accepts the regulated wage, and defection (D), or free-riding, in which it goes for the best wage it can get at the time, using the available means to do so. Let us, furthermore, assume that the pay-offs from these strategies are such that each worker in the group 'obtains a higher payoff if [the group] chooses D than if [it] chooses C, no matter what strategies are chosen by the other players; but every [worker] prefers the outcome (C,C,C, ... C) in which everyone cooperates to the outcome (D,D,D, ... D) in which everyone defects' (Taylor, 1976: 89). With these assumptions, the preference ordering of strategies and pay-offs for the group is as seen in Table 5.1.[5]

TABLE 5.1. *Preferred strategies and their pay-offs for group*

Group	All Others	Pay-offs for Group
D	C	y
C	C	w
D	D	x
C	D	z
	Where: $y > w > x > z$	

It is evident that any group would prefer to free-ride while all others co-operate. But, since all players (in this case, groups of workers) must be assumed to be able to reach somewhat the same conclusions, the outcome of the game will be that all players will defect (D,D) and no wage regulation will be achieved. Our workers will not be happy with this outcome. None the less, under the assumption of egocentric material rationality in the regular one-play n-person PD game, no other outcome is possible. However, this assumption is not necessarily applicable for all situations for which the PD analysis might seem appropriate, and certainly not for that of wage regulation.

To date, the most often questioned assumption of the PD game as applied to wage regulation has been the one defining worker 'interests'. The PD game, after all, assumes an entirely self-interested, materially-oriented and untrusting worker. In the real world, however, workers frequently develop a sense of collective responsibility; and in at least some societies, workers (and others) may be 'interested' in behaving in a way which increases their moral and not just their material worth.[6]

I have no basic argument with those who have made such observations. None the less, they seem to me to have insufficiently explored the *possibility* that even egocentrically rational workers may co-operate with wage regulation. If this were the case, it would mean that the existence of wage regulation need not imply that the rational, material self-interests of union constituents were being over-ridden through coercion or set aside in the pursuit of less self-interested goals. And it would further mean that under certain conditions the public goods attainable through wage regulation could be compatible with the pursuit of individual material self-interests on the part of workers and with unions whose policies were responsive to those workers (Lange, 1984).

The need to explore this possibility is also underlined by a theoretical observation. The standard PD analysis is, as Taylor notes (1976: 84-5) 'entirely static; it is concerned with individual preferences at only one point in time, and proceeds as if the individual [or, in our case, the group of workers] makes only one choice, once and for all, of the amount of his contribution to the provision of the public good.' It is difficult to imagine a situation for which this static analysis is less realistic than wage regulation under institutionalized collective bargaining. For any particular wage-regulation bargain is always *just one in a series of bargains* (wage-regulating and not) between unions and employers. What we have, therefore, is an indefinitely long (and therefore effectively infinite) set of games, with the unions (and employers) and each group of workers deciding at (and during) each play what strategy to follow.[7] Like labour and capital in the analysis of Przeworski and Wallerstein (1982a), workers decide each time wage regulation is proposed whether and how much they want to contribute to the achievement of its goals; and they do so in terms of both present and expected future conditions, and of how those conditions impinge on their interests both at that moment and in the future.

A number of extremely important consequences for the possibilities for wage regulation flow from the fact that the workers are involved in an iterated or 'super-', *n*-person game, made up of an indefinitely long sequence of ordinary *n*-person PD games. These consequences have been systematically analysed by Taylor (1976: chs. 3, 4, 5), and we will not repeat his discussion here. His general conclusion is of the utmost significance, however, for he finds that '*individual voluntary cooperation in every constituent game of the supergame is ... rational under certain circumstances*' (85, my emphasis). We will argue below that Taylor has somewhat overstated his conclusion: 'pure' rational self-interest maximization is unlikely to produce a stable co-operative equilibrium. None the less, with only *a minimal degree of mutual trust and without any altruistic motives* stable co-operative outcomes can be produced.

Why should this be the case? Why should it be rational for workers to co-operate with wage regulation when the game is repeated even though, if it were played only once, co-operation would be foolish; and what are the circumstances which influence the probability of co-operation? The answers obviously lie in the dynamics of both playing and paying when the game is iterated. Two critical consequences of iteration can be identified.

The first concerns player interaction, and its impact on the probability of co-operation over any sequence of plays of the ordinary game. In the non-iterated PD game, the rational strategy for any player is unaffected by whether or not he can communicate with the other player(s). The only thing which counts is whether he can be certain that the other player will co-operate—something which implies coercion. Such is not the case, however, in an iterated PD game such as wage regulation. Here, the decisions taken by any and all workers in any single play of the game are known to any player at the time of the subsequent play. They can thus affect, and be affected by, his and other players' behaviour.

To understand the full significance of this possibility of effective inter-temporal communication, it must be remembered that any player in the game would, in theory, prefer the all-cooperate (C,C . . . C) outcome to any but the outcome in which he defects and all others co-operate (D,C . . . C), which he cannot think likely. The possibility of communication, in the context of re-peated games, means that any player need not entirely rely on the structure of pay-offs in the present game to anticipate how other players will behave; each player can actually wait for one, or even a couple of plays of the game to find out.[8] Furthermore, any player can also think that other players will do so as well.

This opens new strategic vistas. Above all, it means that players can, rationally, play *contingently co-operative* strategies.[9] In doing so, they will be indicating their willingness to contribute to a generally co-operative solution as long as they find out in relatively short order that enough others also are willing to do so—as indicated by their having played contingent or non-contingent co-operative strategies. Should this strategic interplay display enough co-operating players to satisfy the rational self-interests of the contingently co-operating players, a largely co-operative equilibrium could be established.[10] In terms of our problem, a wage-regulation outcome could be stabilized.

The second major consequence of the fact that the (wage-regulation) game is iterated concerns the pay-offs and has already been suggested. In the single game, the only pay-offs which count are those associated with the single game, and the only important feature of those pay-offs is their rank-order ($y > w > x > z$). When these are known, the behaviour of self-interested, rational players and the outcome of the game is also known. In the iterated game, however, this is no longer the case. Instead, the relative sizes of the possible pay-offs from playing different strategies in the ordinary game will be of relevance, and so too will be expectations about future pay-offs of sustained and extensive co-operation and the rate at which they are discounted (Taylor, 1976: 90-3).[11]

Let us imagine a worker who is asked by his union to accept a regulated wage (i.e. one below what he thinks he could get by being more militant) in order to create conditions which, the union argues, will promote national economic growth and, most important for our purposes, the worker's longer-term wage-growth as well. How should he decide whether or not to co-operate, giving up something in the present to gain something in the future? To explore his considerations, we may revert to the rank-ordering of strategies and pay-offs of the non-iterated PD game presented earlier, but substituting 'worker' for 'group'. As should be evident, we are interested in the conditions under which our worker will consider playing C rather than D, at least contingently. These conditions involve (i) the ordinary game about which he is currently deciding what to do, (ii) his expectations about the future, and (iii) the relationship between (i) and (ii). For expositional purposes we will treat each in turn.

(i) Our worker would prefer the outcome of all co-operating to all defecting. Yet he remains materially self-interested. As a result, he will be concerned with what he might lose in the short run by co-operation. There are two types of potential losses which he can incur: those from being suckered by co-operating when all others defect, and those from failing to free-ride by defecting when all others co-operate (these can be considered opportunity costs). The first is represented by the difference between pay-offs x and z; the second by the difference between pay-offs y and w. The larger either or both of these differences, the greater the potential loss which our worker runs by co-operating with the proposed wage regulation, and the less likely *ceteris paribus* he will be to do so. Conversely, the closer both of these differences approach to zero, the more he will be indifferent, as far as pay-offs in the ordinary game are concerned, about which strategy he pursues. If we call the situation in which the differences *all but reach zero*[12] the 'indifference point', we can say that the worker's co-operation with a wage-regulation agreement becomes more likely as the comparisons of potential pay-offs from co-operating and not co-operating in the ordinary game approach the indifference point.

(ii) It is evident, however, that if we retain the structural relationship between pay-offs which is inherent to the PD game ($y > w > x > z$), the worker cannot fail to run some risk of loss in the ordinary game. He will, none the less, be more willing to run this risk if he thinks the advantages of sustained co-operation are sufficient to warrant it. As this suggests, he must make some guesses about the relative advantages of sustained co-operation among a number of workers over some period of time and the accumulated wages he thinks he could get from sustained wage militancy in that same period. Now, it is quite possible that, over time, wage regulation could produce a better accumulated wage than wage militancy (Przeworski & Wallerstein, 1982a). But how much, how soon, and with what certainty, are factors which can vary from situation to situation (see below). What this implies is that our worker, in considering the future advantages of co-operation in the present ordinary game, will utilize a *discount rate* which will be a function both of how much and how soon he thinks co-operation, if it were sustained at some level, would pay and how certain he feels about this calculation. The lower this rate of discount, the more likely he is to be willing to run the risks of loss in the ordinary game.

(iii) If we now bring these considerations together, what we have established is that the likelihood that any worker will co-operate with wage regulation will be a function of his risk of loss in the present contract period and the rate at which he discounts his future advantages from extensive co-operation if it were sustained. The further his comparison of pay-offs in the ordinary game from the indifference point and the higher his rate of discount, the less likely he is to co-operate conditionally with wage regulation in that ordinary game.[13]

It is undoubtedly evident that this relatively abstract analysis conceals the role played by a number of more realistic conditions in determining the behaviour of workers when confronted with the choice of whether or not to co-operate in wage regulation. The remainder of this paper is devoted to exploring those conditions.

Co-operation without Norms?

We have, to this point, stressed the possibility of co-operation among rational and materially self-interested workers. The assumption of egoism however, excludes only altruism, not all forms of solidarity. In fact, under most circumstances, stable co-operation in iterated games (like wage regulation) requires that workers have some minimal sense that their fellow workers are more inclined to co-operate than not when either strategy might be in their self-interest.

To see why this is the case, recall that iteration makes it possible for players to extend the time-horizon over which they calculate their interests beyond the immediate game. They can, as a result, conceive of risking losses in the present in hopes of being better off in the future. But such risks remain. The structure of pay-offs must be such that defection in the ordinary game, treated in isolation, remains preferable to co-operation. If it were not, the situation would be fundamentally altered and the problem of co-operation no longer pertinent. Taylor 'solves' the problem of short-run risk by implicitly assuming that enough players decide to play a strategy which, despite the risk, includes co-operation in the first game. He never makes clear, however, why they should do so.

Furthermore, as we have also indicated, stable co-operative outcomes over an extended series of games depend on a certain number of players co-operating in each game. Under the assumption of pure rational egoism, that number will be just large enough to ensure that conditionally co-operating players find it worth their while to co-operate—i.e. that the expected (discounted) pay-offs of extended co-operation are sufficient to make co-operation in the ordinary game attractive. No player who is rational will want to be a 'superfluous co-operator', that is, one whose co-operation is not necessary to avoid collapse of all co-operation and who could, therefore, free-ride (by defecting) while still gaining the benefits of the others' co-operation. Laver has pointed out that if we assume workers to be rational, egoistic and *without any social commitments,* this feature of the game makes a co-operative outcome extremely unrealistic (1981: 53–6).

How can these two problems be resolved in a way consistent with the basic rationality and self-interest assumptions and with some degree of realism? The answer would seem to be to acknowledge that for co-operation to become likely some normative factor creating the inclination to co-operate rather than defect under conditions of uncertainty must be present. Such a norm would override the risk of co-operation in the first game and would promote co-operation rather than defection when the player was uncertain whether his individual failure to co-operate might provoke the collapse of all co-operation. While the possible sources of such a norm are many, in the case of workers one of the most likely would seem to be a minimal degree of *extensive group commitment*: an identification with workers beyond one's bargaining unit which promoted a willingness to take small, short-term risks by co-operating when this might be consistent with longer-term self-interest and which was tied to a belief that other workers had a similar identification.[14]

It might be asked whether the introduction of a norm of this sort undercuts the entire logic of the analysis based on rational, egoistic players of the iterated game. I would argue that it does not. Players are still assumed to be maximizing only their own material interests. The norm does not lead them to sacrifice their own interests to promote those of others, but only enables them to extend the time-horizon over which they maximize by making them a bit more inclined to run the risk of paying costs in the present as part of conditional strategies intended to improve their own longer-term outcomes. Furthermore, while some normative commitment may be necessary for co-operation to occur, such co-operation cannot occur unless the structure of pay-offs and surrounding conditions (see below) are consistent with self-interest.

To summarize the argument to this point: *workers' (like unions') co-operation with wage regulation is not to be ruled out, even when the workers are assumed to be wholly self-interested.* They can rationally consent to wage regulation under certain conditions, given that they have some minimal normatively-based extensive group identity. It must be stressed, however, that to say that co-operation *can* occur is not to say that it *will.* Workers' strategic decisions are conditional and contingent, based on calculations made at each bargaining round. We have identified the nature of these calculations in the abstract. It is now time to examine how these decisions of workers are affected by various contextual conditions which define the environment within which the decisions are taken.

Contextual Factors and Wage Regulation

The literature on wage regulation, economic-policy concertation and neo-corporatism has generally suggested that three types of factor influence the probability of *union* consent to wage regulation (i) institutional features of the union movement and the collective bargaining system; (ii) factors related to the nature of the government, especially its partisan composition; and (iii) the economic environment in which the decisions on wage regulation have to be made.[15] We would argue that these same factors influence the likelihood that *workers* will consent to wage regulation, but not always in the way that has been suggested in previous discussions of these issues. In particular, we stress how these factors affect the rational, self-interested calculations of workers and the normative commitment which influences the time-horizon over which they make these calculations, rather than the role that these factors play in counteracting the potential effects of the pursuit of rational self-interest.

The Institutional Context

It has generally been argued that, once a collective bargaining system is institutionalized, the likelihood of relatively stable wage regulation increases, the greater the extent of centralization in union decision-making and collective bargaining (themselves related) and the greater the density of union membership. The former two conditions affect the ability of the unions to 'insulate' bargaining from particularistic demands and to 'coerce' their members to accept the terms of a bargain once reached; the latter prevents disruptive competition between the unionized and non-unionized sectors. Together, these conditions make it easier for unions to override the self-interest of their members which, it is maintained, would otherwise undermine wage regulation.

We have however already shown that these conditions are not *necessary* for wage regulation. Workers can self-interestedly consent to regulated wages. Yet, our model is consistent with an argument that these institutional conditions are *conducive* to gaining worker consent. Several specific effects can be noted. First, restrictions on free-riding centrally imposed by the unions (or the state) will have an impact both on the relative pay-offs in the ordinary game, and on the discount rate. On the one hand, by increasing the number of co-operators, they will increase the likely value of co-operation (w) to any worker. If, at the same time, the value of free-riding (y) is reduced by the 'costs' of doing so against effective union opposition, the difference $(y - w)$ will be moved toward the indifference point. On the other hand, such restraints will tend to lower the discount rate which workers apply. The reason for this is that such restrictions increase the probable number of repeated co-operators in the iterated wage-regulation game. Both of these effects can then be expected to improve the chances of any worker's conditional co-operation[16] —although they do not, of course, fully meet the requirements of 'consensual' wage regulation, even if the sanctions for free-riding can formally be treated as 'costs'.

Centralization is also important from a normative standpoint. We have argued that an identity with workers beyond their own bargaining unit—and a belief that this identification is shared by others—enables workers to perceive and act upon their interests with a longer time-perspective. They become potentially willing to run short-term risks *for their own possible longer-term gain* under conditions of uncertainty.[17] Now, it is evident that this extensive identity and its associated norms can have many sources, among which the most important is likely to be the entire historical experience of the workers' movement itself. It is also the case, however, that a centralized union movement is an institutional embodiment of the norm of collective membership and responsibility. It conveys the idea that, whatever their particular industrial location and job, all workers are part of one unified entity sharing a similar identity and similar interests. When centralization is coupled with institutional practices, such as organizational restraints on free-riding or procedures which aggregate worker opinions on union issues at levels above that of the bargaining units and even the sectoral union,[18] this norm is reinforced.

The submission of central wage-regulation agreements to union memberships for their ratification is particularly interesting in this regard. It might be thought that asking the members whether they are willing to accept regulated wages is unlikely to be successful (unless we assume that workers will vote in order to deceive others about their actual feelings and intentions). As Schwerin has shown in the case of Norway, however, workers often and repeatedly do vote in favour of wage-regulation agreements (1980a: 91–2; 1981: 34–7). Furthermore, our general argument would suggest that there is no reason why ratification votes on such contracts should necessarily be negative.

At the same time, two positive effects of formal ratification procedures for the rational consent of workers to wage regulation can be suggested. First, formal, national votes are a procedural embodiment of an extensive, collective identity. To the extent that their outcomes are put into practice, such an identity will be reinforced. Second, they allow workers throughout the union movement to gain some sense of how many of their fellow workers are inclined to co-operate. If this number is sufficiently large, it may reduce the uncertainties of conditional co-operators during the period of the agreement and thus make them less likely to abandon co-operation out of fear that others are doing so.

The preceding points suggest some of the ways that institutional features of national trade-union movements can affect the likelihood of consent to regulated wages by self-interested workers. Yet, these features tend to change rather slowly. Other factors, therefore, are likely to explain more about when workers decide to co-operate with *specific* wage-regulation proposals, and why their willingness to co-operate may shift from one agreement (ordinary game) to the next.

The Political Context

A widely shared hypothesis regarding wage regulation is that it is more—almost only—likely when government is controlled by political parties of the Left. There are, however, numerous arguments about why this relationship holds. From the Marxist or neo-Marxist standpoint, the case is usually made that unions co-operate with the Left in political power because under these conditions union leaders can expect to gain special advantages for themselves or for the unions as institutions (a subtle version of the 'sell-out' thesis); or because the union leadership is willing to sacrifice the economic interests of its constituency to advance the political interests of the party (Panitch, 1977a). Neither of these arguments admits the possibility that such co-operative behaviour could actually be in the interests of the working class or of workers. We should, therefore, be sceptical of them as primary explanations.

Among those who recognize that the working class, and even individual workers, might have an interest in wage regulation, the association between the partisan composition of government and wage-regulation agreements is often explained in terms of some kind of political exchange—between the state and the workers—which 'compensates' (or promises to compensate) the latter for the sacrifices they make in market exchange and thereby relieves potential resistance within the unions to a wage-regulation policy. As examples, an expanded social wage, or alterations in effective tax rates on workers' incomes, might replace the losses incurred in the market (Cameron, 1982; Schwerin, 1980a). There is, in other words, a relatively direct and material quid pro quo.[19]

In terms of the analysis we have developed, this argument seems to misspecify the role which social-wage policies may play. Government and its partisan composition can be important determinants of the strategies of workers less because of their direct impact on the size of pay-offs for different short-run behaviours than because of their potential influence on the normative underpinnings of rational consent and on the discount rate which workers apply to the possible future benefits of wage regulation.

To begin with, government's role as 'compensator' (Lange, 1981) may have an impact on the pay-offs players can expect from pursuing different strategies in any ordinary game; but, if it does, it is likely to be very small. By offering non-market but monetary compensations, government policy is said to make consent to and co-operation with wage regulation more attractive relative to defection. This seems, however, not to be the case. It is generally very difficult for government to target the compensations it offers for wage regulation only on those who co-operate; rather, compensatory policies usually are more like public goods (i.e. they do not permit individual exclusion). A worker who should rationally prefer not to consent to wage regulation without the offer of such side payments, therefore, should continue not to prefer co-operation once they are offered, since he can get them anyway.[20]

If this is the case, why are side payments so commonly argued to be causally related to wage regulation? Here I would suggest three possible responses about whose relative merits I am uncertain. First, perhaps the much observed association is largely spurious. It may be caused by a set of factors which promotes *both* wage regulation and higher social-wage expenditures (Castles, 1978; Korpi & Shalev, 1979; Korpi, 1980). Second, it is possible that the primary role of the side payments is symbolic and normative. They embody the idea that the sacrifices which the workers are making for the public good are linked to a deepening of governmental commitment to the welfare of all citizens—including and especially the working class—through public programme. These effects would tend to reinforce, on the part of workers, an extensive view of the community to which they belong. Finally, the side payments may express the government's longer-term commitment to the working class. Such a commitment may be of little direct importance to the pay-offs of the ordinary game. As we shall see in a moment, however, it can play an important role in how workers discount possible future pay-offs from sustained co-operation in wage regulation. And since this calculation is itself drawn into the worker's determination of how he should play the ordinary game, it can assume immediate, as well as long-range, significance.

In terms of the government's short-term role, what difference does it make which parties are in power? Who governs should be relatively unimportant to workers as far as the short-term compensator role is concerned. What counts—to the extent that it counts at all—is what is offered and its effects on the pay-offs of different strategies, not who is doing the offering. Government's partisan composition will be important, however, because Left governments would seem generally more willing and able to play the symbolic game. In addition, any government, whatever its composition, which delivers on the side payments it has promised for the short-term is likely to increase the credibility of its promises for the future. Success in building credibility in this way, however, may have more to do with the efficacy of the state machinery than with which party is governing.[21]

In addition to a possible but small role as compensator, government can also play a role as 'guarantor' (Lange, 1981), affecting workers' uncertainties about the future, and thus their discount rates. Przeworski and Wallerstein (1982a) underline the fact that, under capitalism, wage regulation can be to the medium-term advantage of workers because of its effects on the investment behaviour of capitalists and, in turn, on growth.[22] Expectations about the extent and pattern of investment by employers at different levels of wages are therefore critical factors in determining the behaviour of workers in the present ordinary game. The further the current pay-offs are from the indifference point, the more security workers need about future economic and wage prospects if they are to pursue even conditionally co-operative strategies.

Now it is evident that there can be no 'guarantees' about whether and at what level employers will invest. None the less, governments and their policies can influence the rate and pattern of investment in the national economy, thereby affecting workers' expectations about future investment. The most obvious way in which government can do this is by giving assurances that it will promote a propitious 'climate' for domestic investment (as contrasted to capital export, speculation, conspicuous consumption, etc.). Such assurances would tend to reduce workers' uncertainties regarding the likelihood of future benefits from current self-restraint.

How effective government is in playing the guarantor role, however, would seem strongly affected by its partisan composition and expectations about that composition in the future. A government of the Left generally gives greater assurance that the policies of the state will favour the interests of labour and of workers, and seek to constrain undesired behaviour on the part of capital. Both electoral considerations and the organizational ties between unions and the Left parties mean that Left governments are likely to be more attentive to workers' concerns and more subject to their pressure and threats.[23] The stronger these are, the more a Left government will tend to be able to reduce workers' uncertainties.

Several observations about this guarantor role are, however, in order. First, it is obviously extremely important that workers have the expectation that the government of the Left will remain in place for an extended period of time. Since the potential benefits for workers of wage regulation require the accumulation and investment of 'surplus' profits over a number of games, workers need to believe that government will stably promote the desired behaviour on the part of capital. This need for an expectation of *stable* Left government may go a long way toward explaining why there seems to be such a marked difference in the character of wage regulation in the strongest 'neo-corporatist' systems and in other European countries (Castles, 1978).[24]

Second, the extent to which the prospect of stable Left government can reduce uncertainty will also be a function of past experience. In reaching conclusions about their discount rates, workers can be expected to take into account the past performance of government with regard to the issues of special concern. This will tend to favour the prospects for wage regulation in political systems which have had stable Left governments and which have successfully pursued wage regulation policies which workers perceive to have worked in their favour. Again the strong neocorporatist systems come to mind.[25]

Third, all of the above considerations once again point to the importance of perceptions of the efficacy of the state. As we have suggested previously, whatever the political composition of the government, if the state is not perceived to be able to implement its policy intentions, workers' insecurities about future prospects are likely to be increased.

This brings us to the fourth, and perhaps most important observation. Governments can influence the economic behaviour of private actors as well as broader economic outcomes, but they cannot control them. This is not only true because governments have different capacities for economic intervention and because capital need not always respond to government policy as expected or intended, but also because national economies are themselves not autonomous but rather interdependent. Workers (and their unions), therefore, can be expected to evaluate the political 'guarantees' about future benefits from wage regulation in the context of their perceptions of the more general prospects for future economic performance as determined by domestic and international economic conditions. Government can help reduce workers' uncertainties about the future, and a Left government may be particularly effective in doing so, but a great deal will still depend on expectations about future economic prospects regardless of what government does.

Wage Regulation and Economic Conjunctures

The institutional and political factors discussed above should be seen as structural parameters influencing the general likelihood of wage regulation in different countries. These factors cannot, therefore, be easily used as the proximate explanation of breakdowns (or outbreaks) of wage regulation in specific cases. Other, more rapidly changing, factors must be at work. Chief among these is the economic conjuncture within which each decision whether or not to co-operate with wage regulation takes place.

There is considerable controversy about what economic conjunctures promote wage regulation. Much of the writing has stressed the association between wage regulation and full employment (Panitch, 1977a) and has suggested that workers' consent to wage regulation would become increasingly difficult under conditions of sustained economic stagnation where full employment was no longer maintained (Panitch, 1981). Schwerin, by contrast, examined data on the post-war wage regulation experience in Norway, and tentatively concluded that *breakdowns* were more probable under conditions of 'rapid economic growth' (1980a: 96). Lange (1981) also found that there was little empirical justification for the oft-assumed association between full-employment and the original establishment of wage regulation in the immediate post-war years. Instead, wage regulation seemed more often undertaken to promote full employment under conditions of a slack labour market and fear that it would continue. Finally, Schmitter (1982: 275) has argued that labour's participation in 'modern corporatism' may not be a 'fair-weather product' alone; workers and their organizations may remain committed to wage regulation in foul economic weather as well. It may, instead, be employers who promote breakdowns under conditions of national economic distress (cf. Streeck, this volume).

Our model does not encourage the formulation of any simple hypothesis about the implications of different economic conjunctures for wage regulation. The reason is that it includes workers' expectations regarding both the relative size of the pay-offs of the present (ordinary) game in which they are engaged, and their degree of uncertainty about future pay-offs. In the light of these complexities, we will examine, first, the implications for behaviour under our model of different expectations about the short-term economic conjuncture, and then the implications of different expectations about the longer-term economic conjuncture[26] (i.e. the cumulative product of the economic conjunctures over the course of a series of ordinary games). If we postulate two states of economic expectation, optimism and pessimism, then four different cases emerge for consideration, as follows.

(i) Short-term (ordinary game): optimistic expectations

Under conditions of optimism about the economic conjuncture which will prevail over the course of the agreement under consideration (the most important of these is that the labour market is tight and will remain so in the near future) the relationship of pay-offs to workers for not regulating, relative to those for regulating their wages, are not conducive to restraint of wage militancy: neither of the critical paired relationships—free-riding to co-operation (y to w), and co-operating to being suckered (x to z) will tend to approach the indifference point. On the one hand, in a tight labour market, workers are likely to believe that there is a good probability that wage militancy will produce pay-offs significantly better than those which will result from any macroeconomically meaningful wage restraint. This is, of course, not the case for all workers: some can expect to do much better with wage militancy (perhaps through wage drift) than others. Yet, most workers may well legitimately think (given that information cannot be perfect) that there is a chance that they would do significantly better.

On the other hand, the risks of regulating and finding oneself the loser not only with respect to one's potential wage but also with respect to other workers (i.e. the risks that accepting a regulated wage will lead to a decay of one's relative wage position) are also significant. The reasons for this are evident from the immediately preceding point. A tight labour market is the best condition for widespread wage drift (induced by workers or employers) and other forms of non-contracted wage gains.[27] As a result, short-term economic optimism, *ceteris paribus*, is not conducive to wage regulation. This does not mean, of course, that wage regulation will not happen, but only that conditions in the ordinary game are less propitious for it and therefore that there needs to be greater certainty about the advantages of longer-term co-operation.

(ii) Short-term (ordinary game): pessimistic expectations

Under less favourable short-term economic conditions, the likelihood of worker co-operation with wage regulation in the ordinary game is better than when the economy is strong. First, the prospects that wage militancy will produce positive results are less. Among other things, employers can be expected to be more resistant and thus the costs of pursuing wage militancy may be higher. As a result, the difference between the regulated wage and any wage which might be extracted by pressing hard on the wage front will be lower than when the market is tight. Similarly, the worker need have less fear that his acceptance of a regulated wage will open the prospect of a significant deterioration of his relative wage position. Thus, both of the critical comparisons are more likely to approach the indifference point than when short-term economic conditions are more optimistic; and worker co-operation with wage regulation in the ordinary game becomes more likely (controlling for longer-term expectations).

Before closing this discussion of the implications of short-term economic conjunctures, some further discussion of the relationship between any ordinary game and the one(s) preceding it is necessary. As we have seen, the likelihood of sustained co-operative outcomes is partially dependent on the number of players willing to play conditional co-operative strategies in each ordinary game. One of the main parameters of such conditional strategies is the number of other players who played some form of co-operative strategy (conditional or not) in the preceding game(s). If that number was below any conditionally co-operative worker's expectations, he can be expected to defect in the subsequent game and a possible cycle of non-cooperation may be set up.[28]

Now, if we ask under what economic conjuncture the likelihood of such a shortfall of co-operators is greatest, it would seem to be one in which there was a rapid (or at least unexpected) improvement of economic conditions (especially in the labour market) in the preceding period. When this occurs, there is a considerable chance of both worker-induced and employer-induced wage drift, and thus of a larger than expected number of workers who appear not to have co-operated. This, in turn, could lead to extensive non-cooperation with any wage regulation proposed in the next game (depending, of course, on the precise nature of the strategies workers were pursuing). Again, fair-weather economic conditions—in this case fairer than expected—would be associated with breakdowns.

To summarize: short-term economic slack appears more conducive to producing worker consent to wage regulation than economic boom; but the extent to which this is the case will be partially dependent on the way workers have behaved in the preceding game(s) and thus on preceding economic conditions. The *ceteris paribus* condition, however, cannot be forgotten. The prospects for extensive co-operation with wage regulation will also depend on economic expectations about the longer-term future.

(iii) Longer-term: optimistic expectations

By optimism, here, we mean that workers think that it is likely that there will be sustained growth of the national economy in the context of sustained growth in the international economy as well.[29] This expectation, in turn, means that they foresee buoyant demand (both in national and international markets) for what is produced nationally, that the prospects for profits are strong, and that so too are the conditions for investment. Put more simply, workers expect a sustained boom.

When this is the case, the impact of longer-term expectations on the discount rate would not seem favourable for co-operation in wage regulation in the ordinary game. The advantages to be reaped from co-operation with wage regulation relative to what would result from wage militancy would appear rather distant, for much of the investment behaviour which wage regulation would be intended to promote could be expected to result even without it. Workers could well expect, in fact, that the 'excess' profits produced by regulative behaviour would not go into investment but would instead end up as dividends or speculative spending, or would be invested outside the national economy. Furthermore, they could also think that a sustained boom would create the conditions for considerable employer-induced wage drift (as a result of the competition for scarce labour) which would, in turn, reduce the likely benefits of the regulation policy in any case. Expectations of a sustained boom, therefore, would seem unpropitious for co-operation with wage regulation.

(iv) Longer-term: pessimistic expectations

When we examine pessimistic projections of future national economic trends, we need to separate out two cases. On the one hand, there can be what we might call *conditional* (or perhaps cyclical) pessimism. This obtains when domestic economic prospects for the immediate future are seen as uncertain—perhaps due to slowed domestic and international demand or a decline in the competitiveness of domestically produced products—but there is no expectation that weak demand conditions will be generally sustained. This would typically be the case in an international recessionary phase or when national inflationary pressures have exceeded those of major trading competitors. On the other hand, it is also possible to conceive of what we might call *structural* pessimism, that is, an expectation that domestic and international economic conditions are likely to remain poor (in terms of the national economy) for a lengthy period of time, unless (and perhaps even if) there is a major restructuring of the domestic economy. This would seem most closely to resemble the most recent phase of economic life in the advanced industrial democracies. These forms of pessimistic expectations are obviously different and deserve separate treatment.

Conditional pessimism can be anticipated to favour co-operation with wage regulation in the ordinary game. The lowered wage costs due to co-operation could make a significant difference in the competitiveness of national products in a constricted market, and thus in profits and the prospects for investment. Furthermore, because the cycle is expected to turn around in the not-too-distant future, there will be good reason to expect capitalists to invest the 'surplus' created by restraint. Finally, the pay-offs of restraint can be expected to show up relatively soon, or at least can be evaluated within a relatively short period (thus further lowering the discount rate).

It is considerably harder to evaluate the impact of structural pessimism on the prospects for co-operation with wage regulation in the present. On the one hand, it might be thought that workers would be strongly inclined to regulate wages, for they would think that failing to do so would condemn the national economy to sustained recession or even depression, and their own wages to real decay. On the other hand, the bleak economic prospects might lead workers to think that there is little to be gained by restraint—things will not get better anyway without major disruptions to their economic lives—and that it is therefore best to try to get as much as possible while it can still be had.[30]

No firm answer about which of these approaches is the more likely can be given. The reason is that workers here need to evaluate between two 'bads': doing terribly if there is sustained non-cooperation or perhaps doing somewhat better (but possibly still badly) if there is sustained co-operation. In either case, there are great uncertainties about their economic future and thus future pay-offs will be discounted heavily. From the standpoint of the iterated wage-regulation game as we have presented it, therefore, structural pessimism would not seem conducive to co-operation with wage regulation in the ordinary game.

Yet, here we need to recall the role that political factors can play in reducing uncertainties about the future. We noted above that these factors can significantly affect how workers perceive the probability that the fruits of their restraint will redound to their future economic advantage. In a condition of structural pessimism, this role would seem to be particularly important. Workers might be especially concerned, for instance, with whether government policy is likely to promote the ability and willingness of capital to exploit whatever small potential for competitive advantage their restraint would provide. Or they might want to increase their direct role in the investment process (perhaps through their unions), feeling more secure when the workers' organizations have a direct role in how investments are made. And they might also want assurances, implicit or explicit, that government will protect their incomes and future wage prospects during a process of industrial restructuring. What this suggests, then, is that when there are structurally bleak economic prospects, the importance of non-economic factors in determining the likelihood of worker co-operation with wage regulation rises sharply.

This observation echoes a point made by Goldthorpe (this volume), among others. It is in conditions of structural crisis—he argues—that choices between the market and political control of the economy are most starkly posed. Workers' co-operation with the kinds of wage-regulation policies which are called for by a crisis is more than usually dependent on reducing uncertainties about the future—which are large—by political means. The willingness of workers to accept regulated wages, therefore, is likely to be accompanied by, and perhaps to be contingent on, attempts to increase their control over the future either indirectly through government policy (in which case a stable government of the Left would be particularly important) or directly by their unions taking a hand in the investment process.

Employers, by contrast, are not only unlikely to be favourable to this kind of extension of control but might well want to abandon centralized wage regulation entirely, thinking that they could do just as well or better by allowing wages to be determined by the (extremely weak) market and dismal prospects, and that they could, at the same time, regain some of their bargaining autonomy and prerogatives (Schmitter, 1982: 275-7). In pursuing such a policy, they would, of course, also have to rely on government, but clearly on one of a different type than that desired by labour. The conditions for a major struggle over the political and economic 'rules of the game' would therefore be in place.

The issue cannot be left here, however. So far our discussion has focused on workers' income expectations from following different strategies. But it is possible in a structural crisis that workers will come to value their current job (even at a reduced real wage) over wage considerations in the short- or longer-term (cf. Streeck, this volume). In this case, it may be possible to gain worker consent to wage regulation more easily than might be expected.[31] What would be required is that the worker have a clear sense that acceptance of the regulated wage would allow him to hold on to his job.

What is interesting about such a possibility, however, is that it implies an extremely decentralized form of wage regulation. Specific jobs can only be 'guaranteed' factory by factory or, at best, firm by firm. As a result, a shift in preferences of this kind would probably be accompanied by a significant institutional change in at least the more centralized collective bargaining systems—something which the unions could be expected most strongly to resist, again leading to considerable potential for political struggle over the basic shape of the political economy. It also seems that efforts to implement this type of 'wage regulation' are most likely in those systems in which wage bargaining is institutionally quite decentralized and which, ironically, are also the systems least likely to be able to gain worker cooperation for wage regulation under other circumstances.

Before closing this consideration of the impact of economic conjunctures, we need to examine one further question: where do workers' expectations about the economic future come from? Two major sources can be suggested. One is institutions in the society, most importantly, the unions and the government. Union officials are likely to be particularly prominent. The second major source would seem to be the recent experiences of workers themselves. The expectation of sustained boom, cyclical crisis or structural crisis is likely to be not only a product of what workers are told the situation is, but also of a comparison that they make between the present situation and their own experiences. Put simply, it would seem—following arguments of Phelps Brown (1975), for instance— that the longer the time since the last structural crisis, the more workers are likely to expect that strong economic conditions (when they exist at the time of the ordinary game) will continue, and that downturns will be only temporary (cf. Salvati, 1981).

There are two interesting implications. First, the longer growth continues, the less likely it becomes that expectations about the future will favour co-operation with wage regulation. Second, there will be a considerable lag before workers come to recognize the full implications of a structural crisis. The shift to a primarily employment-oriented perspective—if it comes at all—is likely to be slow to arrive.

Let us now summarize our conclusions about the impact of longer-term economic expectations on the probability that workers will co-operate with wage regulation in the ordinary game. What we have found is that optimism about the economic future (based on future projections and past experience) is least likely to promote wage regulation. Conditional pessimism, by contrast, would seem most propitious for co-operation in wage regulation. Finally, structural pessimism might also promote co-operation, but major uncertainties about the future, whatever wage policy is adopted in the present, mean that non-economic factors are likely to play a particularly important role. In addition, it is under conditions of structural pessimism that the starkest choices arise about the basic principles by which economic policy will be conducted.

Conclusions

It has generally been argued that agreements to regulate wages, whatever their macroeconomic merits, will founder on the resistance of workers to the self-restraint that is required. Wage regulation cannot be expected to gain workers' consent because it is fundamentally opposed to their interests. As a result, even if trade unions want, and find it in their interest, to support such policies, their freedom to do so will be sharply constrained by the continual danger of internal revolt by their discontented members (cf. Regini, this volume). The possible success of sustained wage regulation, therefore, depends on finding ways either to defuse constituency revolt by side payments (which are likely to undermine the broader goals of the policy), or to repress it, or to impede members' ability to identify their 'real' interests.

Those stressing the internally contradictory and therefore tendentially unstable, repressive or self-defeating character of wage regulation have generally utilized two alternative understandings of the interests which workers are thought to pursue. The Marxist perspective has stressed workers' class interests and has generally operated with a zero-sum understanding of the relationship between labour and capital. A seemingly more telling critique has grown out of the public choice literature with its assumption of rational, individualistic, material-interest maximizers. From this perspective, the outcome of wage regulation may be a public good, and even in the long-term interests of the workers themselves, but their consent to regulated wages is unlikely because of the rationality of free-riding.

This understanding of the weaknesses of wage-regulation policy rests on a very narrow conception of the nature of workers' interests. It allows for no altruism, no collective consciousness, no extensive group identity and solidarity. It is easy, therefore, to fault the conclusion because of the narrowness and lack of reality of its premises.

Yet, it should not be too quickly dismissed. It has a certain theoretical parsimony and elegance. It seemingly accords with some of the experiences with wage-regulation policies in post-war Europe. Its understanding of workers' interests bears some correspondence both with recurrent conceptions of 'market man' and with arguments which stress the breakdown of normative restraints in the contemporary advanced capitalist democracies (Hirsch, 1976; Goldthorpe, 1978). More practically, as long as one acknowledges that rational self-interest plays some role in workers' decisions about whether to consent to centrally regulated wages, it is useful to explore whether material self-interest alone can promote consent and under what conditions.

We have followed this procedure in the preceding pages and have found that the argument that workers cannot rationally consent to wage regulation is sharply overdrawn. It is possible for workers—and not just unions acting on their collective behalf—rationally to consent to centralized regulation of their wages. This can be so even when workers, acting through relatively small bargaining units, are assumed to have a narrow, self-interested, materialistic understanding of their interests and to be unwilling to behave altruistically. The mere existence of wage-regulation agreements cannot be assumed to indicate that workers' self-interests are being overridden. Consent, even under these restrictive conditions, is possible and rational when collective bargaining is institutionalized and the bargaining game between workers and employers is iterated.

At the same time, rational consent to wage regulation by workers is both conditional and contingent. It is not given once and for all but must be repeatedly renewed. Each time it is up for renewal, workers can be expected to re-evaluate whether co-operation is (still) to their advantage. In the abstract this calculation involves a balancing of the pay-offs of different courses of action in the present against the potential benefits of sustained co-operation by a large number of workers over time, discounted for uncertainties about the future. More concretely, the factors which enter into the calculation will be a function of the workers' recent experience of the behaviour of other workers, and of the institutional and political context and particular economic conjuncture within which the decision is made. Furthermore, consent only becomes probable—perhaps even possible—when workers have some inclination to risk some losses in the present by co-operating under conditions of uncertainty about how other workers will behave. This inclination to co-operation, in turn, presumes a degree of pre-existing normative identification with, and commitment to, the maintenance of a more extensive group (e.g. the union, the working class, even the society) than the workers' own bargaining unit. It does not, however, require that the worker be altruistic; consent is possible even when his decision is assumed to be based on his own material self-interest alone.

Our argument, thus very briefly summarized, has significant analytical implications. It allows us to move beyond three types of reasoning which have characterized much of the discussion of wage regulation, concertation and neo-corporatism. First, it breaks with the tendency to treat wage-regulation agreements as imposed on unions and workers by the state, in the interests of the state and of capital. Instead, we have shown—similarly to Regini (this volume) and Przeworski and Wallerstein (1982a)—that such agreements might really be *agreements*, into which each of the actors enters for his own reasons and in his own interests. Second, we push this argument further by asking whether it might hold for individuals or small groups of workers as well as for workers treated collectively and acted for by their unions. We therefore break with the assumption that wage regulation may be in the interests of workers collectively, but cannot be in the interest of individual workers. Whether collective and individual interests are in conflict, even when the latter are narrowly defined, becomes an empirical question. Third, the logic of our argument breaks with the tendency to see institutional and political conditions as 'prerequisites' for wage regulation. Instead, it pushes us in the direction of seeing a variety of conditions—normative, institutional, political and economic—as impinging on any decision, with none having causal precedence over the others in any particular decision, and each contributing positively or negatively to the probability that consent will be achieved.

These shifts in analytical perspective, in turn, have theoretical and normative implications. First, there is no necessary reason why the pursuit of collective or public goods through centralized wage-regulation agreements *must* encounter the resistance of workers and entail repression of their ability to pursue their interests or call for extensive, and potentially self-defeating, side payments to win their consent. Furthermore, this suggests that unions which engage in wage regulation repeatedly and over long periods need not be unresponsive to their members' demands and interests (Lange, 1984).

More broadly, it also follows that neither the critique from the left—that wage regulation is a form of capitalist stabilization undertaken by the state with the collusion of the unions and at the expense and over the resistance of workers—nor the critique from the 'rationalist Right'—that it is a necessarily coercive form of economic management which represents the attempt to impose collective (and collectivist) goals over individual preferences—can be accepted. Rather, the normative and empirical issues raised by wage-regulation arrangements are considerably more nuanced and complex, and judgements need to be grounded in close empirical analysis of the particular situations in which agreements are reached.

Of course, it must also be recognized that consensual wage regulation, to the extent that it rests solely on an individualistic and utilitarian basis, is highly fragile. Even where institutional and political factors are favourable, it is highly susceptible to unavoidable fluctuations in the economic conjuncture. The more workers operate with a narrow, materially self-interested outlook, the less probable it is that consensual wage-regulation can be sustained.

As this suggests, wage regulation, at least with the consent of workers, is not a macroeconomic policy which is equally as available, or likely to be successful, across political systems. Given the importance of institutional, political and normative factors in improving the likelihood of sustained regulation, and the extent to which these factors are historical products, some countries clearly provide much more propitious environments for such a policy than others. The pattern of post-war experiences with wage-regulation agreements only underlines this point. At the same time, however, our analysis brings out the fact that operating within historically given constraints and the pressures of particular political and economic conjunctures, governments can undertake policies which will improve the likelihood that workers, calculating their own advantage, will be willing to accept regulated wages. Recognizing that workers can rationally consent to wage regulation creates the possibility of policy initiatives which, rather than inclining toward restraints on the democratic expression of interest or self-defeating raids on the public purse, will establish a context in which the workers' self-interest can be consonant with the broader public interest. Whether governments and organizational leaders will be able and willing to take such initiatives is, of course, another matter.

Acknowledgements

I wish to thank Peter Hall, William Keech, Gary Marks, Adam Przeworski, George Ross, Michael Wallerstein and the members of the Working Group on Order and Conflict in Western Capitalism for their comments on an earlier draft of this paper. Special thanks to Geoffrey Garrett who provided a continual prod as I worked through the arguments and to John Goldthorpe for his intelligent, thoughtful and stimulating comments, for his light-handed but remarkably efficient leadership, and for bringing us together in the first place. Thanks finally to the German Marshall Fund of the United States for the Fellowship support during the period when this paper was written.

Notes

1. Castles (1978) applies this term to the Scandinavian social democracies. Its more general meaning is, however, that wage regulation becomes part of a mutually reinforcing relationship between policies which support economic growth and the expansion of social welfare programmes, labour restraint in the market, and stable, dominant electoral support for the governments involved.

By wage regulation we refer to peak-level agreements made between unions and employers' associations, with the formal or informal participation of the state, to regulate wage levels throughout the economy (or at least the unionized sectors of it) at levels agreed to be consonant with medium-term national economic performance goals. It thus includes a broader set of policies and outcomes than are usually encompassed by the term 'incomes policies'.

2. The broadest of these conditions is that a transition to socialism—an outcome in which workers take control of the means of production and investment decisions are socialized (1982a: 217)—is deemed by workers as likely to produce economically inferior outcomes for them, as compared to those which are likely to result from class compromise under capitalism (234). Within this constraint, the medium-term value of wage restraint to labour depends critically on the investment behaviour of capital over time. This means that the worth of compromise for labour depends ultimately on the behaviour of capital. Most of the contingencies which labour considers in deciding its strategy are concerned with the risks associated with this dependency.

3. Our analysis throughout this paper assumes group, rather than individual, bargaining. We also assume that the decentralized bargaining units are not large enough for size effects to become a consideration (Olson, 1982).

4. Conspicuous examples of sustained wage regulation, punctuated by eventual (sometimes permanent, sometimes temporary) breakdowns include the Netherlands (Windmuller, 1969), Norway (Schwerin, 1980a: 1981), Sweden (Martin, 1985), and Austria (Marin, 1983). For a general discussion of incomes policies and specific national experiences, see Flanagan et al. (1983). It might be objected that these 'exceptions' (generally taken eventually to prove the rule) simply point to the fact that you can fool some of the workers some of the time. It seems only wise, however, to fully explore the possibility that workers know their interests before attributing the findings to 'irrationalities'.

5. A similar way of presenting the strategic choices and consequences for any individual player in the n-person PD situation is utilized by Elster (1979: 18-20). The ordering of pay-offs ($y > w > x > z$) is consistent with the standard two-person PD game. While in formal terms the pay-off structure in the n-person game is more complex, the underlying logic is the same: for any player, defection dominates co-operation in the single play (Taylor, 1976: chs. 3 and 5).

6. Sen's 'assurance game' develops the implications of this different type of 'self-interest' (1977; see also Elster, 1979).

7. This, of course, requires that the actors expect the system of collective bargaining and its rules to be relatively stable and enduring. The more institutionalized the collective bargaining system, its participant collective actors and the broader political context whose

authority underpins the system, the greater this expectation is likely to be. On the importance of institutionalization and the expectation of endurance, see Hardin (1982: 146–50).

8. How long he will be willing to wait will depend significantly on the relationship between present and expected future pay-offs and on the discount rate applied to these future pay-offs, as well as on normative considerations (see below).

9. There are a vast number of possible such strategies. What they share is that the player co-operates and defects according to a self-selected set of rules (strategy) regarding how he will react to the aggregate co-operation and defection decisions of others. Taylor (1976) explores a few contingent strategies. See also Axelrod and Hamilton (1981) and Hofstadter (1983).

10. More formally, Taylor (1976: ch. 5) argues that, whatever his strategy of conditional co-operation, the player will have some criterion about the number who should co-operate which, if not met, will lead him to retaliate with non-cooperation for one or more games. He will do so because he feels he could do better by himself not co-operating if the number of co-operators remains as low as it has been. It is possible, however, that after retaliating, he will try out a co-operative strategy again. This remains a relatively restrictive condition for the likelihood of co-operation, but not nearly so restrictive as a requirement that all co-operate.

11. Taylor (1976; ch. 5) identifies factors endogenous to the games as generally relevant to players' calculations. It is these which we will informally discuss in order to explore how they can be affected by variables exogenous to the game.

12. If the differences actually reach zero or the relationships between the pay-offs shift so that $y > w > x > z$ does not hold, we are no longer in a PD situation and an entirely different analysis is called for.

13. This is consistent with Taylor's formula showing that the critical relationship is between the discount rate and the ordinary game pay-offs (1976, chs. 3 and 5).

14. An extensive group identity could well be expected to include such a minimal degree of trust because the worker believed that the existence of organization as such was good for his welfare, broadly understood; that other workers also understood this; and that in the absence of any mutual trust, the existence of the organization itself would be thrown into question. For a more general discussion of the relationship between identity and interest and an argument that identity must precede interest for the latter to have any meaning, see Pizzorno (1983).

15. These same factors are noted by Przeworski and Wallerstein (1982a: 220–1) as critical to how collective workers (and employers) judge the uncertainties and risks associated with class compromise, thus affecting their discount rates on future pay-offs. The workers and the union leaders acting on their collective behalf need not, of course, reach similar conclusions about the merits of wage regulation in any particular situation.

16. These effects are not necessarily very large. A great deal depends on how effective the coercion is expected to be. In most union movements, the actual effectiveness of coercion seems to be relatively small: if workers do not want to abide by the wage-regulation agreement and are in a relatively strong market position, they can find ways to get around it. What this suggests is that when workers consent to regulated wages, they do so for reasons other than the fear of coercion.

17. It should be obvious that there are a large number of other factors which, by increasing workers' willingness to make sacrifices for others, will also increase the probability of wage regulation achieving their consent (e.g. Schwerin, 1981, on Norway; Lewin, 1980, on Sweden; Lange et al., 1982, on France and Italy; Regini, this volume).

18. A clear example of this is the 'coupling' of ratification votes in the Norwegian union movement (Schwerin, 1980a; 1981). There are many other examples, however, of procedural rules which normatively support broader rather than narrower consciousness.

19. Schwerin (1980a) has pointed out that this exchange process can often undercut the potential macroeconomic benefits of wage regulation, especially when those policies are intended to reduce inflationary pressures.

20. Here one caveat is in order. When wage regulation involves getting less of a *gain* in the real wage than militancy might produce, the argument we have made would seem entirely applicable. It may be, however, that side payments which promise to compensate for *declines* in the real wage which the wage regulation would create have greater importance,

for maintenance of the real wage has enormous symbolic importance. This may explain why government commitments to cut tax rates for workers, in order to compensate for the declines in the real wage which the regulated wage would produce, have apparently become more common in recent years (Flanagan *et al.*, 1983).

21. One's different expectations about an Italian government of the Left and a German government of the Right which made the same promises on side payments is amply suggestive of this point.

22. It is interesting to note that Przeworski and Wallerstein (1982a) argue that this guarantor function can be effectively carried out without formal concertation between government and the unions and employers' associations. Scharpf's analysis (this volume) would, however, suggest that established concertation procedures with respect to wages (and prices) can have an important independent effect.

23. This point obviously raises the issue of the cross-national differences in the organizational and electoral characteristics of both the Left and non-Left (Castles, 1982), and the consequences of these differences for how, and how effectively, Left parties could play the guarantor role while remaining electorally strong enough to govern.

24. Strong and well-established institutional constraints on capital's behaviour might act as functional equivalents of a stable Left government. Things which come to mind in this regard are legal restraints on dividends, union-controlled investment funds, and even just a long-nurtured normative climate favourable to policies which provide 'guarantees' to labour. Again Castles (1978) concept of a 'social democratic image of society' comes to mind.

25. The obvious comparison here is that of Britain (Panitch, 1976) and neo-corporatist systems (Castles, 1978). It is probably not very important whether past successes really have been due to the wage-regulation policies only that they are perceived as associated.

26. Short-term expectations are those regarding the period of the agreement. As this suggests, the lengths of agreements in different countries and the procedures for their renegotiation between regular bargaining deadlines can have an impact (Sachs, 1984).

27. Of course, past experience of other workers' behaviour, as well as the underlying sense of shared collective responsibility, will play a role in determining how large workers judge the risks of co-operation to be. These will affect how great the temptation is not to co-operate, given any expected distance from the indifference point.

28. This is a simplified form of the situation. As we have already seen, workers who are consciously trying to see how many other workers are willing to co-operate may wait more than one game before again deciding whether or not to co-operate. The conditionally co-operative strategy which posits that the worker will abandon co-operation once and for all the first time that the number of other co-operating workers falls below his expectation in any ordinary game is the most demanding but also seems the least realistic. More probable, in my view, would be a strategy which allowed the worker to wait a couple of games to see how others played and which, even if defection became called for, would allow the worker to return to another attempt at conditional co-operation after one or more games in which he did not co-operate. Such a strategy would seem particularly likely when the long-term benefits of sustained co-operation seemed evident and/or when the normative climate was propitious. It would also be consistent with a pattern of wage regulation agreements in which sustained periods of co-operation were occasionally punctuated by breakdowns for the period of one contract—as, for example, in Norway (Schwerin, 1980a).

29. Particular attention needs to be paid to the interdependence of the post-war advanced industrial economies, and the resultant impact on national labour markets of conditions in the international economy. The literature on neo-corporatism has suggested a relationship between wage-regulation arrangements and the 'openness' or 'vulnerability' of the national economy (Cameron, 1978; Lange, 1981; Katzenstein, 1983).

30. If we follow the reasoning of Panitch (1981), co-operation under conditions of structural pessimism is to be entirely ruled out because even the promise of full-employment has been lost.

31. What is being suggested here is that a fundamental shift in preferences may occur under conditions of a structural crisis. Whereas under other economic conditions workers were heavily wage conscious, assuming general employment prospects to be favourable, they might, under conditions of severe crisis, come to value their *current* job much more highly, fearing that unemployment could be considerably more than a short-term condition.

6

The Conditions for Political Exchange: How Concertation Emerged and Collapsed in Italy and Great Britain

MARINO REGINI

The Limits of Neo-corporatist Analyses of Concertation

Among students of European political economies, some consensus has been reached on how to interpret the relations prevailing between governments and economic interest organizations during the 1950s and 1960s. Three ideal types of these relations have been developed, which largely correspond to the divergent paths followed by different countries in economic policy formation (cf. Salvati, 1982). To increase our understanding of these types, we may see relations between governments and economic interest organizations as depending mainly on the outcomes achieved in regard to two basic problems. The first concerns the role of labour movements in public policy formation. Governments can either develop a strategy of the inclusion of labour in the policy-making process (as in the Scandinavian countries, in Austria, Holland, and for some time in West Germany and Switzerland); or they can pursue a strategy of labour exclusion (as in France and in Italy in the 1950s); or they can let the market determine labour's strength and political influence, without major institutional mediation (as in the US and, for some periods, in Great Britain). The second problem concerns the extent to which centralization is achieved in collective bargaining and in the organizations of the main industrial relations actors. Centralization may be high, as, apparently, in countries pursuing labour exclusion *and* in those in which inclusion prevailed; or low, as in those countries where industrial relations strongly reflected market power and were only slightly modified by political processes.

Following from these outcomes, the three basic types of relation between government and economic interest organizations thus became identifiable. The first was *concertation*. The inclusion of labour unions in economic policy formation and implementation went together with a high degree of centralization of both political and wage bargaining and of industrial relations in general. Several commentators subsequently redefined this type of solution as 'neo-corporatism' (cf. Lehmbruch, 1977). The second type of relation was based on the *political isolation* of labour. The exclusion of labour from state policy-making prevented extensive and significant political bargaining, even though wage bargaining was relatively centralized (Lange *et al.*, 1982). The third type we can call *pluralistic fragmentation.* Wage bargaining was decentralized to the level of the industry or even of the firm; industrial relations were insulated from political processes; and the role of the organizations of both labour and capital in economic policy-making was entirely dependent on their market power, and was generally confined to the exertion of external pressure.

In studies relating to the 1950s and 1960s, then, concertation was explicitly or implicitly seen as just one of these three ideal types of relation between economic interest organizations and the state. However, this perspective changed somewhat when developments in the 1970s came under observation. For many authors, concertation could now be better seen as an end-point on a *continuum* along which most, if by no means all, Western European countries were moving. Many indications were seen that concertation was developing (or would develop) from being just one among several different patterns to become the dominant tendency in Western Europe, even though the pace and exact form of this change could be expected to vary from country to country.

Three factors strongly influenced this, often not fully perceived, shift of perspective. First, the countries which ranked high or medium-high on most indicators of concertation or neo-corporatism—such as Austria, Sweden, Norway, Switzerland, West Germany and Holland—seemed better equipped to face at least some of the many features of the economic crisis that emerged in the mid-1970s. And even if on certain economic indicators the evidence might seem unclear, these countries were further shown (Schmitter, 1981) to be those best able to solve the problems of 'governability'. Their relative success in contending with such problems, which confronted all Western political economies, would, it was implied, bring concertative solutions to the attention not only of scholars but also of political élites, and would foster attempts to reproduce these solutions cross-nationally. Secondly, two major Western European countries which did not previously fit the corporatist model sought rather conspicuously to adopt concertative solutions, thus reinforcing the belief of a more general trend in this direction—Britain during the years of the Social Contract (1974-9) and Italy in the period of *solidarietà nazionale* (1977-9).[1] Then thirdly, the defeat of the dominant coalitions which had been responsible for the political isolation, or for the outright repression, of labour in France, Spain, and Greece further added to the impression that concertation was going to become the generally prevailing pattern of relations between interest organizations and the state.

While circumstances may have changed again in the early 1980s, it is in the context of both the success and the expansion of concertation that one must understand the enormous growth of the literature on neo-corporatism in the late 1970s. As has been noted several times (lately by Schmitter, 1982), one stream of this literature practically equates neo-corporatism with concertation, by defining the former as a 'mode of policy-making' in which major interest organizations are involved in the formation and implementation of state policies (cf. Lehmbruch, 1977). Another influential view sees neo-corporatism, rather, as a 'form of interest intermediation' (Schmitter, 1977). But this interpretation also reflects the growing importance of concertation, since it directs attention to the transformation of interest organizations, under the inducement of the state, from agents of class mobilization and interest representation into partners of government in co-operative policy-making.

Both understandings of neo-corporatism imply, then, a view in which it is the 'state'—rather than organized interests themselves—which takes the lead and shapes relations in a neo-corporatist way. It is the state which grants institutional recognition and monopoly of representation to organizations, sometimes supports them, delegates public functions to them, and involves them in the policy-making process. Such action by the state is usually explained by pointing to the need to solve a series of problems with which Western political economies are confronted (Lehmbruch, 1977; Panitch, 1977a; Offe, 1981; Schmitter, 1981). First, the impossibility of avoiding class conflict through the outright repression of union activity creates the need to regulate such conflict by shifting it into the political arena. The state can give power and material benefits to the organizations of both capital and labour in exchange for their moderation in industrial relations, thus turning a zero-sum conflict into a positive-sum one. Secondly, the increasing ability and propensity of organized interests generally to address their demands to the state results, according to the theorists of 'overload', in a crisis of governability. Some governments can, however, successfully react by co-opting the most powerful groups into the process of policy-making, thereby inducing them to abstain from exerting their veto power *ex post*. Thirdly, some authors propose a scenario in which governments, faced with the crisis of a welfare state which has hitherto confined its action to external support for economic development, are now led to give the state a more 'directive' role in this development in order to ensure sufficient levels of capital accumulation (Winkler, 1974). Democratic governments, however, are normally too weak to perform such a role unaided; hence they try also to involve major interest organizations, which are endowed with sufficient power and legitimacy to make such participation credible, in the state management of the economy.

Such accounts of the development of neo-corporatism in Western Europe were, to repeat, evidently inspired by the apparent success and expansion of concertation in the 1970s, which created the impression of a general trend, prompted by the needs of the state under advanced capitalism. But these accounts had a distorting effect on the treatment of those issues which became the focus of empirical analysis. Since neo-corporatist arrangements were seen as functional in relation to state needs, the empirical question of their varying 'political value'—that is, of the varying extent to which they were consistent with the goals of labour in different countries—was largely overlooked (Regini, 1981). More generally, it could be said that the search for the determinants of neo-corporatist arrangements or of attempts to create them, was not directed towards the interests and strategies of all the actors involved. Rather, attention was concentrated, as already noted, on the 'functions' performed by such arrangements in solving the problems of capitalist economies and democratic polities, and thus on *state* interests and initiatives in such solutions.

This paper is itself intended to make a contribution to the analysis of the conditions that allow concertation to emerge and to become more or less stable. However, it aims to do so by looking—so to speak—at the other, less well-known, side of the moon; that is, by focusing on the strategies of interest organizations rather than on the role of the state. More precisely, I shall, in the next two sections, analyse the conditions which allow interest organizations to pursue a logic of action based on systematic, long-term political exchange, so as to make concertation possible and stable. Then, in the final section of the paper, I shall discuss to what extent these conditions were present in the two new attempts at concertation in the 1970s that were previously mentioned: that of the British Social Contract and that of the period of *solidarietà nazionale* in Italy.

To summarize the argument so far, we might say that the neo-corporatist literature has overestimated the role of 'the state' in fostering concertation—and indeed the very possibility of detecting a consistent strategy and an autonomous initiative on the part of such a multiform actor. Moreover, many participants in the debate on neo-corporatism have not only exaggerated the state's role when describing specific historical realities; they have gone so far as to develop it theoretically into a long-term 'strategic design' of an actor called 'the state' (without further specification) which can be seen as the 'architect of the political order' (Anderson, 1977). In responding to systemic needs, it is held, many states have been led to build a new corporatist order—with the consent of the organized interests involved—by granting privileges to certain organizations in exchange for the limitation of their full autonomy in the market arena.

But why, or to what extent, should interest organizations accept such a design? And why, or to what extent, will they be able to conform to it? Under what conditions will the advantages derived from concertation be reckoned as greater than the costs involved in the limitation of market autonomy and in the strains that are likely to be placed on relations with rank-and-file members? Some leading theoreticians of neo-corporatism seem well aware of the crucial importance of such questions: 'A central problem of a genetic theory of neo-corporatism, thus, is how—in the absence of coercion from the state—the decision of large organizations to enter (or to continue) a "liberal corporatist" cooperation may be explained' (Lehmbruch, 1977: 92). But there can be no clear and satisfactory solutions to this central problem in the corporatist literature, in consequence of the emphasis given to functional requirements and the role of the state.

Neo-corporatist writers pay very little attention to the conditions which may lead organized interests to move autonomously into a corporatist path as a part of *their own* strategy of exchange, by exercising self-restraint in their market actions, and even by implicitly inducing governments to grant them a public status. In fact, in entering into exchange relations with each other and with the state, interest organizations try, on the one hand, to pursue their own objectives, while being led, on the other, to internalize some common constraints or systemic imperatives. Instead, therefore, of conceptualizing neo-corporatism simply as a 'strategy of domination' (Crouch, 1977) and of analysing its functions within this framework, it is, rather, necessary to look more carefully at the conditions which allow a 'strategy of exchange' to be pursued by each actor alike.

The Emergence of Concertation: under what Conditions will Trade Unions Adopt a Strategy of Political Exchange?

Our problem may then be posed in the following way: what makes an interest organization both willing and able to enter a relationship based on concertation? And what makes such willingness and ability stable over time? In this section, I shall try to answer the first question quasi-deductively, by developing an analytical framework which will later be applied to concrete historical cases. As a preliminary, a few concepts should be clarified.

For our purposes, *concertation*[2] may be defined as a mode of policy formation in which major interest organizations participate in the decision-making process; this participation is not merely occasional, but takes place in a context of systematic, long-term exchange between these organizations and government. The emergence of such a situation is possible when the strategies of all the actors involved tend to converge in this direction. However, I shall limit my analysis to the strategies of labour organizations[3] and, hence, to the conditions under which *they* are led to contribute to the establishment of exchange processes of a systematic, long-term kind.

It may next be helpful, in order to clarify the type of exchange through which concertation takes place, to develop the concept of 'political exchange', as used by Pizzorno in a seminal essay (1978b) and by various later authors (e.g. Mutti, 1982). Drawing on these contributions, we may define *political exchange* as a type of relation between the state and labour organizations in which a trade-off of different forms of political power occurs. The state devolves portions of its decision-making authority to trade unions, by allowing them to play a part in policy formation and implementation and, thus, to gain advantage from the material and symbolic resources which the state can distribute. In return for this, trade unions deliver their indirect political power to the state by guaranteeing consensus and by drawing on their own resources to ensure the legitimacy, effectiveness and efficiency of state action. It is quite clear that such a mutual exchange of power implies a limitation of each actor's autonomy—a willingness to accept self-restraint so that courses of action are followed which would not otherwise have been chosen. The mutual benefits which may derive from political exchange necessarily go together with mutual costs. It is, therefore, only in the context of a—however rough and implicit—cost-benefit evaluation that the decision by a trade union to enter, or to continue, a relation of political exchange may be explained.

This is a point largely overlooked in the few attempts that have been made to account for trade unions' interest in accepting—or promoting—political exchange. Such an interest is usually seen to lie in the organizational gains that unions, or their leaders, can obtain from an exchange relation: 'The gains that the union may receive in it are in terms of political power' (Pizzorno, 1978b: 284). Or, as Keeler (1981: 185) puts it, there are two main types of organizational gains: 'The more obvious and more often discussed type is *biased influence*: structured access to the decision-making centres of the state and/or devolved authority for the administration of public policy. But a second type of gain, related to but analytically distinct from the first, is of more fundamental importance for an official union: *competitive advantage* . . . [i.e.] organizational supports from the state sufficient to assure that its unpopular behaviour will not imperil its sectoral hegemony through generating a massive departure of hostile members for rival union movements.'

There are two difficulties with such accounts. First, if the only advantages that a union gets from political exchange are in the form of power for its leaders or of organizational gains, there should be a formidable amount of opposition on the part of the rank-and-file, since self-restraint by workers would be compensated for only by gains for their representatives. But in many cases there are no— or only quite limited—signs of such opposition. Secondly and more important, in these accounts the gains that a union may receive from political exchange are not set against the costs; whereas it is only when the former exceed the latter that a union can 'rationally' estimate such a relation to be in its own interest. Keeler, for instance, readily recognizes that, in exchange for gains of the kind described above, a union 'loses . . . a certain measure of its freedom to articulate the demands of its members' (1981: 185). But under what conditions will the trade-off between gains and losses be viewed as favourable to the union, so as to lead it to political exchange rather than to alternative courses of action? It should be easier to understand why a trade union is, or is not, willing to accept, or to promote, a relationship with government based on concertation and on a stable political exchange if its choice is seen as if it were the outcome of a 'rational' calculation of the benefits and of the costs that are entailed.[4]

For a trade union, the *advantages* of a stable political exchange cannot be seen, as we have said, solely in terms of power for the leaders or of organizational gains, although such considerations may well be important ones. The main benefit is, rather, to be understood as the possibility of modifying market outcomes to labour's advantage. Market outcomes can, of course, be affected via the use of organizational power and mobilization in 'free' collective bargaining. But political exchange, though it involves some degree of under-exploitation of this power in industrial relations, may still be viewed as a better alternative under certain conditions.

First, the degree of responsiveness of state institutions to the unions may be greater than that they can obtain from employers; or, in other words, trade unions may have more power in the political arena than in the industrial relations one. This could result from different factors: for instance, from a structure of industrial relations which makes the unions organizationally weak, or from a pro-labour party being in office which can offer them political support. When such factors are present, trade unions may find it advantageous to shift the locus of distributional conflict away from industrial relations and into the political market (Korpi & Shalev, 1980; Korpi, 1983).

Secondly, the state may be a potentially greater source of benefits than are private employers. For instance, income redistribution via social reforms and fiscal measures may be more important than wage increases, especially when the welfare state is expanding or when industrial productivity is falling. Control over the labour-market and industrial policies of the state may prove more effective in sustaining employment than collective bargaining of work-time reduction. And so on. In such circumstances, the possibility of influencing state decisions will appear more crucial than collective bargaining to the pursuit of labour's objectives, irrespective of trade unions' relative power as between the industrial and political arenas.

Thirdly, the national economy may be in deep crisis or be highly exposed to international competition. In such situations, even a strong trade union may find it very risky to exploit to the full its organizational and market power in collective bargaining. Indeed, somewhat paradoxically, the stronger the union, the more likely it is to be confronted with an acute dilemma. If it uses its strength unrestrainedly in pursuing workers' short-term interests through collective bargaining, then its disruption of the economy may be such as to imperil its future ability to defend its members' employment and in turn the very basis of its own power. If, on the other hand, it merely under-exploits its power by moderating its labour-market action, it will risk arousing internal dissent and weakening the loyalty of its members. Political exchange may then be seen as a way out of this dilemma, since union self-restraint in the industrial arena is—or should be—compensated for by access to the resources which the state can offer.

To summarize the preceding discussion: the advantages which a trade union may draw from a relation with government based on political exchange are to be seen mainly in the possibility of modifying market outcomes, under conditions in which relying on 'free' collective bargaining would be less fruitful or more risky. If these are the potential benefits of a stable political exchange, what, on the other hand, are the potential *costs?*

As we suggested earlier, the limitation of their autonomy in the industrial relations arena and the moderation involved in political exchange are likely to place a strain on unions' relations with their rank and file; and also to limit their ability to act 'on behalf' of other social groups. The unpleasant consequences that may then ensue, range from a weakening of members' loyalty or a decrease in membership to the loss of representational monopoly or the withdrawal of the tacit right of representation given to the unions by social groups outside their membership. These are all serious risks for trade unions to run—so much so in fact as to constrain their willingness to enter a relation of stable political exchange, for fear of provoking a major 'crisis of representation.' However, these risks are the lower, the more trade unions possess instruments to control such a potential crisis. These instruments can be of differing kinds; but their common effect will be to lower the potential costs of political exchange to the unions, thus changing the outcome of their rational calculation. For instance, centralization and representational monopoly, usually considered as conditions for the stability of concertation, may be seen in this light as elements in the unions' cost-benefit assessment. By allowing a relative 'insulation' of internal decision-making processes, they may be able to prevent open confrontation with the rank-and-file from taking place, or potential dissent from finding effective organizational forms. Moreover, though, as we shall see in the next section, these are not the only instruments potentially available to trade unions in avoiding a crisis of representation. For instance, the use of ideology as an 'identity incentive' to retain workers' loyalty may, for some unions, be even more effective.

To sum up the main elements of our analytical framework, we may then suggest that, from the point of view of the unions' logic of action, a stable political exchange leading to concertation will be possible under three conditions.[5]

(i) The ability of unions to modify market outcomes via concertation in a more fruitful or less risky way than via collective bargaining. This will result from: a greater union strength in the political market than in industrial relations; the greater importance of the state than of firms as a source of benefits; or an economic situation in which it appears dangerous for unions to exploit their collective bargaining power to the full.

(ii) A high degree of organizational ability on the part of unions to pursue long-term objectives and to under-exploit their market power. This will be dependent mainly on the availability of various instruments through which unions can control the crisis of representation which is a likely consequence of their strategy.

(iii) A high degree of organizational ability to aggregate or, better, to pre-mediate a plurality of fragmented interests seeking representation in the political market, so that the unions can hold an 'oligopolistic' position in political bargaining with government. This will be a function of trade union organizational concentration and, probably more important, of the readiness of other interest groups to look to the unions to act on their behalf in bargaining with government.

The Stability of Concertation: under what Conditions can Political Exchange Persist over Time?

The analytical framework developed in the preceding section should permit a more satisfactory interpretation than is found in the neo-corporatist literature, not only of the emergence of concertation, but of its varying degrees of stability as well. We have assumed that the actors' willingness to enter into a systematic, long-term political exchange leading to concertation is based on some kind of cost-benefit assessment. However, in the case of any actor involved, such an assessment may prove to be mistaken; and further, the ratio of costs to benefits may, for various reasons, rapidly change to an actor's disadvantage. Where this is so, that actor will be tempted to withdraw from—or to change the terms of— the political exchange, thus making it unstable and the attempt at concertation short-lived and unsuccessful.

From this point of view, then, the stability of concertation depends on the interaction between quite complex strategies and calculations made by the actors involved, and not on any formal prerequisites. Consider, for instance, the most commonly discussed prerequisites of stability: a high degree of centraliz- ation and concentration of interest organizations, representational monopoly, and a pro-labour party in office. All or many of these conditions have character- ized, for longer or shorter periods, the countries most frequently described as neo-corporatist or concertative: Austria, Sweden, Norway, Holland, and West Germany (Korpi & Shalev, 1980; Visser, 1983). Thus a correlation could easily be claimed between the existence of these conditions and the probability of stable concertation. However, such a correlation is called into question by two different phenomena of relatively recent date.

On the one hand, some previously stable concertative arrangements—for example, those of West Germany—have shown growing signs of instability. This appears to be due mainly to the decreasing interest that employers have in concertation and to their increasing unwillingness to pay the costs of it (Streeck, 1983 and this volume). The supposed prerequisites of concertation have re- mained largely unaltered—at least until the recent change in government—but this has not prevented instability. On the other hand, in the mid- and late 1970s, concertative arrangements in some form or other emerged in countries such as Great Britain and Italy, where most of the organizational and institutional conditions usually considered as prerequisites were absent (see Visser, 1983, for a series of indicators). To be sure, one could observe that the 'life-cycle' of those attempts has been far shorter than that of neo-corporatist endeavours elsewhere. Still, the political exchange that underlay them was not merely *ad hoc* and limited, but was, rather, of a systematic kind and entailed long-term objectives. Also, for two or three years, both attempts did resist fairly well the many threats of instability to which they were exposed. What is here suggested is *not* that the above-mentioned organizational and institutional conditions are without influence on the stability of concertation: indeed, they may—and usually do—represent factors that affect either actors' interests in, or their ability to sustain, a political exchange. The point is rather that it is in *this* regard that their importance must be assessed, and in each case separately, for such importance may vary from situation to situation. Other factors, as we shall see, can contribute to the stability of concertation or may even play the role of 'functional equivalents' for 'prerequisites' that are lacking.

Going back to our analytical framework, then, we maintain that the degree of stability of concertation depends on the extent to which both actors' interests in systematic long-term political exchange and their capability to follow such a logic of action, are not subject to major changes.

As regards *capability*, it may be said that a strategy of systematic long-term exchange requires of all the actors involved that they can set limits to the satisfaction of the diversity of short-term demands which they articulate, by moderating, aggregating or choosing among these demands. Also, if these actors are to be reliable partners in long-lasting accords, they will need to show that they can implement a strategy of exchange; that is, that they can ensure the intended outcomes, by successfully overcoming or preventing the reactions that may be expected from hostile interests.

In the case of trade unions, a first crucial variable in this respect is the degree to which they possess what I earlier called *instruments to control a potential crisis of representation*. By seeing the matter in this way, it should be easier to understand the role played by two of the supposed organizational prerequisites for stable concertation that have been noted: namely, union centralization and representational monopoly. A highly centralized decision-making process necessarily implies a high degree of aggregation and modification of rank-and-file demands; hence it makes it difficult for members to assess the degree of responsiveness of union policies to these demands. Again, representational monopoly practically rules out the possibility that outbreaks of dissent can find effective organizational channels. At the same time, though, our formulation of the problem allows us to see how organizational centralization and representational monopoly are but two of the potential instruments on which trade unions may rely in order to prevent a crisis of representation from becoming unmanageable. They are likely to provide the safest solution—even though their effectiveness has proved variable—but they can be complemented by other instruments that may be available or they may prove to have direct functional equivalents. This possibility has recently been recognized by neo-corporatist writers (e.g. Lehmbruch, 1982), but has been generally regarded as of only limited or dubious relevance. The Italian experience in the late 1970s, however, has shown that such functional equivalents for centralization and representational monopoly are rather wide-ranging and can be relatively effective.

First, while formally remaining in three separate labour confederations, Italian trade unions relied on a 'unitary pact' to avoid competition among them, and to prevent dissent within one confederation from finding opportunities for organizational expression within the other two. Secondly, they managed to limit the impact of external competition from so-called *sindacati autonomi* (autonomous unions outside the three confederations), which were becoming strong in such public service sectors as railways, health, education and public transport. They did so, on the one hand, by using their political resources to force Parliament and governments to grant them some degree of privileged recognition, but on the other, by launching an ideological mobilization aimed at delegitimating the *sindacati autonomi* as merely 'corporatist'—that is, in

workers' language, merely sectional and egoistic—unions. Thirdly, the ideology
of class, as opposed to sectional, interests was also heavily used as an 'identity
incentive' (Regini, 1983) to reinforce workers' loyalty to the unions' policies.
By presenting the content and the objectives of the political exchange under way
in terms of solidaristic class interests—employment, the development of the
South etc.—the unions discouraged open dissent among a sizeable portion of
their rank-and-file, namely, the more politicized. Fourthly, labour leaders co-
ordinated plant-level platforms and took part in decentralized bargaining to
such an extent that workers' councils were left with little *de facto* autonomy to
articulate rank-and-file demands that might conflict with national policies.
Finally, while the ample opportunities available in the unions for both 'exit'
and 'voice' (Lange, 1983) were used by dissenting minorities, the majority of
workers did not find suitable procedures within the union democracy (plant
assemblies, not ballots, are used to approve or reject general union policies) for
making their occasional opposition felt. Thus, the potential crisis of representation was never actually realized. The unitary pact, class ideology, the co-
ordination of bargaining, and the lack of effective democratic procedures all
worked as functional substitutes for centralization and representational monopoly in endowing the process of political exchange with some measure of
stability.

A second crucial variable in trade unions' ability to participate in concertation
in a stable way is the degree to which they hold an *oligopolistic position in
political bargaining with government*. While the problem discussed above
concerns the 'intensity' of representation, there is a further problem concerning
its 'extension': that is, a problem of the number of different functional interests
which have access to political bargaining only through the mediation of the
unions.

Concertation, as opposed to pluralistic pressure-group politics, requires few
participants in the game. This is why a high horizontal concentration of interest
organizations, particularly the existence of only a few large industry federations
(cf. Streeck, 1981b; Lehmbruch, 1982), as well as an attribution of public status
to them (Offe, 1981), are often seen as necessary conditions. According to this
view, stable concertation requires that only a few major interests are recognized
as legitimate and incorporated into policy-making institutions, while other
interests are allowed no access. Accounts of concertation in Austria, for
instance, normally stress these features as playing a key role in its outstanding
record of stability (Lehmbruch, 1977; Marin, 1983). However, while the importance of such organizational features is not in question, the possibility of
functional equivalents must again be stressed. And again too the case of Italian
trade unions in the late 1970s lends empirical support to this argument.

In fact, what gave the Italian unions an oligopolistic position in political
bargaining was not a high degree of organizational concentration of interests—
such concentration being actually very low (Visser, 1983)—but rather their
ability to carry out, as part of their own strategy, an effective 'pre-mediation' of

different functional interests to be represented in political bargaining, even though these interests remained organizationally distinct and fragmented. Thus, a sort of internalization of distributive conflict was achieved, which prevented major disruptions of political exchange and of its outcomes, although of course increasing tension within the decision-making processes of the unions themselves. This ability to pre-mediate a wide spectrum of functional interests had two main sources. On the one hand, the egalitarian and solidaristic roots of their own strategy (Regini, 1979), as well as the PCI's pursuit of social alliances, led the unions to a set of demands which could appeal to a wide range of different social groups: to workers in the primary labour market and also to marginal workers, to the unemployed, to pensioners, to consumers, and sometimes even to policemen. On the other hand, the unions' legitimacy as successful agents of social mobilization—stemming from the years following the 'hot autumn' of 1969—was still strong enough to lead most of these groups to delegate to the unions, openly or tacitly, the right to act on their behalf in bargaining with government, rather than seeking to act themselves as independent pressure groups. In this way, then, the Italian unions obtained a *de facto* oligopolistic position in political bargaining, which helped to make a relatively stable concertation possible.

So far we have discussed the extent to which trade unions are capable of following a logic of action based on long-term political exchange, as a major condition for the stability of concertation. But what about the degree of their *interest in* such an exchange? Under what conditions will this be strong and steady enough to ensure continuity of participation? From this point of view, the crucial problem may be the willingness and ability of governments to guarantee the expected results of political exchange; that is, economic and other policies consistent with the unions' objectives as redefined during the bargaining process. Here again, the traditional emphasis on the presence of a pro-labour party in office as a prerequisite for the stability of concertation may mean short-circuiting the analysis. It is certainly true that, as Crouch (1982) argues, 'faith' in a government that is close to labour may fill the temporal gap which opens up, to the detriment of workers, when immediate wage moderation is exchanged against long-term—and uncertain—benefits. But, as the British experience of the Social Contract shows, this condition soon becomes insufficient.

In fact, what is important is government's ability to guarantee the expected results of political exchange. In the terminology of public policy studies, this implies the capacity of government to ensure both the expected 'output' and the expected 'outcome'. But even a pro-labour government may lack this capacity. First, it may have to face strong opposition from social groups damaged by the policies emanating from concertation, or a subtle resistance by a public administration that is both hostile to labour and unable to implement innovative policies. In either case, the expected outcome may fail to materialize. This is in fact what happened in Italy during the last phase of *solidarietà nazionale*, leading the unions to question what real value concertation had for them. Secondly, a pro-labour government may have to face seriously deteriorating economic conditions, which cut back the resources that can be allocated through political bargaining and force it to change the priorities of its agenda. Such a situation led the British unions, during the second stage of the Social Contract, to question the possibility that the initially favourable outputs of legislation could continue, and thus undermined the stability of the political exchange on which the Social Contract depended.

The Growth and Decline of Concertation in Britain and Italy in the 1970s

Both the Italian and the British experience of political exchange in the 1970s can substantially add to our understanding of the complexity—and of the reproducibility—of the conditions which make concertation more or less stable. These historical situations can be seen as ones in which a 'rational' calculation of costs and benefits by union movements led them to accept—to some extent, even to promote—policies of concertation. However, concertation proved unstable, and systematic political exchange eventually ended in stalemate, because of a rapid decline in the extent of the benefits that could be expected from it and in the possibility of controlling its costs; or, one could say, because of a failure to assess realistically the difficulties of obtaining benefits and avoiding costs.

Despite all the differences that must be recognized in political context and historical background, there is a striking similarity in the objectives stated by the British and Italian trade unions at the start of their attempts at political exchange, and in both cases these implied notable departures from their previous strategies (see on Britain Bornstein & Gourevitch, 1983; Crouch, 1980; and on Italy, Lange et al., 1982). Both the TUC's programme (and the Social Contract statements) in 1973-4 and the so-called EUR document approved by the Italian confederations in February 1978 stressed the need for increased state and union control over microeconomic decision-making in industry in order to promote faster growth and employment. And on the other hand, while both union movements rejected statutory incomes policies, they alike accepted the need for voluntary wage restraint. Clearly, too, the state was in both cases seen as crucial for the resources it could provide. Private enterprises had become increasingly dependent on political decisions, especially if expensive programmes of industrial restructuring and reconversion—deemed necessary by the unions—were to be carried out. And likewise, employment levels could only be sustained with the support of the state. At the same time, both union movements were still strong enough to cause substantial disruption within their already declining economies should they decide to exploit their organizational power to the full on the wages front (Lange, 1979). While they could not accept a statutory incomes policy, a trade-off between wage moderation and other types of benefit appeared as an attractive alternative. Partisan and electoral considerations reinforced this assessment of the potential benefits of political exchange. For the

Italian unions—and especially for the largest confederation, the CGIL—it was important to show that the participation of the Communists in the parliamentary majority could change the previously conflictual relationship with government into a more co-operative one. For the TUC, the opportunity to help the Labour party at the next election appeared even more important, since the previous Tory government had posed a serious threat to the unions through its Industrial Relations Act.

In Britain, the first two years of Labour government (1974-5) did in fact produce the expected outputs, as the new Cabinet was quick to implement the agreements reached in 1973 between the unions and the party, which later became known as the Social Contract. These agreements focused on three main types of provision—in regard to social policy, investment control and expansion, and union rights. Incomes policy was not part of the explicit deal but it seems that a future Labour cabinet was tacitly committed not to repeat the policy of the Wilson government in 1966-7, and to aim rather at securing some form of voluntary wage restraint (Crouch, 1977; Coates, 1980; Bornstein & Gourevitch, 1983; Sassoon, 1982). A sizeable package of benefits was, in other words, promised to the unions, and they in turn found it convenient to enter into a relation of political exchange with the new government. To repeat, a large portion of this package was rapidly implemented. Between 1974 and 1975, a series of social reforms brought considerable benefits to workers in the form of increases in old-age pensions, food subsidies, a rent freeze, price controls, and changes in income tax. Probably more important, workers' and unions' rights were strengthened by the Trade Union and Labour Relations Act of 1974 and the Employment Protection Act of 1975.

In this situation, the decentralized structure of British trade unionism and industrial relations did not prevent political exchange from working. Even when, from 1975 onwards, a rapidly deteriorating economic climate forced a shift in the focus of the policies of concertation—from social reform and industrial democracy to wage regulation—the TUC did not at once withdraw from the Social Contract, nor was workers' loyalty to their unions immediately undermined. Of the four phases of incomes policy which followed one another between 1975 and 1979, the first two were in fact negotiated by the Labour government with the TUC. Moreover, they did not meet with any strong resistance from either the rank-and-file or the union militants. The extent to which the costs of political exchange were accepted in the period in question by a union membership both accustomed to decentralized 'free' collective bargaining and provided with the organizational means to pursue it, may seem surprising. Certainly, 'free-riding' behaviour was lower than would be expected on the basis of theory (Olson, 1965), or than was actually anticipated by most industrial relations experts (cf. Coates, 1980; Boston, 1983). The data reveal that wage drift was very limited during the first two phases of incomes policy (1975-7), and that over this same period average earnings rose less than the rate of inflation (Coates, 1980: 32-4). Further, data on industrial conflict show that this declined rapidly in 1975 and 1976, just after reaching the highest peak since 1926. For about three years, therefore, political exchange worked very well in Britain, in spite of the absence of the organizational conditions—that is, centralization and concentration—which are generally regarded as its prerequisites.

From the point of view of the unions, it is easy to see how, in the first period of the Labour government, the benefits of political exchange were higher than the costs. After 1975, the more evident gains of this earlier period could no longer be matched, but three main considerations still led the unions to see the continuation of political exchange as being in their own interests. First, during the Social Contract period they had acquired an unprecedented political influence (Coates, 1980: 57), which they obviously wished to keep. Secondly, they did not want to hinder the Labour government's ability to pursue its own programmes, as this would strengthen the Tories' electoral chances. And thirdly, a return to collective bargaining without the constraints set by political exchange, as was demanded by groups of workers with above-average market power, would have further deepened the crisis of the British economy, and thus threatened the unions' power and legitimacy. On the other hand, though, by persisting in a relation of political exchange, the unions were running the risk of a slowly accumulating crisis of representation. Strikingly enough, for about three years this risk did not materialize, and the TUC showed its ability to adhere to a logic of long-term political exchange, even though effective instruments to control a crisis of the kind in question were not readily available. The most powerful device which unions may use in such a situation is, after all, ideology; that is, an instrument usually missing from the British union leader's tool kit. But in fact, egalitarianism and the protection of the low paid—that is, the goals pursued by the TUC through setting a common ceiling to pay rises for all groups of workers (Boston, 1983; Bornstein & Gourevitch, 1983)—probably gave a normative justification for the acceptance of incomes policy in which values of class solidarity were effectively expressed.

However, in the end, the lack of safer instruments to control a crisis of representation made the costs of continuing political exchange overwhelming. In 1977, rebellions at plant level and resolutions against wage restraint supported by important unions became widespread. By the summer of that year, the list of affiliated unions opposed to an endorsement of Stage III of incomes policy was so impressive that the TUC was forced to withdraw its support for government policy (Coates, 1980; Sassoon, 1982). From then on, up to Labour's defeat at the election of 1979, the guidelines for wage policy set by the government were no longer the outcome of concertation, and the whole edifice of the Social Contract collapsed. The only advantage that could remain for the unions, were they to continue with political exchange, would be that of avoiding an electoral triumph by the Tories. However, important as this was felt to be, it could no longer match the costs entailed. It was, in other words, not only the decrease in evident gains but, especially, the growing inability to control the costs, which led the British unions to terminate their experiment in political exchange.

The relationship between the trade unions and government in Italy during the period of *solidarietà nazionale* shows a number of similarities with that which prevailed in Britain under the Social Contract. Of course, there are many and well-known differences: in the Italian case, unlike the British, there was no previous experience of concertation which the actors could draw upon; no formal agreement between the unions and the parties of the Left—there being of course more than one—was reached; and the government, though it was the first not to isolate the Left since 1948, could be considered as pro-labour only with qualification, having in fact more of a 'consociational' form. Nevertheless, Italian trade unions did, like the British, accept, and to some extent promote, a systematic long-term political exchange, and with rather similar objectives. A trade-off between wage moderation and influence over industrial and labour-market policies aimed at fostering growth and at sustaining employment was, in fact, deemed necessary in a period of economic recession and growing inflation. Moreover, while this was the rationale officially assigned to trade-union partici-pation in economic policy-making, there was also a political interest in support-ing a relatively pro-labour government, even though not to the same extent or as openly as in Britain.

As was earlier noted, the Italian trade unions were better equipped than their British counterparts to control the potential costs of political exchange and were, therefore, more capable of following through its logic, in spite of their lack of centralization and of representational monopoly. Why, then, one may ask, did their initial engagement in concertation not last for more than two years—their willingness to withdraw from it being clear even before the 1979 elections which brought *solidarietà nazionale* to an end? My hypothesis is that the crucial problem which persuaded the Italian unions to abandon their strategy of political exchange was not, as in the case of the British Social Contract, the difficulty of enforcing wage restraint (which was formally proclaimed in the 'EUR document' of February 1978) and of controlling workers' dissent over this policy. Rather, it was the unions' growing awareness of their miscalculation of the benefits which could in fact be obtained from concertation.

To be sure, the unions' new policy of supporting wage moderation and greater labour flexibility met with some internal opposition (which was at times highly visible, as in April 1977 when dissenting minorities held a meeting at the Teatro Lirico in Milan), and was not evenly implemented over all industries and areas of the country (Golden, 1983). Nevertheless, such difficulties should not be exaggerated. At the peak level of the labour confederations, the new policy was put into practice even before it was formally adopted by the unions, when, in January and March 1977, two agreements were signed with *Confindustria* (the private employers' association) and with the government respectively. While successfully resisting pressures to place restrictions on plant-level bargaining, the labour confederations accepted through these agreements a less favourable working of wage-indexation mechanisms, and also provisions to increase industrial productivity (fewer days off, a different distribution of vacations,

checks on absenteeism, and norms governing internal mobility). One can interpret these two agreements as involving concessions on the unions' side in
exchange for future participation in the decision-making process at the levels
both of the firm and of national economic policy (Perulli, 1982). Moreover,
the unions exercised self-restraint both in plant- and industry-level bargaining,
with demands for investment and for rights to information and control generally
replacing more traditional claims for higher wages or better working conditions.
In turn, data on industrial conflict show a sharp decline in 1977 and 1978 (Cella,
1983). The difficulties of implementing a policy of moderation, one must then
conclude, did not substantially impair the unions' ability to pursue the logic of
political exchange.

The benefits anticipated by the unions consisted in a programme of legislation, negotiated with government, the most important items in which were
measures on industrial restructuring and reconversion (1977), on youth employment (1977), on vocational training (1978), and a bill on pensions reform
(1978). Trade unions saw in such legislation potentially innovative instruments
not only to foster employment, but further to increase political control over the
economy and to achieve redistributive goals. Consider for instance the law on
industrial restructuring and reconversion (cf. Regalia, 1984). It required government to elaborate 'sectoral plans' to set the criteria for granting public funds to
firms which wished to restructure. It required the firms which sought to take
advantage of public funds to inform the government of their 'programmes of
investment and of entrepreneurial activity'. And it required public inspectors to
certify that assisted firms had preserved previous levels of employment before
they could obtain further funds. All of these provisions were seen as elements of
a more *dirigiste* industrial policy and of planning in accordance with union
objectives. Or again, take the bill negotiated between government and the unions
on pensions reform, which never actually passed Parliament (Regini & Regonini,
1981). Its goals were: a redistribution from high-income to lower-income
pensioners; a greater equality in the contributions-to-benefits ratio as between
wage-earners and self-employed workers; and wider responsibilities—that is,
more power—for the public agency which administers pensions and in which the
unions hold a majority position.

However, the benefits expected from these policies largely failed to materialize. In the case of the bill on pensions, for instance, the interests which would be
damaged mobilized against it, put pressure on political parties, and were able to
prevent Parliament from passing it. In other cases, failure was due to different
factors. First, the public bureaucracy was neither able nor willing to take an
active role in the implementation of innovative policies, being accustomed to
respond only to more established interest groups and to work in routinized ways
through which change could be achieved only very slowly. Secondly, the government itself was neither able nor willing to take the further decisions often
required for policy implementation—for example, to produce the detailed
sectoral plans for industrial reconversion. Consequently, the unions realized that,

even after the passing of agreed legislation, they had to continue to put pressure on government and to bargain over its implementation. Finally, in some cases areas of decision-making were compartmentalized, and the unions discovered that they had little influence within the more important ones. For instance, the law on industrial restructuring gave the task of managing labour mobility and redundancy compensation to regional commissions on which the unions are strongly represented; but it reserved the distribution of public funds and other incentives to firms engaged in restructuring to a strictly governmental body.

After their initial expectations of major benefits, the unions became thus deeply disillusioned. Even a relatively pro-labour government could not provide them with the outcomes of concertation that they had looked for. Although the costs of political exchange for Italian unions were not as high as for the British, they came to realize that the actual benefits were not such as to match even the potential risks. Both in Britain and in Italy, therefore, the same 'rational' calculation which had led the unions to accept or to promote concertation may be seen as leading them eventually to withdraw from it. In both countries, political exchange proved unstable and concertation short-lived.

In brief conclusion to this analysis, we may again observe that the elements which enter into a cost-benefit assessment of the kind in question are obviously subject to change. Hence, in any country, periods in which a systematic political exchange is possible, because it appears advantageous to all the actors involved, may alternate with others in which such exchange is not possible. Further research should focus on the variability of the conditions for political exchange in the above sense, rather than on supposed organizational or institutional pre-requisites, which, for all their importance in some situations, may be shown to be neither necessary nor sufficient in others.

When the likely scenarios for the 1980s are considered, a focus on the changing and complex conditions of actors' rational choices implies that some doubt must fall on the possibility of discerning linear trends of either decline or development in concertative arrangements. To be sure, the weakening of trade union power, which is a consequence of prolonged recession, makes a continuation of the type of political exchange which prevailed up to the mid-1970s rather improbable. To seek the deregulation of markets and to dispense with the costly institutions of concertation may be a growing temptation for both employers (Streeck, this volume) and governments (Carrieri & Donolo, 1983). West Germany and Great Britain provide good examples of these possibilities. But such circumstances will not necessarily bring concertation to an end. The weaker actors may well accept less favourable 'terms of exchange' in order to preserve it. The stronger ones may come to think that, if new terms of exchange emerge which correspond to the changed power relations, it may still be in their own interests to govern by agreement rather than by unilateral authority or by relying on unregulated market forces—to revert to the three basic forms of resource allocation discussed by Salvati (1982). This possibility is demonstrated by the most recent phase of political bargaining and of tripartite agreements in

Italy (Regini, 1984). After all, the assessment of the relative costs and benefits of the different alternatives is not only difficult for social scientists; it is also a quite complex matter for the actors themselves.

Acknowledgements

I wish to thank John Goldthorpe for his revision of my English text and Peter Lange for his useful comments. Research on the Italian and British cases has been made possible by funds provided by the Italian Research Council (CNR).

Notes

1. The period known as 'national solidarity' or 'national unity' was one in which the Italian Communist party (PCI), i.e. the major party of opposition since 1947, entered a parliamentary coalition of six parties, supporting the government. Faced with a deep economic crisis and with the threat of terrorism, the six parties, including the PCI, reached a 'programmatic agreement' on a series of policies, which secured the parliamentary abstention of the PCI in 1977 and then its vote in 1978. 'National solidarity' officially ended in 1979, with the elections of that year.

2. While in the preceding section I have used the terms 'neo-corporatism' and 'concertation' interchangeably in order to discuss the literature which focuses on the former concept, I shall, from now on, use only the latter term, for two reasons: first, to partially accept Schmitter's (1982) suggestion to reserve 'neo-corporatism' for situations in which a system of interest intermediation displays the features he describes; secondly, to avoid confining the concept of 'concertation' to the limits of the neo-corporatist literature previously discussed.

3. There are two main reasons which make this concentration on labour unions strongly advisable for the time being: first, the need to simplify the analytical framework that is to be presented; and secondly, the relative abundance of studies of the strategies of unions as compared with those of other relevant actors. However, to understand fully the conditions under which concertation is likely to emerge (or to terminate), it will clearly be necessary to develop a similar analytical framework for these other actors. As far as governments are concerned, the current literature already provides many hints as to the conditions and limits of their interest in concertative solutions, as well as of their ability to pursue them. As regards employers' associations, we have to rely on mainly speculative analyses, which are hardly based on a comparative observation of their logic of action (e.g. Offe & Wiesenthal, 1980; Crouch, 1982). Hopefully, when the comparative studies currently under way (Schmitter & Streeck, 1981) have clarified the differences and the similarities between this logic and that of trade unions, it will become possible to apply to the study of employers' associations an analytical framework analogous to the one developed here.

4. Of course, this raises the problem of the limits of rational action models, especially for such actors as trade unions. In fact, they may have to rely on ideology as an orientation for their action far more than on utilitarian calculation, since ideology itself is for them an important 'identity incentive'–i.e. a means to recruit members and to keep their loyalty. While sharing some of the concerns about these limits, our task here is not to assess to what extent trade unions actually *are* rational actors. Rather, by assuming that their action may be analysed *as if* it followed a logic of utilitarian rationality, we can develop an interpretative framework which is, we maintain, both internally consistent and more able to account for a large body of empirical evidence than competing explanations. More specifically, it is not necessary to maintain that all unions actually go through a conscious process of cost-benefit evaluation of the type we develop here. For our purposes, it is sufficient to show that, by assuming such a decision-making process, we can improve our explanation of the similarities and differences in union behaviour which are suggested by comparative research.

5. Obviously, these conditions are seen as necessary, but not sufficient, for concertation actually to emerge. For this to happen, the logic of action of other actors must to some extent also lead towards this outcome (see note 3).

7

Social Democracy, Corporatism, Labour Quiescence and the Representation of Economic Interest in Advanced Capitalist Society

DAVID R. CAMERON

Introduction

During the past decade, the advanced capitalist nations experienced simultaneously a diminution in the rate of economic growth, an increase in the rate of unemployment, an increase in the rate of inflation, and numerous associated macroeconomic maladies. The halcyon days of the early 1960s, when most nations experienced relatively full employment *and* price stability, increasingly appeared as a unique and atypical phase in the life of modern capitalism.[1]

While all the advanced capitalist nations shared in the experience of stagflation, it is also true, as Scharpf (this volume) notes, that the nations responded in very different ways to the economic crisis. As a result, one observes a *greater* degree of variation in most indicators of economic performance than had existed in the immediate pre-OPEC era. This chapter examines that variation in detail and attempts to assess why the macroeconomic performance of the advanced capitalist nations varied as much as it did. In particular, we shall consider why some nations were much more successful than others in maintaining near-full employment in an era of world recession and stagnation. We shall consider why some nations were able to contain the acceleration in prices that followed the oil shocks of 1973 and 1979 without forsaking the commitment to full, or high, employment that had become widely accepted in the post-Second World War era. And we shall consider why other nations were able to stabilize prices only by bludgeoning labour with sharp increases in unemployment to levels that had not been seen since the 1930s. Why did some nations respond to the economic crises of the 1970s and 1980s with deflationary policies that imposed severe costs on the labour force, while others did not? Why did countries as diverse as Britain, Spain, the Netherlands, Belgium, and Denmark respond with policies that increased the rate of unemployment by six percentage points or more between the mid-1960s and early 1980s? (See Table 7.1) And how did other countries, such as Switzerland, Japan, Austria, Norway, and Sweden, maintain almost full employment throughout the period and limit the increases in the rate of unemployment to less than one per cent of the labour force?

TABLE 7.1. *Unemployment in eighteen nations, 1965–82*

	% of Total Labour Force, Unemployed[a]			
	Average 1965–82	Average 1965–67	Average 1980–82	Increase 1965–67 to 1980–82
Switzerland	0.2	0.0	0.3	0.3
Japan	1.6	1.3	2.2	0.9
Austria	1.8	1.9	2.6	0.7
Norway	1.8	1.6	2.1	0.5
Sweden	2.1	1.6	2.5	0.9
Germany	2.2	0.6	4.5	3.9
Netherlands	3.2	1.0	7.5	6.5
Finland	3.6	1.9	5.4	3.5
Australia	3.7	1.7	6.2	4.5
France	3.8	1.7	7.2	5.5
Denmark	4.1	1.4	8.7	7.3
Britain	5.1	2.6	10.4	7.8
Belgium	5.2	2.1	11.0	8.9
Spain	5.4	2.4	13.7	11.3
United States	5.7	3.9	8.0	4.1
Canada	6.2	3.6	8.6	5.0
Ireland	6.3	4.8	8.2	3.4
Italy	6.4	5.4	8.2	2.8

[a] Unemployment is measured as the *total* number of unemployed as a proportion of the total labour force.
Sources: OECD, *Labour Force Statistics, 1960–71*, Paris, 1973; *Labour Force Statistics, 1968–79*, Paris, 1981; and *Economic Outlook*, 34, 1983.

In investigating why nations responded in such different ways to the endemic crisis in the world economy, we shall concentrate on two plausible sources of variation. The first involves political parties—in particular, the differences in public policy that may occur when parties of distinct ideological hues govern. We shall consider whether, and if so to what extent, the ability to maintain full employment and price stability in an era of economic stagnation has been associated with—and, by inference, may therefore depend upon—government by leftist (or non-leftist) parties. The second source of variation involves the organizations of the major producer groups in advanced capitalist society and their relations with each other and government. In particular, we shall consider whether the variations in response to economic crisis reflect the presence or absence of corporatist institutions and practices—whether, that is, the existence of corporatist arrangements of negotiation, collaboration, and compromise between employers, workers, and public officials seem to contribute to the maintenance of full employment and price stability in an era of stagflation.[2]

In attempting to evaluate whether differences in the ideological centre of gravity of governing parties, or the organizational characteristics of labour movements, or both, account for the differences among nations in success in coping with the economic crises of the last decade, this chapter reflects several concerns. First of all, the paper represents an attempt to evaluate the impact of government by leftist (or non-leftist) parties and of corporatist arrangements upon the economy. Given the several significant developments within the European Left in recent years—for example, the departure of the German SPD from government after almost two decades of participation in various coalitions, the historic victory of François Mitterrand and the Socialist party in France in May–June, 1981, the return to government of the Swedish Social Democrats after six years in opposition, and the entrance into government of the Spanish Socialist party in late 1982, as well as the bitter ideological conflict within the British Labour party—what leftist parties wish to achieve in office, what they are capable of achieving (especially in an era of economic stagnation and frequent recession), and what they do in fact achieve (and in whose interest and at whose expense) remain among the most important issues confronting students of European politics.[3] And given the fashionable attraction of the concept of 'corporatism' (usually accompanied by some prefix such as 'neo', 'liberal', or 'quasi'), the relationship between the organizational characteristics, political resources, and programmatic ambitions of labour movements and the macro-economic policies of governments represents an important and relatively unexplored domain of inquiry.

In assessing the impact on the economy of government by leftist parties and of corporatist structures and arrangements, we inevitably confront a larger political and intellectual issue—one that has pervaded the discourse and demarks the major schisms within the European Left between Marxist-Leninism, Marxism, and non—Marxist socialism; between those who deny, and those who believe in, the possibility of a reformist, revisionist, parliamentary path to socialism; between those who accept and those who reject Leninist strategies of party organization and revolution; between those who believe that leftist parties are incapable of doing anything other than administering, reforming, and legitimizing capitalism, and those who believe that such parties represent the interests of the working class and are capable of engineering a transition from capitalism to socialism.[4] The issue—which, at least in principle, can be assessed empirically—involves (at least in part) the notion of representation: to what extent are the economic interests of workers, and more generally those of all wage earners in advanced capitalist society, represented when leftist parties, rather than non-leftist ones, govern? And to what extent are those interests represented when workers participate, through their labour organizations, in corporatist arrangements? *Are* the interests of labour in fact represented when leftist parties govern and/or when labour participates in corporatist arrangements? Or are leftist government and corporatist arrangements simply forms by which labour is co-opted, compromised, controlled, and subordinated? To answer these questions, we must explain not only why national variations occur in response to stagflation but also how those different responses affect citizens.

In addition to representing one of the central issues in the above-mentioned schism, the question of whether the interests of a particular economic group or class are served by the participation of leftist parties in government and labour organizations in corporatist arrangements also underlies contemporary scholarly debate among students of comparative political economy. While there is considerable disagreement among the scholars who employ the concept of corporatism, most would agree with Schmitter (1974: 107-8) that: 'societal corporatism can be traced primarily to the imperative necessity for a stable, bourgeois-dominant regime . . . to associate or incorporate subordinate classes and status groups more closely within the political process'. And some, if not all, would agree with Panitch (1981: 33) in attributing the integration of labour organizations into corporatist institutions and practices to:

the commitment of the state to maintaining a high-employment fiscal and monetary policy . . . the attenuation of the reserve army of labour as a result of nearly full employment . . . that critically further strengthened the organized working class at the industrial level . . . [and] closed off the possibility of securing the necessary rate of exploitation via labour market mechanisms alone.

Most again would agree with Lehmbruch (1977: 107) that 'cooperative incomes policies have been developing as a core element of corporatist management of the economy'. Or as Panitch (1980: 174) expressed it:

Corporatist structures, in the form of economic planning and incomes policy bodies, involved the integration of trade unions in economic policy making in exchange for their incorporation of capitalist growth criteria in union wage policy and their administration of wage restraint to their members.

In short, corporatism can be seen as a system of institutionalized wage restraint in which labour, acting 'responsibly', voluntarily participates in and legitimizes the transfer of income from labour to capital.

While most students of corporatism—especially those concentrating on the British and German experiences and those using Marxian categories of analysis— view the arrangements as benefiting capital, many of those who have concentrated their attention further to the north and examined the impact of Social Democratic government in Norway and Sweden reach a different conclusion. Scholars such as Martin (1975), Hibbs (1977), and Korpi and Shalev (1979, 1980) have argued that enduring control of government by leftist parties—especially when accompanied by many of the attributes associated with corporatism, such as highly centralized peak associations and economy-wide collective bargaining— benefits the working class. Korpi and Shalev (1979: 170), in elaborating their 'power resources' model, argue that:

with more extensive organizational power resources, the political arena will become increasingly important for labour. To the extent that labour is successful in acquiring control over political institutions, it can exercise its power through these means and will not be limited to the industrial arena. On the other hand, the possibilities for employers to exercise political power will decrease.

Thus in describing the Swedish experience since the mid-1930s, they convey (1979: 172, 177) an image of a shift in the relative balance of power between capital and labour in favour of the latter:

the entrenchment of the Social Democrats as the dominant governmental party opened up new courses of action for the labour movement . . . it now became possible to move from a 'zero-sum type of conflict to a 'positive-sum' type, where both parties could expect to gain from cooperation to increase economic growth. . . . For the labour movement, having a hold on political power offered great advantages. The level of employment, of crucial importance for the welfare of workers, could now be raised and maintained at a high point. . . . Fiscal, social, labour market and educational policies could affect the distribution of income and the welfare of citizens. . . . For the representatives of capital, however, the new situation placed limitations upon their courses of action. Their ultimate weapon, the large lockout, was now much more difficult to utilize, since the 'positive neutrality' of the state could no longer be assumed. . . . [In] the Swedish case, a labour movement which had developed sufficient organizational strength and political support to achieve durable control of the polity altered the balance of power in society. . .

In the same vein, but more general in its application, is Hibbs's argument (1978: 165-6) regarding the decline of strike activity in nations such as Sweden, Norway, the Netherlands, Belgium, and Denmark:

nations experiencing a sustained decline or withering away of strike activity during the post-war era are largely those where Social Democratic and Labour parties based on the working class and trade unions successfully mobilized mass political support in the electoral arena, gained control (or at least shared control) of the state, and sharply expanded the scope of collective consumption and distribution. This historical development in the political economy of distribution in these societies represented a massive shift of political power away from business interests and their middle-class allies to the 'organized working class'.

The suggestion that labour benefits in a significant way when Social Democracy rules for an extended period obviously differs from the view of corporatism as a system of class collaboration and compromise that benefits capital. What makes the difference in interpretation especially intriguing is the fact that both sets of scholars are, to a large extent, talking about the *same* nations! Thus, five of the seven most 'societally corporatist' nations, in Schmitter's (1981) classification, are also among the seven nations that, according to Korpi and Shalev, have the greatest degree of working class mobilization and most enduring control of government by leftist parties.[5] The fact that those five nations—Austria, Norway, Sweden, Denmark, and Belgium—are relatively corporatist, compared to other nations, *and* relatively Social Democratic, in terms of the control of government, suggests that any effort to disentangle the effects of corporatism and leftism will be, at best, very difficult. More important, it also suggests that the fundamental difference in the two approaches rests upon a significant difference in understanding a common experience—that of the smaller nations of Europe[6]—that represents the baseline for generalizations about *either* Social

Democracy *or* corporatism. What is required, perhaps, is a more extensive and empirical investigation of that particular experience. In examining the impact on economic policy and performance of Social Democracy and several of the social characteristics associated with corporatism in the advanced capitalist world, we hope to offer evidence that will inform the debate—a debate that, at its core, concerns the issue of the circumstances under which the interests of groups and classes are represented.

Economic Performance in Comparative Perspective

Unemployment and Inflation

All the nations of the advanced capitalist world experienced rising unemployment in the wake of the recessions of the 1970s and 1980s. As Table 7.1 demonstrates, the rate of unemployment increased sharply in most nations in the 1970s, and by the early 1980s it exceeded 10 per cent in Spain, Belgium, and Britain, and surpassed 7 per cent in Denmark, the Netherlands, France, Ireland, Italy, Canada, and the United States. Only in a handful of nations—Switzerland, Japan, Austria, Norway, and Sweden—did unemployment increase by less than one per cent of the total labour force between 1965-7 and 1980-2. In all other nations, unemployment increased by at least two and a half percentage points. Taking the average of the eighteen years between 1965 and 1982, unemployment exceeded 5 per cent in seven nations—the United States, Canada, Britain, Italy, Belgium, Ireland, and Spain. Conversely, unemployment was less than 3 per cent in six nations—Germany, Sweden, Austria, Japan, Norway, and Switzerland—and remained in that range in the early 1980s in five of the six (i.e. all but Germany).

While the advanced capitalist world experienced a dramatic increase in the rate of unemployment during the 1970s and 1980s, it also experienced a sharp increase in the rate of change of prices.[7] As Table 7.2 demonstrates, almost every capitalist democracy experienced a marked increase in the average rate of change in consumer prices between the mid-1960s and the early 1980s. In two-thirds of the nations, prices were increasing by 10 per cent or more a year in the early 1980s, and in some—for example, Italy, Spain, and Ireland—the annual rate of change was between 15 and 20 per cent. In other nations, however—most notably, Japan, the Netherlands, Germany, Austria, and Switzerland—the average rate of change in prices increased by no more than 3 per cent between the mid-1960s and the early 1980s.

Ever since Phillips (1958) observed an inverse relationship between the level of unemployment and the rate of change in nominal wages, conventional macroeconomic wisdom has perceived a trade-off between unemployment and inflation or, conversely, between full employment and price stability.[8] According to that wisdom, inflation, defined in terms of acceleration of the rate of change of prices, is a function of the rate of change in money wages, which depends on the bargaining power of labour, which, in turn, depends on the

TABLE 7.2. *Inflation in eighteen nations, 1965–82*

| | Average Annual % Change in Consumer Prices | | Increase in Average % Change in Consumer Prices |
	1965–7	1980–2	1965–7 to 1980–2
Italy	3.5	19.1	15.6
Ireland	3.4	18.6	15.2
France	2.7	12.9	10.2
Britain	3.7	12.8	9.1
Canada	3.2	11.2	8.0
Norway	4.0	11.9	7.9
United States	2.5	10.0	7.5
Australia	3.4	10.4	7.0
Sweden	5.2	11.5	6.3
Finland	4.8	11.0	6.2
Spain	8.6	14.8	6.2
Denmark	6.7	11.4	4.7
Belgium	3.7	7.6	3.9
Germany	2.8	5.6	2.8
Austria	3.7	6.2	2.5
Netherlands	4.4	6.4	2.0
Switzerland	4.0	5.4	1.4
Japan	5.2	5.2	0.0

Sources: As for Table 7.1.

tightness of labour markets, as reflected by the aggregate rate of unemployment. Hence, as unemployment increases, the rates of change in money wages and inflation *de*crease; as unemployment approaches zero, the rate of change in money wages (and thus in prices) increases at an accelerating rate.

In an important article, Hibbs (1977) extended the logic of the Phillips curve across the advanced capitalist nations. He suggested that the same inverse relationship which Phillips observed *within* a nation over time could be expected to hold in a comparison *across* nations, reflecting the difference among nations in the degree of aversion to high unemployment relative to inflation. And when he compared the average rate of change in consumer prices with the average rate of unemployment during 1960–9 across twelve capitalist democracies, he found that, indeed, there *was* a strong, inverse relationship ($r = -.45$). In other words, nations with relatively high levels of unemployment (e.g. the United States and Canada) had relatively low rates of inflation compared to nations with relatively low rates of unemployment (e.g. Denmark, Finland, the Netherlands, Sweden, and Norway).[9]

Figure 7.1 arrays the average rate of unemployment over the eighteen years between 1965 and 1982 with the increase in the average rate of change in consumer prices between 1965–7 and 1980–2.[10] Figure 1 indicates that, contrary to Hibbs's conclusion, there is a strong, *positive* relationship between inflation and unemployment ($r = +.70$). Nations with high rates of unemployment,

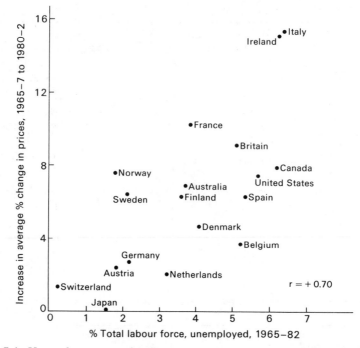

FIG. 7.1. *Unemployment and inflation in eighteen nations, 1965–82*

relative to other nations, also experienced the greatest *increases* in the average rate of change in prices between the mid-1960s and the early 1980s! Conversely, the nations with the lowest levels of unemployment tended to have the *smallest* increases in the rate of change in prices. In other words, relative full employment is not associated with price *acceleration* but, instead, with price *moderation* (relative, that is, to the rate of change in other nations).[11]

The array in Figure 7.1 is of particular interest because it suggests that nations are *not* inevitably fated to suffer either high inflation or high unemployment. In some—most notably, Switzerland, Japan, Austria, Germany, the Netherlands, and, to a lesser extent, Norway and Sweden—the maintenance of unemployment at or below the three per cent level did not produce the relatively great acceleration in prices that a good Phillipsian might expect. And in other nations—most notably, Italy, Ireland, the United States, Canada, Britain, France, and Spain—the tolerance of relatively high unemployment in the range of four per cent or more over nearly two decades did not produce the moderation in prices that might have been expected. Of the two clusters of nations, one—composed of Japan, Germany, and the latter's smaller neighbours—enjoyed, relative to other nations, the best of both worlds—that is, relatively stable prices and relatively full employment.[12] The other, less fortunate cluster—composed largely of Britain and its former colonies—enjoyed, relatively speaking, the *worst* of both worlds—that is, accelerating prices *and* high unemployment!

Inflation and Increases in Earnings

The acceleration in prices throughout the advanced capitalist world after the mid-1960s can be attributed to many factors—the fiscal, foreign, and monetary policies of the Johnson administration, which eroded the value of the dollar at a time when it was still the reserve currency in the international monetary system; the devaluation of the dollar in 1971 and the subsequent realignment of currency values; the increase in commodity prices; the increase in OPEC's crude oil price as it sought to recoup its losses in real income over the previous half-decade (as well as punish the West for its stance *vis-à-vis* the Yom Kippur War), etc.[13] As important as these (and other) time-specific reasons were, the inflation of the last two decades undoubtedly reflected other more enduring processes in capitalist economies. One of these involved the efforts of suppliers of goods to raise their income—including, among the more important suppliers of goods, wage-earners who supply their labour to employers and who will generally tend to ask for a higher price for that labour when the economy is booming, when there is little surplus labour (as reflected in a low rate of unemployment), and when employers are ready to pass on increases in their labour costs to consumers.

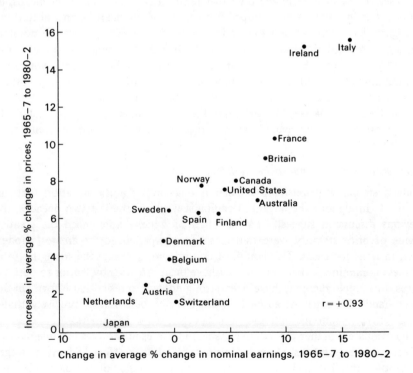

FIG. 7.2. *The relation between change in earnings and inflation in eighteen nations, 1965–82*

While it would be exceptionally simple-minded to attribute the global inflation of the last two decades to wage push, and equally naïve to believe that the considerable differences among nations in inflation therefore reflect differences in the degree of economic militancy among wage earners, it is nevertheless plausible that the acceleration in the rate of change in prices is, to some degree, the product of acceleration in the rate of change in wages. Figure 7.2 demonstrates that while a simple statistical association between changes in wages and prices says little about the causal process of inflation, the variation across the advanced capitalist world in the rate of inflation closely parallels the cross-national variation in the rate of change in workers' earnings. This Figure arrays the measure of inflation—i.e. the increase in the average rate of change in prices between 1965-7 and 1980-2—with a measure of the increase in nominal earnings of production workers in manufacturing.[14] We observe a very close relationship ($r = +.93$) between the two. In other words, the difference across nations in the magnitude of the increase in the rate of change in prices since the mid-1960s reflects, to a very large degree, the difference in the extent to which labour has pushed for, and obtained, larger increases in pay.[15]

The very close relationship in Figure 7.2 between the magnitude of the increases (or decreases) in the rates of change in earnings and prices means, of course, that the nations are grouped in clusters that are nearly identical to those in Figure 7.1. Thus, among the nations with the largest increases in nominal earnings (and inflation) are Italy, Ireland, Britain, Australia, and France, followed by the United States and Canada. In contrast to those nations, where the average annual rate of change in nominal earnings of manufacturing workers increased by at least five percentage points between the mid-1960s and early 1980s, Germany, Japan, Austria, and the Netherlands experienced relatively large *de*creases in the average annual rate of change in nominal (and real) earnings.

Increases in Earnings and Strike Activity

While a simple wage-push model can not account for the inflation that has occurred throughout the advanced capitalist world in the last two decades, the previous discussion suggests that the nations which experienced the greatest degree of price stability were the ones which experienced the greatest moderation in wage increases. This could, of course, simply reflect the strength of the business community; there might well have been *attempts* by labour to push up wages, but employers may have been strong enough to resist that effort. On the other hand, the apparent absence of wage push could reflect precisely that— the absence of economic militancy among organized wage-earners.

To evaluate whether the relatively small increases in earnings in some nations reflect the successful resistance by business to labour's effort to increase wages or, on the other hand, the absence of economic militancy on the part of labour, one can compare the relationship between the changes in earnings and strike activity. If the small increase occurred in spite of a strong effort by labour to push up wages—an effort that might plausibly have included the use of the strike as a bargaining weapon—we should not find a close relationship between the magnitude of the increase in earnings and the degree of strike activity. Whether labour obtained large or modest increases in earnings would therefore depend more on the political and economic strength of business than the extent and use by labour of its collective resources. On the other hand, if relatively modest increases in earnings occurred primarily because wage earners did not use their ultimate weapon (withholding their labour from employers via the strike), we would expect to find a strong *positive* relation between the magnitude of the increase in earnings and strike activity, with the smallest increases being registered in the nations in which labour abstained from extensive strike activity.

TABLE 7.3. *Strike activity in eighteen nations, 1965-81*

Working Days Lost in Industrial Disputes per 1000 in Total Labour Force	
Italy	849
Canada	707
Ireland	484
Australia	427
United States	411
Britain	375
Finland	358
Spain	334
France	278
Belgium	156
Denmark	148
Sweden	95
Japan	71
Norway	28
Germany	28
Netherlands	22
Austria	10
Switzerland	1

Source: International Labour Office, *Yearbook of Labour Statistics,* Geneva, 1983.

Table 7.3 presents a measure of strike activity in the eighteen nations during 1965-81 and Figure 7.3 presents the relationship between strike activity and the measure of the increase in the rate of change in earnings between 1965-7 and 1980-2. Our measure of strike activity is identical to that used by Shorter and Tilly (1974) and Hibbs (1978) and represents the average of the number of days lost each year in industrial disputes per 1000 members of the total labour force.[16] Figure 7.3 demonstrates that a strong, *positive* relationship exists between the volume of strike activity during 1965-81 and the magnitude of the

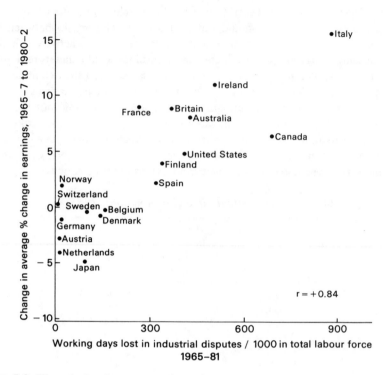

FIG. 7.3. *The relation between strike activity and the increase in the rate of change in earnings*

increase in the rate of change in nominal earnings ($r = +.84$). The close association between the two suggests that the variation across the advanced capitalist nations in the acceleration of the rate of change in nominal earnings (and ultimately prices) reflects, to a very considerable degree, the difference among the nations in the frequency, duration, and size of strikes by labour. Thus, whether the rate of change in earnings increased depended less on the ability of business to resist labour's efforts to push wages up than on labour's willingness to be economically militant. In nations with a relatively high degree of strike activity throughout the period—nations such as Italy, Canada, Ireland, Australia, and, to a somewhat lesser degree, Britain, the United States, Finland, and Spain (since Franco's death)—the rate of change in earnings generally increased by five percentage points or more between the mid-1960s and early 1980s. In contrast, nations with very low levels of strike activity, relative to other advanced capitalist nations, experienced very small increases—and often, in fact, *decreases*—in the rate of change in earnings. In those nations—Switzerland, Austria, the Netherlands, Norway, Germany, and, to a lesser degree, Japan, Sweden, and Denmark—the characteristic posture of labour throughout the period was one of economic quiescence rather than militancy.[17]

Strike Activity and Employment

Why do the advanced capitalist nations vary so dramatically in the extent to which labour uses the strike? Most who have studied strike activity turn immediately to the political arena and search for the key to that variation in the composition of government or the fiscal policies of government and the relation of labour to political élites and the government. (See Hibbs, 1978; Shalev, 1978; Korpi & Shalev, 1979, 1980) But it is equally plausible that the variation in strike activity reflects variation in other aspects of working life that are especially salient to labour. Whether labour uses its ultimate weapon, the strike, may depend as much, or more, on its situation in the market and its relations with employers. It may be the case, for instance, that labour will readily concede increases in earnings that can be obtained through wage militancy, as exemplified by the frequent use of the strike, if it attains other objectives that are more highly valued. One of those more highly valued objectives may be employment. In fact, Calmfors (1983: 13) asserts that the 'usual assumption' in the literature on union behaviour is that the typical union: 'cares about the real wage and about the level of unemployment. When it sets the wage rate, it thus trades off the positive effects of a higher real wage against increased unemployment.'

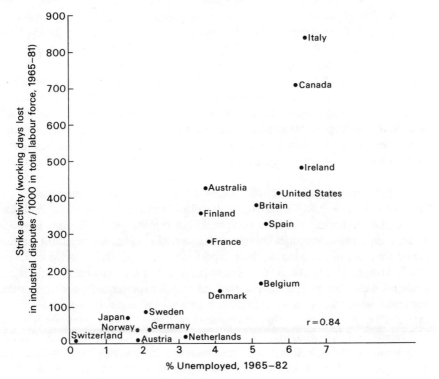

FIG. 7.4. *The relation between unemployment and strike activity in eighteen nations, 1965–82*

Figure 7.4 presents the relationship between the degree of strike activity and the average rate of unemployment in the eighteen nations during 1965–82. We observe a *very* strong relationship between the two (r = +.84).[18] The nations with relatively high levels of strike activity—nations such as Italy, Canada, Ireland, the United States, Britain, and Australia—all experienced relatively high levels of unemployment throughout the eighteen years after 1964. In contrast, the nations in which labour largely abstained from using the strike weapon in most years—Switzerland, Japan, Austria, Norway, Sweden, Germany, and the Netherlands—were the only ones in which the average rate of unemployment over the eighteen years did not exceed three per cent. In the former group—nations in which most workers were unorganized but in which those who were organized were militant in the sense of using the strike to push for wage increases—the organized segment of the labour movement struck frequently, in spite of the relatively high rate of unemployment. In striking, that segment promoted its short-term economic interests, but only at the cost of maintaining and accentuating the considerable wage differentials that already existed between organized and unorganized labour[19] and, more important, at the cost of jobs for other members of the labour force. In contributing to the acceleration in the rate of change in earnings and prices, that militant segment of labour gave employers an incentive to shed more labour by shifting production to lower-wage regions either within the nation or in other countries. In the latter group of nations, labour apparently traded economic militancy and large wage increases for near-full employment. It generally abstained from using its ultimate weapon in the distributional struggle with capital and, as a result, experienced relatively small increases in earnings (in spite of the existence of tight labour markets). But while organized labour may have forsaken the maximum possible short-term wage gains, the moderation in wages and the labour costs of firms may have provided sufficient profits to dampen the labour-shedding tendencies of employers, thereby contributing to the maintenance of a high level of employment.

We have now closed the circle linking the four aspects of economic performance, and Figure 7.5 demonstrates the close relation between the variations across the advanced capitalist nations in unemployment, inflation, wage increases, and strike activity. In recent decades, the advanced capitalist nations varied dramatically in each of these aspects of economic performance, but what is of particular interest is the extent to which performance in one aspect covaried with that in the others. Nations which experienced, relative to other nations, low levels of strike activity and modest increases—or decreases—in the rate of change in earnings also experienced relatively modest increases in prices *and* relatively full employment. In contrast, nations which experienced relatively high levels of strike activity and large increases in nominal (and real) earnings also experienced, simultaneously, relatively large increases in prices *and* relatively high levels of unemployment. Thus, distinct clusters of economic performance appear—one composed of Germany, Austria, Switzerland, the Netherlands,

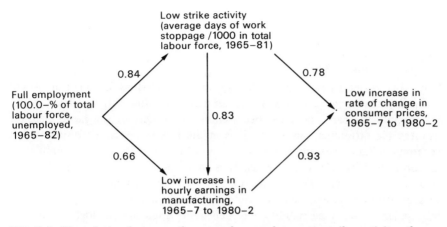

FIG. 7.5. *The relation between the rate of unemployment, strike activity, the increase in earnings, and the increase in prices in eighteen nations, 1965-82*

and Japan (and, to a lesser degree, Belgium, Denmark, Norway, and Sweden), the other composed of Italy, Ireland, Britain, Canada, the United States, and Australia (and, to a lesser degree, France, Spain, and Finland).

The relationships presented in Figures 7.4 and 7.5 suggest that the simultaneous occurrence of price stability and full employment in some nations, and inflation and unemployment in others, reflects a complex causal relationship between the two, in which the relative quiescence or economic militancy of labour plays a critical intermediary role. Where full employment is maintained, labour is relatively quiescent and thus earnings, and prices, increase at only a modest rate. Where labour is relatively militant, earnings and prices tend to increase at a rapid rate, thereby providing employers with a rationale for further increases in unemployment. In both cases, there exists an implicit trade-off between the *immediate* economic gains of *organized* workers and the *long-term* likelihood of jobs for *all* workers. In some countries, labour is economically militant and opts for the former; in others, labour is quiescent and opts for the latter—and in so doing enables those nations to experience relatively full employment *and* price stability.

Social Democracy, Corporatism, and Economic Performance

Having identified two clusters of nations that differed dramatically in economic performance after the 1960s, we now turn to an examination of the social and political bases of that variation in performance. Our concern will be twofold: first of all, to investigate the extent to which performance in the several related domains depends on the domination of government by leftist parties or the existence of corporatist institutions and practices (or both); secondly, to examine the extent to which the performance typified by one or the other of our two clusters—that is, labour quiescence or militancy in the economic realm—can be said to represent the economic interest of labour in capitalist society.

Leftist Parties in Government

Why have the advanced capitalist nations varied as much as they have in rates of unemployment, change in prices and earnings, and strike activity? Many plausible hypotheses can, and have been, enumerated. One of the more plausible involves the differences among nations in the interests that are represented in government (and that are, therefore, presumably influential in the formulation of public policy). The extensive analysis of economic policy by Kirschen and associates (1964: 224-9) suggested that the objectives of government in regard to such issues as growth, employment, the distribution of income, the balance of payments, and price stability vary depending upon the ideological centre of gravity of government. For example, the ranking of macroeconomic priorities—such as the relative preference for price stability, even at the cost of unemployment, or for full employment, even at the cost of inflation—depends, Kirschen *et al.* suggest, on whether government is controlled by (i) Social Democratic and Labour parties, (ii) Christian Democratic and other centrist parties, or (iii) Conservative parties. Recent studies of various aspects of economic policy by Tufte (1978), Cowart (1978), Hibbs (1977, 1978), and Korpi and Shalev (1979, 1980), among others, have—while concentrating almost exclusively on the distinction between leftist and non-leftist parties—generally supported the Kirschen argument. These studies suggest that cross-national differences in a variety of macroeconomic and fiscal policy domains such as inflation, employment, taxation, spending, and industrial relations depend, to some degree at least, on the extent of control of government by leftist parties or their opponents.

The most elaborate explanation of why differences among nations in the partisan composition of government—in particular, the control of government by leftist or by non-leftist parties—are associated with differences in policy is offered by Korpi and Shalev (1979, 1980). In their elaboration of a 'power resources' explanation of strike activity (1979: 170), they argue that the working class is more powerful, relative to capital, when its organizational power is maximized—that is, when there is:

an integrated labour movement with strong support among workers. This implies . . . a high density of unionization, industrially based unions unified by a strong union central, and close cooperation between this central confederation and a party that clearly dominates on the left and commands a sizeable proportion of the nation's electorate. Where these characteristics are present, the working class can be said to act as a 'class for itself'.[20]

Do the differences among nations in the several domains of economic performance and, in particular, in the degree of economic quiescence or militancy of organized labour reflect differences in the balance of power between workers and employers in advanced capitalist society? More precisely, does the magnitude of the *im*balance in power between capital and labour diminish dramatically when leftist parties govern? And does that change in the degree of imbalance of power between classes manifest itself in macroeconomic performance? To answer these questions, we have measured the extent of control of government between 1965 and 1982 by leftist parties, broadly defined to include Communist, Socialist, Social Democratic, and Labour parties, as well as several small parties that are to the left of centre on a Downsian (1957, ch. 8) ideological continuum.[21]

To accurately portray the strength of leftist parties in government we have created a measure that combines two distinct properties: (i) the extent to which leftist parties control government, as indicated by their control of portfolios in the cabinet; and (ii) the strength of governing leftist parties in parliament. By using the control of portfolios, rather than simply the presence in government, the actual strength of leftist parties relative to that of other (non-leftist) governing parties is taken into account. And by using the strength of governing leftist parties in parliament, we take into account the extent to which leftist governing parties enjoy a secure position in parliament, in contrast to the insecurity that must confront any minority government. The measure was calculated by obtaining the partisan composition of all governments in all nations over the eighteen years, calculating the proportion of cabinet seats held by each party for each month of each year, and taking an average of the proportion held by the leftist parties in each year. These data were then multiplied by the proportion of all seats in parliament held by the governing leftist parties divided by 50 per cent. The values for each year were then summed and divided by thirteen to yield an average measure of leftist party control of government.

Table 7.4 presents our measure of the extent of leftist control of government during 1965–82. Significant differences exist among the nations: leftist parties controlled government most frequently in Austria, Sweden, Britain, Germany, Denmark, and Norway. In all other nations, government was more frequently than not controlled by non-leftist parties. And in six nations—Japan, Spain, the United States, Canada, Italy, and Ireland—leftist parties either did not exist or held less than 10 per cent of the portfolios over the eighteen years between 1965 and 1982.[22]

Social Democracy and Economic Performance

To what extent does the variation in economic performance across the advanced capitalist nations—in particular, their propensity to display the macroeconomic products of labour quiescence, on one hand, or militancy, on the other—depend on the extent of control of government by leftist (or, conversely, non-leftist) parties? Table 7.5 presents the statistical relations between our measures of leftist control of government and the several aspects of economic performance.[23]

Every correlation coefficient in Table 7.5 between the measures of economic performance and leftist control is negative. They indicate that nations with frequent leftist governments tended to experience low unemployment and strike

TABLE 7.4. *The control of government by leftist parties, 1965–82*

% of cabinet portfolios held by leftist parties × % of minimum parliamentary majority held by leftist parties	
Austria	76
Sweden	65
Britain	63
Germany	55
Norway	53
Denmark	53
Finland	38
Australia	17
Belgium	16
Switzerland	15
Netherlands	13
France	10
Italy	7
Ireland	4
Spain	0
Japan	0
Canada	0
United States	0

Sources: Keesing's Contemporary Archives and Thomas Mackie and Richard Rose, *The International Almanac of Electoral History*, New York, 1982.

activity and modest increases in earnings and prices, relative to the levels and rates found in nations dominated by non-leftist governing parties. More precisely, nations in which leftist parties frequently controlled government after 1965 tended to experience, relative to nations dominated by non-leftist parties, *lower* average levels of unemployment over the entire period ($r = -.44$)[24] and relatively *smaller* increases in the rate of unemployment between the mid-1960s and the early 1980s ($r = -.24$).[25] In addition, the data in Table 7.5 indicate that nations in which leftist parties most frequently controlled government also had relatively *small* increases in the rate of change in nominal and real earnings ($r = -.28$ and $r = -.29$) and in consumer prices ($r = -.21$) and, in addition, relatively low levels of strike activity ($r = -.47$).

TABLE 7.5. *The relation between the extent of control of government by leftist parties and economic performance in eighteen nations, 1965–82*

	Unemployment		Strike Activity 1965–81	Increases in Rates of Change 1965–7 to 1980–2	
	Average 1965–82	Increase 1965–7 to 1980–2		Earnings, Nominal (Real)	Prices
Leftist Party Control of Government	−.44	−.24	−.47	−.28 (−.29)	−.21

The analysis in Table 7.5 indicates that nations in which leftist parties most frequently and most extensively controlled government tended to experience labour *quiescence* rather than militancy. That quiescence was reflected in an infrequent use of the strike and the acceptance of relatively modest increases in earnings (and thus in prices), in return, apparently, for the maintenance of relatively full employment. Nations dominated by non-leftist parties, in contrast, tended to experience labour *militancy* in collective bargaining, as reflected in frequent and large strikes and large increases in earnings (and prices), in spite of the existence of relatively high levels of unemployment.

Our finding that leftist governments are *more* likely than non-leftist governments to moderate the acceleration in price increases is surprising. Kirschen *et al.* (1964: 227) suggested that the primary economic priority of conservative governments is price stability, while that of leftist-controlled governments is full employment, with price stability being much less important. And using the Kirschen framework, Hibbs (1977) reached a similar conclusion—that is, that leftist-controlled governments are less averse than others to increases in prices. Accepting the inherent logic of the Phillips curve—that a trade-off exists between inflation and unemployment for the reasons noted earlier—Hibbs found a correlation of +.74 across twelve nations between the presence of leftist parties in government during 1945-69 and the average rate of inflation in 1960-9.[26] Although Hibbs (1979) later reported a more modest association (generally in the range of .3), after adding several nations and changing the measurement of the two variables in response to criticisms, the sign remained positive and the argument remained intact—that leftist parties are less averse to inflation than non-leftist parties and, when in government, are more likely to generate or tolerate inflation.

Plausible as the argument is that leftist-dominated governments tolerate higher levels of inflation than non-leftist governments, Table 7.5 suggests that it is simply wrong—or at least time-bound and true only for an era when inflation was not a significant macroeconomic problem for most nations.[27] Compared to governments dominated by other ideological *tendances*, then, governments dominated by leftist parties not only are more likely to preside over higher rates of employment but, also, are more likely to achieve that essential objective of conservative politics—price stability—by inducing labour to forsake the use of the strike as a weapon in collective bargaining and to restrain its increases in wages.[28]

If the relationship between leftist control and acceleration in the rate of change in prices differs in sign from that predicted by several scholars, those in Table 7.5 between the extent of leftist party government and unemployment are—while in the 'correct' direction—weaker than we might expect. Figure 7.6 arrays the average level of unemployment upon the measure of leftist party control of government. As expected, most of the nations in which leftist parties frequently governed—for example, Austria, Sweden, Norway, and Germany—had relatively low rates of unemployment while most of those in which leftist parties

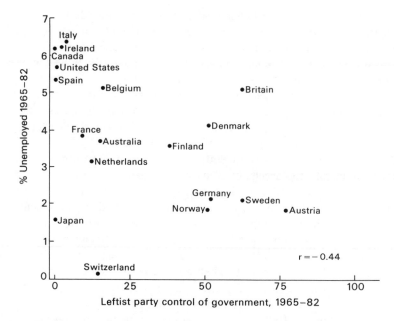

FIG. 7.6. *The relation between leftist party control of government and
unemployment, 1965–82*

(if they existed at all) governed infrequently or not at all—for example, Ireland,
Canada, the United States, Italy, and Spain—experienced the highest levels of
unemployment. However, Figure 7.6 also indicates that the relationship is not
nearly as strong as one might infer from Kirschen *et al.* (1964) and Hibbs's
(1977) initial analysis.[29] We observe several nations which deviate from the
expected relationship, most notably, Britain and Denmark, which have higher
rates of unemployment than we might expect given the frequency of leftist
control, and, conversely, Japan and Switzerland, which have much *lower* levels
of unemployment than might be anticipated on the basis of the partisanship
(and, presumably, macroeconomic priorities) of government.

Figure 7.7 presents the relationship between the extent of leftist control of
government and the increase in unemployment over the 1970s. This array reveals
that while leftist-controlled governments tended to preside over smaller increases
in unemployment than typically occurred under non-leftist-dominated governments, the relationship was hardly perfect. Some nations, such as Japan and
Switzerland, remained at full employment in spite of the weakness or exclusion
of leftist parties from government; others, however—in particular, Denmark and
Britain—experienced sharp increases in unemployment in the 1970s and 1980s in
spite of frequent control of government by the Social Democratic and Labour
parties.

The relationships described in Table 7.5 and Figures 7.6 and 7.7 suggest the
existence of a *statistical tendency* between the control of government by leftist

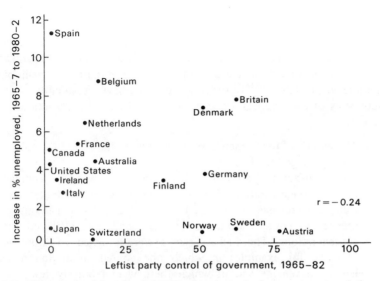

FIG. 7.7. *The relation between leftist party control of government and the increase in unemployment, 1965–82*

parties and the preservation of near-full employment over the long term and through an era of world economic crisis. But we have not found a relationship that is strong enough to warrant the inference that leftist control represents a *necessary and sufficient* condition for full employment and economic quiescence. Therefore, we must turn to other factors that may help to account for the cross-national variation in the several aspects of macroeconomic performance. It is to one of these—the organizational resources and power of the labour movement—that we now turn.

The Organizational Resources of Labour, Corporatism, and Social Democracy

Does the distinctive pattern of macroeconomic performance that tends to occur when leftist parties dominate government—high employment, relative price stability, and labour quiescence on the wage front—also occur in nations in which the labour movements possess distinctive characteristics? For example, does it tend to occur where the labour movements are relatively inclusive, in terms of membership, and relatively centralized, in terms of the number and bargaining powers of the confederations? Does the statistical relationship between that distinctive pattern of macroeconomic performance and government by leftist parties simply reflect the close relationship between governing leftist parties and labour movements that possess those characteristics? Should we therefore attribute the distinctive pattern of macroeconomic performance to the political influence of those relatively powerful labour movements rather than simply to the partisanship of government?

The notion of 'power' is notoriously illusory, imprecise, and difficult to specify; nevertheless, we have sought to determine whether the difference among nations in the extent of government by leftist parties, and in the pattern of macroeconomic performance, reflects important differences in the organizational strength of the major economic classes of advanced capitalist society—in particular, the strength of labour.[30] In order to do so, we have measured the following characteristics of the organization and locus of activity of each nation's labour movement.

(i) The extent of union membership, relative to the size of the total labour force, averaged for 1965 and 1980.

(ii) The organizational structure of the labour movement—specifically the unity or fragmentation of organized labour at the confederation level. Nations were assigned scores between 0 and 1.0 depending on the number of confederations and number of unions affiliated with the confederations. The highest scores were assigned to those nations (Austria, for example) in which one confederation dominated the labour movement and in which there were relatively few industrial unions. The lowest scores were assigned to those nations (such as France) in which a multiplicity of confederations organized wage-earners and in which there were numerous unions.

(iii) The power of labour confederations in collective bargaining. Nations were assigned values between 0 and 1.0 on a four-item scale depending on whether the confederation (a) consults with unions about wage negotiations prior to collective bargaining; (b) participates itself in collective bargaining; (c) possesses the right to veto negotiated settlements; and (d) controls the distribution of strike funds for unions, thereby effectively controlling the ability of unions to call strikes.

(iv) The scope of collective bargaining, ranging from restrictions on collective bargaining on the one hand to economy-wide bargaining on the other. Nations were assigned values between 0 and 1.0 on a seven-point scale that, in ascending order, moves from restricted collective bargaining (as in Spain in the Franco era), to highly decentralized company-level bargaining with company unions, to decentralized bargaining with national unions, to partially centralized bargaining with company and regional or multi-employer negotiations, to partial industry-wide bargaining, to full industry-wide bargaining, and finally to industry-wide bargaining with economy-wide formally negotiated agreements.

(v) The existence of schemes for worker participation in decision-making in enterprises on the plant floor and on company boards. Specifically, we distinguish between those nations which established some type of Works Council or comparable institution and *also* instituted schemes for the participation of employee representatives on company boards, and those which established neither form of worker representation.

(It is of interest to note that only those nations which implemented Works Councils—usually in the late 1940s—implemented the schemes for representation on boards—usually later in the early 1970s.) Nations which have legislated requirements for Works Councils (or comparable institutions such as *comités d'entreprise* and their equivalents) and representation on company supervisory boards are given a score of 1.0. Those which have only Works Councils (or equivalent bodies) receive a score of 0.5. In addition, several nations—Britain, Ireland, and Australia—are given a score of 0.3 to recognize the importance of shop stewards in articulating the grievances of workers within the enterprises.

Table 7.6 presents the scores for the eighteen nations on these five characteristics of the organization and locus of activity of labour. Figure 7.8 presents, in simplified form, several of the relationships among the characteristics of the labour movement identified here, as well as the relations between them and the measure of leftist party control of government.[31] The bivariate relations in

TABLE 7.6. *Structural attributes and* loci *of activity of labour movements in eighteen nations, 1965-80*

	Average % of Total Labour Force Unionized	Organiz-ational Unity of Labour	Confederation Power in Collective Bargaining	Scope of Collective Bargaining	Works Councils and Co-determination
Sweden	70	0.8	0.7	1.0	1.0
Norway	65	0.8	0.7	1.0	1.0
Belgium	55	0.6	0.6	0.8	0.5
Denmark	54	0.8	0.4	0.9	1.0
Austria	50	1.0	0.8	1.0	1.0
Finland	47	0.8	0.6	1.0	0.5
Britain	45	0.4	0.3	0.6	0.3
Italy	41	0.2	0.2	0.6	0.1
Australia	40	0.4	0.3	0.6	0.3
Ireland	32	0.4	0.4	0.9	0.3
Germany	32	0.8	0.2	0.6	1.0
Netherlands	28	0.6	0.6	0.8	1.0
Canada	27	0.4	0.0	0.4	0.0
France	24	0.2	0.0	0.5	0.3
Switzerland	24	0.6	0.4	0.8	0.3
United States	21	0.4	0.0	0.5	0.0
Japan	16	0.2	0.1	0.2	0.0
Spain	14	0.2	0.0	0.3	0.0

Sources: For union membership and the organizational unity of labour, the *Europa Yearbook*; for confederation power, Headey (1970), amended and supplemented; and for Works Councils etc., *The Annals*, May, 1977, Schregle (1976), Cordova (1982) and Diamant (1982). The scale of scope of collective bargaining is taken from Cameron (1978) and represents an elaboration of one originally devised by Hibbs (1976).

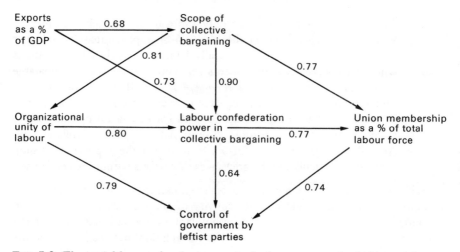

FIG. 7.8. *The social bases of enduring control of government by leftist parties, 1965–82*

Figure 7.8 demonstate the extent to which enduring or frequent dominance of government by leftist parties (or, if we were to reverse the signs of the co-efficients, by centrist and rightest parties taken together) rests on the inclusive-ness of unionization, the organizational unity of the labour movement, and the internal power, within the labour movement, of its central organizations.[32]

The schematic representation in Figure 7.8 of the close relationship between, on one hand, the inclusiveness of the labour movement, its organizational unity, and the power of confederations to control the negotiating positions of their affiliates and, on the other, the control of government by leftist parties suggests that when such parties govern, they do so as the political representatives of the organized wage-earners of society. And to the extent that government by leftist parties is founded upon a highly organized, unified labour movement (although, as France since 1981 demonstrates, this need not always be the case) we can perhaps say, with Korpi and Shalev (1979: 170), that government by leftist parties represents *political* (albeit not necessarily economic) control by the working class.

In order to demonstrate the close relationship between the domination of government by leftist parties and the several organizational attributes, we have combined the latter into a measure that better reflects the organizational power of labour. This measure involves the product of the average proportion of the labour force that is unionized in 1965 and 1980 and the sum of the measures of organizational unity and labour confederation power in collective bargaining. That is:

organizational power of labour = (organizational unity of labour + collective bargaining power of the labour confederation(s)) × per cent of labour force unionized.

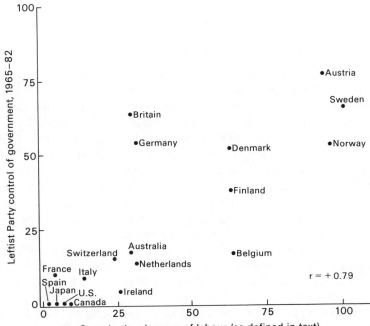

FIG. 7.9. *The relation between the organizational power of labour and leftist party control of government*

Figure 7.9 arrays the proportion of cabinet portfolios held by leftist parties during 1965–82 upon this measure of the organizational power of labour. We observe a very strong relationship between the two (r = +.79). In short, whether a nation's government is dominated, over the long run, by leftist or non-leftist parties depends very much on the organizational structure of the labour movement. Where the labour movement is highly inclusive in membership, highly unified in the sense of having a relatively small number of industry-wide unions, and capable of speaking with one voice in the sense of delegating considerable power to the confederation (as in Sweden, Norway, Austria, and, to a lesser degree, in Finland, Belgium, and Denmark), the parties linked to that movement are likely to control government most of the time (in spite of occasional losses of power as in Norway in 1965–71 and since 1981, and in Sweden in 1976–82).[33] Where the labour movement is less inclusive of all workers, where it is less unified, and/or where the confederations enjoy less power over their members, as is true (to varying degrees) in Britain, Germany, and the Netherlands, the Social Democratic (or Labour) party is less able to act as the party of the organized working class when in power (and, partly because of that, is more likely to suffer electoral erosion and loss of power). And where the labour movement includes only a small fraction of workers, suffers from numerous internal schisms, and lacks a single voice that can articulate its collective interest, the leftist parties—if they exist at all—are likely to enjoy at best only sporadic control of government.

It is worth noting that our composite indicator of the organizational power of labour closely resembles—both in content and in the nations to which it assigns the highest values—those used to define and identify corporatist polities. Thus, two of the characteristics included in the composite measure of the organizational power of labour—the organizational unity of the movement and the bargaining power of the central confederation—are virtually identical to those with which Schmitter (1981) measures 'societal corporatism' in fifteen nations.[34] What is intriguing, of course, is the fact that we have developed an indicator that is virtually identical to one used to define corporatism without using the term—instead, casting the discussion in terms of the organizational power of labour. The fact that identical concepts can be used to characterize labour's organizational strength or to identify corporatist polities suggests some of the conceptual difficulty associated with the latter term—in particular, the tendency to assign labels fraught with behavioural connotations (such as the implications of élite coalescence, co-optation, and participation in such wage-restraining acts as incomes policies) to structural attributes. Because the characteristics identified and examined here are simply aggregate indicators and say nothing whatsoever about whether corporatism—defined in terms of the coalescent, co-optive, and collaborationist behaviours of labour and business élites—has or has not occurred, we prefer to view them as representative only of the *structural preconditions* for behaviour that *may* (or may *not*) occur among labour élites and that alone warrants the label 'corporatist'. For that reason, we shall continue to speak of the organizational power of labour rather than of corporatism, although we shall ask the reader to keep in mind the near identity of the two in measurement and empirical reference.

To what extent do the differences across the advanced capitalist world in economic performance—and, in particular, in the propensity to opt for the macroeconomic by-products of labour militancy or quiescence—reflect differences in the organizational structure and locus of activity of labour? To what extent does the pattern of quiescence—that is, avoidance of high strike activity and acceptance of wage restraint—often found in nations governed by leftist parties for extended periods reflect the impact of those aspects of labour organization? And, while recognizing the close temporal and spatial relationship between Social Democracy and corporatist structural pre-conditions (if not actual behaviour), to what extent does labour quiescence depend more upon the organizational characteristics of the labour movement than the extent of government by leftist parties?

Table 7.7 presents the relations between the several aspects of economic performance and the measures of the structure and locus of activity of labour—and, for comparative purposes, the measure of leftist party control.[35] As was the case with the relations between the economic measures and the extent of leftist party control of government, virtually all the correlations in Table 7.7 are

TABLE 7.7. *The relation between the structural attributes and* loci *of activity of labour movements and economic performance*

	Unemployment 1965–82	Strike Activity 1965–81	Increases in Rate of Change 1965-7 to 1980-2 Earnings, Nominal (Real)	Prices
% of Total Labour Force Unionized	−.16	−.20	−.04 (−.27)	.01
Organizational Unity of Labour	−.52	−.59	−.52 (−.49)	−.42
Labour Confederation Power in Collective Bargaining	−.44	−.51	−.36 (−.46)	−.23
Scope of Collective Bargaining	−.29	−.34	−.12 (−.34)	.02
Works Councils & Codetermination	−.51	−.66	−.50 (−.58)	−.33
Organizational Power of Labour	−.40	−.47	−.35 (−.52)	−.18
Leftist Party Control of Government	−.44	−.47	−.28 (−.29)	−.21

negative—and some are very strong. Each of the several attributes of labour's organizational strength and locus of activity is associated with the pattern of labour quiescence. That is, nations in which there is a relatively high level of unionization; a single labour confederation composed of relatively few, industry-based unions; a considerable amount of collective bargaining power vested in the labour confederations; economy-wide bargaining between labour confederations and employer associations; and in which Works Councils and codetermination schemes exist tended, relative to other nations, to experience *low* levels of strike activity and unemployment and *small* increases in nominal and real earnings and prices.

Especially impressive in Table 7.7 are the strong relations between unemployment, strike activity, and increases in earnings and prices, on one hand, and the measures of the organizational unity of the labour movement, the power of labour confederations in collective bargaining, and the existence of schemes of worker representation and participation within enterprises, on the other. For example, we observe a very strong correlation between the existence of Works Councils and labour quiescence, defined as modest increases or decreases in nominal and real earnings (r = −.50 and r = −.58, respectively), and low strike activity (r = −.66). And we observe comparable correlations between the organizational unity of labour and wage restraint (r = −.52 for the increase in nominal earnings, r = −.49 for the increase in real earnings) and strike activity (r = −.59). These two aspects of labour organization—the second of which is central to most empirical measures of corporatism—are more closely related than are the measures of the scope of collective bargaining and the inclusiveness of unionization to all five aspects of economic performance. And they are *far* more closely related to the pattern of labour quiescence than is the measure of leftist party control. To a large extent, then, the existence of labour quiescence depends less on the class-compromising policies of Social Democratic governments than on certain characteristics of labour movements—characteristics that are most frequently found in the nations in which leftist parties frequently govern. Specifically, quiescence seems to be most likely to occur when only one major labour confederation (e.g. the Austrian ÖGB and the Norwegian LO) exists; or if more than one confederation exists, when the several differ only by occupation and thus each enjoy a monopoly position within one of the major segments of the labour force (e.g. the German DGB, DAG, and DB; the Swedish LO, TCO, and SACO). In either case, the confederations are composed of a relatively small number of unions which thus draw their membership from workers in one or more industries (e.g. metalworkers). In addition, quiescence seems to occur when Works Councils and codetermination schemes exist—both of which displace unions to some extent and institutionalize precisely the kind of 'class collaboration' associated with most notions of corporatism.[36] Conversely, the data in Table 7.7 suggest that economic *militancy* by labour, in the sense of high levels of strike activity and wage push—a militancy that was most evident in Italy, Britain, Canada, and Ireland—may derive less from the weakness (or non-existence) of Social Democracy and its frequent absence from government than from the organizational fragmentation of the labour movements, the multiplicity of confederations or the existence of single major confederations having very large numbers of affiliated unions organized by narrow craft and industry criteria, and, finally, the absence of any institutionalized form of participation in decision-making within firms.

Labour Quiescence and the Representation of Economic Interest

In this paper we have investigated the economic performance of the advanced capitalist nations in regard to employment, inflation, increases in earnings, and strike activity. Distinct clusters of economic performance were identified, one of which reflected a pattern of labour quiescence—in the sense of infrequent strike activity and wage restraint—and the other of which reflected a pattern of labour militance—in the sense of high strike activity and wage push. We examined whether labour's propensity to be quiescent or militant (in economic terms) was associated with the partisan control of government and certain attributes of the labour movement. We found that quiescence was, in fact, associated with both the control of government by Social Democratic parties and the existence of the structural pre-conditions of corporatism—especially the latter. That being the case, we can now turn to the issue posed initially. Do substantial differences exist among the advanced capitalist nations in the extent to which the interests of particular economic groups are represented—in the 'hard' sense of having their interests articulated, communicated, considered, *and* satisfied in actual performance? To what extent does an economic performance characterized by labour quiescence, on one hand, or militancy, on the other, 'represent' the interest of wage-earners in general? And, in particular, to what extent—if at all—does the pattern of labour quiescence associated with lengthy Social Democratic rule and corporatist structural pre-conditions (if not actual practices) represent the interests of labour? Does the apparent 'exchange' of economic militancy for near-full employment represent the best that can be obtained by labour in capitalist society? Or does it simply represent another manifestation of the subordination of labour and is it best conceived in terms similar to those used by Marx (1852, 1963: 50) in describing social democracy in nineteenth-century France?

The peculiar character of . . . Social-Democracy is epitomized in the fact that democratic-republican institutions are demanded as a means, not of doing away with two extremes, capital and wage labour, but of weakening their antagonism and transforming it into harmony. However different the means proposed for the attainment of this end may be, however much it may be trimmed with more or less revolutionary notions, the content remains the same. This content is the transformation of society in a democratic way, but a transformation within the bounds of the . . . bourgeoisie.

To a considerable extent, of course, these questions are unanswerable—or, more precisely, are best answered by recourse to ideology (hence the long-standing, and unresolved, schism noted earlier within the European Left). Nevertheless, it *is* possible to identify empirical evidence that pertains to the questions, and Table 7.8 presents some of that evidence. Table 7.8 presents the relationships, across the eighteen advanced capitalist nations, between two of the most important indicators of labour quiescence—a relatively small increase (or *de*crease) in the average rate of change of real earnings between the mid-1960s and early 1980s and a low level of strike activity—with several macroeconomic outcomes that can plausibly be assumed to be important to labour. These involve:

(i) The maintenance of relatively full employment throughout the years of economic crisis in the 1970s and early 1980s, as measured by the size of the increase in the percentage of the total labour force that was unemployed between 1965–7 and 1980–2 and the level of unemployment in 1980–2.

(ii) The attainment by labour of a high, and increasing, share of factor income relative to that received by capital, as measured by the average percentage of domestic factor income received by all employees in compensation during 1980–2 and by the increase in that proportion between 1965–6 and 1980–1.

(iii) The establishment of a relatively high 'social wage', as measured by the percentage of GDP represented by all Social Security benefits and

TABLE 7.8. *Labour quiescence and the benefits thereof*

	Small Increase in Real Earnings 1965–7 to 1980–2	Low Level of Strike Activity 1965–81
Employment		
Low Unemployment 1980–2	0.18	0.52
Small Increase in Unemployment, 1965–7 to 1980–2	0.10	0.21
Factor Income		
High % of Domestic Factor Income received by Employees 1980–1	0.05	0.15
Large Increase in Employees' Share of Domestic Factor Income 1965–7 to 1980–2	0.08	0.09
Social Spending		
High % of GDP accounted for by Social Security and Social Assistance, 1980–1	0.41	0.35
Large Increase in % GDP accounted for by Social Security and Social Assistance, 1965–7 to 1980–2	0.58	0.38
Total Government Spending		
High % GDP accounted for by Total Government Spending, 1980–1	0.53	0.18
Large Increase in % GDP accounted for by Total Government Spending 1965–7 to 1980–1	0.64	0.23

Source: OECD, *National Accounts, 1964–1981,* Paris, 1983.

Social Assistance grants during 1980–1 and by the increase in that percentage between 1965–6 and 1980–1.

(iv) The extent to which the consumption and distribution (if not the production) of the economic product of the society has been 'socialized', as measured by the percentage of GDP represented by all government spending during 1980–1 and by the increase in that percentage between 1965–6 and 1980–1.

The data in Table 7.8 indicate that labour quiescence was generally associated with the attainment of the various outcomes that might plausibly be assumed to provide workers with material benefit, although most of the relationships are quite modest. Labour quiescence *was* associated with a slightly smaller increase in unemployment after the mid-1960s (and it remained strongly associated with a low rate of unemployment in the early 1980s, as it was throughout the period). Thus nations in which the average rate of change in earnings increased by a relatively small amount (or decreased) between 1965-7 and 1980-2 experienced somewhat smaller increases in unemployment over that period than nations with large increases in earnings (r = .18). And nations with relatively low levels of strike activity tended to experience relatively small increases in unemployment between 1965-7 and 1980-2 (r = .21) and, perhaps most importantly, maintained relatively full employment throughout the economic crises of the 1970s and early 1980s (r = .52 between the low strike activity and low unemployment in 1980-2).

Labour quiescence was associated, also, with a somewhat higher proportion of domestic factor income received by employees in the early 1980s and a relatively large increase in labour's share of income between the mid-1960s and the early 1980s. However, the correlations are quite negligible and perhaps the most important conclusion to be drawn is that neither quiescence nor militancy over the long term has a great deal of impact on the distribution of income between capital and labour. Quiescence does not appear to produce any marked diminution of labour's share of income (contrary to what critics of wage restraint and 'corporatist collaboration' might suggest). And, conversely, militancy does not appear to produce any marked improvement in the labour's share of income (as such critics might imply).

While labour quiescence had little effect on the allocation of shares of income between labour and capital over the past two decades, it *was* associated quite strongly with a high, and expanding, 'social wage'. We find that the nations with the smallest increases in the average rate of change in real earnings were the ones in which government spent a relatively large share of GDP on social programmes during 1980-1 (r = .41) and in which that share increased by a relatively large amount between 1965-6 and 1980-1 (r = .58). In short, labour was compensated—to some degree at least—for its quiescence. Of course, much of this compensation for wage restraint may have been paid to persons who were not in the active labour force—e.g. the elderly, the long-term unemployed, the sick, etc. To that extent, labour—defined to include those who are actually working (and restraining their wage demands)—may in fact have received little *immediate* material compensation for its quiescence. On the other hand, since most individuals move back and forth between the two categories of active and inactive worker, it would be naïve to conclude that, in obtaining a 'social wage' consisting largely of insurance payments for temporary or permanent inability to work in return for wage moderation, labour did not benefit over the long term.

The analysis presented here suggests that labour exchanges wage militancy and, more generally, militancy in collective bargaining for employment. Important though the other material benefits are that we have described—e.g. increase in labour's share of factor income, expansion of the 'social wage'—the heart of the exchange involved employment. The essential *quid* for the *quo* of labour quiescence is full employment over an extended period. In a few of the advanced capitalist societies—most typically those in which leftist parties have dominated government and in which those leftist governments are supported by an inclusive, centralized, and powerful labour confederation—virtual full employment has been maintained in spite of global stagflation. All the attributes of labour's power—inclusiveness, an ability to speak with a single voice in collective bargaining, organizational coherence, a representational role within enterprises, and affiliation with leftist parties in government—do not constitute a fundamental transformation of the imbalance of power between the classes of capitalist society. And maintaining near-full employment hardly constitutes the first step in the transformation of a capitalist economy to socialism. Nevertheless, it is also true that where labour movements have possessed those attributes and where they have, with their allies in leftist governing parties, been able to maintain virtual full employment over the long term, wage-earners have at least been able to avoid the fate experienced in countries where labour is organizationally weak and leftist parties do not govern. Such 'power resources' have not transformed capitalism. But they *have* enabled labour, in Scharpf's words, 'to largely decouple employment opportunities from the development of the capitalist economy' (this volume: 267). That obviously has not produced, and has little prospect of producing, a transition to socialism. But, given the enormous costs of high unemployment, it is nevertheless a very significant achievement. To some, militancy may appear to be the best means of 'bringing capital to its knees', and quiescence may appear to be nothing more than a strategy of co-optation, collusion, and collaboration that only maintains labour's subordination to capital. Nevertheless, whatever gains are obtained by a militant labour movement may be neutralized by the perpetuation and creation of unemployment among the unorganized. And whatever immediate, short-term economic sacrifices are experienced by a quiescent labour movement may be more than fully compensated for by the knowledge that the state and employers are more likely to maintain full employment over the long term.

Acknowledgements

Earlier versions of this paper were presented at the Conference on 'Representation and the State: Problems of Governability and Legitimacy in Western European Democracies', Stanford University; and at the Seminar on 'The State and Capitalism', Harvard University. I wish to thank the participants of each for their many helpful comments—especially Peter Lange, Adam Przeworski, Fritz Scharpf, and Hans Weiler at Stanford, and Gösta Esping-Andersen, Peter Hall, George Ross, and John Stephens at Harvard. Also, I wish to thank Stefanie Cameron, Robert Dahl, Peter Katzenstein, and Susan Woodward for their comments and suggestions.

Notes

1. For a discussion that conveys the naive faith of that era in perpetual economic growth, see Shonfield (1965), who believed that 'the average rate of growth in the Western industrial world will continue to be higher than that of even the most prosperous periods before the Second World War' and that 'a major set-back of Western economic growth seems on balance unlikely' (pp. xiv–xv).

2. For discussions of the meaning of 'corporatism', see Schmitter and Lehmbruch (1979), Lehmbruch and Schmitter (1982), Panitch (1980), Marks (1983), Lange and Garrett (1983) and Lehmbruch (this volume).

3. There has, of course, been a great deal of disputation about the impact of party on policy in recent years. See, for example, Rose (1980) and Castles (1982).

4. Among the many works that are informative about the schism, see Schorske's (1955) outstanding treatment of the German SPD in the era between the Erfurt programme (1891) and World War I. On the British Labour Party, see Miliband (1961).

5. Schmitter ranks Austria, Norway, Denmark, Finland, Sweden, the Netherlands, and Belgium as the seven most 'societally corporatist' among a set of fifteen capitalist democracies. Korpi and Shalev (1980: 317) rank Sweden, Austria, Norway, Denmark, New Zealand, United Kingdom, and Belgium as the seven nations (among eighteen) with the highest degree of working class mobilization and most enduring Social Democratic control. On the intimate connection between corporatism and Social Democracy, see also Panitch (1981).

6. On the political consequences of small open economies, see Cameron (1978), Katzenstein (1983, 1984), and Schwerin (1980b, 1982).

7. There is, of course, a vast literature by economists on the inflationary experience of the advanced capitalist nations since the mid-1960s. For analyses that give primacy to the *political* and *social* sources of inflation, see Hirsch and Goldthorpe, eds. (1978) and Lindberg and Maier, eds. (1985).

8. It should be noted, of course, that most monetarists would dispute the view that there is any long-term trade-off between the two. See Friedman (1977).

9. We should note, however, that Germany represented a significant and unexplained deviation for Hibbs, having the third lowest rate of inflation in spite of having the *lowest* rate of unemployment during the 1960s.

10. Figure 7.1 employs a measure of the *increase* in the rate of change, rather than the average rate of change, because we believe the former to provide a better representation of the inflation process. On inflation as the *acceleration* in the rate of change in prices, see Friedman (1977).

11. The positive relationship described here between inflation and unemployment is also reported in Schmidt (1982b).

12. The fact that this cluster of nations includes not only Germany but several of its neighbours as well is not, of course, coincidental; the modest rate of inflation in Germany's smaller neighbours reflects the importance of international factors—in particular, the dampening impact on prices in the small European nations (e.g. Austria, Switzerland, Denmark, Belgium, and the Netherlands) which have explicitly linked their currencies to the Deutsche Mark and which have thus incorporated Germany's fiscal and monetary priorities—in particular, its aversion to inflation—via the impact of a strong currency on interest rates and trade. For discussions of this international effect, see Schwerin (1980b), Calmfors (1983), and Lindbeck, ed. (1979).

13. For discussion, see Calleo (1982), Cagan (1979), and Lindberg and Maier, eds. (1985) especially the paper by Keohane.

14. To ensure the greatest possible validity, the index for each year is the latest or last reported for that year.

15. The increases in nominal earnings do not reflect—as some might hypothesize—simply the maintenance of real income in the face of rising prices. Instead, the largest increases usually *exceed* the rate of increase in prices and thus cause an increase in real earnings. Thus, we observe a strong correlation ($r = + .70$) across the nations between the magnitude of the increase in the average rate of change in nominal earnings between 1965-7 and 1980-2 and that of 'real' earnings (i.e. the rate of change in nominal earnings minus the rate of change in prices).

16. Strike activity is defined as the total *volume* of strikes, defined as the product of the *frequency* of strikes (number of strikes per 1000 in the total labour force), the average *duration* of strikes (number of days of work lost per striker), and the *size* of strikes (number of strikers per strike). The product is the number of days lost per 1000 in the labour force. Korpi and Shalev (1979) argue that this measure aggregates three distinct components of strike activity (which is true) and they distinguish between *duration* (defined as it is here) and *strike involvement*, defined as the number of strikers per 1000 in the work force (that is, the product of *size* and *frequency*). While useful for some purposes, their measure suffers from the explicit exclusion of any differentiation between very long and very short strikes. Largely because they exclude duration they find, for example, that Japan has a *higher* level of strike activity than the United States, Canada, Britain, Belgium, and Ireland—all of which have much larger scores when one takes account not only of size and frequency but duration, too.

17. It is important to note, of course, that several of these nations experienced on occasion unusually large levels of strike activity—for example, in Germany in 1971 (166.6) and 1978 (163.3), in the Netherlands in 1973 (121.6), in Denmark in 1973 (1594.3), in Norway in 1974 (189.1), in Sweden in 1971 (211.8) and 1980 (1037.2), in Japan in 1971 (116.3), 1974 (182.0), and 1975 (150.6). (Parentheses contain strike volume for the year.) If those few years of abnormally high strike activity were eliminated from our measure (for example, by calculating the median rather than the mean), all of these—especially Denmark and Sweden—would receive lower values on the measure of strike activity.

18. Figure 7.4 suggests a curvilinear relationship and, in fact, we find a stronger relationship ($r = +.89$) when the rate of unemployment is correlated with the natural log of strike activity. We might note, also, that the relationship is far stronger than that reported in the only other study to systematically compare unemployment and strike activity; see Korpi and Shalev (1980), who report a correlation of .49 between unemployment in 1959–76 and strike involvement in 1949–76.

19. On segmentation within labour, see Piore (1979) and Gordon *et al.* (1982).

20. The reader will immediately note the extent to which this model is drawn from the Scandinavian—especially the Swedish—experience. The phrase 'class for itself' is, of course, from Marx's famous distinction between a class *an sich* and a class *für sich*. For a discussion of the importance of organization and consciousness in Marx's conception of class, see Miliband (1977, Chs. 2 and 5).

21. Kirschen *et al.* (1964) suggested a threefold distinction among parties, differentiating between centrist and Christian Democratic parties and other more conservative non-leftist parties. Few have used that original threefold distinction; one study that does is Cameron (1982). Castles (1982) has suggested that the rightest vs. leftist and centrist dichotomy produces slightly stronger correlations than the leftist vs. centrist and conservative distinction used by most scholars.

22. The measure does not distinguish between a situation in which a leftist party moves in and out of government—perhaps controlling all the portfolios when it governs (e.g. Britain)—and a situation in which it forms a long-lasting coalition with non-leftist parties (e.g. Germany). Obviously, that distinction may be consequential.

23. Because some of the cross-national variation in the increase in the rate of change in nominal earnings undoubtedly reflects differences in increases in the rate of change of prices—i.e. workers 'catching up' with inflation and attempting to maintain real income—the table also includes the measure of the increase in the rate of change in real earnings between 1965-7 and 1980-2—that is, the increase in the rate of change in nominal earnings minus the increase in the average rate of change in prices—in addition to the four aspects of economic performance discussed earlier.

24. The nations vary a great deal in the change in the absolute size of the labour force over the period. Canada, the United States, and Australia in particular experienced large increases in the work force, compared to negligible increases in Germany, Switzerland, and Austria. Some of the cross-national variation in unemployment rates undoubtedly reflects that considerable difference. Thus, we have repeated the analysis in Table 7.5 of the relation between the rate of unemployment and the control of government by leftist parties controlling for the change in the total labour force between 1965 and 1980. The relation with the measure of leftist strength remains moderately strong (Beta = $-.34$).

25. While the simple correlations are illuminating, it is of course true that each of the attributes of economic performance is influenced by factors other than the partisan control of government and a more sophisticated analysis would take those factors into account. We have regressed the increase in unemployment between 1965-7 and 1980-2 on the measure of government and a more sophisticated analysis would take those factors into account. We derive from the prior level of unemployment as well as the average rate of growth in real GDP during 1965-82. The standardized regression coefficient for the measure of leftist control is —.26.

26. If Hibbs had reported the regression coefficient, rather than the correlation co-efficient, however, the effect of a year, or even a decade, of leftist representation in govern-ment on inflation would have appeared extremely small.

27. It might be argued that our results are distorted by the inclusion of Spain, which experienced relatively large increases in the nominal earnings of workers (in excess of 20 per cent a year in 1974-9) after the termination of authoritarian rule with Franco's death in 1975 and the elimination of Franco's restraints on collective bargaining and strike activity. However, we find a correlation of only .03 between the number of years under authoritarian rule during 1965-81 (Spain = 1, others = 0) and the increase in the average rate of change in prices, and we have not felt it necessary to exclude Spain from the analysis.

28. An inverse association of about the magnitude reported here between leftist party control of government and inflation is also found by Schmidt (1982b) and by Lange and Garrett (1983).

29. Hibbs (1977: 1474) reports a correlation of r = —.68 between the percentage of the years during 1945-69 in which leftist parties were in the executive and the rate of un-employment in 1960-9. In a subsequent reanalysis for eleven nations, he reports corre-lations between —.27 and —.53, depending on the measure of partisanship. (1979: 188).

30. In speaking of strength, we are of course thinking in relative terms—specifically, the power of labour *relative* to that of capital. See Korpi and Shalev (1979, 1980).

31. Figure 7.8 also includes a measure of the openness of the economy, which is closely related to several of the labour movement characteristics (and which also serves as a surro-gate variable for size of nation). On the impact of openness, see Cameron (1978).

32. Figure 7.8 is not intended to indicate the *only* sources of leftist domination of government but, rather, the close relationship between the several characteristics of the labour movement and the domination of government by leftist parties. If our concern were the elaboration of all the reasons why leftist parties frequently control government in some nations and not others, several characteristics of the electoral system would have been added. For example, enduring leftist domination appears to depend (notwithstanding the victory of the French socialists in May-June 1981 and that of the Spanish socialists in October 1982) on the structure of the party system and, in particular, on the existence of a *single* major leftist party. Thus, we find a correlation of +.7 between the measure of leftist control and a dummy variable indicating whether a nation has a leftist party that gains at least 30 per cent of the vote and confronts no rival on the left that receives, on average, in excess of 10 per cent of the vote. This measure assigns values of 0 to nations that either have no leftist party (e.g. the US), have one that is electorally weak (e.g. Canada), or have two large parties on the Left (typically one that is Communist and another that is social demo-cratic) that compete against each other and are seldom, if ever, in alliance (e.g. Italy, Spain, Finland, Japan, and France prior to 1972 and in 1977-81).

33. We should note that all of the implied causal arrows in Figures 7.8 and 7.9 can be reversed. That is, enduring control of government by leftist parties has frequently had very significant consequences for labour in terms of strengthening its organizational resources—for example, by extending collective bargaining, mandating union recognition, facilitating centralization of power within federations, developing the practice of economy-wide bargaining, etc. It may well be the case that these effects of leftist governments in trans-forming the organizational resources of labour *after* coming to power are among their most consequential actions over the long term. For this reason, one of the most significant (and least noticed) aspects of government policy in France since May 1981 involves its legislation in the domain of labour relations i.e. the Auroux legislation.

34. Schmitter (1981: 293-4) combines the rankings of the fifteen nations on 'associ-

ational monopoly' (which is quite similar to our measure of organizational unity) and 'organizational centralization' (nearly identical to our measure of the power of labour confederations in collective bargaining). In his combined ranking, Austria is the most 'societally corporatist' nation, followed by Norway, Denmark, Sweden, and Finland, and then the Netherlands, Belgium and Germany. The least corporatist nations are Canada, Ireland, the United States, France, Britain, and Italy. For other rankings of nations according to the degree of corporatism, see Wilensky (1976) and Schmidt (1982b) and also Lehmbruch (this volume).

35. Logically, we would like to use regression analysis to compare the impact of leftism and the structural pre-conditions of corporatism (by comparing regression coefficients). Unfortunately, the very strong correlation between the two means that simultaneous inclusion would violate one of the fundamental assumptions of regression analysis. This would apply also if we were to include in the regression analysis the measures of leftist party control and organizational power of labour *and* an interaction term between the two, as Lange and Garrett (1983) suggest.

36. Seen from this perspective, the German experience ceases to be the unexplained deviation that it is in Hibbs's (1977) analysis of inflation and Korpi and Shalev's (1979; 1980) analysis of strike behaviour. In comparison with other nations, German labour was relatively quiescent, in the sense of abstaining from a high degree of strike activity and accepting modest wage increases, during most of the post-war period—not only after the SPD entered government in 1966 but prior to that as well, during the long period of Christian Democratic government. Most explanations of this pattern of quiescence give considerable weight to the role of Works Councils in German firms and, to a lesser degree, the existence of *Mitbestimmung*. For discussions of the German case, see Kerr (1957), Conrad (1981), von Beyme (1980), and Sturmthal (1983).

8

Social Policy as Class Politics in Post-War Capitalism: Scandinavia, Austria, and Germany

GÖSTA ESPING-ANDERSEN AND WALTER KORPI

Introduction

To be able to appreciate the role of political factors in the development of the welfare state during the post-war period, it is necessary to understand the contexts of power in which different actors evaluated their alternatives for action and in which they made their strategic choices. Underlying conflicts of interest need not necessarily have become manifested in political conflicts of the kind that can be easily grasped by quantitative indicators. Care is also required in the definition of the dependent variables, that is, the choice of policies that are to be studied. Here, the traditional focus by students of social policy on core programmes of social insurance and on social security expenditures becomes inadequate.[1] While social insurance programmes were unevenly developed in the capitalist democracies at the end of the Second World War and considerable conflicts emerged in their completion, other arenas of political strife have been equally or perhaps more important during the post-war years. Thus, one major source of conflict was the extension of political measures to influence distributive processes and outcomes in areas such as the labour and housing markets. That is, conflict arose over the extension of the boundaries of social policy. A more traditional arena of strife concerned the form of the institutions through which citizens become organized into the welfare state—institutions which contribute in significant ways to the definition of collective interests among citizens, and which thus influence collective action.

The role of politics in welfare state development is not of course something which first emerges in the post-war period. From the very beginning political factors have been central to social policy. Thus, the politicians who pioneered the introduction of social insurance in the 1880s, Otto von Bismarck in Germany and Eduard von Taaffe in the Habsburg empire, did not see themselves as reacting to factors such as demographic changes and increasing economic resources in their nations. Instead, taking warning from the Paris Commune, they consciously used state power to develop social policy as the second leg of a strategy to undercut the threat to the existing social order from the growing organizational strength of an emerging industrial working class; the first leg of the strategy was the use of repressive measures.

The approach to the *Arbeiterfrage* which these conservative politicians came to adopt was to a significant extent shaped by Catholic thinkers, such as von Ketteler and Hitze in Germany, Lichtenstein and Vogelsang in Austria. The Catholic *Soziallehre* combined a basic acceptance of capitalism with a criticism of its exploitative excesses in early industrialism. Farmers and urban petit-bourgeois groups just as much as workers were seen as suffering from the advances of industrialism. Therefore, the *Mittelstand* came to play a strategic role in Catholic reform strategy. The long-term task of social reform was seen as the creation within capitalist, industrial society of a new *Volksordnung* based on occupational communities or estates (*Berufsstände*), which would include employers as well as workers. The essentially corporatist nature of this type of solution to prevailing social ills was underlined by Catholic thinkers and became clearly expressed in the papal encyclical *Quadragesimo anno* of 1931. It was, in turn, manifested in institutional structures of social policy which divided wage-earners into different occupational groups and, in particular, separated manual workers from salaried employees. In this strategy the state was accorded a subsidiary role in support of the efforts of individuals, families, neighbourhoods and occupational groups (Messner, 1964).

Such conservative initiatives in Germany, Austria, and elsewhere met with resistance and counter-strategies from some privileged as well as from the under-privileged sectors of the new industrial society. Yet, with only a few exceptions, the welfare states of Western nations developed up to 1945 as a result of social policy imposed 'from above', where the working class was the *object* of the concerns and worries of the traditional ruling élites. As a result of improved capabilities for collective action during the first post-war decades, manifested for example, in significantly higher levels of unionization and leftist voting, the representatives of the working class increased their influence in legislatures and governments (cf. Korpi, 1983, ch. 3). This improved power position then enabled social democratic parties to become—in differing degrees—the *subjects* of welfare state development. But the alternative courses of action that were open to these parties depended not only on their relative power positions but also on the existing institutional structures of social policy that were the residues of the previous phase of development 'from above'.

As the result of bourgeois class politics before the Second World War, social policy had become instituted in very different ways across nations. Two broad approaches are readily distinguished.[2] In nations such as Germany and Austria where capitalism became established under neo-absolutist, statist auspices, an active social policy had emerged at an early date. It was explicitly designed to preserve stability and arrest socialism by granting rights independent of market participation. Social reforms pursued a corporatist,* status-segregated order

---

* *Editor's note:* As will be evident from the context, the term 'corporatist' is used here, and subsequently in this paper, in a sense quite different from that adopted by other contributors. The connection between the different usages is however indicated in Lehmbruch's paper, above.

designed to reward loyalty and traditional privilege, and to discourage wage-earner unification. The leading concern was to preserve pre-capitalist conceptions of organic social integration rather than to facilitate the free development of market relations.

This contrasts with the liberal bourgeois response that prevailed in the Anglo-Saxon and Scandinavian nations. The overriding objective here was to minimize state interference in private property rights, to block the emergence of distributional mechanisms outside the market, and thus to incarcerate labour in the market. The punitive poor law was the favoured response to the social question for classical liberalism, while reformist liberals looked to corporate welfare or contractual insurance schemes.

The working hypotheses of this paper are the following. Rather than the making of social policy during the post-war period being, as is often supposed, consensual and depoliticized, significant conflicts of interest between different collectivities or classes have been present. The extent to which these conflicts of interest have become manifest in political strife is influenced by the distribution of power resources among actors. The different collectivities or classes have had specific objectives in welfare policy and have developed more or less clearly conceived strategies to attain these objectives. In part, conflict over the welfare state has concerned the relative role which should be accorded to markets and to politics in distributive processes. Such conflict was centred not only on social insurance programmes but also on the extension of politics to other areas of distribution, that is, on the issue of the boundaries of social policy. Additionally, significant conflict has been concerned with the institutional structures of social policies. Besides economic and demographic factors, conflicting political efforts have thus also shaped welfare state development.

As a result of the opportunities afforded by the relatively similar occupational and class structures of the advanced capitalist democracies, as well as of cross-national diffusion, the opposed strategies of the Right and Left concerning the institutional development of social policy can be expected to be broadly similar across nations. Labour movements have tended to strive for institutional structures which unify as large sectors of the population as possible into the same institutional contexts, and the Right has favoured attempts to divide the population through the creation of separate programmes and institutions for different sectors and groups. The extent to which the labour movements in different countries have achieved their goals is here expected to be influenced not only by the strength of their power resources relative to those of their adversaries, but also by the extent to which pre-war bourgeois social policy had already created vested interests in occupationally segmented institutions—interests which are difficult to overcome.

We will here attempt to substantiate our hypotheses by case studies of the Scandinavian countries—especially Sweden—Austria and Germany. In terms of indicators of manifest conflict such as strikes and shifts in governments, these countries have been, over the post-war years, among the most 'peaceful' and stable in the world. If the development of social policy has generally been depoliticized and consensual, this pattern would be especially likely to emerge in our selection of countries. Before World War II, conservative class politics led to a strong institutionalization of corporatist social insurance programmes in Germany and Austria. This bourgeois heritage was much weaker in the Scandinavian countries. The nations we have chosen for study thus also vary considerably in terms of the distribution of power resources, our key independent variable.

We assume that the distribution of power resources between different collectivities or classes is an important baseline influencing the conditions for societal bargaining and conflict, that is, in setting the contexts in which strategic and tactical choices are made, as well as influencing the chances of their success. The consequences of the choices and strategies that are put into action will, in turn, feed back to and affect the distribution of power resources. In the industrial Western democracies, the two major types of power resources can be assumed to be, on the one hand, the ownership of capital, and on the other hand, the labour power and numbers of wage-earners. The effectiveness of these basic power resources can be increased through organizations for collective action, such as juristic persons, business organizations, political parties, and labour unions. To decrease the costs associated with the use of power resources, it is advantageous to invest resources in attempts to shape institutions for decision-making and for the regulation of the behaviour of citizens (Korpi, 1983: chs. 2–3). From this point of view, then, the institutional structures of social policy and of the welfare state generally emerge as significant targets for such investments.

In our perspective, the relative power position of labour in a capitalist democracy comes to depend on a multitude of factors affecting not only wage-earners but also employers, farmers, and other interest groups. However, for the postwar period, the level and type of political and union organization has probably been the single most significant source of cross-national variation in the power position of wage-earners.

The relative power position of wage-earners is probably more favourable in Sweden than in any of the other countries in question. The overwhelming majority of Swedish manual workers are organized, via industrial unions, into one strong and centralized union confederation (LO), which acts in close cooperation with a social democratic party (SAP) that has an undisputed position on the Left.[3] Salaried employees are also highly organized, and, again, primarily in the industrial type of union (TCO). However, largely as a response to union strength, employers and other business interests have in turn become highly organized; and furthermore, to a greater degree than in most other western nations, Swedish capital is in private hands and highly concentrated.

The Austrian labour movement shares many characteristics with the Swedish one. Both salaried employees and manual workers belong to one highly centralized union confederation (ÖGB). However, institutionalized religious and political cleavages exist in the form of fractions, and the membership ratio is significantly lower than in Sweden. The co-operation between the unions and the Socialist Party (SPÖ), which dominates on the Left, has been very close. However, in contrast with the divisions among the Scandinavian bourgeois parties, the Australian People's party (ÖVP) forms a coherent political force on the Right. While the Swedish Social Democrats have narrowly managed to dominate governments and have initiated policy development over a very long period, up to 1970 the Austrian socialists found themselves, at best, as the junior partner in coalition governments where the ÖVP effectively held veto power. On the other hand, the position of Austrian capital is relatively weak because of the large nationalized sector of the economy. Its most significant organizational representation comes through the statutory *Bundeskammer der gewerblichen Wirtschaft*, an arrangement which is unique among the OECD countries.

Finally, the German union movement is much weaker than its Scandinavian or Austrian counterparts in terms of membership ratios. It maintains a relatively close co-operation with the German Social Democratic party (SPD). Yet the party has been comparatively weak electorally and remained in opposition until 1966. The position of the Right in German national politics is strengthened by the dominance of the religiously based CDU-CSU coalition and by the marked strength of organized business interests (Zinn, 1978).

Social Democratic Strategy in Social Policy

The reformist socialist parties have always seen social policy as an integral and even central part of their political strategy. In this context the overriding principle has been to utilize political power as a means to substitute democratic distribution for market exchange; social rights for property rights (Heimann, 1980; Kalecki, 1972). This implies that social democracy recognizes no boundaries to social policy; that, given the power to do so, social rights would be extended progressively—for example, into such areas as housing and employment. A primary objective behind this strategy has been to weaken wage-earners' dependence on market forces, both to assure that consumption capacities could be socially guaranteed and to reduce the individual's degree of reliance on his or her own labour power. In this sense, social policy contains an effort to 'de-commodify' wage-earners. De-commodification can be defined in terms of the extent to which individuals and families can uphold a normal and socially acceptable standard of living regardless of their performance in the labour market. The degree of de-commodification is accordingly a function of the extent to which citizenship rights supplant market distribution.[4]

Both trade unions and socialist parties gradually came to the understanding that income maintenance schemes, social services, and other social policy programmes, which were initially organized via the unions or fraternal societies, would have to be universal and national in scope.[5] One important thrust in the direction of legislating social rights with universal coverage arose from the internal divisions within the working class. As the socialists learned during economic slumps, failure to come to the aid of the unorganized and those most desperately in need of immunization from market compulsion creates dualities and conflicts among workers (Esping-Andersen, 1984).

A second important strategic objective behind the social democratic goal of encompassing social-policy programmes was the necessity of avoiding splits between manual workers and salaried employees. The pursuit of this objective was combined with efforts to form broader class alliances, especially with farmers and urban petit-bourgeois groups. Social policy institutions that compartmentalized occupational groups, status categories, or classes would easily consolidate traditional lines of cleavage and even generate new, separate interests. This, in turn, would induce competition rather than nurture solidarity. A universalistic strategy should help to promote the mobilization of the largest possible number of citizens for collective action. Besides its egalitarian and redistributive intent, the broadly defined solidarity implied by universal social policy was explicitly a means for political mobilization and for increasing the chances of promoting a more far-reaching social transformation (Heimann, 1980; Jungen, 1931).

The equalization of social status, resources, and also burdens, through universalistic schemes, involves the socialization of financial obligations, the elimination of status differentials with respect to conditions and benefits, and attempts to divorce benefit distribution from initial inequalities or performance. Such de-corporatization or de-individuation of social welfare marks socialist party platforms across Western Europe; for example, under the banner of *Volksversicherung* in Austria and Germany, 'unification' in Italy, or 'peoples' pensions' in Scandinavia. Closely attached to the principle of universal and equal coverage in public programmes is the necessary fight to avoid private market alternatives to public schemes. This, as labour has come to experience in countries such as Denmark and Britain, may severely undercut popular loyalty to the public welfare system and introduce new invidious cleavages that are difficult to bridge.

The extension of parliamentary democracy and universal suffrage after World War I acted as a catalyst in the battle for de-commodification at the national level. The targets of the Social Democrats were surprisingly similar across nations. Typically, the first-order task was to reform, and hopefully marginalize, the traditionally punitive, means-tested relief programmes for the poor, replacing them with income maintenance entitlements across the entire range of social risk (cf. on Germany, Preller, 1949; Heimann, 1929, 1980; and on Scandinavia, Rasmussen, 1933; Esping-Andersen & Korpi, forthcoming). A precondition for de-commodification was not just the creation of rights, but also the strength of rights. With regard to social insurance, conflicts therefore came to be fought over the conditions for entitlement (such as waiting days, contribution requirements, employment experience and benefit duration) as well as over the scope and generosity of benefits. The pursuit of generous benefits was not a sign of frivolity, but a concerted effort to effectively shield wage-earners from the whip of the market place.[6] Strategically even more important was the right to work, guaranteed through policies to achieve full employment; this, in fact, became the most cherished goal of the reformist socialists. In contrast to the Liberals, Social Democrats argued that economic growth, labour productivity and economic efficiency increasingly *depend on* firm social rights and broad social services (Wigforss, 1932; Kuusi, 1964).

Using Titmuss's well-known typology (1974: 30-1; cf. Korpi, 1983: 188-92), we can say that socialist labour movements attempt to create 'institutional' welfare states, in which politics assumes as natural a place in the distributive processes as the market and the family. Bourgeois forces, in contrast, strive for 'marginal' types of social policies, where public policy is appropriate only when the market and the family fail in their natural role as providers for the individual.

Scandinavia: The Social Democratic Type of Welfare State

In contrast with Germany and Austria, where the institutional contours of welfare policy were established long before the First World War, the Scandinavian model is of recent origin.[7] Its implementation largely coincides with the political consolidation of social democracy between the 1930s and the first decades of the post-war period. At the onset of the Great Depression, social policy in the Scandinavian countries was exceptionally retarded. At that time, especially in Sweden and Norway, social expenditure levels fell below most Western countries, while Germany and Austria were international leaders. (See Table 8.1.)

TABLE 8.1. *Social security expenditure as a percentage of GDP in Scandinavia, Austria and Germany, 1933-77*

Year	Denmark	Norway	Sweden	Austria	Germany
1933	6.2	4.1	3.5	7.0	11.4
1950	7.5	4.6	8.8	10.1	11.7
1977	23.3	19.1	29.7	20.1	22.4

For sources for this and subsequent tables, see Appendix.

By the 1970s, however, the Scandinavian countries displayed some of the largest ratios of public, non-military collective consumption in the West, and led in terms of total social security expenditure. Their income distributions were also relatively egalitarian, but even more significant are the institutional characteristics of Scandinavian social policy. Thus, social policy has deliberately sought to make the need for public assistance peripheral, and to eradicate strictly insurance-type elements in income protection. One of social democracy's clearest objectives has been to establish a comprehensive network of income and consumption maintenance as an unrestricted and unconditional citizenship right. Another principle has been that social policy should strive to eliminate income and status differentials between welfare-state clientele and market participants. Since the 1950s, benefit levels have been pushed upward—in pensions through second-tier insurance—to match normal working incomes. Whether it be health care, education, social transfer payments, or social services, deliberate attempts were made to set the quality of public provision at levels sufficiently high to discourage private alternatives.

At the ideological level, Scandinavian social democracy came to defend the reformist 'social citizenship' strategy as constituting a preconditional stage for 'economic democracy'; it would equalize the distribution of social resources, raise the capacities of citizens, and create a broad social solidarity on which the long-run socialist project could be based. At the pragmatic level, the Social Democrats contradicted the edicts of classical liberalism by insisting that equality and social protection support efficiency; that the welfare state is a cornerstone for productivity and growth under conditions of full employment (Kuusi, 1964; Johansson, 1982). And at the strategic level, government welfare policy was designed to be in harmony with labour-market policy, union wage-bargaining practices, and government macroeconomic management. A defining characteristic of the Scandinavian welfare state model is, therefore, the absence of clear boundaries between social policy and other policy domains.[8]

In contrast with their counterparts elsewhere, the Scandinavian Social Democrats were in a position to forge cross-class alliances with the agrarian parties of independent farmers. The presence of distinct farmers' parties, a unique feature of the Scandinavian polities, helped bring about the social democratic breakthrough. Not only did the capacity for a 'red–green' alliance help the Social Democrats to escape from their isolation as urban working class parties, but it also weakened the bourgeois party bloc. And, since the inter-war Depression hit both farmers and workers very hard, a mutual pact between the two class parties was made possible. This political alliance permitted the Keynesian welfare state politics of the post-war era.

The Social Democrats, in Sweden especially, also profited from the absence of a strong bourgeois legacy in social policy. As a consequence, the labour movement's policy initiatives did not clash with historically institutionalized interests, and the party could therefore profit politically by spearheading long awaited reforms. This was clearly the case when, in the mid-1930s, the Swedish Social Democratic party (SAP) inaugurated deficit-financed anti-cyclical policies and employment creation schemes at market wages. Along with agrarian price supports, this was the political capital upon which social democracy could undertake its programme for a post-war reconstruction of capitalism. The SAP was able to exploit its post-war position of power and the terms of the 'historical compromise' of the 1930s to embark upon a full-blown welfare state strategy (Korpi 1978; ch. 4). Within a brief span of years, the old poor laws were transformed into non-punitive assistance schemes and the replacement levels of the universal peoples' pension were markedly increased. A system of universal child allowances replaced earlier tax deductions for children, a universal sickness insurance scheme was passed, and key institutional structures for labour-market and housing policy were established.

Social policy was framed, especially in Sweden and Norway, under the assumption of constant full employment. Indeed, precisely because its function was meant to be marginal, unemployment insurance in Sweden was, rather ironically, allowed to remain as a second-rate system of publicly subsidized, union-controlled funds with relatively meagre benefits. The emphasis was rather placed on moulding social policy to assure full employment and high productivity. The Swedish and other Scandinavian Social Democrats came to pioneer strong family allowance schemes and social services that would free women from the home and permit easier labour-market entry, but which would also have a sizeable income-redistributive effect. And the vast network of training, mobility, and employment programmes that evolved in Sweden with the expansion of the Labour Market Board in the late 1950s was designed to facilitate industrial restructuring, enhance productivity, and allow unions to engage in 'solidaristic' wage-bargaining without the need for a government-imposed incomes policy. But it was also a social policy aimed at establishing the wage-earners' rights to employment and job-training, and, equally important, at socializing the risk of lay-offs due to modernization. From the mid-1950s onward, the bourgeois parties also came to accept a political commitment to full employment.

That social welfare policy should bolster rather than stifle economic efficiency was an objective that had the commanding force of necessity. Post-war Swedish social democracy confronted the dilemma of how to achieve price stability and balanced growth with full employment. As in Britain, governments faced a possible scenario of endless stop-go policies coupled with mandatory wage controls or, alternatively, the risk of unemployment. But the Swedish labour movement further elaborated the logic of Keynes and Beveridge. With the active labour-market policy as the core component, numerous subsequent policy developments owed their design to the search for positive-sum solutions to the dilemmas of full employment capitalism. Centralized and solidaristic wage-bargaining went hand-in-hand with a strategy of facilitating industrial reorganization via manpower policy. In turn, wage pressures on companies were offset by their rather lenient fiscal treatment, with particular emphasis on support for industrial investment and expansion. Social policy came increasingly to act as a facilitator in this policy-mix. This logic permeated the educational reforms of the first post-war decades, the major pension reform of the late 1950s, and the housing policy of the 1960s.

As elsewhere, the inadequate levels of compensation afforded by flat-rate schemes compelled a pensions reform. Obviously, one alternative would have been to promote or permit private individual or occupational schemes to cater for additional needs, something which already had developed quite extensively among various groups of salaried employees. This, however, was difficult for the Social Democratic party to accept, for reasons of equality and wage-earner unity and solidarity. Contrary to social democratic objectives, it would reaffirm market dependencies, segmentation and stratification.

The other alternative, chosen in the three Scandinavian countries, but implemented only in Sweden and Norway, was a national system of earnings-related supplementary pensions. The two principal criteria involved were that coverage should be universal, granting identical status to all categories of wage-earners (with the possible inclusion of the self-employed as well), and that the huge amount of savings that would result from the funding of the system should be placed under public jurisdiction rather than in private hands. In the latter case, the aim was explicitly to strengthen the public steering of the credit market so as to establish greater collective assurance of investment behaviour. The main bourgeois alternative was to extend the individual or occupational pension schemes already in existence, and to keep their sizeable funds under private control. This strategy would have introduced a considerable degree of occupational segmentation into the Swedish welfare state.[9]

The politics of the Swedish pension reform were extraordinarily polarized, and involved a prolonged struggle. Opposition was mounted by all three bourgeois parties; the Conservatives, Liberals, and Agrarians—the latter armed with a proposal favouring farmers and small entrepreneurs. The pension issue generated both an advisory referendum and the first and only extraordinary parliamentary election in Sweden since the advent of universal suffrage. And then, in 1959, the legislation passed only because one member of the Liberal parliamentary group, a former manual worker, abstained from voting. However, after its implementation, both employers' organizations and the bourgeois parties—with considerable hesitation among the Conservatives—came to accept the new situation.

The pension reform itself prompted further extensions of the boundary between politics and markets, especially with regard to housing policy. Aside from general problems of scarce housing and high dwelling-costs in a rapidly urbanizing society, housing proved also to be a particular bottleneck for industrial expansion and manpower policy. The labour mobility required for economic restructuring came to depend on an adequate and affordable housing supply in growth areas. Under the rubric of the 'Million Programme', involving the construction of one million apartments over ten years, the Social Democrats used the pension fund capital in an attempt to drive the market out of the housing sector, favouring co-operative builders with credit at low interest rates for large-scale housing construction. Until government moved towards a greater reliance on market incentives in the 1970s, Swedish housing development was, by and large, part of the institutional expression of the principles of social citizenship.

Income and property equalization seems to be the Achilles' heel of social-democratic welfare politics. In Sweden, income inequalities decreased moderately during the first decade of the post-war period but thereafter remained relatively stable (Spånt, 1976). During the 1960s, the pressures for a new attack on inequalities impelled both the unions and the party into action. The trend toward central wage agreements with special commitments to lower-paid workers was associated with a substantial wage and income equalization during the 1970s (Åberg et al., 1984). But aside from wage policies, which to some extent decreased differentials also between workers and salaried employees, the decline in income inequality was the result of political measures to increase labour-force participation rates, improve pension benefits and enhance tax progressivity.

Yet, the very success of the wage-solidarity policy generated new incompatibilities as the logic of markets clashed with the principle of equality. Wage pressures in weak industries squeezed profits to the point of disinvestment; but in expanding sectors workers were under-selling their human capital and permitting 'super' profits. The strains created by this situation provided the main motivation for LO's proposals in the mid-1970s for collective wage-earner investment funds. Such funds would be financed by a combination of an increase in employers' social security contributions and a transfer of 'excess profits'. Their purpose was to buy shares in the larger industrial firms and, as a consequence, permit wage-earners—as collective shareholders—greater influence over the economy (Meidner et al., 1978). These new proposals provoked a curtailment of the tradition of co-operation between labour and capital that had marked Swedish class relations since the 'historical compromise'. In response to the proposals, the Swedish Employers' Confederation (SAF) launched an intense campaign designed to weaken the strength and cohesion of the labour movement. Their attacks focused on the centralization and unity of union organization since this was seen as the key to its power (Korpi, 1983: ch. 10). An opportunity to drive a wedge into the labour movement offered itself in the 1983 wage negotiations when tensions between workers in private industry and in public employment allowed the employers to break with the very same tradition of economy-wide agreements that they had themselves been instrumental in developing during the 1950s. Dominant sections among private sector employers now came to favour decentralized bargaining with larger wage differentials.

The six-year period of bourgeois party rule in Sweden, from 1976 to 1982, indicates that the social-citizenship state can become a significant social-democratic power resource. Rather than risk the political repercussions of even mild increases in unemployment, the bourgeois cabinets semi-nationalized the shipyards and the steel industry, fuelled inflation and raised the public debt. Subsidies to firms escalated as did expenditure on the active labour-market policy. During their last year of office, however, the bourgeois governments shifted course and proposed welfare-state roll-backs. Since 1982, the Liberal and Conservative parties, in concert with the SAF, have developed markedly neo-liberal plans for income-tested benefits, policy targeting, the privatization of social services, and a general retreat from the institutional type of welfare state.

With the return of a Social Democratic government in 1982, a limited version of the plan for wage-earner funds, implemented in 1984, introduced a new dimension in welfare policy. Its positive-sum element is that wage-restraint can obtain as long as wage-earners in turn receive a share of the resulting profits and greater influence in industry through the collective ownership of shares. The strategy is therefore to introduce a new set of citizen rights to collective capital ('economic citzenship') as a means of resolving the existing contradictions between social citizenship with full employment and economic growth. This strategy continues to draw an extremely determined opposition from the bourgeois parties and the employers, and its future is accordingly uncertain.

Austria: Social Democratic Power in a Conservative Welfare State

The context in which the Austrian labour movement found itself at the end of the Second World War differed greatly from the Scandinavian one, both in terms of historical traditions and power relationships.[10] The foundations of the Austrian welfare state had been laid in the 1880s—in a period of economic downswing—by the Taaffe government, a coalition against big industry which drew its support from clerical, feudal, and middle-class forces, as well as from the Slavic minorities within the Habsburg empire. The internally divided Austrian labour movement was significant only as a potential threat when Taaffe introduced sickness and accident insurance for industrial workers. These insurance programmes were to be financed by workers and employers, and jointly administered by them through self-governing bodies.

By the 1890s, the Conservatives had lost interest in the further development of workers' insurance, in part because social policy had failed to stifle the growth of the socialist labour movement. Instead, the Catholics within the Christian Social party, together with the Liberals, turned to a strategy designed to divide wage-earners, essentially by devising advantageous policies for salaried employees which were, however, withheld from workers. A first important step in this direction was the 1907 pension act for salaried employees in the private sector. The political overtones of this act are indicated by the fact that it coincided with the extension of universal and equal suffrage for men. Since the turn of the century, then, the labour movement has been the driving force in Austrian social-policy development (Talos, 1981: 75).

The Social Democrats became the largest party in the 1918 elections of the new democratic republic, and joined in a coalition government over the next two years. Within the broader context of the revolutions in both Russia and neighbouring Hungary and Bavaria, many of the reform proposals which the Social Democrats had struggled for in vain during the pre-war years, were now hurriedly rushed through the bureaucracies and parliament—in spite of adverse economic conditions. To the Austro-Marxists, social policy was an important means of persuading the working class that significant reforms were possible even within a capitalist state.

But by 1920 social policy had again stagnated and the employers launched a powerful campaign to roll back existing legislation. At the same time the bourgeois parties' *Mittelstand* strategy was given new life, especially in the direction of strengthening the principle that salaried employees were a category distinct from workers, enjoying a privileged relationship with their employers (Talos, 1981: 183). Thus, sickness insurance was introduced for the *Beamten* and improved for other salaried employees, their employers being now required to continue full wage payment during illness. In 1926, pension, sickness, and accident insurance for private-sector salaried employees was consolidated within a single legal framework. But meanwhile, pension insurance for workers was postponed. In fact, a workers' pension system was not introduced until 1939, when the German scheme was extended to Austria. The corporatist strategy of the bourgeois parties was continued through efforts to combine the various social insurance programmes into separate packages targeted for discrete occupational statuses, such as private salaried employees, public sector employees, industrial workers, and workers in agriculture and forestry.

The Austrian Social Democrats remained a strong oppositional force during the inter-war years. But the bourgeois parties managed successfully to confine them to the role of a strictly industrial working-class party. Thus, the Social Democrats were unable to penetrate electorally into categories such as the farmers and salaried employees. They tried, instead, to use their Vienna stronghold as a showcase of what socialist policies could achieve. But class conflicts intensified in the late 1920s. An authoritarian regime was established in 1933, and this was followed by the *Anschluss* to Nazi Germany in 1938.

The post-war occupation by the four allied powers posed a threat to the very existence of the Austrian nation. In the election of 1945, the ÖVP emerged as the strongest party, but a grand coalition with the Socialists and Communists was formed for the sake of national unity. Between 1949 and 1966, Austria was governed by a series of coalition governments between the ÖVP and the SPÖ, with the ÖVP in a dominant position. Informal institutions for consensual decision-making, and a system of proportional representation within the higher civil service for 'blacks' and 'reds', evolved gradually over the years. In addition, the traditional *Kammer* system of statutory representation of wage-earners, farmers, and employers in the legislative process was reintroduced. Between 1966 and 1970, the ÖVP ruled as a one-party government but this was followed by a succession of SPÖ one-party cabinets until 1982.

The SPÖ controlled the Ministry of Social Affairs in all the years of coalition government. As a consequence, the Socialists once more asserted their role as the motor of Austrian social-policy development.[11] In the aftermath of World War II, SPÖ's chief social policy goals were to abolish the corporatist organization of social insurance schemes, to place the benefits and rights of workers on a par with those that obtained for salaried employees, to enhance the position of workers within the self-governing social insurance institutions (which play a significant political and economic role) and, finally, to improve the benefit levels of social insurance. Throughout the era of coalition government, all social policy legislation was passed unanimously in the parliament. Yet, the Socialists encountered strong opposition from the ÖVP over most of their policy initiatives.

The first important clash erupted immediately after the war, when the process of 'Austrifying' social legislation from the Nazi era was undertaken. Already in its 1945 programme, the ÖGB demanded that social insurance for workers and salaried employees be equalized. The Ministry for Social Affairs, the SPÖ, and the *Arbeiterkammern* made proposals for the unification of the existing 58 social insurance bodies (44 of which were concerned with sickness insurance). In contrast, the ÖVP demanded further extensions of the corporatist basis of social insurance, and the dissolution of the integrated sickness insurance scheme for workers and salaried employees that German legislation had brought about. All in all, the ÖVP plan was for a total of 83 separate social insurance bodies.[12] The two parties also clashed over questions of financing and representation in the self-governing insurance institutions. The ÖVP demanded greater employer influence, while the SPÖ proposed an increase in the government's financial responsibilities.

Following two years of strained bargaining, a compromise on the *Sozial-versicherungsüberleitungsgesetz* was reached in 1949. The new law retained the existing system of sickness insurance, but halved the number of separate pension and accident insurance bodies. The ÖVP was relatively successful in defending its interests on the issues of financing and representation. A new unemployment insurance programme was also introduced in 1949. The Socialists demanded, as they had done already in 1920, that this scheme should also be made self-governing, but the old system of state administration was maintained.

Although their expectations probably were tempered by the powerful resistance they had met, the SPÖ and ÖGB continued to struggle for a major reorganization of the social insurance system. SPÖ programmes for 1947 and 1952 demanded an *Allegemeine Volksversicherung* (general peoples' insurance) that would include the self-employed and equalize the status of workers and salaried employees. In December 1950, the Socialist minister of social affairs, Karl Maisel, declared that the ministry had begun the task of realizing a comprehensive scheme that would include accident, sickness, old age, and invalidity insurance.[13] In the 1953 elections to the works' councils, the Socialists further proposed the introduction of a *Volkspension* (peoples' pension).

The ÖVP, however, continued its opposition to a restructuring of the social insurance system, while simultaneously attacking the status quo. In 1949, the party demanded the introduction of voluntary sickness insurance as well as the separation of workers and salaried employees within the existing sickness insurance schemes. In 1951, Maisel declared that the differences in party positions on social insurance were so great that no reform could be carried through.[14]

However, when the *Allgemeine Sozialversicherungsgesetz* (ASVG) was finally passed in 1955, it was the result of a classical Austrian *Junktim,* in which capital-market legislation, favourable to ÖVP interests, was traded against the new law. The ASVG formally brought the social insurance of all wage-earners within the same legislative framework but coverage remained largely unchanged. The pension system lost some of its insurance character, since pension levels were to be proportional to wages during the last five years of employment. Separate pension insurance schemes for workers and for salaried employees were however maintained, although their rules were made similar. The employers were able to strengthen their position to some extent on the self-governing boards. As an indirect consequence of the intense conflicts that had arisen, the goal of the SPÖ and ÖGB of a unified *Volksversicherung* was apparently abandoned.

The formation of the one-party SPÖ government after 1970 (with a parliamentary majority from 1971) led to a series of social policy reforms. The inegalitarian system of tax deductions for children was abolished; instead, the formerly miniscule child allowances were substantially increased. Against strong ÖVP opposition, the SPÖ passed the twenty-ninth amendment to the ASVG in 1972. This amendment decreased the amount of regressivity in social insurance contributions and equalized the contributions of workers and salaried employees. It simplified the organizational system by bringing down the number of sickness institutions from forty to twenty-nine. A statutory sickness and pensions insurance for trades people, with eventual universal coverage, was also introduced. After many futile attempts during the previous decades, the Socialist majority was finally able, in 1974, to pass legislation providing for wage continuation for workers during illness, thereby equalizing the conditions of workers and salaried employees in one key area of social protection. Finally in 1979 a measure was passed, against strong ÖVP opposition, which guaranteed workers the right to a lump sum from their employers if, for some reason, they had to quit employment—a right traditionally held by Austrian salaried employees.

During the phase of post-war reconstruction, the SPÖ and ÖGB were compelled to give economic growth priority over improved living standards. To combat inflation, they agreed to restrictive wage policies. While economic growth was rapid, both unemployment and inflation remained high, and workers' earnings trailed behind those of other groups in the labour force (Traxler, 1982: 178). Eventually, the restrictive policies generated splits within the SPÖ and, in 1950, provoked a massive wave of unofficial strikes, over which the Communists tried to establish control.[15] However, the protests failed.

In the early 1950s, the ÖVP responded to the inflation-unemployment dilemma with a package of restrictive monetary and fiscal policies and public expenditure cuts—which led to increased unemployment. This so-called *Raab-Kamitz Kurs* was vehemently attacked by the Socialists, who scored a victory in the 1953 elections. Within the inflationary context, the ÖGB had been demanding price controls to supplement wage restraint. These were finally instituted in 1957 in the form of the well-known *Paritätische Kommission für Lohn und Preisfragen*. As a result, the ÖGB obtained some influence over the determination of prices and, as a quid pro quo, the employers received improved guarantees that wage increases would conform to economic growth.[16]

However, the labour movement was unable to persuade the government to adopt an expansive, anti-cyclical budget policy until the recession of 1958–60. In 1961, the number of registered unemployed dropped, for the first time, below 3 per cent. Since then, this has constituted the Austrian full employment target, and has become generally accepted as a goal of the 'partnership' policy. During the period in which the ÖVP governed alone, a law to improve labour-market functioning was passed, but the pursuit of full employment has been chiefly through general economic and wages policies rather than through 'active' labour-market policy in the Scandinavian sense (cf. Scharpf, this volume). Compared to Sweden, as well as to countries such as Germany, the United States, and Britain, Austria continues to dedicate an insignificant proportion of its GNP to employment creation policies. To some extent, the large state-owned industries serve to cushion the impact of downswings and, in addition, the ÖGB has exercised an unusual degree of self-discipline in its wage demands. In contrast to the Swedish strategy of a solidaristic wages policy, the Austrian unions have refrained from pushing the lowest wages above what the least efficient firms in each branch of industry are capable of paying. The net result of these policies has been to decrease the wage-earners' share in the functional distribution of income. Since the global economic crisis of 1973–4, Austria is one of the few nations in which unemployment has remained low. But, in comparison with Sweden, the labour-force participation rate remains relatively modest and has not increased markedly, and Austria reduced its number of *Gastarbeiter* substantially after 1975.

Rent controls, public financing, and construction under co-operative arrangements have been quite dominant in housing policy since the war (Langer, 1982; BWS, 1981). But SPÖ's desire for a more concerted social housing programme was frustrated because of ÖVP's ability to insist that major policy decisions be delegated to regional authorities rather than the central government.

From the point of view of social policy, then, the great difference between Austrian and Swedish social democracy is that the former has lacked the power of initiative exercised by the latter over the past four decades. For the Austrian SPÖ, the price of full employment has been a sanctioning of the remnants of corporatist status segregation in the welfare state, unbroken guarantees of wage restraint, and, perhaps most significantly, the tolerance of high wage, income and property inequalities. Despite repeated programmatic promises to attack such inequalities, there is little to suggest that the SPÖ governments have achieved any major redistributive changes.[17] What scanty data exist, suggest mounting inequalities over most of the post-war period, resulting in one of the most inegalitarian overall income distributions in the West (Chaloupek & Ostleitner, 1982; Walterskirchen, 1979; Bundesministerium, 1982).

Germany: Subordinate Social Democracy and Delayed Realignment

Because of similarities in timing, and in the early influence of Conservative-Catholic reformism, the development of the welfare states of Germany and Austria show many parallels: for example, the persistence of corporatist occupational divisions and institutional fragmentation. However, in the reconstruction period after 1945, the German labour movement was considerably weaker than its Austrian counterpart. After the end of the Second World War, it took German capitalism barely ten years to reconstitute itself in the form of an extraordinarily concentrated economy, dominated by interlocked industrial and banking oligopolies (Lieberman, 1977). Faced with high unemployment and a constant supply of new manpower from the East, the trade unions stood relatively powerless against their adversaries. When the German Trade Union Confederation (DGB) was constituted in 1949, it unified both Christian and Socialist members along industrial lines. But alongside the DGB, there arose independent associations of salaried employees and civil servants. Except in select industrial branches, trade-union organization and power has remained low by both Austrian and Scandinavian standards.

The post-war party system obviously broke with the Weimar legacy but many connections remain (Loewenberg, 1978). Presenting itself as a non-ideological peoples' party, the CDU-CSU alliance brings together in denominational terms northern Protestants and southern Catholics, while in class terms it unites German business with the old middle classes, especially the farmers, and the salariat. This mobilizing capacity (with or without the help of the Liberals in the small FDP) tends then to force the SPD into political isolation—in the same way as the SPÖ—as the party of the urban workers.

With an electoral return only slightly inferior to that of CDU-CSU in the first post-war elections, the SPD chose the strategy of non-collaborative opposition; programmatically, it searched back to the Weimar past, calling for nationalization, economic controls, and a planned economy. Thus, the SPD let itself be cornered into a twenty-year period of exclusion from political power, and in consequence the institutional framework within which post-war class conflicts and negotiation took place was one largely created by bourgeois forces. The trade unions were forced to pin their hopes on the future full-employment dividend of economic growth, financed by low wages and high savings.[18]

The duality of the social base of the CDU-CSU alliance expresses itself in its social politics. The dominant neo-liberal wing, initially exemplified by Ludwig Erhard, has always stood for minimal public responsibility and has favoured a classical self-help approach that relies on individual thrift, market provision, private insurance, and a close approximation of benefits to market differentials. The Social-Christian wing, in part under the influence of Christian unionists, is much less enthusiastically wedded to the cash nexus. Its position, most clearly represented in the 1955 *Rothenfels Denkschrift*, implies a thoroughly corporatist reorganization of social security, in which welfare-state responsibilities would be transferred to occupational bodies. As with Austrian Social-Catholicism, government's primary task is seen as that of increasing the capacity of intermediary associations and of the family to protect themselves. The ideal is an organic but paternalist integration of workers and employers (Hockerts, 1981: 327; Messner, 1964). To a large extent, an ideological synthesis of the two strands of neo-liberalism and social-catholicism found concrete political expression in the social legislation of the period of CDU-CSU hegemony, from 1945 to 1965.

Until the 1959 Bad Godesberg programme and SPD's electoral realignment, the Social Democrats' main strategy was to attack the CDU with its conventional package of policy alternatives. Thereafter, the SPD advocated a typical mix of welfare state improvements and Keynesian-style management of the private economy, but in neither respect did it exert real influence until after the mid-1960s. A Social Democratic plan for social policy crystallized during the early 1950s and took shape with the 1957 *Sozialplan*.[19] It was premissed on the principle that social security must be linked to full employment, and that the latter is only possible with the former (Hockerts, 1981: 324). It proposed a universal pension system with a guaranteed, uniform and non-contributory first tier, coupled with an earnings-graduated contributory second tier—a system that is essentially the same as the Swedish one. The plan stressed the necessity of strong and comprehensive social rights to 'basic life-chances in health, work and human dignity' (Rimlinger, 1971: 158). It permitted benefit differentiation, but insisted on strong redistribution and a guaranteed floor.

As in Austria, the Social Democrats have fought hard for the elimination of occupational segregation and for the equalization of the status of workers and salaried employees. These principles and demands were repeated and additionally stressed in the later SPD plan for 'Peoples' Insurance', drafted by Schellenberg in the 1960s (Bartholomäi, 1977: 162 ff.). But, to a degree not found among the Austrian socialists, both the SPD and the DGB have emphasized active manpower policies, co-determination, and also social housing.

At the end of the war, the system of social security in Germany, as in Austria, was in need of de-nazification and major overhaul.[20] As the immediate problems of the massive influx of refugees and of political stabilization were gradually resolved, the question of reform began to take on greater importance. The crisis in housing compelled a major public commitment, and, after 1949, the government promoted massive construction with huge grants, loans and subsidies to private builders. The 1952 *Bauspargesetz* introduced public grants to supplement private savings for housing. But as the worst of the housing crisis was overcome, the CDU took the opportunity to gradually roll back public action in favour of private initiative. Against fierce but ineffective SPD opposition, the last steps towards complete privatization were taken in 1960; regulations and controls were lifted, the old law on tenant protection was abolished except for certain localities, and housing was thus restored as a market commodity. A means-tested rent allowance was introduced for the poor (Alber, 1980).

A political debate over the glaring inadequacies of existing pensions, and the pressures brought to bear by the proposals from the SPD and the DGB for a two-tier peoples' pension, made the CDU initiate a pension reform in 1957. Initially, CDU's neo-liberal wing proposed to scale down existing public insurance schemes (by lowering the income ceiling for compulsory contributions) and instead to encourage private pensions for the majority of wage-earners. The abolition of public subsidies to workers insurance was also suggested. However, under pressure from Catholic unionists and the Social Christian wing, such neo-liberal elements became only marginal to the wage-indexed scheme that was eventually advanced.

Adenauer saw wage-indexed pensions as a powerful electoral asset against the SPD, and also as a show-piece of West German achievement to set against East Germany (Zöllner, 1982: 65).[21] With wage-indexation and assuming fifty years of contribution, the aim was to arrive at a 75 per cent pension replacement rate (Hauck, 1981: 23). This implied sharply increased contributions and a reaffirmation of the link between past performance and future reward. The reform was designed to ensure the preservation of status, and to strengthen the insurance principle by widening differentials among beneficiaries.[22]

As a result of cumulating demands for improvement, and the rising power of the SPD and the unions, sharp political conflicts erupted in several other areas of social policy during the late 1950s and early 1960s. The most divisive of these concerned sickness insurance, where the DGB asserted its demand for full wage compensation for manual workers. The CDU, in alliance with employers' organizations, proposed cost-sharing for the entire health sector. In the event, the CDU was forced to back down in the face of insistent SPD and DGB opposition (Immergut, 1984; Muhr, 1977: 481).

The period of the Grand Coalition between CDU and SPD, from 1966 to 1969, marks a watershed in post-war German politics. A combination of structural forces and the onset of a recession weakened the CDU's grip on the German political economy, and with its post-Bad Godesberg profile and under Willy Brandt's leadership the SPD made substantial electoral gains which brought it a share in power.

The first reactions to the recession that began in 1966 were not auspicious. Budget cutbacks and reduced public subsidies to pension insurance provoked tensions within the coalition. Still, in both economic and social policy the first steps towards a social-democratic programme were taken. Erhard's neo-liberalism was shelved in favour of Keynesian counter-cyclical policies, and 'concerted action' marked a step towards a settlement on incomes between unions, employers and the government. In social policy, the SPD came closer to one of its chief aims when, in 1967, pension schemes for workers and salaried employees were financially co-ordinated and the ceiling for compulsory insurance was lifted. However, the avalanche of social-democratic reforms came only after 1969, when the SPD governed with FDP support.

Two objectives to which the SPD had given high priority were immediately achieved. The job promotion act of 1969 committed the government to an active manpower policy very similar to the Swedish one, and workers were guaranteed the same status as salaried employees as regards full wage continuation during sickness. In addition, as a complement to the active labour-market programme, the SPD took the first steps toward a regional investment policy.

With the SPD in power, widespread hopes were attached to the introduction of universal social insurance, advances in industrial co-determination, educational reform, and the reintroduction of a social housing policy. The first target was pensions, where the SPD wanted to extend the principles of peoples' insurance by fully equalizing the burden of finance, by consolidating and harmonizing various existing schemes, and by abolishing the remaining corporatist vestiges. However, in the face of massive resistance from the CDU, the employers, and private insurance companies, the SPD's goal of a major reform resulted only in a compromise in 1972 (Muhr, 1977: 482). The SPD won the battle for a basic guaranteed pension, but, as in Austria, the socialists could not abolish occupational segregation. In the case of sickness insurance, the SPD extended coverage to farmers and the self-employed. And in housing policy, they managed to reintroduce tenant protection and to augment housing allowances, but were relatively unsuccessful in reversing the CDU's liberalization of the housing market.[23] One of the labour movement's few victories in the later years of the SPD's period of office was the tumultuous passage of an anti-trust bill and the new codetermination law of 1976.

The ambitions that marked the beginning of the Social Democratic era were, then, more often than not frustrated, and after the mid-1970s, the SPD was increasingly forced to administer self-negating policies. It made no further headway toward the goal of government economic steering, proposed under the rubric of *Globalsteuerung*. In response to stagflation after 1973-4, the Bundesbank effectively enforced compliance with a tight monetary policy and high interest rates (Medley, 1981) and, as the rate of unemployment began to rise, the active labour-market programme was allowed to erode.

Furthermore, as the interaction of demographic pressures and economic stagnation began to strain insurance finances, the SPD was again forced to roll back earlier achievements. In 1977, health expenditures were cut and pension adjustments were delayed. Still harsher measures were invoked in 1978 when contribution rates were raised, sickness benefits reduced for the aged, and pension indexing once again delayed.[24] At the same time, the government's failure to maintain the active labour-market programme, combined with its restrictive fiscal and monetary policies, helped to push unemployment rates to high levels, despite the export of hundreds of thousands of foreign workers.

Finally, it should be noted that, as in Austria, the boundaries of social-democratic choice were drawn in such a way as to bar any major redistributive advances. The heavy reliance on direct employee contributions to the financing of social insurance, coupled with the highly income-differentiated benefit structure, severely restricted the possibilities for redistribution via welfare policies. Neither wage differentials nor fiscal incidence were, or are, as inegalitarian as in

Austria, and clearly some of the SPD's reforms—such as the guaranteed minimum pension and various allowance schemes—have had a certain equalizing effect. But the CDU's preference for a system of income distribution that reflects the market rather than politics has essentially been upheld.

Comparative Welfare State Characteristics

In comparing the extent to which the labour movements in Scandinavia, Austria and Germany have been able to achieve their social policy objectives we can use different types of indicators. Of central relevance is the degree to which social rights have become institutionalized. This can be captured by showing the extent to which the role of the traditional kind of means-tested poor relief or social assistance schemes becomes marginal. In 1950, expenditures on individually means-tested social programmes in relation to total social security expenditure was sizeable in all of our countries. By the mid-1970s, this ratio had decreased markedly across the board, but more drastically so in Scandinavia than in Germany. (See Table 8.2.)

TABLE 8.2. *Selected welfare state characteristics in Scandinavia, Austria and Germany during the post-war period*[a]

Indicator	Years	Denmark	Norway	Sweden	Austria	Germany
Means tested social assistance expenditure as a percentage of total social security expenditure	1950	13.2	11.0	11.8	10.1	15.4
	1974–5	1.0	2.1	1.0	2.8	4.9
Private pension expenditure as a percentage of public pension expenditure	ca 1975	32	2	9	3	5
Individual social security contributions as a percentage of total social security revenue	1950	13.0	29.0	10.0	26.0	21.0
	1977	3.0	30.0	2.0	32.0	38.0
Fiscal redistribution	1978	17.0	16.5	23.5	9.0	13.0
Unemployment as a percentage of total labour force	1950–9	(4.5)	(2.0)	(1.8)	(3.9)	(5.0)
	1967–73	(1.0)	1.7	2.2	1.5	1.0
	1974–83	(7.4)	2.1	2.2	2.3	4.5
Labour-market expenditure as a percentage of GDP	1975–8	1.4	0.6	1.6	0.0	0.6

[a] For explanations of indicators, see Appendix and text.

The relative importance of markets as opposed to politics in the determination of the distribution of welfare can be captured by showing the mix of public versus private provision. Since they constitute such a huge share of social security costs, pensions offer a good starting-point for comparisons in this respect. Table 8.2 presents estimates of the ratio of expenditure on private, occupational-type pensions to total public expenditure on pensions in our five countries (individual life-insurance plans have been omitted from the analysis). The figures indicate that private occupational pensions are rather insignificant in Germany, Austria, and Norway. They play a modest role in Sweden, something which reflects the legacy of collectively bargained pensions for salaried employees and the subsequent attempts of manual workers to obtain parallel arrangements. But Denmark is clearly the case where markets are allowed to play a central distributive role. The large ratio of expenditure on private pensions here testifies to the Social Democrats' frustrated efforts to legislate a second-tier system of the Swedish type, and to the bourgeois parties' victory in nurturing market solutions.

Contemporary social insurance programmes are nowhere strictly actuarial. Yet considerable differences can be found in the extent to which the financial burdens of social insurance fall upon individuals through often regressive social security contributions, or conversely in the degree to which they are more widely shared through taxation or employers' contributions. In Table 8.2 we see that Sweden and Denmark relied only marginally on individual contributions in 1950 and that by the late 1970s this share had become insignificant. In Norway, Austria, and Germany, however, there has been a heavy reliance on individual contributions throughout the post-war period, and in Germany this reliance has even increased.

Another relevant variable is the extent of progressivity in the combined system of income taxes and social security contributions. Let us look at the percentage of gross income paid in these two ways by families with one working spouse and two dependent children, and then measure the degree of progressiveness by taking the difference between the percentages paid by those earning the wage of an average production worker and those with twice the average production worker's wage. Measured in this way, 'fiscal redistribution' can be seen from Table 8.2 to be highest in Sweden and lowest in Germany and Austria.

For the period 1967–73, immediately before the onset of the international economic crisis, all our countries had low levels of unemployment. In the period immediately after World War II and throughout the 1950s, however, Germany, Denmark, and Austria experienced relatively high unemployment rates. During the years of the economic crises from 1974 to 1983, unemployment rates remained low in Sweden, Austria, and Norway, but in Denmark and Germany they have escalated. Table 8.2 shows that in the late 1970s expenditure on labour-market programmes were insignificant in Austria, considerable in Norway and Germany, but very large in Sweden and Denmark. The overwhelming share of the Danish labour-market expenditure, however, is used to finance unemployment insurance, whereas most Swedish expenditure goes on active labour-market policies (Esping-Andersen & Korpi, forthcoming).

How far have the major social insurance programmes of the post-war period succeeded institutionalizing the rights of citizens to income security? This can be captured by examining the extent of coverage by these programmes of relevant population groups, by the number of waiting days, and by the duration and levels of earnings replacement. For Sweden, Austria, and Germany in 1950 and in 1980, we find that as far as work-accident and unemployment insurance are concerned, the degree of coverage (of the labour force and of employees, respectively) has become near universal (see Table 8.3). The pensions and sickness insurance systems, however, exclude considerable proportions of the working-age population in Austria and, especially, in Germany; whereas in Sweden these systems have also achieved near universal coverage. Waiting days have largely disappeared for sickness, work-accident, and unemployment

TABLE 8.3. *Coverage of relevant population groups, waiting days, durations and earnings replacement levels, in the four main social insurance programmes in Sweden, Austria and Germany in 1950 and 1980*[a]

	Old Age Pensions		Sickness Cash Benefits		Work Accident Cash Benefits		Unemployment Insurance	
	1950	1980	1950	1980	1950	1980	1950	1980
SWEDEN								
Coverage	100	100	66	87	73	100	45	100
Waiting Days	–	–	3	0	0	0	6	5
Duration (weeks)	–	–	104	∞	∞	∞	30	60
Earnings Replacement:								
Single person	18	82	18	90	79	90	37	67
Couple[b]	28	82	21	90	88	90	57	67
AUSTRIA								
Coverage	42	65	42	58	57	90	72	87
Waiting Days	–	–	3	0	3	0	7	0
Duration (weeks)[c]	–	–	26	26	26	26	30	30
			(52)	(78)	(52)	(78)		
Earnings Replacement:								
Single person	67[d]	57	50	65	50	72	34	41
Couple[b]	67[d]	57	50	79	50	83	50	50
GERMANY								
Coverage	48	59	39	50	92	100	72	92
Waiting Days	–	–	3	1	3	0	7	0
Duration (weeks)	–	–	26	78	26	78	13	52
Earnings Replacement:								
Single person	33	39	39	85	50	85	23	78
Couple[b]	33	39	39	85	50	85	32	84

[a] For explanations of indicators, see Appendix.
[b] Assumed, where relevant, to have two dependent children.
[c] As indicated, the statutory minimum duration of Austrian sickness and work accident cash benefits has remained at 26 weeks. Many insurance funds have, however, extended the duration of these benefits up to a maximum number of weeks shown in parentheses.
[d] 1960.

insurance—the exception being Swedish unemployment insurance, which in this respect remains a second-rate programme. Durations for sickness and work-accident benefits are still limited in Austria and Germany, while such limits have been abolished in Sweden. The duration of unemployment insurance is particularly short in Austria.

To find a meaningful base for comparing earnings replacement levels across countries and over time, we can relate benefit levels to the wages of an average production worker in manufacturing. The expected pension of a worker with thirty-five years of contribution in 1950 was from about a fifth to a third of contemporary worker earnings in Sweden and Germany. In 1960 the replacement level of the ASVG pensions in Austria was about two-thirds of the average production worker's wage, a level which has slipped considerably during the 1970s. In 1980, pension levels remain low in Germany, while in Sweden they approach average worker earnings.[25] In 1950, sickness cash benefits were much lower in Sweden than in the two other countries, but they now also approach average worker wages, while in Austria and Germany the level of improvement has been less dramatic. Sweden had the most favourable work accident scheme in 1950 but, since then, work accident insurance has become co-ordinated with sickness insurance in all three nations. Finally, unemployment benefits have improved most significantly in Germany and only modestly in Sweden, while in the Austrian case they have remained at a stable, but low, level of earnings replacement.

Conclusions

In almost all Western nations, post-war welfare-state developments mark a sharp break with the past, not just with regard to social expenditure and consumption, but also in terms of the underlying principle of social rights to income and welfare independently of the market. A universal feature is therefore some transfer of distributive conflicts from the market into politics. But the degree of transformation varies greatly among the advanced nations. In fact, there is no evidence of convergence, but rather substantial indications that differences are greater today than they were thirty or fifty years ago. The absence of convergence would appear to be especially pronounced in those aspects of welfare-state development that are especially difficult to reconcile with capitalism, such as the promotion of full employment, collective consumption and 'de-commodification'.

Cross-national comparisons indicate that the balance of political power is closely related to the extent to which the boundaries of social citizenship have been expanded. However, there are aspects of social policy, among them the degree of corporatism and redistribution, where the strength of labour movements is less obviously the key to national variation. A closer scrutiny suggests that there are other social or political forces that can either constrain or facilitate the process of social democratization in post-war capitalism. This is where comparative historical studies of the leading European social democracies become relevant.

The case studies of Scandinavia, Austria, and Germany permit a comparison of nations in which reformist social-democratic parties, with strong ties to national union movements, have dominated working-class politics over the past century. Despite their starkly contrasting historical fates, the labour movements in these countries share a common ideological heritage, and have espoused almost identical blueprints for social policy. Social-democratic parties played only a peripheral role in pre-war, or pre-1930s, policy-making, but have in all cases governed, alone or in coalitions in a majority or minority position, for a decade or more during the post-war era. Yet, their capacity to 'social-democratize' their respective societies has differed considerably more than would be expected in terms of relative degrees of union strength and centralization, working-class political mobilization, and parliamentary power. The boundaries of social-democratic reform appear substantially narrower in Austria than in Scandinavia, and seem in fact much more similar to Germany, where the labour movement has been comparatively weak.

The number of significant circumstances that differentiate these nations is certainly large. Especially important in our view is the fact that in Austria and Germany, working-class parties were politically and socially ghettoized to a degree never experienced in Scandinavia. The political fragmentation of the Weimar period and the splits in the First Republic notwithstanding, the bourgeois parties in Germany and Austria emerge as a solid and hegemonic bloc, without the divisions between independent farmers and the urban bourgeoisie from which Scandinavian socialists could benefit.

But although the differences in historical causation are multiple, they resolve into the terms under which the post-war political settlements among the classes were negotiated. In Sweden, the Social Democratic mandate that emerged during the 1930s was narrow with respect to changing property relations within the economy, but very broad with respect to distributive change through parliamentary power. The Scandinavian Social Democrats could strengthen their political and organizational positions by building an institutional type of welfare state. The wide political support for welfare policies pressed the bourgeois opposition into compliance with the social-democratic agenda, even if political conflicts continued to emerge as, for example, over the goals and means of employment policy.

However, on account of changing class structure and a growing need to escape from the political confines of the inter-war settlement, a Social Democratic realignment became the prerequisite for continued power. If the conflicts over the 1959 pension reform in Sweden signaled the arrival of the realignment, the real issue was more than pensions. In essence, the growing dilemma for social democracy was how to reconcile economic policy for full employment with the consolidation of the social-citizenship state. Their tentative answer to this dilemma, which emerged during the 1970s, was to challenge the rights of capital ownership, implanted in the 'historical compromise', by demanding industrial democracy, collective capital formation and the rights to capital of wage earners.

Despite strong unions and a major left-wing party, the post-war settlement that was forged in Austria was of a wholly different kind. One explanation is that during the first twenty-five years of the post-war period, the Austrian Socialists were the weaker party in a coalition government and faced interests solidly vested in the conservative social policy established in the pre-war years. The nationalization of the large firms and banks introduced a class-based duality in which the ÖVP came to represent an amalgam of small-scale capitalists, farmers, the urban petit bourgeoisie, and also in large part the salaried strata. Thus, up to the 1970s the socialists remained a working-class movement without cross-class allies.

The institutions of 'social partnership', together with the nationalized sector of the economy, became a crucial setting for distributive conflict and nego- tiation. Since neither of the two class and political blocs between which this conflict chiefly lay could gain a decisive supremacy, bloc-based collaboration and consensual decision-making became the main alternative for Austrian social democracy (cf. Lehmbruch, this volume). But the Left being the weaker partner within this political order, the mandate for a 'social democratization' of Austria was strictly circumscribed. Neo-liberal social market economics and Social- Christian *Mittelstandspolitik* largely came to define the boundaries for social democracy, at least until the 1970s.

If the changing balance of power gradually eroded these boundaries, exemp- lified in the decisive shift in the 1960s from liberal to Keynesian economic policy, they could not be completely transcended. The SPÖ government cer- tainly introduced significant reforms during the 1970s; yet strong interests remain in the maintenance of corporatist segmentation in social policy and in wide economic inequalities. And the precondition for sustained full employment is still the labour movement's willingness to let market forces dictate wage behaviour. Thus, politics have not been permitted to interfere with markets to the degree we find in Sweden.

The political balance in Germany during the early post-war years was very similar to that in Austria. In both nations the labour movement had spent more than a decade in exile and had re-emerged with a degree of social legitimacy that stood in sharp contrast to that of the bourgeoisie. Yet, the limits for Germany's post-war political economy were defined and institutionalized by the CDU-CSU coalition without socialist, and with only peripheral trade union, participation.

Like the ÖVP in Austria, the CDU upheld a broad bourgeois coalition. But this coalition achieved far greater political dominance in Germany because labour was organizationally weaker and politically isolated until the 1960s. Hence, the neo-liberal-cum-Social-Christian policy model prevailed for two decades and the achievement of labour's goals had to await the arrival of full employment. The policy shift after the mid-1960s was clearly a product of the changing balance of labour-market and political power. Growth could no longer proceed on the basis of low wages and abundant surplus manpower; it required political negotiation.

Under the umbrella of their coalition with the FDP, it is clear that the Social Democrats sought to build a broad wage-earner alliance for a 'social-democratization' of Germany along the same lines as in Scandinavia. But, after a short burst of initiative, the project was abandoned and the Social Democrats were essentially compelled to govern with CDU-style social-market policies.

Our case studies thus indicate that the post-war development of social policy has been highly conflictual, even in such outwardly peaceful and stable democracies as those of Scandinavia, Austria, and Germany. Opposing interests have not only battled over the scope of social policy, but have also pursued distinctly class-specific strategies and goals in their policy choices. Conflicts have centred on the extent to which wage-earners should be dependent on the market mechanism, the ways in which class interests should be institutionalized in the organization of welfare-state programmes, the boundaries of social policy, and of course, the allocation of financial burdens created by an expanding welfare state. And the contemporary resurgence among the bourgeois parties of Germany, Denmark, and even Sweden of neo-liberal programmes which aim to return the welfare state to a marginal role, suggest the arrival of a new era of conflict of a yet sharper kind.

Clearly, in the countries we have considered, the relative power position of wage-earners has been of central significance for the development towards an institutional type of social policy. The importance of the strength of labour movements is perhaps best indicated by the efforts made to sustain full employment under adverse economic conditions. Among the Western nations since 1973, it is only the three with the most powerful labour movements—Sweden, Norway, and Austria—which have utilized macroeconomic, wage- or labour-market policies in order to hold unemployment at relatively low levels. But the relationship between power and policy is not a simple linear one. The conditions for social-democratic ascendancy involve, beyond the labour movement's own power resources, the constellation of political forces emerging from the formation of class and group alliances. It is this which has ultimately defined the boundaries of post-war political settlements and the limits of political choice.

Acknowledgements

This chapter is one of the interim products of a comparative study of social-policy development in 18 OECD countries over the period 1930–80. The project is directed by Walter Korpi and Gösta Esping-Andersen and supported by the Swedish Delegation for Social Research, The Bank of Sweden Tercentenary Foundation, and the German Marshall Fund of the United States. We wish to thank Jens Alber, Peter Katzenstein, Gaston Rimlinger, Emmerich Talos, and Helmut Wintersberger for critical consideration of earlier versions of the Austrian or German sections of this paper and John H. Goldthorpe, Gunnar

Olofsson, Sven E. Olsson, Joakim Palme, and Joseph Schwarz for valuable comments on the manuscript.

Notes

1. For example, the influential pioneering study by Wilensky (1975) concluded that ideologies were of little significance for the development of social security expenditures, while factors such as the proportion of elderly in the population and the level of economic development of a country were of major importance. Comparing Sweden and Britain, Heclo (1974) came to the conclusion that political conflicts were of little significance in social policy development. In an excellent study of the historical development of welfare states in Western Europe, Alber (1982) argues that, in contrast with the period before World War II, political factors have by and large been insignificant for social-policy development during the post-war era. This result, however, may reflect the limitations of his major dependent variable: the number of social insurance laws passed by different types of governments.

2. For a detailed historical overview, see the superb account by Rimlinger (1971).

3. Note that many of the indicators that some 'neo-corporatist' writers view as signs of working-class co-optation and incorporation into a 'mixed economy' are here taken as indicators of the relative power position of the labour movement (for a discussion cf. Korpi, 1983: ch. 2).

4. 'De-commodification' as used here does not refer to the complete abolition of labour power as a commodity in the labour market (cf. Esping-Andersen, 1981).

5. Unemployment insurance remains a partial exception to this strategy. In many countries the Ghent system of union-controlled unemployment insurance funds with public support has become dear to the unions, since it gives them control over relatively large economic resources. In contrast to pensions and sickness insurance, unemployment insurance has for long been a concern primarily of manual workers.

6. The idea of non-contributory social insurance was especially popular among labour movements in Scandinavia and the Anglo-Saxon countries, but was also adopted by the German and Austrian Socialists as a first-tier pension, even if they had to come to terms with the earnings-graduated principle of Bismarckian social insurance (SPD, 1957; Bartholomäi, 1977; Hockerts, 1981).

7. The model of social reform is sufficiently congruent in the Scandinavian countries for us to take Sweden, the most developed, as largely representative. Where decisive deviations exist between Denmark, Norway, and Sweden, we will give them special treatment. This section draws upon Esping-Andersen and Korpi (forthcoming), and also Esping-Andersen (1984).

8. These characterizations hold less for Denmark, where the Social Democrats have been stifled in their efforts to institutionalize active labour-market policies or the public steering of credit and investment behaviour.

9. In Finland, where the labour movement has been divided and considerably weaker than in Sweden, occupationally-segmented supplementary pensions were legislated in the 1970s. Their funding is accumulated in private insurance companies.

10. The historical data in this section are largely based on Berchthold|(1967), Hofmeister (1981), Talos (1981), and Traxler (1982).

11. In spite of Catholic political dominance in Austria up to 1970, welfare-state politics have largely been the domain of the Socialists and the trade unions. They have favoured the expansion of the welfare state and supported social policies that were often uncongenial to the ÖVP. This fact is easily missed in clsssifications which, on a global level, relate Catholic political power to social-policy outcomes (e.g. Wilensky, 1981b).

12. ÖVP's opposition to universalism was based on the arguments that it would bring benefit levels down to the lowest common denominator, and that the financial obligations imposed on the government would push Austria dangerously close to socialism |(*Wiener Tageszeitung*, 12 December 1950).

13. Cf. *Weltpresse*, 4 December 1950.

14. On ÖVP positions, see, for example, *Das kleine Volksblatt*, 25 May 1949. Maisel's speech is reported in the *Wiener Kurier*, 4 October 1951.

15. The internal conflicts included the expulsion from the Socialist party in 1948 of a member of the parliament, Erwin Scharf. He opposed co-operation with the ÖVP, and advocated closer contacts with the Communist party. Scharf formed his own splinter party, which never became significant.

16. The *Raab-Kamitz Kurs* was named after the ÖVP Chancellor and the Minister of Finance. The price controls covered about a third of all consumer prices.

17. At the party congress in 1972, Chancellor Bruno Kreisky spoke on the classless society and stated that it was a 'categorical imperative' for the SPÖ to achieve 'more equality' (Eppel & Lotter, 1982: 68; cf. also the 1978 SPÖ party programme).

18. For more than a decade, wage increases fell below increases in productivity and profits and, aided by the Bundesbank's tight money policy, the CDU governments used high (and quite regressive) taxes, initially imposed by the Allied Powers, to create budget surpluses for investment and to allow tax exemptions to business (Lieberman, 1977: 58, 210; Wallich, 1955; Edinger, 1977; Sontheimer, 1977).

19. See the *Sozialplan für Deutschland* (1957). Its basic principles were already published by the party executive in 1953 under the title *Die Grundlagen des Sozialen Gesamtplans der SPD*. Walter Auerbach and Ludwig Preller were its primary architects. The influence of Beveridge is not surprising, since Auerbach spent the war years in London participating in the preparation of the Beveridge report (Hockerts, 1981: 328 ff.).

20. Among the most pressing problems were the very heavy overload (which resulted in cuts of benefits between 1945 and 1949) and the severe housing shortage in urban areas (which led to rationing). Benefits were raised again after the 1949 currency reform. In addition, a minimum pension was introduced for the many who had lost benefit rights during the Nazi period. Also, the unemployment insurance scheme was re-established in accordance with its Weimar format.

21. A social assistance type of pension to farmers was appended to the reform. This pension was simultaneously an agricultural policy: it would only be granted to farmers who transferred, or sold, their farm. The intention was to accelerate the rationalization and consolidation of agriculture.

22. As intended, the gap between salaried and worker benefits grew sharply. According to Rimlinger (1971: 180) the spread between the highest and lowest pensions increased from 1:3 to 1:10. Although income-graduated benefits everywhere maintain inequalities, the goal of increasing differentials appears to have been especially emphasized in Germany.

23. The rent allowance scheme, moreover, remains closer to a poverty programme than a rights programme since only 7 per cent of households (in 1976) received an allowance compared to about a half in Sweden (Alber, 1980; Esping-Andersen, 1978).

24. The ratio of old-age pensions to normal workers' earnings has fallen slowly but steadily over the past 15 years.

25. Both Germany and Austria, however, allow pensions to rise with increasing contribution periods. With 45 years of contributions pension levels, in 1980, were 50 per cent in Germany and 70 per cent in Austria.

Appendix to Tables 8.1–8.3

In Table 8.1 social security expenditures are taken from ILO, *International Survey of Social Services*, Geneva, 1933; ILO, *The Cost of Social Security*, Geneva, 1955 and 1978. In Table 8.2 the figures on expenditures on means-tested programmes as well as on the relative size of individual social security contributions have been estimated by the authors and Martin Rein, also on the basis of *The Costs of Social Security*. Private pension expenditure data derive directly from national ministries and statistical offices. The figures on fiscal redistribution are based on data from the OECD series, *The Tax/Benefit Position of Selected Income Groups in the OECD Member Countries*, Paris, 1981. Data on unemployment for Norway, Sweden, Austria and Germany for the period 1967–83 (only the first three-quarters of 1983) are standardized and based on OECD, *Historical Statistics 1960–81*, Paris,

1983 and on *OECD Economic Outlook*, 34, December, 1983. However, other un-employment data are presented according to national definitions (cf. Maddison, 1982: 207–8). Estimates of labour market expenditures are taken from various OECD sources.

The more specific data bases for Table 8.3 will be described in future publications by the authors. In this Table, coverage refers to the number of insured with the right to cash benefits in relation to the population aged 15–64 years (pensions and sickness insurance), the labour force (work accident), or the number of employees (unemployment insurance). Replacement levels are calculated on the basis of the cash benefits that would accrue to a 'standard worker' with 35 years of contri-bution (pensions) and up to five years of service in his present place of employ-ment. Pension benefits refer to the expected pension of a worker who became a pensioner in 1950 or 1980; for the other programmes, the average benefit refers to the first 26 weeks after waiting days. Benefit levels are expressed as ratios of the wage for an average production worker in manufacturing (metal) industry. The role of taxation for benefit levels has not been considered.

9

Market-Independent Income Distribution: Efficiency and Legitimacy

RUNE ÅBERG

Introduction

In a lecture before a group of American economists in 1980, Tibor Scitovsky took up the familiar theme: 'Can capitalism survive?' Like many economists before him who have pondered over this problem, Scitovsky gave vent to both anxiety and doubt. His main line of reasoning was that capitalism is losing its ability to exploit opportunities, absorb shocks and adapt itself to changed circumstances. In a nutshell, the flexibility, which is one of the good sides of capitalism and which is especially important for giving the system legitimacy, is disappearing. And this is taking place at a time when the division of labour has fragmented the economy more and more and when technical development has speeded up the rate of change. The need for adaptability has grown, while the ability to carry it through has been weakened.

Capitalism achieves flexibility by means of the market mechanism, where price changes play a decisive role in resource allocation. The problem today, according to Scitovsky, is that these price signals deviate more and more from the signals that a freely functioning market would produce. At the same time, the various 'actors' in the market have become less sensitive to the signals that exist. This is especially true for the labour market. One can find a number of reasons for this development. To begin with, one can assume that the long-term growth in the standard of living has shifted priorities somewhat away from further material improvements and in favour of measures aimed at providing a secure and stable social situation. This implies diminishing marginal returns to wage increases. And this, in turn, means that wage rises must be more substantial and differentials greater if they are to maintain their ability to allocate labour power effectively. Secondly, it is reasonable to assume that the influence of non-market factors over wage determination has increased. The growing strength of the trade unions plays an important role here.

But even if wage differentials were to widen and compensate for the diminishing marginal utility of wage increases due to changed preferences, it would not suffice for a restoration of the market. Another 'anti-market' force has grown stronger and stronger during recent decades and that is what is usually called the welfare state. Lindbeck (1980) has studied this question and concluded that state policies on transfer payments, which go beyond helping the unfortunate victim of special circumstances, lead to a number of disincentives. In the first place, comprehensive social insurance systems take the initiative away from the individual for doing something about his situation. Secondly, a developed welfare state brings in its train high taxation levels and, often, high marginal tax rates. As a result, the individual can never keep more than a small proportion of pay increases. Sensitivity to alterations in the wage level then lessens, with a subsequent worsening in the function of the market.

Scitovsky's and Lindbeck's concern about the effects of the welfare state and income equalization represent a reaction to one of the important tendencies of our time—the politicization of areas of activity earlier regarded as the exclusive preserve of the market. Economic life has been more and more subjected to institutional regulation. From a neo-classical point of view this is regarded as a threat to the efficiency of the economic system and to economic growth. What is recommended as the solution to the economic crises which logically follow is a reduction of the influence of institutional arrangements, i.e. to free market forces and restrict the influence of unions and politics. For example, Meade (1982) suggests that if the present problem of stagflation is to be solved, wage determination must not serve equity goals. Rather, wages must be allowed to reflect differences in market conditions. Only then will labour market flows serve the goals of full employment and stable prices.

But unions and political parties which are trying to influence wages and redistributive policies have hardly grown in size without reason. Collective action through such bodies must be seen as a conscious attempt to correct the welfare distribution which would have resulted from a free market. The degree to which such corrections can be accomplished is, above all, a question of organizational strength among those who have an interest in changing the outcome of the market. For most wage-earners, union and political organization are the main means of protection against the market, but their immediate needs as well as their conception of how the market should be restricted vary. Therefore, it is difficult to establish organized co-operation among different wage-earners' interests. However, the larger the extent to which such organized co-operation between wage earners is accomplished, and the more its base rests on common interests, the more far-reaching market interference can be. But this also means that the welfare distribution can no longer be regarded as an automatic outcome of an impersonal market. Instead it is the result of decisions made in organizations and parties. The more politics penetrate into the market, the more interesting it becomes to ask how political decisions are made and what they lead to.

Much of the research on 'corporatism' has focused on these questions. Some have interpreted the growth of various forms of interest mediation as indicating a tendency for power to shift from politics and parliament over to organizations. Others seem to believe that the state or capital has become more powerful and, together with the organizations, 'rules' the people. The latter idea is based upon the assumption that rank-and-file members lose their influence and that power becomes concentrated among the leaders of the organizations. If growing union and political influence over the market is followed by such tendencies there will be problems in preserving legitimacy. The temptation to use measures of force or persuasion in order to maintain organizational strength will be strong and steps away from democratic ideals will be taken.

Legitimacy, if it is to be based on what Weber called 'legal-rational' grounds, is always problematic when an organization is built on subgroups with many divergent interests. This is the case for unions and political parties which pursue long-term goals for the majority of wage-earners. In the short-run there are always those who would have preferred the outcome from the market rather than the results achieved by collective effort. If such groups are large, there is a potentially severe problem of legitimacy. Therefore, the maintenance of legit-imacy and the prospects for continued mobilization are much better if there are ample resources to satisfy different interests.

Furthermore, it is easier to obtain support for a collectively decided distri-bution if this does not lead to labour-market disequilibrium, with growing differences in market opportunities and thereby growing heterogeneity in interests among the supporters. This means that the goals of efficiency and economic growth are almost as important for those who want to correct a market-determined welfare distribution through unions and politics as they are for the defenders of the market economy.

In the following discussion we will address these problems more throughly. The principal questions are (i) how do unions and welfare policies influence the process of distribution? (ii) what are the effects on efficiency, especially on the functioning of the labour market? The problem will be pursued both theoretically and empirically. Data from two countries, Sweden and the USA, which are very different with respect to market intervention, will be compared.

Wage Differentials and Trade Unions

Wage relations are crucial for income distribution. Their economic function from the standpoint of market theory is clear. The perspective usually relied on is some variant of Hicks's (1964) application of the theory of supply and de-mand in this field. This theory assumes that wages tend to rise in those partial labour markets with excess demand for labour. In the opposite case, wages tend, if not actually to fall, at least to remain stationary. Equilibrium of supply and demand in the various partial labour markets, therefore, plays a key role in the development of wage levels. A shortage of labour in certain areas and unemploy-ment in others should accordingly change wage differentials to the benefit of the labour-shortage area.

A number of factors, which affect the demand for and supply of labour, can give rise to disequilibrium conditions: expansion or contraction of the various commodity markets, technical innovations, productivity changes, price fluctuations, demographic developments, reforms in the areas of education, taxation, family policy, etc. Productivity differences have a special status in economic theory. The shape of a firm's demand curve for labour depends on its marginal productivity. Firms with a high marginal productivity have much to gain from employing additional labour and can increase wages to attract more workers. According to this model, whatever the causes of disequilibrium on the labour market are, they should be reflected in wage differences. The model thus has a normative aspect. It is thought to be a good thing that wage differences develop in this way. If not, disequilibrium would become even greater, since the function of wage differentials is to be the incentive to redress disequilibrium. Labour power should be attracted to areas with rising relative wages and repelled from those areas where the relative wage is falling. In this way, the labour market is self-corrective and moves towards equilibrium.

But the problem with the 'market model' is that wage differentials in most cases are only partially determined by market forces. Other factors, often pin-pointed by sociologists who have studied wage determination, cannot be ignored. For example wage differentials are often seen as a result of *conceptions of justice* and of the *distribution of power* (Phelps-Brown, 1977; Goldthorpe, 1974). Sometimes, however, the effects of these factors coincide with those of the determining factors of the market model. If the rationality of the market dominates social consciousness, most people will regard those wage differences imposed by the market as being in the general interest. Accordingly, they gain legitimacy. If market forces benefit particular categories of workers, they strengthen not only the position of individuals, but also the trade unions in these sectors. Conceptions of justice and organizational strength can, then, go hand in hand with wage determination through the market.

To constitute an alternative to the 'market model', it is necessary for 'socio-logical' theories to demonstrate that conceptions of a fair wage and/or power relationships have determinants other than the actual market situation. This is probably so in most cases. There is hardly any country where the rationality of the market has become an unchallenged way of thinking among the general public. Most people's ideas about what constitutes a reasonable wage are based on their own situation in relation to others. The factors usually taken into account can range from wages *per se* to those involved in the more complex notion of a net reward, where wages are viewed in relation to work effort and the demands placed on the individual. Normally, conceptions of a 'fair' wage are rather stable and tradition bound. In fact, actual wage relativities are seldom altered very dramatically. (Hyman & Brough, 1975, ch. 3 esp.)

An explanation for the absence of dramatic changes can be found if one considers the value structure of the entire system as composed of the values of a number of subgroups, all of whom evaluate their own situation in relation to nearby reference groups. To the extent that such a value system is allowed to determine actual wage determination, the wage structure will naturally be stable. If category A receives a relative wage improvement, without there being any tangible changes in A's work conditions, categories B and C will experience this as unjust if they have A as a reference group. Discontent and compensatory wage demands are created. The net effect will be that wage relativities will tend to return to the point of departure but at a higher average wage level. This assumes of course that B and C can drive through compensatory wage claims that do not reflect prevailing market conditions. They must be sufficiently well organized to be able to bring pressure on their employers. Relatively strong trade unions are thus needed, and also a decentralized union structure, which permits expression to the special interests of various occupational groups. Such groups can become strong in a society which is characterized by an advanced division of labour, where the whole is dependent on the parts. Small groups can, at little cost to themselves, cause extensive disruption by strikes. If most employees are organized in many independent unions, wage determination can be expected to show the above pattern: i.e. stable wage relativities but with the general wage level out of control.

However, if unionization is low in some parts of the labour market and high in others, wages can be expected to change in another way. People working in unorganized or poorly organized parts of the labour market do not have the protection that a union can give them in times when such support is needed. Some people, like certain white-collar workers and specialists with very high market capacities, seldom find themselves in such situations. But most workers are vulnerable to market fluctuations. When the general demand for their type of labour decreases and the competition for jobs sharpens, they will face growing difficulties in defending their relative wage positions. The harder the competition, the lower the wages will be. This might have positive effects on employment in these areas if the relative decrease in wages makes labour cheap compared to productivity. Low-paid workers will grow in number.

Those who work in organized parts of the labour market are not in the hands of the market to the same extent. Among them, wage relations do not develop in the way the market would imply. Rather, we would expect stable wage relativities at comparatively high average levels. Relatively high wages in these sectors also provide an incentive to improve productivity by making production more capital intensive or by reducing the number of low-productivity jobs. Workers usually accept such changes if they are guaranteed security in employment. This is more easily accomplished with strong unions. Barriers to entry in these sectors will be high in down-turn periods. Then highly-paid workers will not grow in number, but will decrease from 'natural' drop-out. The consequence will be an enlarged wage gap between the increasing number of low-productivity, low-paid workers in the unorganized sector, and the decreasing number of high-productivity, highly-paid workers in the organized sector.

Thus, decentralized trade unionism gives the market an important role in wage determination but a role which is different from that under the ideal neo-classical model. Incentives to increase protection against market fluctuations are always present. Therefore, it is often regarded as rational for a union to limit the supply of labour within its specific area or profession. This can be done by agreements on an exaggerated professionalization or on other measures aimed at creating a lasting disequilibrium to a group's own advantage. But there are also incentives to build alliances with other groups. Such strategies tend to push the fragmented trade union movement towards co-operation and eventually towards a greater degree of centralization. For such a strategy to occur, it is important that market opportunities do not differ too much between members of the potentially co-operating unions. It is also important that wage demands claimed by one group are accepted by the others. This often means that there are incentives to determine wages more and more by values of fairness and equality rather than by market conditions.

In the first place, a development towards co-operation and centralization means a change in points of reference. Important here is that the trade-union structure and the negotiating system itself produce changes in how conceptions of fair wages are formed. A relatively centralized structure, where wages for widely differing occupational groups are determined in centralized negotiations, makes comparisons between groups unavoidable. Those who put forward wage demands must justify them not only to their employers but to other occupational groups.

This leads us to the second point. Solidarity is essential for the stability of a united labour movement. A prerequisite for a lasting alliance between different groups of wage-earners is that one group's struggle is regarded as legitimate by the others. Much of the mutual jockeying for position between groups is, in this case, removed from the sphere of the market and taken into the negotiating room. In this situation, the need for more neutral criteria for evaluation will become acute. As a consequence, there will be a need for some kind of work evaluation. The firm's ability to pay wages, as well as changing market conditions can be included in a such system, of course, but will be weighed against factors like the nature of the work, how skilled, responsible and risky the work is etc. With such 'total' comparisons, it is difficult to justify extremely low wages and to accept the moods of the market. The demand for explicit criteria for evaluation results in a shift of factors determining wages. Greater weight will be given to non-market criteria.

Thirdly, it is reasonable to expect that a co-ordinated system of negotiations, to the extent that it is built up in a democratic way, will strengthen the position of the weakest. The greater the inequality that exists to begin with, and the more the arithmetically average wage exceeds the median wage, the easier it will be for the deprived majority to dominate collective decisions and vote down the better paid minority. (For similar reasoning applied to political democracy see, for example, Downs, 1957; Lenski, 1966). Such a possibility is greatest in a union structure of the centralized type. This kind of structure should, therefore, encourage a development towards diminished wage differences—both as a result of changed power relationships and of changes in the conception of a fair wage.

Let us now look at some empirical data and compare two countries with different union structures and collective bargaining systems. The choice of countries is designed to represent the two ideal-type situations previously discussed, but has also been guided by the availability of data. The dual economy case is represented by USA and the case of high union coverage and co-operation is represented by Sweden.

Union membership is low in the USA—less than 30 per cent of the employed work-force in the mid-1970s. The degree of organization of white-collar workers in the private sector is especially low (about 10 per cent). About 50 per cent of manual workers are organized. In particular, the automobile, steel, and paper and pulp industry unions are strong. About 70 per cent of the workers in these industries are organized and collective agreements apply to more than 80 per cent of their labour markets. The cloth and timber industries, on the other hand, are poorly organized with only 20–30 per cent being members and 25–35 per cent being covered by collective agreements (Freeman & Medoff, 1979).

The AFL-CIO (American Federation of Labor-Congress of Industrial Organizations) carries out some co-ordination and information work but does not participate in any negotiations. Centralized wage policies do not exist. It is instead the local trade union which forms the key element in the structure of the union movement. It is at the local level that negotiations on wages and working conditions take place. Agreements in the leading firms tend to set the norm for others in the same branch. Some collaboration has occurred between unions during the 1970s but the American trade union movement still gives the impression of being a fragmented movement. There are no fewer than 200 trade unions, in some cases organized by occupation and in other cases by industry.

In Sweden, a very different situation prevails. About 95 per cent of manual workers are organized, and the figure has been high throughout the entire post-war period. Among white-collar workers, the corresponding figure is 70 per cent. Blue-collar and salaried employees belong to separate union confederations, the LO (*Landsorganisationen*) and the TCO (*Tjänstemännens centralorganisation*). The principle of industrial or vertical unionism clearly dominates within both organizations. Within the LO, a 'solidaristic wages policy' has, since the end of the 1950s, been aimed at decreasing wage differences, independently of prevailing market conditions. In recent years, the TCO has also aimed at higher wage increases for its lowest-paid members. A smaller white-collar confederation, SACO (*Sveriges akademikers centralorganisation*), is organized according to professional affiliation. This organization has become less important in recent years. The central union organizations have a strong position. Wage negotiations have been conducted centrally and have covered the entire labour market. Agreements have been made at the level of individual trade unions and finally at the level of the firm. The agreements that the higher levels conclude have formed the framework for bargaining at the lower levels. In 1982, however, for the first time since 1956, one union within LO did not participate in central negotiations, and in 1983 no such negotiations took place at all. No doubt, the present situation is a sign of the vulnerability of the 'Swedish model' but it is probably too early yet to conclude that it has come to an end. At all events, for the period covered by our data, Sweden was a good example of a country with a centralized and co-ordinated collective bargaining system.

If institutional arrangements are of significance for wage determination, the differences in union structure between the two countries should be reflected in differences in the development of wages during the 1960s and 1970s. Among US industrial workers, both organizational density and the numbers covered by collective agreements vary greatly from branch to branch. According to our earlier line of argument, this should imply that wage differentials will vary with the rate of unemployment. The gap between the well-organized and the badly-organized branches can be expected to grow with rising unemployment. In the well-organized sector, the union organization can—at least partially—resist the pressure for wage reductions exerted by unemployment. That is not possible in those areas where trade unions are weak.

Figure 9.1 shows that during the 1960s, when unemployment in the USA was low and continuously decreasing, wage differences were rather stable. But during the 1970s, when unemployment was on the rise, wage differences also increased. Figure 9.2 shows that increased wage differentials during the 1970s coincide with a widening gap between wages in the organized and the unorganized sectors. From other studies we also know that wage differences among organized workers are considerably less than among the unorganized (Freeman, 1980).

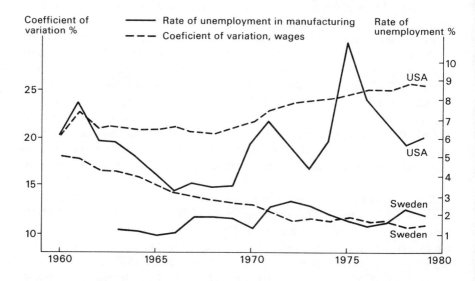

FIG. 9.1. *Unemployment and wage differentials for workers in US and Swedish manufacturing industry 1960–1970*

Sources: Svenska Arbetsgivarföreningen, *Wages and Total Costs for Workers*; OECD, *Labour Force Statistics.*

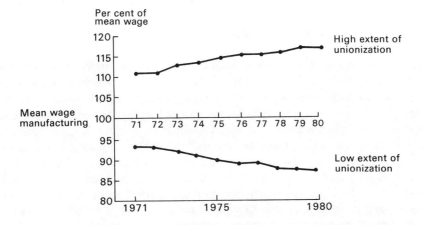

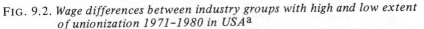

FIG. 9.2. *Wage differences between industry groups with high and low extent of unionization 1971–1980 in USA*[a]

[a] A high extent of unionization is operationally defined as a collective bargaining coverage higher than the average for all manufacturing. Industry groups with high extent of unionization are those with ISIC numbers 311–13, 314, 341, 351–2, 353, 354, 36, 37 and 384.

Sources: Freeman & Medoff (1979); ILO, *Yearbook of Labour Statistics,* 1982.

This pattern does not apply in Sweden. There are no branches of industry with weak trade-union influence. Wage bargaining, moreover, has been co-ordinated and centralized and since the mid-1960s, shaped by conscious efforts to improve the situation of the most poorly paid. Figure 9.1 shows that wage differentials in Sweden have diminished regardless of variations in the number of unemployed.

The data presented here support the hypothesis that the organizational structure of trade unions and the nature of collective bargaining are important explanations for differences in wage determination in the two countries. In the USA, the influence of the market is still strong and the developments of the last decade have therefore resulted in widened wage differentials. However, these differentials seem to be determined by union strength rather than by supply and demand in various labour market segments.[1]

Market-Independent Income Determination, the Functioning of the Labour Market, and Strains on Union Co-operation

As mentioned in the Introduction, the greatest problem with a centralized type of trade-union structure and co-ordinated negotiations is how to maintain legitimacy and unity. One may wonder why workers with strong market power are interested at all in participating in this type of negotiation. Why not leave the organization and negotiate independently? And moreover, could we not expect the market to correct wage agreements that are out of tune with prevailing market conditions, so that wages in any case will rise for those able to achieve higher wages? A contrary problem exists for those who achieve higher wages than the firm is capable of paying. Will not this labour price itself out of the market?

The tensions in a centralized bargaining system are undeniably great and varied. Yet, such systems do persist. Moreover, in a number of industrial countries the trade union movement is moving towards larger units and increased centralization (Windmuller, 1981). The reasons for this may be economic concentration or other structural changes which promote conscious attempts at strengthening the trade unions through co-ordination. In the long run, it might be the best policy to allow short term 'egoistic' interests to suffer for the longer-term common goal. Furthermore, increased interdependencies also mean more equal power distributions. If any one actor can greatly harm every other, it is of course rational to avoid conflict and look for acceptable forms of co-operation. As earlier mentioned, such strategies also mean that more can be accomplished with political measures. The efficiency of organization as a power resource increases (Korpi, 1978).

But, economic rationality does not always decide what is going to happen. As we know, union structure and collective bargaining systems differ between countries. For a more complete answer to the question of why some countries have more centralized systems than others, it would be necessary to take into account historical, political, religious and ethnic factors. This task falls outside the scope of this paper. What we want to do here is to stress the importance of one factor—the ability to simultaneously handle the problem of efficiency and legitimacy. It is our belief that the extent to which the labour market becomes unbalanced, as a result of measures undertaken in order to make wages independent of market conditions, is of crucial importance for how well this problem can be handled. Following the assumptions of neo-classical economists, one would expect that even minor deviations from the ideal of market-determined wages would mean distortions in the functioning of the labour market. However, these assumptions can be challenged for various reasons.

(i) The transfer of labour power from one branch to another only partly consists of people who move from low-wage (declining) branches to high-wage (expanding) ones. Instead, adjustment takes place through the filling of vacancies in expanding branches by new recruits to the labour market. For them, the choice is made almost independently of the relative wage levels of the various branches of industry. Very few jobs will exist in the declining branches, while there will be a lot in the expanding ones. Even if jobs in the declining branches were better paid, most job seekers would still be faced with no other option than to take jobs in the expanding sector. The net effect will be a transfer of labour to the expanding branches.

(ii) As Marx recognized long ago, labour is not a commodity like other commodities, since when a worker sells his labour power he also sells a large portion of himself. The choice of work is affected by social connections, the nature of the work in relation to individual abilities and needs, status considerations of various types, other family members' situations, etc. For some, these can be reasons to change jobs; for others, reasons for staying in the jobs they already have. Therefore these factors do not necessarily act as a hindrance to mobility. What is important is that many other factors apart from wages play an important role in the determination of the individual's behaviour on the labour market. Moreover, it is not unreasonable to accept, as Scitovsky does, that these other factors increase in relative importance in a developed economy, where social welfare improvements are given a higher priority than narrowly economic improvements. Similar implications stem from arguments developed by Fromm (1966), Bell (1976), Ingelhart (1977) and other commentators on cultural changes in modern societies. According to these writers, our civilization is moving towards a value structure which, in the field of work, will mean that values of 'expressive success' will grow in importance relative to values of 'material success' (cf. also Zetterberg, 1983). By this is meant that more weight is given to what is necessary for human inner growth.

(iii) A change of work, and perhaps of place of residence, involve initial economic costs which must be deducted from the eventual benefit of a rise in wages. Such costs are, for example, travel costs, costs of moving, or of education. If the market functions in the way predicted by economic theory, the discounted present value of the net gain from the pay increase will be quite small. This is due to the fact that the relative wage advantage should not last especially long, if more workers behave as expected, i.e. move to jobs with higher wages thereby creating a downward pressure on wages. If the costs of mobility were to be included and the short discounting period considered, wage differentials must be large, and be allowed to change quickly, if they are to have a regulatory function. Alternatively, one can assume that people are not aware of this situation. If this is the case, then one must be careful not to inform them, since otherwise the system would not work as expected and market adjustment for many people would be something of a fraud and lead to disappointment. This in turn will mean incentives for organized protection against market outcomes and exit from the unstable 'market case'.

(iv) Employers have a capacity to adapt to changing circumstances. Thus, if wages cease to be an efficient means of getting people to behave as required, other measures may be used: for example, jobs can be moved to areas with an excess of workers; in large companies, more attention can be given to training and to recruitment strategies within internal labour markets; workers can be rewarded by other things than money, etc. These possibilities should not be exaggerated, but it would seem reasonable to suppose that increased rigidity on the side of labour can to some extent be offset by the flexibility in organizing work and employment relations that employers possess (cf. Goldthorpe, this volume).

Wages are, then, only one of many allocative instruments of the labour market, and their importance is probably exaggerated by main stream economists. None the less, we cannot suppose that their importance is negligible. Thus, the more wages are determined by factors other than market ones, the more one has to rely on other measures for achieving balance between supply and demand in various segments of the labour market.

Labour-market policy is one such measure. It entails provisions such as labour exchanges, career services in schools, labour-market retraining schemes and various types of financial grants and aid to those who have to move to find a job. But labour-market policy need not be concerned only with helping individuals to improve their chances on the market. Job opportunities can also be created in areas where a substantial surplus of labour exists; new industries can be located in areas where firms have closed down; and various other steps can be taken with the aim of easing the processes of market adjustment.

A further important task for labour-market policy is to maintain employment during periods when the market cannot sustain sufficient employment and when general economic policy measures are not in themselves adequate to redress this situation. In this case labour-market policy involves the creation of various types of public work, and government funding for the allocation of labour to short-term employment or to protected employment for those who cannot compete effectively on the open labour market. The handicapped fall into this category, as do unemployed persons who cannot move away from an area of high unemployment for some reason. During periods of very weak demand for labour power, all types of unemployed may be involved. Job support measures can be aimed at firms, too. Support can be given to the production of inventories, direct state orders can be placed, and grants given to enable workers to be retrained rather than dismissed.

Institutional arrangements of this type, if they work according to plan, should improve market adaptability. Since it is made easier for the expanding parts of the labour market to find labour power, wage increases will be less than would otherwise have been the case. Moreover, the remaining employees in the declining sectors will be in a stronger bargaining position than would otherwise have applied, since labour power can more easily move away from this sector. Those who are given alternative possibilities of employment through governmentally subsidized jobs or similar arrangements, reduce the numbers of unemployed and thus soften the wage-diminishing effects of unemployment in areas with a large labour surplus.

Well-developed labour-market policies should thus contribute to an allocation of labour power which is less dependent on wage differentials, and therefore contribute to the basis for trade-union wage policies aimed at satisfying conceptions of justice and equality. Thereby, such policies are important in a strategy for creating a united labour movement.

By introducing labour-market policy we have shifted our focus towards the political side of institutional arrangements which affect the distribution of welfare. Labour-market policy is in itself important in this respect, since its primary goal is to keep unemployment low and thus reduce economic hardship and mitigate the many other problems associated with unemployment. But the same arguments for regarding labour-market policy as a prerequisite for market-independent wage determination can also be invoked for regarding it as a prerequisite for other social policy measures aimed at more market-independent living conditions. This is especially important if social policy is constructed according to the 'institutional model' (Korpi, 1983).

According to this model, most people receive some form of aid and economic protection at a fairly high economic level. Generous transfer payments are made when people have children or high housing costs and low incomes, when they are sick, unemployed or retired, when they need hospital care or education. Food prices are subsidized etc. Most people benefit one way or another from these transfers and most people have to contribute to their financing. They are equalizing to the extent that people with low incomes receive more and people with high incomes pay more. Most important for our discussion here is the fact that social policy following the institutional model is expensive and requires high taxes, often progressive ones. This also means that income changes will have minor effects on changes in disposable income. Thus social policy of this kind can be assumed to have similar effects on the incentive structure of the labour market as market-independent, diminished wage differentials.

Social policy of the 'marginal' type does not have these effects. In this case, support is only given to the poorest on occasions of great need. Even if this model is an efficient one in the sense that inequality is reduced to a relatively great degree at little cost, it cannot have far-reaching effects. As it is primarily limited to people outside working life and as it is cheap, the incentive structure of the labour market should not be much affected.

On the subject of social policy, we can reason in the same way as in the case of union and collective-bargaining models. The answer to the question of why some countries develop a social policy of the institutional type while others pursue a social policy of the marginal type falls outside the scope of this paper. But again we believe that if social policies of the institutional type are to survive, their effects cannot be allowed to damage economic efficiency and the functioning of the labour market.

Let us again compare the USA with Sweden. As we already have seen, wage relativities have developed differently in the two countries. In Sweden wage differences have diminished, in the USA they have increased. The tendency towards more equality in Sweden is further strengthened by differences in social policy in the two countries. Social policy in the USA is generally of the marginal kind. The public sector's share of GNP is comparatively small and consequently taxation is low. As an example, we can mention that a metal worker only pays around 25 per cent marginal tax.

Social policy in Sweden has long been constructed according to the institutional model. For 1981, about 34 per cent of total disposable income was in the form of transfers. For 1968 the corresponding figure was 15 per cent. Social policy has thus reached a high level, and so have taxes. A metal worker in Sweden could not in 1982 *keep* more than 25 per cent of his increase in income.[2]

Given these differences, we may hypothesize strong variations between these countries where economic incentives for changing jobs and using market opportunities are concerned. But before we analyse whether these differences actually influence labour-market performance, we must again mention labour-market policy.

Labour-market policies have some similarities in the two countries. In 1973, the USA supplemented its battery of labour-market policies with the so-called CETA programme (Comprehensive Employment and Training Act). This programme included a number of measures to retrain manpower, to create jobs for especially hard-hit groups and regions, and to improve the matching process between job-seekers and employers with vacancies. In 1979, the estimated cost of these measures was $12 billion dollars or 0.57 per cent of GNP. The lion's share of this expenditure, about 55 per cent, was invested in various forms of labour retraining programmes, about 40 per cent in job creation, and the remainder in the organization of labour exchanges. Since then, great cuts in expenditures on labour-market policies have been made and the CETA programme abandoned.

Labour-market policy in Sweden has a long history. It began to be built up in the late 1950s. It, too, embraces various types of programme to improve workers' skills, to smooth the 'matching process', and to create jobs. About 8 billion kronor were invested in these activities in 1979, equivalent to 2.1 per cent of GNP. The proportions spent on job creation and various types of training and retraining programmes were about the same as in the USA. The main difference between the USA and Sweden is that much greater efforts have been made in this area in Sweden. This has meant that during the 1970s in Sweden unemployment was held down to between 2 and 3 per cent. In the USA, the figure has been more than 8 per cent in some years. Consequently, 70 per cent of the total expenditure on the unemployed has been used for unemployment benefits and 30 per cent for labour-market policy measures. The corresponding figures for Sweden are about 10 and 90 per cent (Stafford, 1981).

Since the late 1960s, the relative importance of measures in the Swedish labour-market policy has changed. Measures for creating jobs and avoiding lay-offs have increased much more than mobility-stimulating measures. Sometimes, this has been taken as a sign of a shift in goals. But the main reason for the change seems to be that a decrease in demand for labour and an increase in supply have resulted in a reduction of mobility opportunities. Thus, the possibilities for reducing unemployment by stimulating mobility have decreased and the need for job creation has increased.

The problem now is whether the labour market in the USA is more flexible, and more efficient in adjusting to changes in supply and demand in different sub-markets, than is the labour market in Sweden. This is what one would expect if economic incentives have the decisive importance for labour mobility assumed by most economists. But if economic incentives are of minor importance or if labour-market policy can be a substitute, the countries should then not differ so much where labour-market behaviour is concerned. It is not easy to treat this issue on the basis of available evidence. There are no generally accepted empirical indicators of labour-market adjustment, and existing data are frequently not comparable from country to country. The following data do, however, bear some relevance to the problem.

(i) At first sight it would appear that the US labour market functions better than the Swedish one. *Labour-market mobility* is higher in the USA. Furthermore, mobility in Sweden has decreased during the 1970s, while no clear downward trend can be observed in the USA. In the USA, 'accessions' and 'separations' hovered around 3.5 per cent per month during the 1960s and 1970s. In Sweden, the corresponding figures have fallen from about 3 to 1.5 per cent since the middle of the 1960s. These data are only available for workers in the industrial sector. However, these factors can hardly be accepted as proof of a better functioning labour market in the USA. When we compare mobility statistics in the two countries, we should take into account the large number of temporary lay-offs during periods of work shortage in the USA. Many people are laid off and re-employed. In this way, both 'accession' and 'separation' increase without any real mobility taking place. Temporary lay-offs are about five times greater in the USA than in Sweden (Björklund & Holmlund, 1981). But from our point of view, where differences in mobility patterns are assumed to result from differences in incentive structures, 'quits' are a more valid indicator. Available data on quits show no difference between Sweden and the USA. During the 1970s the average monthly quit rate per 100 workers is 2.1 in both countries (Table 9.1).

(ii) The ability of the labour market to adjust itself is frequently studied by looking at *the relationship between vacancies and the number of unemployed*. If the labour market functions well, the number of unempoloyed should go down when vacancies increase and vice versa. If the relationship between vacancies and unemployment changes so that unemployment becomes higher at a given rate of vacancies, this will be a sign of a worse functioning labour market. This is usually, illustrated graphically by diagrams such as those in Figures 9.3 and 9.4. The further from the origin that the observations move, the poorer the market's ability to pair the unemployed and vacancies.

TABLE 9.1. *Monthly lay-off and quit rates per 100 workers in Sweden and USA 1969–1977*

	Lay-off rate		Quit rate	
	USA	Sweden	USA	Sweden
1969	1.2	0.2	2.7	2.9
70	1.8	0.2	2.1	2.9
71	1.6	0.4	1.8	2.1
72	1.1	0.3	2.3	1.9
73	0.9	0.2	2.8	1.9
74	1.5	0.2	2.4	2.2
75	2.1	0.2	1.4	2.0
76	1.3	0.1	1.7	1.8
77	1.1	0.2	1.8	1.5
Mean values	1.4	0.2	2.1	2.1

Source: Stafford (1981).

There are no direct statistics on the number of vacancies in the USA. Available instead is information on 'help wanted', based on advertisements in a representative sample of newspapers. The statistics which are presented are aggregate figures for the whole labour market. Figure 9.3 shows the relationship between 'help wanted' and unemployment. Since 'help wanted' is published as a relative number with 1975 as a base year, these relative numbers have been subtracted from the number of employed expressed as a relative number with the same base year. In this way, one gets a measure of demand which does not reflect the general expansion of the labour market. The same holds for unemployment which is expressed as a percentage of the labour force. Figure 9.4 shows the same thing for Sweden. The demand for labour is based here on the number of vacancies expressed as a percentage of the labour force.

It is clear from these two figures that, contrary to what one would have expected on the assumption of market-directed behaviour by the labour force, the American labour market seems to have developed a higher degree of disequilibrium—as shown by the line drawn in Figure 9.4—while this is hardly the case for the Swedish labour market.

So far we have mainly been concerned with efficiency in terms of the labour market's ability to allocate labour when demand shifts. Intervention in the process of income determination has been discussed in terms of effects on relative income. However, economic performance can also deteriorate as a result of an uncontrolled development of mean wages and other labour costs. In the long run, problems arise when labour costs deviate too much from productivity.

FIG. 9.3. *Demand for labour and unemployment in USA 1960–1982*
a For definition of these measures, see text p. 224.
Source: OECD, *Main Economic Indicators.*

Two opposing views exist about the effects in this respect of unions and government expenditure.

In the 'public choice' literature, there are many examples provided to support the general idea that interventions in the market, regardless of their good intentions, lead to unintended negative results. For example, labour-market policy is supposed to have such results since its existence implies that the government takes responsibility for employment. Strong unions can then disregard the effects of their wage claims and use their power exclusively to the benefit of those in work: government will take care of the eventual problems. Temptations to increase wages and other labour costs faster than productivity increases can also be expected to grow out of the fact that it is difficult to hold the union organization together. This will be easier if everybody can receive something. Even if the negotiators knew the rational wage level, they would be forced by divergent internal interests to exceed that level. 'Wage-drift' is another important problem. If negotiated wages depart too much from market conditions, wage-drift will appear and demands for compensation will be raised in the next round of negotiations so that the general wage level will move upwards.

On the other hand, it could be questioned whether a fragmented union structure would be a better alternative. In that case, nobody could afford to adopt considerations beyond his own interests. As we mentioned earlier, this

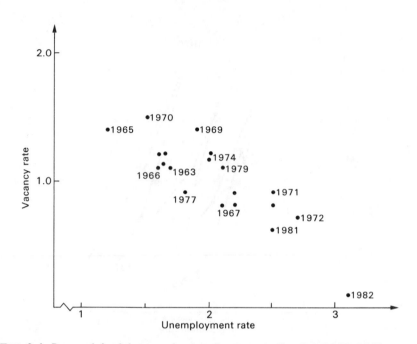

FIG. 9.4. *Demand for labour and unemployment in Sweden 1963–1982*
Sources: Statistiska Centralbyrån, *Labour Force Surveys;* Arbetsmarknadsstyrelsen, *Labour Market Statistics.*

must lead to endless wage competition. Such a process can either be controlled through union co-operation and a co-ordinated collective bargaining system or by government incomes policies. However, these measures must alike be built on consent if they are to function according to plan. But consent is almost impossible to achieve if there are many bargaining units without links between them. Therefore, a more centralized bargaining system based on internal consent is assumed to be a prerequisite for incomes policy to be efficient. Furthermore, market forces should not be allowed to create differences in market opportunities, with wage-drift and disunity as a result. Thus, labour-market policy is important for every strategy aimed at controlling mean wages. Whether this takes the form of government incomes policy or is handled by the unions themselves does not matter from a strict economic perspective but is an important democratic problem which falls outside the scope of this paper.

However, a federation of unions which can offer discipline also has power. Consequently, demands can be pressed on governments and employers. Such a federation also has its own long-term interests, among which a stable economic development is one. Thus, it has nothing to gain from raising wages more than the economy can bear. Nor of course does it have any interest in holding wages back more than necessary.

Union structure, as earlier mentioned, can vary with the degree of coverage.

This also can be assumed to affect union influence on the mean wage level. In a fragmented structure with high unionization covering the whole labour market, the wages struggle which is characterized by the jockeying for position of various groups, can be expected to leave the general wage level out of control.[3] In a dualistic situation with high union coverage in some parts of the labour market, the mean wage level may be easier to control since some of the necessary wage decreases can be shifted over to the poorly organized sectors.

To illustrate these mechanisms empirically, one should have an indicator of the extent to which the wage level is adapted to economic resources. For that purpose, we have chosen to relate changes in real GDP per capita to changes in real wages (Figure 9.5). As real wages are determined not only by available resources, but also by power relations between employers and employees, we have included profit rates in the figure.

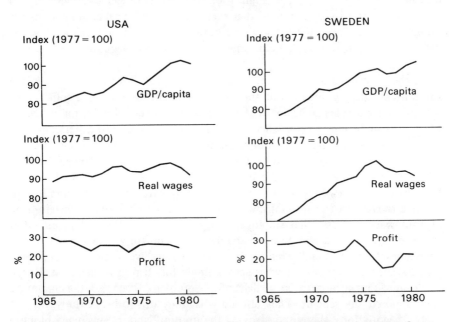

FIG. 9.5. *Real wages of workers in manufacturing, real GDP per capita and profit shares for the USA and Sweden, 1965-1980*
Sources: OECD, *Historical Statistics*, 1982, Svenska Arbetsgivarföreningen, *Wages and Total Labour Costs for Workers.*

The curves in Figure 9.5 show that for the USA a relatively good correspondence exists between real GDP per capita, real wage and profit share. In most years, it can be observed that production is associated with increases in real wages as well as profit shares. The mean wage level has not increased faster than the GDP per capita.

In the case of Sweden, mean wages have followed real GDP per capita rather closely and have changed almost independently of profit shares. But the interesting observation here is that real wages increased continuously until 1976, and since then they have decreased. Although the turning point came a few years too late, this gives the impression of a controlled development of mean wages.

Another empirical illustration can be found in OECD statistics (1983b: 48), where real-wage rigidity in industry has been calculated for eleven OECD-countries. The USA, Canada, and Sweden are the countries with the lowest rigidity, i.e. those in which real wages react strongly to a rise in unemployment but little to the acceleration of inflation. Thus, Sweden and the USA seem to be two countries which have been comparatively efficient in controlling mean wages. But, as demonstrated earlier, they have done it in very different ways.

Now, let us return to the problem raised in the introduction to this section—is a centralized and co-ordinated collective bargaining system compatible with efficiency and legitimacy? The implication of our theoretical arguments as well as of the empirical illustrations is that such systems *are* capable of handling the problem of efficiency, at least so far as behaviour in the labour market and the development of real wages are concerned. The problem of legitimacy is however, more complicated.

In the above-mentioned sense, efficiency is probably a necessary condition for consent and legitimacy, but the present tendencies towards a split among Swedish wage-earners indicates that it is not sufficient. Of vital importance is the long-term decline in economic activity in Sweden, as in most other countries. Income has stopped increasing but government spending has not. Consequently, budget deficits have grown. To turn the economy back into a balanced situation again will mean that strong efforts must be made to increase production with little or no return going to labour but rather towards reducing deficits. This places a heavy burden on unions, which in many cases are asked to abstain from securing wage increases that employers can afford to pay. After a long period of real-wage decreases, it will be more and more difficult for workers in high-profit companies to understand why they should not receive some share of these profits. The introduction of wage-earner funds (cf. Esping-Andersen & Korpi, this volume) must be seen in the light of this problem. Of course, the employers have opposed the scheme. They also do what they can to break the system of central negotiations, thereby destroying the unity of labour. This makes it more difficult to achieve income-policy goals, and consequently a heavier burden is placed on the political branch of the labour movement. The most likely alternative therefore seems to be a reduction and privatization of the public sector, together with tax increases and increases in prices for public services. Such measures will be difficult to implement without the social democrats, in government since 1982, losing electoral support. Further reductions in working class power may be the result.

When considering these different options, we must realize that they are partly determined by the limits set by macroeconomic realities and partly by actions undertaken and strategies chosen by the main actors in the arena—the organized interests around capital and labour. It is useless to try to predict the outcome of this class struggle; but the Swedish case shows that the stability of institutional arrangements which affect distributional processes in society is not only determined by their ability to stand up against ideals of economic rationality. It is also dependent upon the distribution of power and the strategies used in the continuing class struggle.

Summary and Conclusions

In many countries intervention through political and union channels in the process of income determination has grown in importance, but the forms this intervention take differ. In some countries there are new tendencies towards more co-ordinated collective action. In others, such strategies have been in operation over quite a long period. These tendencies have brought some old, but nevertheless important, questions to the centre of the political debate and have stimulated social scientists to take them up again. These questions are (i) whether intervention in the process of income determination is compatible with efficiency and (ii) whether the increasing importance of collective action at the expense of the market is compatible with democratic ideals. Much research within the tradition of neo-classical economics, or concerned with such topics as 'public choice' or 'corporatism', would seem to give negative answers to the above questions.

The problems of efficiency and democracy are separate but there are nevertheless important links between them. One is legitimacy, here used in the sense of the extent to which the actual distribution of income deviates from (or changes in the direction of) the prevailing value structure of a society. Market interventions through working class mobilization, based on strong links between various political and union organizations, are likely to produce two important conflicting tendencies. First, there are tendencies towards a more egalitarian value structure and towards increased demands for the inclusion of other work criteria than market conditions in wage determination. Secondly, if more egalitarian evaluations are put into practice and if wage differentials have some importance for allocative efficiency in the labour market, then it may be supposed that the labour market will be thrown into disequilibrium and the opportunity structure made more unequal and out of line with the value structure, so that growing internal tensions result. This dilemma is much easier to solve if efficiency and economic growth are high. It is also easier to solve to the extent that the labour market can be brought into equilibrium without the help of market-determined wage differentials.

It is argued in this paper that efficiency, at least in the sense of a well-functioning labour market, is compatible with rather extensive intervention in income determination. The overriding importance of wages as allocative instruments in the labour market is questioned and, further, it has been argued that their importance in this regard can be reduced by labour-market policies. Some empirical support for these arguments has been given by comparisons between the USA and Sweden, two countries which differ greatly in wage distribution and social policy, but very little in allocative efficiency in the labour market. Even if this does not prove that the idea of a trade-off between equality and efficiency is wrong, at least it indicates that equality and market-independent income determination are within rather wide limits, compatible with efficiency. This has led us to believe that rather extensive interference in the process of income determination is possible. Whether institutional arrangements responsible for this interference will survive is dependent upon the extent to which interference is made in accordance with people's conceptions of justice. However, that in turn is a question of macroeconomic realities as well as of the power distribution between classes in society.

In conclusion, it may be noted that the alternative to collective action through class-based organization is hardly the free market in the classical sense, as one might be led to believe from much of the debate on this issue. In Western democracies, where the right to organize exists, it is collective action in some more fragmentary and differentiated form which is the alternative. How, in such political systems, income distribution and economic efficiency will be affected will then depend, among other things, on the pattern that the organizational structure takes. Two main possibilities would seem to exist, each with its attendant problems. One is the emergence of a 'dual economy', which can be expected to appear to the extent that organizational strength varies in the labour market. This, however, must lead to very great inequality. The other possibility is that the whole of the labour market is well organized, but still fragmented. In this case, the difficulty will be that of achieving income-policy goals and the consequent threat to the society at large of reduced economic performance. Finally, then, it may be said that how fully either of these possibilities can stand up to test against democratic ideals remains itself an open question.

Notes

1. The general conception that a strong, co-operative union structure will lead to wage relativities determined more by fairness than by market conditions and will also gradually lead to decreasing wage differentials is supported by the above data. But we are well aware that some other countries do not fit into this picture. Austria, for example, has a union structure which, perhaps, is even more centralized than the Swedish. Nevertheless, wage differentials in Austria seem to have developed towards inequality at an even faster rate than in the USA. The Netherlands is another deviant case. Wage differences in that country have changed in a way similar to that in Sweden without a centralized union structure of the Swedish type. Such deviant cases make it difficult to generalize about the relation between union structure and wage relations. It seems plausible that the above-mentioned mechanisms exist, but perhaps only under certain circumstances. As always, other factors are also important. The importance of union structure relative to other factors remains to be determined.

2. Since then a tax reform has been decided on. This reform aims at a reduction of the marginal tax rate to 50 per cent by 1985.

3. The United Kingdom seems to be a good example of this case. For most of the 1970s, wages were too high in relation to economic resources. Thus, the wages struggle became a zero-sum game, in the sense that wage increases seemed to be matched by reductions in profits and vice versa.

10

Historic Compromise and Pluralist Decline? Profits and Capital in the Nordic Countries

DON S. SCHWERIN

Introduction

There is a paradox between Olson's thesis of pluralist decline (1982) and the conditions for capitalist production elaborated by Lancaster (1973), Przeworski and Wallerstein (1982a) and Schott (this volume). So-called historic compromises in social-democratic societies are held responsible for the survival of a capitalist mode of production—which otherwise would be in question in the face of an unprecedented redistribution of political resources in favour of labour: yet the compromise itself and the organizational conditions underlying it would, by Olson's thesis, lead to a progressive deterioration of economic efficiency and growth. The democratic capitalist solution itself becomes the problem. Class compromise is self-defeating, while the alternative, at least in political economies where labour is able to resist capitalist domination, is oscillating political stalemate between labour and capital and consequent economic stagnation.

Capitalist economic growth depends on capitalists diverting profits from consumption to investment. Historically, capitalists' rates of saving and investment choices were substantially unilateral decisions taken by owners and hierarchically imposed on labour. The development of democratic governing institutions and of trade unions shifted power resources to labour (Korpi, 1983) and threatened not only capitalists' discretion about what to do with their profits but also the capitalist mode of production. The maintenance of capitalism in the face of growing labour power called for a compromise recognizing the institutionalization of labour's political resources and its claims to improving standards of living in exchange for security of private property and capitalist determination of savings and investment. The stability of the compromise entailed labour's restraint in using its institutional leverage to appropriate profits and capital's commitment to sufficient investment to ensure economic growth.

The combination of private ownership of the instruments of production with representative political institutions based on widespread suffrage constitutes a compromise between workers, who consent to the private appropriation of profit by owners of capital, and capitalists, who accept the democratic institutions through which workers can make effective claims for an improvement of their material conditions (Przeworski & Wallerstein, 1982a: 215).

It is organization which pushes historic compromise into pluralist decline. Uncertainty is the chief threat to class compromise and reduction of uncertainty through organization is its rationale (Przeworski & Wallerstein, 1982a: 231 f; Schwerin, 1980b). Historic compromises and organization go hand in hand. Compromises ratify the outcomes of a power relationship at a particular point in time and project that balance of power into the future. Each side forsakes risky maximizing strategies for a more modest but more certain share of a long-term joint outcome. Neither capital nor labour can afford, politically or economically, to commit itself to a moderate strategy without some assurance that the other has the intent and the capacity to adhere to the settlement. The question of capacity is raised by the public goods character of the outcomes and the consequent incentives for constituent elements of capital or labour to defect. The inclusive and hierarchic organization of capital and labour alike thus contributes to the mutual assurance of capability to implement what are necessarily regulatory agreements (Schwerin, 1982; cf. Lange, this volume). Organization between sectors indicates intent, and is expressed in formal contracts and the development of norms and procedures of joint decision making, enforced to varying degrees by the state. Organizational enforcement of co-operative tactics and strategies reduces uncertainty and the risks of moderation. In sum, organization, both between sectors and within, provides the information and predictability critical to optimal joint outcomes (Frohlich & Oppenheimer, 1978: 61).[1]

By Olson's (1982) reasoning, the attempt to regulate present and future incomes through institutionalized class compromise is misguided. The only dispensation Olson allows is reserved for 'encompassing' organizations, similar, for example, to the sectoral organizations found in Scandinavia: 'Clearly the encompassing organization, if it has rational leadership, will care about the excess burden arising from distributional policies favorable to its members and will out of sheer self-interest strive to make the excess burden as small as possible' (1982: 48). However, Olson quickly hedges even this hint of a U-shaped relationship between the degree of interest organization and economic performance. Large organizations, he reports, have many decisions to make, take a long time to make these decisions, and so labour under 'clogged agendas' (54-8). The result is neglected problems and delayed, often inappropriate, reactions. Olson further suspects the lack of pluralism that is characteristic where encompassing organizations prevail: 'If a political system is composed only of highly encompassing organizations and institutions, there also may be less diversity of advocacy, opinion, and policy, and fewer checks to erroneous ideas and policies'. Any eventual success of such systems is fortuitous: 'Encompassing organizations and institutions may therefore perform unusually badly in some cases or periods and unusually effectively in others' (52). Moreover, since 'the degree of monopoly power often increases as an organization becomes more encompassing' (49), a 'kinky', or broken, curve with a relatively wide band of indeterminate behaviour may better capture the swings of 'nearly' encompassing organizations between private rent-seeking and social responsibility. What is rational behaviour becomes increasingly problematic as organizations approach the inflection point of the U-shaped curve. Certainly, large sectoral organizations use their monopoly position to bargain for favourable distributional outcomes from even socially responsible policies and to threaten socially irresponsible—and even self-defeating—behaviour in order to make a political point.

Olson has, in other words, little confidence in the implications grounded in his own theory of collective action. He so hedges his discussion of encompassing organizations that we cannot take it as a serious amendment to the thesis of 'pluralist decline'. Olson resorts to the ambivalent formulation that his discussion 'refers to the incentives that face encompassing organizations rather than to their choices in particular cases' (53), thus leaving the argument available merely for covering deviant cases (90–2).

Olson's critique is of course primarily directed at 'distributional coalitions': 'organizations for collective action [that are] overwhelmingly oriented to struggles over the distribution of income and wealth rather than to the production of additional output' (44). The greater the accumulation of such organizations, the slower the rate of economic growth. Distributional coalitions lobby (successfully) for self-serving redistributions from the public purse and insulate their advantages with complex regulations. They restrict factor mobility, make prices sticky downward, slow the rate of innovation, and frustrate adjustment to external change; in short, distributional coalitions shield their members from competition and thereby build in inefficiency and guarantee slow growth. In theory, at least, encompassing organizations are partially excepted from this critique since such groups must supposedly consume the fruits of their own policies, rather than push the costs off on to third parties. Increasing organizational size and inclusiveness tends to shift strategy towards social responsibility.

Unlike Olson's distributional coalitions, the organizations of class compromise mix distributional and production goals. For labour, production is of no interest without a satisfactory distribution rule but distributional advantage without growth is myopic. For capital, holding on to the dominant share risks losing it all, yet property is little pleasure without a pay-off. Even if the sectoral organizations of the Nordic countries can be regarded as encompassing groups, however, the logic of class compromise and its historic circumstances conserves distributive shares, restrains competition, and avoids conflict, and so should lead to the path of pluralist decline blazed by distributional coalitions. Such compromises are economic peace treaties which freeze a particular power relationship. Again, the paradox is that where labour is strong and potentially militant, economic growth within a capitalist mode of production is greatest in a class compromise regime; yet both the conserving character of class compromises and the organizational context of such agreements run counter to liberal prescriptions for economic growth.

This paradox is, however, less a contradiction of empirical laws than, as in a dictionary definition, 'an inconsistency of opinions'. In several countries, including those of the Nordic region, there have been developments which may be labelled historic compromises and which resemble class compromise.[2] The inconsistency concerns the consequences of these compromises. The one explicit opinion, or proposed developmental path, is that of Olson which suggests that such compromises are not economically viable over the longer term, due to deteriorating growth. The implicit contrary opinion is embraced in the Scandinavian variety of a social-democratic planned economy. The Scandinavian social democrats of the 1920s and 1930s, on the one hand, pledged commitment to democratic political institutions and accepted private property and, on the other, built organizations: a strong centralized trade-union organization, a competitive and disciplined parliamentary party, and an active state pursing fiscal stimulation, industrial planning, and capital regulation. The social-democratic path is one characterized by solidaristic workers, wage increases adjusted to productivity, external markets, and investment requirements, state-led investment in the economic infrastructure, and steeply progressive personal income taxes. The goals are sustained growth, full employment, and an equalization of economic welfare. The social-democratic path is both more optimistic and less deterministic than the prospect of pluralist decline.

While the paths of pluralist decline and of social-democratic planning differ on expected consequences, both assume that the historic compromise remains roughly intact. However, a more familiar evaluation of historic compromises is that the compromise itself is unstable and vulnerable to subversion from, alternatively, the Left or the Right. These are more clearly political arguments. The political counterpart to the thesis of pluralist decline is the liberal-conservative view of social-democratic 'middle ways' as simply rest stops on the road to full-blown socialism. The Right lacks confidence that labour in government will resist the temptation to appropriate increasing shares of profits for public consumption and social transfers. This third path, 'socialist exploitation', projects declining profits, increasing wage shares, and eventually a capital flight and an investment crisis.[3]

The Left, for its part, forecasts capitalist subversion of the social-democratic compromise. Capital will use its leverage over investment to force labour acceptance of conventional capitalist prerogatives regarding profits and investment, thus leaving labour with neither a fair distributive share nor control over the means of production. The left has no confidence in the social productivity of capitalist investment. Capitalist savings and investment practices—not labour's consumption demands—are held responsible for economic stagnation and unemployment.

It is capital that is rent-seeking, not labour. Far from being a threat to market processes, the Left sees organization as the necessary instrument for redressing the imbalance of power resources in society and for creating the conditions for socially productive economic growth. The Left expects a persistent capitalist political assault on the institutions of the historic compromise and thereby on the power relations underlying it: 'The erosion of the historic compromise of the 1930s began with the gradual emptying of its political formula' (Korpi, 1983: 210). This is the fourth developmental path: 'capitalist *revanche.*'

In sum, historic compromises may work (social-democratic planning), may degenerate in pluralist decline (Olson), may be undermined from the Left (socialist exploitation), or may be subverted by the Right (capitalist *revanche*). In the next section, I show that evaluations of 'social-democratic planning' and of 'pluralist decline' give contradictory results with respect to economic growth, depending on the specification of the independent variable. I further note that evaluations of two other dimensions of economic performance, employment and distribution, give the advantage to social democracy.

Pluralist decline vs. social-democratic planning

The overall results of this cross-sectional study of advanced industrial countries seem to support strongly Olson's theory of the political economy of comparative growth (Choi, 1983: 71).

So summarizes Kwang Choi his operationalization and testing of Olson's central arguments. He reports strong relationships between an index of institutional sclerosis and growth rates of GDP, total and per capita, from eighteen advanced democratic countries for the period 1950–73 (1983: 59). Olson boldly reasons that the density of interest groups will increase with the 'age' of a modern democratic polity, with age adjusted for suspension of democratic liberties during periods of, for example, foreign occupation. It is then, through age, in this sense, that Choi operationalizes institutional sclerosis, rather than by any direct measures of interest group density, policy institutions, or economic regulation. In contrast, Cameron (this volume) constructs an index of the 'organized power of labour' from proportion of work-force unionized, organizational unity of labour, and power in collective bargaining. Cameron's index directly assesses the extent of labour organization and indirectly indicates the influence of labour over wage levels and wage structures, conditions of employment, and, to a lesser extent, employment levels. Schmitter (1981: 294) labels a composite measure, which produces a similar rank ordering of nations, an 'indicator of societal corporatism'.

I find that for fifteen of the eighteen nations studied by Choi, there is no significant relationship between Cameron's more direct indicator of 'distributional coalitions' and mean annual percentage change of GDP at market prices, 1960–80 (Pearson's $r = -.05$). There is, however, a weak positive relationship between Cameron's index and the trend slope of annual percentage changes in real GDP, 1962–80 (Pearson's $r = +.34$; $b = 0.0008$). In other words, growth rates in more organized societies have been dropping off at a slightly slower rate. There is no difficulty in accounting for the difference between these correlations and Choi's findings. Choi's index of institutional sclerosis and Cameron's index are, if anything, inversely related (Pearson's $r = -.21$). Social-democratic planning, to the extent that it varies with Cameron's index, apparently does not injure economic growth.

Social democracy adds employment and income equality to GDP growth as goals. Cameron's analysis (this volume) supports the social-democratic claim regarding employment while van Arnhem and Schotsman (1982) find that Left and labour strength are related to income equalization. (See also Lindbeck, 1983.) These findings are neither unique nor irrelevant. Added to the, at worst, inconclusive findings for growth, the social-democratic record in employment and distribution suggests that the promise of historic compromise has been realized, at least for labour and in relative terms. Class compromise, however, concerns not only economic performance but also the protection of institutions. Has half a century of adjustment fundamentally altered the terms of historic compromises in this latter respect?

The question of institutional stability introduces the scenario of socialist exploitation where the Left is charged with defecting from the terms of class compromise and using its democratic leverage to appropriate profits for consumption. In the remainder of this paper I evaluate socialist exploitation using the Nordic social democracies as a best-case test. I leave evaluation of the capitalist *revanche* scenario for another effort. The current political temper, especially in the United States, puts social democracy on the defensive and makes the present task one of confronting the socialist exploitation scenario.

Profits and Savings

This section is provoked by the observation of a regular fall in operating surplus as a percentage of GDP in the Nordic countries over the last thirty years. If for no other reason, this decline warrants examination as a major structural development of the post-war period. But, of course, the appearance of a falling profit share is also of interest as possible evidence of what I have labelled, somewhat inflammatorily, the path of socialist exploitation. Declining operating surplus, or profits, as a percentage of GDP signals systematic changes in capitalist industrial economies, affecting the holding of real and financial assets, and with obvious consequences for the control of capital and the distribution of power resources.

In the following, I take up the questions of operating surplus, returns to capital, savings, investment, public sector finance and finance of industry in a preliminary evaluation of the hypothesis of socialist exploitation in the Nordic countries. These countries offer here a best-case test. The Nordic economies are highly organized, labour is strong both at the work-place and in government, and the countries historically have been social-policy pioneers and have correspondingly large public sectors. (See Scharpf, this volume, for a Nordic–Germanic comparison.)

Few time-series for the post-war period are as impressive as data on the decline of operating surplus as a percentage of GDP, this being often termed

TABLE 10.1. *Net operating surplus as percentage of gross domestic product*

	Denmark	Finland	Norway	Sweden		France	West Germany	UK	US
1950	40	35	–	35					
1951	38	37	–	36					
1952	37	35	–	32					
1953	37	33	–	31					
1954	35	36	–	31					
1955	34	37	–	29					
1956	35	35	–	29					
1957	34	33	–	29					
1958	33	34	–	29					
1959	34	34	–	30					
1960	33	34	–	27					
1961	32	34	–	26					
1962	31	33	25	23					
1963	30	28[a]	25	23	22[b]	29	28	20	23
1964	31	27	26	23	22	29	28	20	23
1965	29	26	26	22	21	29	27	20	24
1966	27	25	24	20	20	29	26	19	24
1967	26	24	21	20	20	29	26	19	23
1968	25	25	22	18	18	29	28	19	22
1969	26	26	21	19	19	29	26	19	21
1970	25	25	21	19	19	28	26	18	18
1971	23	23	18	15	17	28	24	18	19
1972	25	23	17	15	17	28	24	20	19
1973	26	23	18	16	19	28	23	20	19
1974	23	23	18	16	19	25	22	16	17
1975	21	21	18	14	18	23	22	14	18
1976	22	20	15	10	15	22	22	15	18
1977	22	20	13	07	11	22	22	17	18
1978	22	21	15	09	13	22	22	18	18
1979	21	22	20		15	22	22	16	18
1980	21	20	24		16	21	21	14	17

[a] New series.
[b] 1963–78 data revised in 1982.

Note: Net operating surplus is defined as gross output minus the sum of intermediate consumption, compensation of employees, indirect taxes minus subsidies, and consumption of fixed capital. Gross operating surplus equals net operating surplus plus consumption of fixed capital.

Sources: OECD *National Accounts 1962–1979*, Vol. II, Paris, 1981; OECD *National Accounts 1963–1980*, Vol. II, Paris, 1982.

profit share (P/Y, where P is operating surplus and Y is value added). Table 10.1 shows the decline in profit share for several welfare economies. As a verdict on the fate of capitalists, the trend is at least partially spurious. The extent of the decline mostly reflects the changing structure of the economy. Unless otherwise corrected, farm incomes count as operating surplus. Agriculture's falling share of national income, therefore, shows up in the relative decline of operating surplus.

Likewise, the relative growth of government has reduced the operating surplus share of national product, since operating surplus is undefined for the production of services by government.[4]

Even these spurious sides to declining operating surplus, however, have real effects. Agricultural investment requirements remain, perhaps even increase, as farm incomes and savings have shifted, in part, to household consumption and saving. It is not a matter of political or economic indifference that new cars replace new tractors. Likewise, the effect of government growth on the relative decline of operating surplus is more than just an accounting technicality. The shift of resources from tradeable to non-tradeable production implicit in the relative expansion of government services jeopardizes the nation's external balance, quite apart from the usual charges laid against big government.

Table 10.1 indicates that there is nothing distinctive about the Nordic social democracies. Both the levels of profit share and the rates of decline in profits of the Nordic countries are similar to the profit levels and trends in political economies as diverse as those of France, West Germany, the United Kingdom, and the United States. Sweden's revised figures do not look seriously different from those of the US or the UK, whereas Denmark and Finland resemble France and Germany. Cyclical effects are more apparent in the Nordic data, as might be expected in relatively more open economies, but not necessarily in social democracies.

Disaggregated profit-share trends for industry and, more narrowly, for manufacturing and specific branches in manufacturing, are much less smooth than the trends in Table 10.1. In Table 10.2, the trend slopes for profit shares are reliably negative for Sweden and Denmark for both manufacturing and industry. No trend, however, can be assigned to profit shares in Finland and the uncertain downward trend before 1977 for Norway is reversed when the time series is extended to 1980.

TABLE 10.2. *Gross profit shares (P/Y) for manufacturing and industry. Linear trends for 1963–80, N = 18*

| | Denmark[a] | | Finland | | Norway | | Sweden | |
	manuf.	indus.	manuf.	indus.	manuf.	indus.	manuf.	indus.
b =	−.35	−.43	−.11	+.05	—	−.13[b]	−.60	−.32
r =	−.65	−.84	−.16	+.10	—	−.35	−.72	−.59
mean	25.7	33.7	36.3	36.3	—	35.6	25.1	29.5

[a] 1966–77; N = 12.
[b] 1963–77; N = 15. For 1963–80, b = +.30 and r = +.40, owing to a sharp upturn in profit share after 1977, attributable to the oil sector.
Source: OECD *National Accounts 1963–1980*, Vol. II, Paris, 1982.

A declining trend seems most marked for Sweden: 'Other countries have also experienced large shifts in factor shares but the level of profits in Swedish industry seems to have fallen relative to most other countries' (OECD, 1982b: 28). The current path of Sweden's manufacturing profit shares is, however, obscured by very strong cyclical effects. Net profit share went from 16 per cent in 1972 to 24 per cent in 1974, and then down to 4 per cent in 1977; profit share in 1983 is expected to rebound to 18 per cent (*Konjunkturläget*, 1983: 128). Manufacturing profit shares in Britain and the United States (since 1965) are similar to Sweden's in trend and level. German profit shares are somewhat higher but also declining, though with plateaux in the mid-1960s and after 1973. Canada, on the other hand, shows movement around a slight upward slope (OECD, 1982b: 28).

The OECD is, however, convinced that profits, overall, are tending to decline: 'Measurement difficulties aside ... there is a general secular decline in profitability which is not well understood' (OECD, 1983b: 57). The OECD uses both profit share (P/Y) and rate of return on capital (P/K) to argue its case. Profit share and rate of return tend to follow each other through business cycles as declining (increasing) production increases (decreases) both labour/output ratios and capital/output ratios.[5] But just as the case for declining profit share can be qualified, there is also disagreement with respect to rates of return. Differences stem largely from varying methods of estimating the capital base which can lead to a confusion of 'operating rate of return' and 'total rate of return' (Bertmar, 1979: 107). 'One of the implications of [total rate of return accounting] is that real capital gains on stocks and fixed assets and real changes in the value of monetary assets and liabilities are incorporated in profits' (Bergström & Södersten, 1979a: 48).[6] The discrepancy between approaches thus increases during rapid inflation. With these and other adjustments being taken into account, Bergström and Södersten conclude for Swedish industry that 'the only reasonable assessment based on this [*sic*] data is that no longer-term trend for profitability exists—neither rising nor falling' (1979a: 54).[7]

A finding of no trend for an accountant's total rate of return may be scant solace for an industrialist with liquidity problems. Even the Swedish Social Democratic finance minister, for example, concedes that 'all interests responding to the long term economic report accept increased industrial profits as a necessary condition for industrial expansion' (*Finansplan*, 1982: 7). For management purposes, operating surplus and saving are the most relevant indicators of industry's current ability to finance expansion, absorb fluctuations, and increase equity. Saving is the difference between current disbursements and current receipts, where operating surplus adds into current receipts along with property and financial earnings. By national accounting convention, savings plus depreciation (and capital transfers) finance gross accumulation, that is, investment in real assets. A recurrent corporate savings deficit reduces the rate of capital accumulation by industry and requires increased external funding for sustained investment. Non-financial corporate savings, data on which are available for Finland and Sweden, are only slightly less cyclically sensitive than operating surplus. Finnish non-financial corporations are recovering from four consecutive years of savings deficits from 1975 to 1978. Sweden's industry enjoyed booming savings from 1970 to 1975 and then lost even more in the following four years (corrected for inflation).

The sectoral savings structure in both Finland and Sweden is in fact dominated by the financial institutions' increasing share of savings. Financial institutions have increased both their share of total savings and real savings in each year, almost without exception. The cyclical vulnerability of the non-financial sector is only very faintly reflected in the balance sheets of the financial institutions. Especially in Finland, insurance companies account for much of the growth. Employers' contributions paid into the national supplementary pension plan are administered by private insurance companies and are included in the accounts of the financial sector. A broadly similar supplementary pension scheme in Sweden is administered by public sector funds and is included in the government sector. The effect is not only an underestimate of the size of the Finnish public sector but also an increase in the financial leverage of the Finnish insurance companies.

TABLE 10.3. *Percentage distribution of savings by sector, 1965–80*

	Finland				Sweden			
	Sector[a]				Sector[a]			
	H	G	N–F	F	H	G	N–F	F
1965	19	59	03	18	23	59	09	09
1970	20	53	15	12	15	65	10	10
1975	31	49	−05	25	20	43	19	19
1980	32	29	05	34	48	−09	03	57

[a] Sectors: H(ousehold); G(overnment); N(on)-F(inancial) (corporate and quasi-corporate enterprises); F(inancial institutions).
Source: OECD *National Accounts 1963–1980* Vol. II, Paris, 1982.

The relative affluence of the Swedish financial sector parallels a decrease in industry's 'solidity': that is, the ratio of equity to total capital. The solidity of Swedish industry has decreased every year since 1970 except for 1979; from 0.31 in 1970 to 0.25 in 1981 (SOU 1982b: 272; SOU 1980: 430). Comparable data for Denmark and Norway indicate different levels and rates of decline. The solidity of Danish industry declined from 37.9 per cent in 1977 to 34.0 per cent in 1981, a decline of approximately one percentage point per year (OECD 1983a: 32). The solidity of 'traditional' Norwegian industry (i.e. excluding oil and shipping) is comparatively low at 16.5 per cent in 1981, but it has not deteriorated since 1975 (*Nasjonalbudsjettet*, 1983: 82).

Declining Swedish solidity carries with it an increase in the ratio of debt to equity, from 2.24 in 1971 to 2.75 in 1979. (Cf. *Konjunkturläget*, 1983: 132.) Increasing relative debt produces a leverage effect. This leverage means that changes in return to total capital produce exaggerated movements in return to equity (Bertmar *et al.*, 1979). This relieves pressure on the firm during a recovery but seriously jeopardizes the firm's stability in downturns. Savings deficits also appear in self-financing trends for industry. Self-financing (the ratio between gross savings and investment) in Swedish mining and manufacturing in 1979 stood at 0.50; prior to OPEC I, the self-financing ratio stood close to or above unity (*Konjunkturläget*, 1983, Appendix: 26).

There are three conclusions to this discussion. Two are conclusions of inconclusiveness:

(i) Assessments of profit levels and trends are nearly meaningless without a full specification of the definition of profit (e.g. profit share, return to capital, return to equity), of the definition of, and method of estimating, capital (e.g. total rate of return vs. operating rate of return; cost of acquisition vs. replacement cost), and of the time period covered.

(ii) Most statements regarding profit trends in Scandinavia can be contradicted by evidence from at least one of the Scandinavian countries, not to mention Finland. With respect to profit trends, however defined, these countries do not constitute a homogeneous region. National boundaries do make a difference, and the differences within the region are not clearly insignificant relative to the differences between Norden or Scandinavia and other OECD countries and groupings thereof. A more precise statement is not possible with the data presently available.

(iii) The conclusive item is that sectoral savings have shifted markedly from non-financial to financial corporations.

Strikes, Taxes, and Wages

Fears that the Left would defect from historic compromises and maximize short-term labour outcomes would be realized if the Left were either to disavow the labour-market institutions that were part of the Scandinavian historic compromises or to exploit its democratic leverage and manœuvre the state to appropriate capital for labour's advantage. Neither of these has happened. The first would be reflected in strike rates and the rejection of co-ordinated wage settlements. Nothing has happened in Scandinavia in recent years to seriously shake the image of internationally low strike rates, although Finland's strike rate is consistently higher than that of the Scandinavian countries. Co-ordinated wage settlements are always politically precarious but the most troublesome political cleavages run vertically within labour and capital, not horizontally between the class organizations. If any one element recently has disrupted labour-market institutions, it has been the state under bourgeois, not social-democratic, governments—that is, the Schülter government in Denmark and the Willoch government in Norway. Capitalists in Sweden, on the other hand, acted directly in the massive lock-out in 1980. Capital came to an agreement and lifted its lock-out only on request from the bourgeois government, thus ending Sweden's largest industrial conflict ever. Labour, if not all interests within labour, remains committed to co-ordinated wage settlements.

Evidence that labour has used its democratic leverage to appropriate profits must be found in (i) taxes on corporations, (ii) non-wage labour costs, (iii) public sector wages, and (iv) barriers to labour rationalization. It can also be claimed that (v) high wages are an indirect effect of social-democratic fiscal stimulus. Except with (iv), simple tests can in each of these respects be applied.

(i) For the Nordic countries, the trend for taxes on corporate profits and capital gains as a percentage of total taxation and as a percentage of GDP is, if anything, downward sloping since 1965;[7] the exception is Norway's swelling revenues from the oil sector. Corporate taxes in the United States, for example, are considerably more significant than in the Nordic countries, as a proportion of both tax revenues and gross domestic product.

TABLE 10.4. *Tax on corporate profits and capital gains as percentage of total taxation and as percentage of GDP*

	1965	1970	1975	1980
Denmark				
% taxation	4.54	2.64	3.12	3.21
% GDP	1.36	1.07	1.29	1.47
Finland				
% taxation	8.24	5.47	4.22	4.45
% GDP	2.48	1.76	1.52	1.57
Norway				
% taxation	3.81	3.28	2.85	13.22
% GDP	1.27	1.29	1.28	6.26
Sweden				
% taxation	6.10	4.40	4.34	2.45[a]
% GDP	2.19	1.79	1.91	1.21
United States				
% taxation	15.81	12.71	10.79	10.13
% GDP	4.19	3.83	3.26	3.11
EEC mean				
% taxation	6.77	7.33	5.43	6.73
% GDP	2.06	2.48	2.47	2.71

[a] 1981 = ca. 0.9 per cent.
Source: OECD: *Revenue Statistics of OECD Member Countries, 1965–1981*, Paris, 1982

(ii) No interesting generalization can be made about the level and rate of increase of non-wage labour costs (NWLC) in the Nordic social democracies. As is often the case, Sweden defines the stereotype of an aggressive social democracy but, again, it is not a stereotype which usefully describes the other Nordic social democracies pursuing similar social policies within the context of similar institutions. Sweden's NWLC are distinctively high with a high growth rate over the last decade. Payroll taxes increased at an annual average of 3.7 per cent from 1973 to 1977, exceeding the contractual wage increase in 1974 (OECD 1982b: 12). Denmark, on the other hand, is distinctively low with respect to NWLC; NWLC accounted for 20 per cent of total labour costs in Denmark in 1980 compared with an OECD mean of about 35 per cent and 27 per cent in the United States. NWLC in Finland have increased at twice the rate of the OECD mean but have remained stable at about the OECD mean since 1976. Norway's NWLC pattern is indistinctive (see also OECD 1982a: 42).

TABLE 10.5. *Non-wage labour costs as percentage of total labour costs*

	Denmark	Finland	Norway	Sweden	Mean of 13 OECD[a] countries
1969	14.2	21.6	24.7	21.4	27.5
1970	14.0	23.0	25.3	22.0	28.2
1971	14.6	22.8	26.5	22.8	28.7
1972	15.6	26.0	27.9	23.5	30.5
1973	16.8	28.9	30.1	26.0	31.7
1974	17.5	30.1	30.3	29.4	32.8
1975	17.1	32.7	29.9	32.2	33.7
1976	17.4	35.0	29.3	41.6	35.0
1977	17.5	36.0	29.2	35.3	35.0
1978	17.6	35.7	31.1	38.1	35.7
1979	18.8	36.0	32.4	39.5	36.2
1980	20.4	36.6	32.4	40.1	34.8[b]

[a] Belgium, Denmark, Finland, France, Italy, Netherlands (1972–80), Norway, United Kingdom, United States, Federal Republic, Sweden, and Austria.
[b] N = 11; Data not available for Italy and Austria.
Source: Swedish Employers' Confederation. *Wages and total labour costs for workers, 1969–1979*, Stockholm, 1982.

(iii) The size of government employment, its rate of growth, and the increasing organization of government employees attach a certain plausibility to the charge that government wage policy has made the public sector wage-leading. However plausible, the evidence is lacking. Public sector salaries in the Nordic countries follow closely what happens in the private sector in the annual or biennial wage rounds, with public sector salaries falling behind in the interims between negotiations, despite *post hoc* catch-up clauses. Data reported by the OECD for Denmark support the impression of public sector wage lag: in only one year from 1971 to 1980 did gross nominal income for 'public employee' increase faster than that for 'LO wage-earner' (OECD 1982a:

16). Public employees in Finland likewise have trailed behind. Setting earnings level in 1975 at 100, the earnings of employees in public administration, education, and health, stood at 178, 177, and 173, respectively, in 1981, against an overall mean of 188 (*Ekonomisk översikt*, 1982: 112). Data for Norway in Table 10.6 show roughly the same relationship.

TABLE 10.6. *Mean average annual increase in wage income before taxes 1973–80, Norway*

Industry:	Percentage change
Industrial worker	11.1
Upper-level management	9.8
State	
Skilled worker	
(rail and telephone)	9.8
Office clerk	10.5
Upper-level management	8.6

Source: NOU, *Om grunnlaget for inntektsoppgjörene 1983*, Oslo, 1983.

Rather than public employees, the two groups which seem to have been income-lending in the 1970s are farmers and pensioners, neither of which lend themselves to elegant class compromise analysis, but which were implicitly part of the Nordic historic compromises.

(iv) Social-democratic governments have plausibly made it more difficult for employers to lay off and fire workers. Direct cross-national data relating government employment regulation to employer lay-off calculi are not available—understandably so. Productivity data (change in real value added per employee: Y/L) are a conventional proxy, in spite of their contamination by independent variations not only in labour force and output volume and price but also in capital intensity (K/L) and capital productivity (K/Y): $Y/L = K/L : K/Y$. Productivity data do not therefore lend themselves to straightforward interpretation.

The productivity data in Table 10.7 indicate generally lower productivity increases in the Nordic economies. Norway and Sweden, especially, have had low productivity growth rates in the period 1973–80, while Denmark and Finland had rates slightly above the EEC mean. The productivity trends for Norway and Sweden are not surprising. Both maintained high employment even while production was stagnating. Unemployment rates of under 2 per cent in Norway and Sweden throughout the post-war period meant that employers faced a chronic shortage of skilled workers. Reasonable employer calculation as well as government regulation may therefore account for employer reluctance to lay off skilled labour during what are expected to be only cyclic declines.

TABLE 10.7. *Real value added in manufacturing per person employed (Average annual percentage change^a)*

	Denmark	Finland	Norway	Sweden	EEC[c]
1960-67	4.8	4.3	3.4	5.3	4.8
1967-73	4.2	4.0	3.9[b]	5.6	5.9
1973-80	3.4	2.9	0.3	0.8	2.7

[a] Geometric means. The differences between geometric and arithmetic means in these data are substantial.
[b] 1967-71.   [c]Weighted mean.
Source: OECD, *Historical Statistics,* Paris, 1982.

The effects of declining productivity on capital, even if induced by restrictive government employment regulation, cannot be assessed in isolation from compensating policies. Inventory loans and direct subsidies, used by both Sweden and Norway, cushion the effect of declining labour productivity on profitability. Norway's 1979 wage freeze and Sweden's devaluations in 1981 and 1982 more dramatically intervene between labour productivity and profitability. The lesson is that productivity declines should quicken our curiosity, not conclude the argument.

(v) Comparative wage rates are of interest for what they do not show. Table 10.8 does not corroborate, for example, the simple expectation that wage rates in the Nordic social democracies are notably high (cf. Cameron, this volume). What Table 10.8 does demonstrate is that exchange rate variations make a great deal of difference.

Government Finance and Crowding Out

The predicted subversion of the historic compromise from the Left has not happened. There has not been an exploitative increase in corporate taxes, non-wage labour costs have not increased at an unusually rapid pace, the government has not become wage-leading, and estimates of declining returns to capital are sensitive to variations in data and method. This does not disguise, however, the fact that there have been structural changes in the flows of capital which have substantially modified economic relationships.

Three things have happened: (i) industry has become increasingly dependent on external financing; (ii) surplus assets have accumulated in financial institutions; and (iii) government borrowing has come to dominate credit markets. Capital is not being squeezed, at least not in the short term. Industrialists, how-ever, are being forced to pay higher prices for working and investment capital, as

TABLE 10.8. *Increase in hourly earnings for adult industrial workers,*
1971–81 (per cent)

| | Total percentage increase, 1971–81 | |
	In national currency	Converted to Norwegian kroner[a]
Norway	193.2	193.2
Denmark	224.7	177.0
Sweden	171.4	124.6
Finland	280.3	201.2
Belgium	232.9	256.4
France	292.2	221.5
Netherlands	167.5	206.5
Great Britain	321.5	185.3
Switzerland	97.0	237.9
Germany	109.0	163.2
United States	123.5	83.1
Canada	179.6	92.8
Japan	229.1	323.2
Unweighted mean	201.7	189.7

[a] The Norwegian krone is used as the common currency for convenience. The choice of any specific common currency produces distortions, the Norwegian krone perhaps fewer than most.

Source: NOU, *Om grunnlaget for inntektsoppgjörene 1983*, Oslo, 1983.

are government debt managers. The emerging cleavage is between big finance and big government, on the one hand, and entrepreneurs and industrial workers on the other. This process goes under the rubric of 'crowding out'. Crowding out has policy implications and implications for the administration of public sector borrowing, but to the extent that it describes a longer-term phenomenon, it also implies a structural change to the detriment of traditional industry as well as to new ventures.

Crowding out signifies the effects of financing a public sector deficit on the availability of capital to non-financial borrowers and/or on the cost of capital. The usual scenario of crowding out begins with the development of a large state budgetary deficit which is financed by borrowing from the public (households, business, local government) and from banks and other financial institutions (insurance companies, public pension funds). So much is required, in fact, that industrialists and consumers are pushed out of the regular market or are required to pay significantly higher interest rates. The increased return required from capital projects leads industrialists to postpone or cancel planned investment. The consequent reduction in economic activity worsens the budgetary balance at the same time that future economic growth is compromised. The more precise effects of government deficit finance depend on (i) the level of private economic activity; (ii) the extent to which the deficit is financed by increasing the money supply; and (iii) the term structure of that portion of the debt that is financed by borrowing.

Broader uses of the idea of crowding out include crowding out by inflation (SOU, 1982a: 137). Deficit financing acts directly on the monetary base and indirectly on prices when the state borrows from the central bank (crudely referred to as 'running the printing presses') or imports capital by borrowing abroad. The latter effect, however, is countered to some extent by fixed exchange rates owing to the current account consequences of domestic monetary expansion. The price effect of an expansive credit policy varies, *inter alia*, with the state of the economy.

The alternative is to borrow directly from the general public, here including insurance companies, or banks. It is usually assumed that bank financing resembles borrowing from the central bank in its effects on monetary expansion. This is, however, misleading unless additional assumptions are made. Borrowing from the banks can resemble monetary financing when (i) there is monetary accommodation by the central bank, such as easing bank borrowing terms from the central bank, (ii) banks have excess reserves, or (iii) banks can quickly increase their borrowing from the public. There is an expansionary effect, for example, if banks are pushed to acquire government bonds over and above their usual portfolio preference and do so by issuing highly liquid bank certificates (SOU, 1982a: 94). The expansionary effect is minimal, on the other hand, if banks are required to draw down private lending in order to increase holdings of state bonds.

Borrowing is usually steered into the short-term markets in order to insulate the longer-term rates which are important for industrial investment and housing construction. The trade-off, however, is that the high liquidity of short-term assets compromises the intended effects of loan financing on prices. Short-term assets can resemble money holdings for some consumers. Further, flows of international credit in open financial markets neutralize national authorities' attempts to minimize the money supply effects of deficit financing. Attempts to market government securities with an interest rate differential attract inward flows of capital with direct liquidity effects. Complicating policy at this point is the fact that policy-makers specifically intend some import of capital in order to cover the balance of payments deficits which often accompany budget deficits. Likewise, there are limits to the interest rate differentials that can be tolerated between different segments of the financial market. Excessive pressure on the short-term markets spills over into longer-term markets as capital is attracted from the latter to shorter-term assets bearing comparatively high interest rates. The eventual spill-over of debt financing into the longer-term markets realizes the crowding-out scenario of reduced industrial investment by making extravagant demands on its profitability.

Eventual crowding out begins, then, with government deficits. In Norden, only Denmark and Sweden have run sufficiently large deficits over several years to give rise to crowding out as a problem. Both Finland and Norway have run budget surpluses each year save two since 1970. The data in Table 10.9, however, are sanitized. Excluded from expenditures are funds which are loaned to businesses and households either directly or through state banks. Still included,

TABLE 10.9. *Central government deficit before loan transactions as percentage of GDP at purchasers' values*

	Denmark[a]	Finland[b]	Norway[c]	Sweden[d]
1970	3.3	2.5	0.4	1.9
1971	0.5	2.8	0.2	2.6
1972	1.9	3.3	1.0	0.0
1973	0.5	4.3	2.5	−0.2
1974	−1.0	2.9	1.3	−1.8
1975	−5.4	0.3	1.2	0.0
1976	−3.4	5.3	0.5	1.5
1977	−3.8	1.3	−1.7	−1.6
1978	−5.1	0.2	−2.4	−5.2
1979	−8.3	−1.2	0.2	−6.9
1980	−7.0	−0.5	3.7	−7.3
1981	–	1.4	2.9	−8.6
1982	–	–	2.8	−10.1

[a] The entry is 'nettofinansieringsbehov' minus 'netto udlån'. The conventional figure reported is DAU (Drifts-, anlegs- og udlånsoverskudd). The figure used here excludes the state's lending but adds certain transfers and capital expenditures related to pension financing. This is judged to be roughly equivalent to the budget balance data for Finland and Norway. (Both the latter include investment in and transfers to state enterprises. Norway's entry includes, in addition, transfers to the public pension administration; Finland's corresponding post is small. The entry for Sweden excludes its substantially larger state enterprise sector but includes transfers to the social insurance sector.) The Danish entries for 1970 up to the end of 1977 are fiscal year balances over calendar year GDP for the first year of the respective fiscal year. The magnitude of the ratios are, therefore, slightly exaggerated. (*Sources: Tiårsoversigt*, Copenhagen, 1981; *Ökonomisk oversigt* 3, Copenhagen, 1983).
[b] Inkomstöverskott: balance before loan transactions and amortization. (*Source: Statistik översikter*, Helsinki, 1983).
[c] Statskassens overskudd för lånetransaksjoner. Data from 1973 on are adjusted for lag in tax collection ('skatteinnkreving'); data are 'påløpte' as opposed to 'bokförte'. The difference in some years is substantial. Norway is the only Nordic country which uses a separate accounting sector outside the state budget for this purpose. (*Source: Ökonomisk utsyn*, Oslo, 1983).
[d] Net lending as defined by OECD, *National Accounts*. The entries for 1981+ are 'finansielt sparande': i.e. 'totalsaldo-utlåning och andra finansiella transaktioner och korrigeringpost'. Conventional figures reported for Sweden include financial transactions. Adding financial transactions adds about 3 percentage points to recent budget deficits as percentage of GDP. (*Sources:* OECD, *National Accounts 1963-1980*, Paris, 1982; *Konjunkturlägetz* 1983).

however, are subsidies to industry and investment in, and capital transfers to, state enterprises. Funds which are channelled back into the capital market, albeit on special terms, presumably contribute to, rather than draw on, available credit.[8]

Any eventual crowding out for Denmark or Sweden has been through access to, or cost of, capital rather than through inflation. To finance deficits in these open, export-oriented economies primarily through monetary expansion would jeopardize external competitiveness and further worsen both government finances and the current account deficit—hardly acceptable trade-offs for reduced financing costs. Foreign borrowing, which is a form of monetary financing, has aimed first at supplying the necessary capital import to cover foreign obligations, including current balance deficits and amortization of outstanding private and public debt. Prior to 1975, private capital imports largely financed Denmark's apparently structural current account deficit. Domestic interest rates were intentionally pushed above those of competing foreign capital sources in order to stimulate capital imports. Private capital imports dropped to an average 38 per cent of the current balance deficit in the 1976–80 period and further to 23 per cent in 1980; in 1981 there was a net private capital export, reflecting in part a decline in private demand for finance capital. Slack domestic activity also provided room for the monetary expansion implied by capital import. The result is that 30 per cent of Denmark's state debt is financed by imported capital, against Sweden's 17 per cent.

The sheer volume of state deficit financing has come to dominate domestic credit markets. All of Denmark's state borrowing is financed through the sale of bonds quoted on the national stock exchange. Up to 1975 there was effectively no state activity in the bond market. In 1980, on the other hand, the state was responsible for 46 per cent of all net issues. Nearly all of the remainder of the bond market in Denmark is in mortgage bonds, fully 40 per cent of which is subsidized or otherwise rent-regulated. Business finance is obtained primarily through commercial banks. While state domestic debt totaled 90.8 billion kroner in 1980, total approved bank credits for business purposes was 63.4 billion kroner. Households owed the remaining 34.2 billion. In all, the state took 40 per cent of the 1980 increase in combined bank and bond market credit.

Sweden's greater relative reliance on its domestic credit market pushed its share of the increase of domestic credit up to 60 per cent in 1981 and 1982 (46 per cent in 1980) and to 50 per cent of the smaller capital market for longer-term finance. Already in 1978 state gross borrowing surpassed business borrowing. Business took only about 10 per cent of the increase in domestic credit (1981); its share of borrowing in foreign currencies, however, was about two-thirds.

The expansion of state borrowing has been absorbed to some extent by the stagnation in credit demand from business for investment purposes, even while short-term liquidity demands have increased. The Swedish government of Olof Palme, for example, talks about crowding out in terms of a possibility: 'the public sector's increased demands on the credit market *risk* driving up interest rates, crowding out business investment, and retarding economic growth' (*Finansplan*, 1982: 18; emphasis added). Crowding-out, according to the government, remains primarily hypothetical because the private sector's net lending has increased to approximately the same extent that the public sector's net lending has decreased:

There are several reasons for this. In part, savings in insurance arrangements financed by contractual employer contributions have increased. In part, profits have increased in banks, insurance companies and other financial companies. But this increased private savings has not led to increased private investment; on the contrary, it has fallen (*Vissa Ekonomisk-politiska Åtgärder m.m.*; 1982: 15).

The result has been that the combined increase in net lending of the financial and non-financial sectors has nearly met the state's net lending deficit since 1980. Deterioration of household net lending in 1982, however, increased Sweden's savings deficit, equal to its balance of payments deficit, from 14 billion kroner in 1981 to 23 billion kroner in 1982. The Palme government's devaluation strategy significantly improved profits of the non-financial sector in 1983. A crucial question is whether these profits will go into capital investment, eventually bolstering state finances, or whether profits will be held as financial investment in state bonds, offering relief on the credit markets but contributing to a structural state deficit.

The Swedish government is, in fact, caught between, on the one hand, discouraging investment with high interest rates and nullifying its fiscal stimulus and, on the other, eating up the benefits of its 16 per cent devaluation by feeding an inflationary money supply. In July 1982, it introduced a new short-term bill (initially, terms of 180 and 360 days) in order to take pressure off the commercial banks, its principal source of finance, and to attract liquidity from the public. The effort succeeded. Forty-three per cent of the state's 1982 borrowing was placed with the public, chiefly business and local government, up from 9 per cent in the previous two years. The success in attracting the public's liquidity, some of which presumably was withdrawn from the banking sector, was at a price: 'The interest rates on these bills for most of the period have remained above the interest rate on bank certificates ...' (*Finansplan*, 1982: 20). Even before the new bill was introduced, the OECD judged that the decline in private demand for investment capital is not simply cyclically coincident with the increase in government borrowing; there has been crowding out but 'the main mechanism at work appears to be the higher cost of borrowing rather than through outright availability effects' (OECD, 1982b: 48).

The relatively higher cost of credit as a result of the state's attempts to control the liquidity effects of its deficit has not only increased the price of investment to private business, it has also shunted capital investment aside in favour of financial assets. It is partly this shift to financial assets that motivates the proposal, and the subsequent legislation, to establish a wage-earners' fund. Yet the Social Democratic government is sensitive to the role that the state itself has played in promoting the erosion of capital investment: 'State finances have been undermined with the effect that returns on financial assets have increased in relation to returns on industrial investment' (*Vissa*, 1982: 15). The ratio of industry's financial assets to real assets increased from 0.86 in 1970 to 1.16 in 1979, even as industry's solidity declined from 0.31 to 0.26 (SOU, 1980: 430) and the 'contribution of financial investments to total profits . . . increased from 30 per cent at the beginning to 50–60 per cent at the end of the decade' (OECD, 1982b: 48).

Whether crowding out private investment or simply taking up slack, the effect is damning: 'Somewhat simplified, recent developments can be seen as a replacement of private sector investment in buildings and machines for productive activity by purchase of government bonds with which the state directly or indirectly has financed private and public consumption' (*Vissa*, 1982: 15).

Denmark's solution to crowding out is similar to Sweden's. An increase in private savings along with a decline in private investment has made room for the state's financial borrowing. Table 10.10 shows a striking shift in savings and net

TABLE 10.10. *Savings and investment in Denmark, 1978–82*
in billion kroner

	1978	1979	1980	1981	1982
Gross savings	58.4	57.8	53.0	51.1	54.7
Public sector	13.8	11.1	4.0	−11.7	−23.9
Private	44.6	46.7	49.8	62.8	78.6
Private gross investment	53.5	59.1	51.7	48.1	58.2
Private net savings	−8.9	−12.4	−2.7	14.7	20.4
Institutional pension saving	13.5	15.8	17.7	20.9	23.5
Other financial saving	−22.4	−28.2	−20.4	−6.2	−3.1

Source: Det Ökonomiske Sekretariat, *Ökonomisk Oversigt,* Copenhagen, 1983; *Finanstidende,* 15 April 1983.

lending. Saving is the difference between current receipts and current disbursements. There is a smooth inverse relationship between (total) public sector savings and private sector savings. The sharp deterioration of public sector savings in 1981 was met by a marked increase of private savings and a decline of investment. The result was a dramatic increase of private net lending (savings minus investment) which was then available to finance the state deficit. 'These conditions have meant that the state's credit demands have exerted only a limited upward pressure on interest rates' (*Finanstidende,* 15 April, 1983). Indeed, banks in the first half of 1983 had significant surplus credit available within the guidelines set by the central bank.

The cost of Denmark's solution to crowding out, however, has been a 30 per cent drop in investment volume (at 1975 prices) from 1979 to 1981. (Over the same period, investment volume in Sweden grew by about 4 per cent.) This drop in investment is unavoidable without a very substantial drop in private consumption necessary to produce an increase in private saving, leaving aside augmenting domestic savings with foreign borrowing. The ratio of government's overall borrowing requirements to private savings (i.e. before private investment) reached 45 per cent in 1981 and 60 per cent in 1982. Similarly, the ratio of public sector borrowing to private savings in Sweden reached 31 per cent in 1981 and 41 per cent in 1982. This puts Denmark and Sweden in the same league as Belgium and Italy, except that the latter two countries have been in such a position for several consecutive years (OECD, 1983a: 21).

The problem is simply that the cyclic squeeze on private profits and state deficits have sharply reduced the national savings available to meet requirements of the state, households, and private enterprise. Danish net savings as a percentage of GDP have dropped from 17 per cent in 1973 to 11 per cent in 1978 to 3 per cent in 1981. (The figures for Sweden are 15, 7, and 5 per cent, respectively.) Even with the decline in private investment, national savings are not sufficient to cover domestic credit needs. Denmark's balance of payments deficit, including amortization of state foreign debt, increased from 11.2 billion kroner in 1978 to 19.8, 16.2, 17.4, and 27 billion kroner in 1979, 1980, 1981, and 1982, respectively, with the figure expected to be 32 billion kroner in 1983. It is characteristic of a small, open economy that the fiscal stimulus of budgetary deficits leaks to foreign economies.

As is apparent, then, from the trends that are still developing in the most recent data available, any conclusive judgement on crowding out in Denmark and Sweden is premature. It can be said, however, that state finances have exercised some unspecified upward pressure on interest rates and that if crowding out in terms of volume has been avoided, it is due to the fall-back of private investment in real assets, possibly attributable in part to the comparative attractiveness of state bonds. There is a cyclic relationship between state deficits and private activity on the down side. It remains to be seen whether the very magnitude of state borrowing delays an eventual recovery.

This begs the question of a structural change in capital markets. There can be no question that state borrowing in Denmark and Sweden has very significantly redirected capital flows. The size of present state borrowing, moreover, means that the burden of debt servicing in the future will prolong state deficits, and state borrowing, at least to the end of the decade even under favourable circumstances. Part of the argument of a structural change in capital markets is that while the state is dominating the demand side, financial institutions are dominating the supply of capital. This is implicitly a two-pronged argument that profits and savings have shifted from non-financial firms to banks and to insurance and pension funds, and that investment has shifted from real assets to financial assets. The argument must be affirmed on each of these points, given the data presented. (Table 10.3 summarizes savings data for Finland and Sweden; comparable breakdowns of national accounts data are not available for Denmark and Norway.) The long-term trends are clearly in favour of financial institutions. In itself, the domination of capital markets by the state means that financial investment presently dominates real investment.

To complete the mutual alignment of financial institution and state, commercial banks in Sweden hold 30 per cent of the state's domestic debt and private and public insurance and pension institutions hold another 28 per cent (31 December 1981). In 1980 and 1981 the state accounted for 53 and 69 per cent, respectively, of the commercial banks' lending and about a third of private insurance companies' loans and half of the lending of the public pension funds. The increase of general public lending to the state in 1982 as a result of the new short-term bill came at the expense of the commercial banks' share. In Denmark, banks in 1981 held 51 per cent of the state's domestic debt with 'other financial' accounting for another 24 per cent; three-quarters of the state's domestic debt is held by financial institutions. The growth sector in Denmark is the pension funds and insurance companies. This sector took 20 and 23 per cent of the state's net placement of domestic debt in 1980 and 1981, against only 1 per cent in 1979 and 1978.

The significance of this discussion of crowding out for the theme of class compromise and socialist exploitation is twofold. First, there is the possibility that crowding out as a problem is generated either by the terms of historic compromises or by socialist defection from class compromise. Secondly, there is the possibility that class cleavage has been fundamentally altered by an increasing separation of financial capital and industrial ownership; and that the contemporary historic compromise is between the state, with its maintenance demands for finance, and the financial community, with its secure supply of capital from state-mandated insurance schemes. I suggest this in a provocative voice and without a ready answer.

Conclusion

I posed the problem for this paper by contrasting very different ways of organizing economies, or not organizing as the case may be. I set Olson's liberal distrust of organizations and 'distributional coalitions' against Scandinavian historic compromises, whose pre-condition and consequence are, precisely, organization. The suggestion that organized political economies are hostile to economic growth was found to fail a simple test.

Suggesting that historic compromise is as much protection of institutions as promise of performance, I evaluated a 'socialist exploitation' scenario of capital erosion. The crucial question of a decline in industrial profits is confounded by variations in data and method and differences between an accountant's total rate of return and a manager's operating profit. What is not obscured, however, is the shift of savings and, hence, accumulation of financial and real assets, to the financial sector. Social democracy and capital are fully consistent, and may be symbiotic—although at the expense of industry.

A brief review of corporate taxes, non-wage labour costs, public sector wages and, more tentatively, productivity and wage developments adds to the conclusion that the predicted subversion from the Left has not occurred. The institutions of the Scandinavian historic compromises, although renewed and adapted, have been roughly respected. (Some recent support for this assessment comes from the Swedish capitalists' charge that the Social Democrats' wage-earner fund breaks precisely with this respect.)

The shift of savings to financial institutions and the cyclic domination of state borrowing in domestic credit markets raise the prospect of a structural change in credit flows through a crowding out mechanism. Will the massive credit demands of the state in the present recession leave a structural mark on capital markets? The other side of the cyclic downturn and reduced demand for investment capital is that the worst scenarios of crowding out for Denmark and Sweden have not been realized. There remains a question, however. Government borrowing has maintained high interest rates and depressed the net return on investment in real assets. The gap between return on financial assets, chiefly government bonds, and real assets has widened. The critical next step is the disposal of operating profits when they recover—as they have in post-devaluation Sweden—between financial investment, real investment, and distribution to shareholders.[10]

Much of the argument in this paper is expressed in passive terms. Phrases like 'not distinctive' and 'no interesting generalization' recur. Indeed, it is critical for the argument that in many respects the Nordic countries *are not* distinctive. The variations within the Nordic region are as interesting as the variations between these countries and other Western industrial economies. And the indistinctiveness of the Nordic economies on many of the issues raised in this paper is all the more significant in the light of the exceptional character of the Nordic nations in the importance they give to collective consumption and in their policy performance in regard to employment and distributive equality.

Notes

1. Cameron suggests a complementary scenario where the government in a small open economy may promote sectoral consolidation and an organized settlement of shares.

2. I use class compromise in a theoretical sense and historical compromise, usually in the plural, in a historical sense referring to the historical circumstances of the labour market and parliamentary settlements between labour and capital. The Scandinavian historic compromises can be dated from the mid-1930s with full effect from about 1948. It may not be appropriate to use historic compromise with respect to Finland at all. The Social Democratic party won an absolute majority of the parliamentary vote already in 1916, tried an ill-fated minority government in 1926, and formed a 'red earth' coalition government with the Agrarians in 1937, roughly in line with developments in the Scandinavian countries. In 1944 capitalists formally recognized collective agreements. In no real sense, however, was there the mutual acceptance either in the labour market or in parliament that was characteristic of the Scandinavian countries. Splits in both the trade-union movement and in the labour parties made post-war industrial relations and parliamentary politics disruptive, topped off by five general strikes from the end of the war to 1956. Social-Democratic participation in government—the party held portfolios in 16 of the 19 governments from 1937 to 1957—came to an end after 1958 when the foreign policy opposition of Kekkonen and the Centre Party to V. Tanner, the Social Democratic leader who had been finance minister during the war, froze the Social Democrats out of government. Tanner's retirement

in 1963 began a thaw in the parliamentary situation and opened the way for a Social Democratic-led popular front government in 1966. Parallel moves in the labour market-led to the reunification of the trade-union organizations in 1971. (I use Scandinavia throughout to refer to Denmark, Norway, and Sweden, and Norden to include Finland. Iceland appropriately belongs in Scandinavia.)

3. Some readers may not be persuaded that this view is serious. I appeal to authority. Paul Samuelson provides an American (i.e. non-political, non-structural) version of the socialist exploitation path (1980: 666):

Here is (what, prior to hearing some of the speakers at this conference, I thought to be) a caricature, almost a parody, of what most businessmen believe. In a lower-keyed version, but still in essentially the same thesis, I suspect it is a view that the majority of college graduates would essentially subscribe to. The thesis follows:
  '[T]his last half century has witnessed an overshoot of government regulations, taxation, and deficit spending. The vigor of the market economy has thereby been sapped—just as it has been in so many of the mixed economies abroad. United States inflation, stagnation in productivity, class struggle, and popular unrest is the inevitable consequence of the cancerous growth of the public sector engineered by power-seeking bureaucrats and politicians.
  'Britain provides an archetypical case to prove that the hand of government withers progress and efficiency, and fails to make good on the 'equity' it promises. As well, a comparative survey of all the mixed economies will bear out the same perverse correlation between the usurpations of the public sector and shortfalls of economic performance—Switzerland versus Sweden, Japan and West Germany versus Italy and the United States, and so forth.'

4. The following shows the components of a structural shift in operating surplus, in terms of percentage of GDP.

	Denmark		Finland		Norway		Sweden	
	1960	1980	1960	1980	1960	1980	1960	1980
Value added in agriculture	11.2	5.2[a]	16.7	8.2	9.0	4.5	6.2	3.1[b]
Government final consumption	13.3	26.8	11.9	18.6	12.9	18.9	15.8	29.2

[a] 1977.   [b] 1963.
Source: OECD, *Historical Statistics 1960–80,* Paris, 1982.

5. 'Declining rates of return in Europe have been fairly consistently associated with falling shares of profits in value added' (Hill, 1979: 119; cf. also, *Konjunkturläget*, 1983: 131).

6. The operating rate of return is often used in macroeconomic descriptions but under different designations, e.g. current operating profit, expressed as a percentage of assets at replacement cost. This is often presented as a real rate of return concept but is, rather, a nominal concept since the profit measurement takes no account of the effect of the fact that assets have been possessed during a period of changed value of money. If we add holding gains or losses and financial income to the profit measurement of the operating rate of return, all the relevant profit elements as regards the measurement of the rate of return on total capital are taken into account' (Bertmar, 1979: 108).

7. In rebuttal of Bertmar's finding of a declining rate of return, Bergström and Södersten (1979b) observe that 'neither Bertmar's nor our trend line differs significantly from zero. Furthermore, a 95 per cent confidence interval around Bertmar's estimate of the slope of the trend line only just includes our estimate' (1979b: 118). They conclude that the entire difference can be traced to 'how corporate net profits should be treated in the calculations' (1979b: 119). The difference is that Bergström and Södersten 'equate deferred corporation taxes (due to accelerated depreciation, including allocations to stock reserves and investment funds) with equity capital' (1979a: 54).

Lacking these refinements, published OECD data for return to capital (P/K) show the more familiar negative linear trend for Swedish manufacturing, 1963–80 ($b = -.42$, r = −.85, mean = 9.3) and a less severe trend for industry plus transport and communication (b = −.25, r = −.85, mean = 8.4) (OECD, *National Accounts, Vol. II*, Paris, 1982). Return to capital net of depreciation for Norway, 1963–79, shows a slight negative trend (t = −.09, r = −.39, mean = 5.3) for industry plus transport and communication (OECD, *National Accounts, Vol. II*, Paris, 1982); see also Lensberg (1982).

Likewise, Hill (1979) concludes from his semi-logarithmic trend analysis for 1955–76 for a set of European countries that 'on balance, the data clearly support the view that profit shares and rates of return have fallen significantly in some countries and certain industries. Moreover, there is next to no evidence anywhere pointing in the opposite direction of increasing profitability' (121).

8. Bergström and Södersten (1979b) reason that the tax burden for Swedish companies was halved during the 1966–76 (Social-Democratic) period: 'These changes included more favourable depreciation provisions for buildings, special investment relief for investment in machinery and an increasingly more frequent use of the system of investment funds. As a result of these changes, the effective tax burden−that share of "real" profits which was paid in tax−was more than halved from 1966/1969 to 1973/1976 . . .' (1979b: 120).

9. The OECD disagrees: 'it is not sure that given the nature of central government lending operations (higher risk, lower interest rates and longer maturity) other investors than the state would be ready to make such credits. In other words, it may not be relevant to claim that government loans, *per se*, lead to a net reduction of credit demand addressed to other lending institutions' (OECD, 1982b: 43).

10. I have omitted in this paper two important items: the bullish share markets in the Nordic countries in the last two years, and the substantial lending role of the state in the Nordic countries.

11

Economic and Institutional Constraints of Full-Employment Strategies: Sweden, Austria, and Western Germany, 1973-1982

FRITZ W. SCHARPF

Introduction

For the purposes of this paper, the following propositions are assumed to be true without further detailed discussion (Uusitalo, 1983; Schmidt, 1983; Scharpf, 1981):

(i) Western European economies which had performed rather successfully during the 1960s have, on the whole, performed much less well after the early 1970s. Even more important, while the variance of performance measures (using conventional indicators of economic growth, inflation, and employment/unemployment) had been reasonably small during the 1960s, it increased dramatically after 1973 (Table 11.1).

(ii) The general decline of economic-performance measures since the early 1970s is usually explained by reference to three interrelated changes in world-wide economic conditions: the inflationary momentum which was generated when the United States chose to finance the Vietnam war without tax increases (Garrison & Mayhew, 1983); the subsequent destruction of the international monetary system when the Bretton-Woods regime of fixed exchange rates was replaced by generally fluctuating exchange rates in the spring of 1973; and, of course, the oil-price crises of 1973-4 and of 1979-80. Rapid increases in the price of an essential resource meant that a massive cost push was added to inflation rates that were already alarmingly high. On the other side, the transfer of purchasing power exceeded the short-term absorption capacity of oil exporting countries. OPEC surpluses rose to 55 billion US dollars in 1974 and to 120 billion dollars in 1980, leaving a corresponding gap in the world-wide demand for industrial goods and services. Thus, Western economies were, at the same time, confronted with rising inflationary pressures and with a weakening of aggregate demand resulting in the underemployment of the existing capital stock and of the labour force.

TABLE 11.1. *Economic growth, inflation, employment and unemployment in seven industrialized countries, 1973–82*

	Average yearly GDP Growth (in %)		Average yearly increase in consumer prices (in %)		Average yearly rates of unemployment (in %)		Total change in employment (in %)	
	1963–72	1973–81	1963–72	1973–82	1963–72	1973–82	1963–72	1973–82
Austria	5.1	2.9	3.9	6.4	2.6	1.9	7.3	6.1
West Germany	4.4	2.4	3.2	5.2	1.1	3.8	0.3	−4.8
France	5.5	2.8	4.7	11.1	1.9	5.1	7.5	0.6
Sweden	3.9	1.8	5.4	10.0	1.9	2.2	4.8	8.8
United Kingdom	2.9	1.3	5.9	14.2	2.0	5.4	−3.1	−5.7
Japan	9.9	4.6	6.0	8.8	1.2	2.0	11.6	7.2
United States	3.9	2.6	3.7	8.8	4.7	7.0	2.1	17.0

Sources: OECD Economic Outlook, Paris, July 1983; Sachverständigenrat, 1982; Abele, et al. (1982); Wifo-Monatsberichte 8/1983; Aktuelle Beiträge zur Wirtschafts-und Finanzpolitik 35/1983.

(iii) But while the general decline of economic performance during the world-wide recession may be plausibly explained by reference to these important changes in the international economic environment, there seems to be no single, straightforward economic explanation for the increasing variance in the performance measures of individual countries. While all were exposed to the same external economic shocks, their responses could hardly have been more different. Looking only at Western European countries with socialist or social-democratic governments politically committed to full employment, economic growth was relatively high in Austria, and very low in the United Kingdom and in Sweden; inflation rates were low in Germany and Austria, and very high in the United Kingdom and in Sweden; and unemployment was very low in Austria and Sweden, and very high in the United Kingdom. At the same time, however, employment increased the most in Sweden, while Germany suffered employment losses during the 1970s. There seems to be no obvious correlation between rates of economic growth and rates of inflation, between inflation and unemployment, or even between economic growth and employment growth. Instead, it seems that in a generally worsening world-wide economic environment individual countries have chosen specific national profiles of economic performance, favouring or neglecting specific measures of performance.

In the absence of plausible economic explanations, attempts to account for the variance of economic-performance measures during the world-wide recession have focused primarily upon structural or institutional factors, such as the relative political strength of the labour movement or the existence of 'corporatist' institutions facilitating peak-level bargaining between the organizations of labour and capital, and the state (Wilensky, 1981a; Schmitter, 1981; Schmidt, 1982b; 1983; Cameron, this volume). As far as cross-country quantitative studies go, these efforts have been reasonably successful, especially when both factors were used in combination. On the whole, it seems that countries with powerful and centralized unions, with politically dominant socialist or social-democratic parties and with arrangements for centralized bargaining, over wages as well as over certain aspects of government economic policy, were generally more successful in weathering the international economic crises than other countries.

Nevertheless, much of the variance remains unexplained, and results seem to be highly sensitive to the selection of countries included, the periodization of the data, the choice of economic performance measures and, of course, the choice of indicators for the independent variables representing differences of political and institutional structure. Some of these difficulties may be reduced by further improvements in the conceptualization of dependent and independent variables and further refinements in the operationalization of indicators and in the selection of data. But, in a more fundamental sense, any attempt to explain variance in economic performance exclusively by reference to differences in the institutional structure of various countries is bound to remain unsatisfactory simply because it is based upon a theoretically incomplete model of the underlying real-world processes.

While I generally subscribe to an 'institutionalist' perspective (Scharpf, 1983), I also think that institutional explanations of economic performance, taken by themselves, must miss two crucial aspects of economic policy. The first is the element of strategic choice. Different countries may differ in their performance profiles because they have *chosen* to pursue different priorities by different means. The second is the 'goodness of fit' between a chosen strategy and a given state of the economy. Strategies may fail because they are *economically* inappropriate in a given situation.

Both points may seem trivial, but they need to be emphasized against hopes to explain performance differences mainly by structural or institutional conditions (Korpi, 1983). Of course, structural factors, such as the relative power position of the labour movement, the existence or absence of corporatist institutions and, I would add, characteristic differences of governmental institutions, are important as constraints. If power resources are inadequate, it may be impossible to adopt certain strategies at all, and if institutional arrangements are inappropriate, strategies which have been adopted may not be implemented. But within such constraints, the adoption of a strategy is still an act of creative choice; and the institutional feasibility of a strategy does not, by itself, guarantee its economic success.

My emphasis upon the importance of *strategic choice* derives from a perception of the complexity and interdependence of economic-policy decisions. Exchange rates and tariffs, interest rates and the availability of credit, taxes, social security contributions and wage settlements, public expenditure and public borrowing, regional and sectoral industrial policy, labour-market training and job creation, working-time and retirement decisions, and many more, will all influence the course of the economy and the level of employment and unemployment. Inevitably, these decisions will have to be taken by a plurality of separate and relatively independent actors; unions and employers' associations, parliamentary committees and regulatory agencies, finance ministers and central banks, central, regional, and local governments, insurance funds and labour-market authorities. If they work at cross purposes, the effective interdependence of their actions could stifle even the most vigorous economy; at the same time, any attempt at central, hierarchical control of all these decisions (if it were constitutionally permissible) would surely overstrain the information capacity and power of even the most centralized government. Thus, successful economic policy does depend upon mechanisms which facilitate self-coordination for which I have here used the term 'strategy' (Katzenstein, 1984). It refers to an overall understanding, among those who exercise effective power, of a set of decision premises integrating world-views, goals and means. Such an understanding need not be highly specific in order to be effective in practice. But unless there is a roughly common view of the dominant factors influencing the course of the economy, of the rank-order among economic-policy priorities, and of the relative effectiveness and desirability of different courses of action, national economic-policy decisions are unlikely to achieve the minimal degree of coherence and consistency which is essential to their overall success.

It is necessary to emphasize three points, however: that national 'strategies' are *contingent*, that they are *fragile*, and that they are *resistent* to purposeful change. Obviously, the choice of an economic strategy does depend upon the relative power positions of classes and interest groups in a society. It is the dominant interests that have the best chance to define national strategies. But even when that is allowed for, there will be differences in the interpretation of an uncertain economic environment, in the rank-ordering of priorities, and in the evaluation of the efficacy of different courses of action, leading to differences in strategy choices that cannot be explained entirely by differences in relative power. Secondly, in order to be effective, any national strategy must be shared to some extent by groups and institutions whose interests and goals are different from, or in conflict with, those of the dominant political forces. Unless they also see their interests well served (as compared to the best available alternative), a national strategic understanding is unlikely to emerge. By the same token, strategic understandings remain fragile, always in danger of disintegration if important interests should 'opt out' because of changes in circumstances, priorities or evaluative judgements.

Thus, the ability to achieve, and maintain, a strategic understanding among important interest groups and institutions remains problematic in principle. Certain countries will have more difficulties than others, but all will have to struggle against the entropy law of dissensus, conflict and disintegration in economic policy. Their very fragility, however, also tends to immunize national economic strategies, once achieved, against proposals for purposeful change. Individual groups or institutions will have come to expect, and to rely upon, each other's specific contributions to an overall strategy, and each of them could unilaterally change its own course of action only at the risk of upsetting the pattern of co-operation altogether. At the same time, efforts to change overall strategic perspectives are up against all the difficulties of reaching agreement in the first place, as well as against the 'sunk costs' of institutional commitments to the existing strategy. Countries with the ability to develop and implement a relatively coherent economic strategy will profit from all the advantages of concerted action in a relatively stable economic environment. When confronted with rapid change, however, they are also likely to suffer from 'policy inertia', being unable to abandon or modify strategies which may no longer fit a changing economic environment (Scharpf, 1981). Poor economic performance is likely to follow if a country should be unable to develop and maintain a coherent economic strategy at all, but also if it should be stuck with a strategy which, even though successful in the past, is no longer economically appropriate.

The problematical character of the *economic appropriateness* of a strategy is often overlooked in institutionalist as well as in 'class-theoretical' analyses. Focusing upon the political dimension of the political economy, they often seem to suggest an omnipotence of power, where relative power positions determine the degree to which group or class interests are realized. While this view may be appropriate for some policy areas, it seems inadequate for the field of economic policy under capitalist conditions. Of course, a relative preponderance of power, and the absence of institutional constraints, will increase the potential control over the choice of economic policies; but it does not ensure control over economic outcomes.[1] National economic performance is, after all, the resultant of a myriad of microeconomic decisions of producers and consumers, investors and savers, employers and job-seekers, and so on. In a capitalist economy (and, to a somewhat lesser extent, under socialism as well), these microeconomic decisions are only incompletely controlled by the available instruments of government policy and they are, at the same time, highly interconnected. The lack of direct policy control over microeconomic decisions, and their inter-connectedness, taken together with the likelihood of external shocks, necessarily imply the ever-present possibility of dynamic, cumulative processes of macro-economic change which policy makers may try to exploit, reinforce or dampen, but which they cannot hope to control completely. Thus, the appropriate analogue for successful economic policy cannot be steering (where all relevant variables are under direct control) but, at best, small-boat sailing (where goals are reached through the skilful adaptation to, and exploitation of, circumstances beyond the skipper's direct control). Under capitalist conditions, therefore, even the most powerful and institutionally unconstrained class or interest associations may fail economically if their strategies should not fit the economic environment, resulting in business failures, disinvestment, run-away inflation or a rapidly deteriorating international balance of accounts. On the other hand, strategies which are well designed economically may equally fail if institutional conditions should prevent their adoption or frustrate their implementation.

In the following sections, I will first focus upon a comparison of Sweden and Austria in order to illustrate the importance of strategic choice, and I will then examine, and try to explain, performance differences between Austria and West Germany which, pursuing the same overall strategy, have operated under different institutional constraints. The bulk of the analysis will be focused upon the 1973-9 period, with only a brief glance at the early 1980s, when the economic environment was changing once more.

Sweden and Austria: The Importance of Strategic Choice

The importance of strategic choice can best be demonstrated by the differing economic performances of two countries which are generally considered to be highly similar in their structural characteristics. Sweden and Austria (together with Norway) are inevitably listed among the countries with the greatest power-resources of the labour movement. Union density in Austria is close to 60 per cent and in Sweden around 85 per cent and in both countries union organization is highly concentrated, with a limited number of non-overlapping industrial unions tightly integrated into central organizations at the national level (von Beyme, 1977). In both countries, the 'political wing' of the labour movement, the social-democratic or socialist party, has been able to influence or dominate government policy all through the post-war period (with a brief interlude from 1966 to 1970 in Austria, and a longer one from 1976 to 1982 in Sweden). At the same time, Austria and Sweden are invariably at the top of anybody's rank-order of neo-corporatism, meeting all the institutional requirements of representational monopolies for the associations of labour and capital interests, centralized decision-making and peak-level bargaining between capital, labour and the state (Schmitter, 1981). In Austria the institutional arrangements of social partnership rest upon an infrastructure of official chambers of business, agriculture and labour with compulsory membership paralleling (and reinforcing) the structure of voluntary associations and culminating in the Paritätische Kommission für Preis- und Lohnfragen which, with the subtle support of the government, exercises a powerful influence not only upon wage settlements but also upon prices (Marin, 1982). In Sweden, corporatist arrangements appear to be less elaborate and formalized, and the government seems to be even more hesitant to interfere visibly with 'free collective bargaining', but its informal influence on peak-level negotiations appears to be quite strong nevertheless.

The organizational and political strength of the labour movement, and the institutional capability of corporatist arrangements, have indeed enabled Austria and Sweden to defend successfully the single most important economic-policy objective of the labour movement: throughout the 1970s, open unemployment remained at, or below, the full-employment level of 2 per cent in both countries, and even under the rapidly deteriorating economic conditions of the early 1980s, Austrian and Swedish (and Norwegian) unemployment rates were still among the lowest in Western Europe. Thus, if one believes that full-employment must be the paramount goal of the labour movement because 'it generally removes the need for servility, and thus alters the way of life, the relationship between classes . . . [and] the balance of forces in the economy' (Balogh, 1982: 47), the labour movements in Austria and Sweden (and in Norway, where similar institutional conditions prevail) have been highly successful during the world-wide recession.

But if Austria and Sweden have been similarly successful in avoiding open unemployment, a look at other performance indicators reveals strikingly different patterns. While Austria had about the highest rate of economic growth in Western Europe during the 1970s, Swedish growth rates were among the lowest. Conversely, price stability in Austria was second only to Switzerland and Germany, while Swedish inflation rates were definitely above average for industrialized Western Europe. And even 'full employment' seems to have had rather different connotations in the two countries. While Sweden had by far the largest increase in the number of persons employed, and a labour-force participation rate (of the population between 15 and 64) rising from 77 per cent to 81 per cent between 1974 and 1980, Austria had a much more modest increase of civilian employment and a labour force participation rate stagnating at around 65 per cent. In addition, full employment in Austria was helped considerably by the emigration of foreign workers after 1974, while there was no similar reduction of the foreign labour force in Sweden.

Apparently, therefore, Sweden was able to maintain full employment by somehow managing to translate rather modest economic growth into very large gains in employment, while Austria used its rather vigorous economic growth merely to avoid open unemployment. The difference also shows in the rise of labour productivity, which was very high in Austria and extremely low in Sweden during the recession period.

I do not interpret these striking differences in the overall performance of two full-employment countries as accidental or as the result of unintended policy failures. Instead, they seem to be the manifestation of two divergent, but equally coherent, strategies of powerful alliances between labour movements and governments in the face of a world-wide crisis of capitalist economies. If this strategic interpretation is accepted as a working hypothesis, the underlying logic of the Austrian and the Swedish 'models' could be characterized, in ideal-type fashion, as follows.

In the 1973-80 period, Austria seems to have pursued a reasonably successful strategy satisfying labour interests through the skilful management of economic growth under adverse international conditions. While the social partnership institutions managed to maintain wage restraint and price stability at home, the government assisted private investment in order to achieve productivity increases comparing favourably with Japan or Germany. Being able to rely upon a generally vigorous and internationally competitive economy, the usual instruments of neo-Keynesian demand expansion were then used to just the degree that was necessary in order to avoid open unemployment. To that extent, Austrian policy makers were quite willing to pay the inevitable price of demand reflation in a world-wide recession, a negative balance on current accounts and rising budget deficits. But the Austrians were unwilling to pay more for additional increases in civilian employment in order to pursue the much more idealistic Swedish goals. For them, it was of paramount importance to maintain the health and competitiveness of the Austrian economy; and the labour movement had to be satisfied with the achievement of its minimal goal, the avoidance of open unemployment. Compared to Germany, which attempted to pursue the same strategy with much less success, this was no mean achievement. But apparently Sweden was much more ambitious (Table 11.2).

The 'Swedish model' must be seen in its historical evolution (Hedborg & Meidner, 1984), and it is even likely that the implications of its inherent logic are not yet fully unfolded. As a consequence, therefore, an ideal-type reconstruction which is attempted here is always in danger of over-interpreting current practice.

TABLE 11.2. *Employment, unemployment and employment effects of labour-market policy in Austria, West Germany, and Sweden, 1973–82*

	Employment (in 1000 persons)			Employment (Index 1973 = 100)			Unemployment[a] (in % of the Labour Force)			Employment-Substituting Effects of Active Labour Market Policy (in % of Labour Force)		
	Austria	West Germany	Sweden	Austria	West Germany	Sweden	Austria	West Germany	Sweden	Austria	West Germany	Sweden
1973	3015	26 849	3879	100.0	100.0	100.0	0.4	1.0	2.5			
1974	3023	26 497	3962	100.3	98.7	102.1	1.3	2.2	2.0	0.2	1.0	2.9
1975	2969	25 746	4062	98.5	95.9	104.7	1.8	4.1	1.6	0.3	1.6	2.5
1976	2977	25 530	4088	98.7	95.1	105.4	1.8	4.1	1.6	0.3	1.1	3.0
1977	3015	25 490	4099	100.0	94.9	105.7	1.6	4.0	1.8	0.3	1.2	3.3
1978	3055	25 644	4115	101.3	95.5	106.1	2.1	3.8	2.2	0.3	1.3	3.9
1979	3034	25 986	4180	102.6	96.8	107.8	2.1	3.4	2.1	0.3	1.3	4.0
1980	3105	26 225	4232	103.0	97.7	109.1	1.9	3.4	2.0		1.4	2.9
1981	3147	26 030	4225	104.4	96.9	108.9	2.5	4.8	2.5			
1982		25 550	4219		95.2	108.8	3.5	6.9	3.2			

[a] Unemployment rates are established from labour force surveys.

Sources: ILO (1982); *Aktuelle Beiträge zur Wirtschafts- und Finanzpolitik,* 35/1983; Schmid (1982); Wösendorfer (1980); OECD, *Labour Force Statistics,* Paris, 1982.

Nevertheless, two crucial premisses of the Swedish strategy were already explicit in the original 'Rehn-Meidner model' discussed and adopted by the union movement and the social democratic party during the 1950s. The first was that wage bargaining should *not* be instrumentalized for the purposes of macroeconomic management. Instead, it was accepted that a 'solidaristic wage policy', attempting to reduce wage differentials between regions, sectors, and skill groups, might reduce employment in the weaker segments of the economy. The second premiss was that government should not try to eliminate all un-employment through the macroeconomic management of aggregate demand—which could only lead to inflationary overheating in the stronger segments of the economy and, worse yet, to increasing wage-drift that would frustrate the very goals of a solidaristic wage policy. Instead, unemployment was to be countered by selective policy measures, primarily through increasing the effec-tiveness of placement services and of demand-oriented training and retraining services offered by the Swedish labour market administration. During the 1960s, when this 'active labour market policy' went into full operation, the facilitation of labour mobility from the weaker to the stronger regions and sectors of the economy was, indeed, very successful. In a generally vigorous economic environ-ment, Sweden was able to maintain full employment without having to rely upon an explicit incomes policy and without the disadvantages of British-style stop-go demand management.

In the 1970s, however, two things changed. First, the Swedish labour move-ment raised its level of aspirations. While labour mobility had been accepted as inevitable during the 1960s, it was now considered increasingly problematical to move people to where the jobs happened to be, instead of moving jobs to the people. Secondly, the world-wide recession reduced the number of available jobs in the private sector, creating for the first time an aggregate employment deficit which could not be eliminated by simply increasing the efficiency of labour mobility even if that had still been politically acceptable. To these new challenges to the original Rehn-Meidner model, Sweden seems to have developed three related responses.

First, *active labour-market policy* was expanded from an instrument of facilitating labour mobility to an instrument providing substitute employment in deficit areas. Regional employment subsidies became one of the major responsibilities of the labour-market administration, and all its other instruments were expanded in volume to the point where up to 4 per cent of the total labour force were actually absorbed in the various programmes of active labour-market policy by 1979. In other words, in the absence of these programmes, open unemployment in Sweden would have been close to 6 per cent instead of around 2 per cent during the late 1970s (Johannesson, 1979; 1981; Schmid, 1982).

The second response was an increase in *public-sector employment*, especially at the local level. According to OECD data, in Sweden the share of the public sector in total employment rose from 20.6 to 29.8 per cent between 1970 and 1979, while in Austria and West Germany the corresponding figures were much lower, with increases from 14.1 to 18.5 per cent in Austria and from 11.2 to 14.7 per cent in West Germany (OECD, 1982c: 12). The same difference holds if one refers to the ILO's functional classification of 'community, social and personal services', whose share in total employment increased from 29 to 35 per cent in Sweden between 1972 and 1980, as compared to 23 to 24 per cent in Austria and 19 to 23 per cent in West Germany during the same period (ILO, 1982, Table 3B). By either measure, Sweden now has the highest share of publicly financed employment of any country in Western Europe.

Finally, Sweden has increased its share of *part-time employment* to the point where, by now, about a quarter of all wage-earners are employed in part-time jobs. Again, this is by far the highest rate in Europe. Part-time work, drawing married women into the labour market, enabled Sweden to further increase its already very high female participation rate during the 1970s. As many of the new part-time jobs were created in the public sector, the public sector was in fact mainly responsible for the expansion of female employment. On the whole, Swedish observers hesitate to interpret the expansion of part-time work as the result of a conscious strategy of sharing available work to combat potential unemployment, but it has had that effect in practice. While the number of persons employed increased by 9.6 per cent between 1972 and 1980 (and while the number of women employed increased by an incredible 21.6 per cent) the total volume of hours worked in Sweden was actually reduced during the same period (Schmid, 1982: 34-5). Hence, the expansion of part-time employment effectively allowed a much greater number of persons to share a slightly shrinking total volume of work.

Taken together, these three responses have enabled Sweden to largely de-couple the creation of employment opportunities from the development of the capitalist economy. To be sure, the Swedish labour movement has not pursued strategies, since the 1930s, which were hostile to the private sector, and neither did the bourgeois coalition governments that were in office after 1976. Never-theless, the Swedish strategy had the effect of reducing the dependence of the labour movement upon the ups and downs of the business cycle, and it has at the same time reduced the need for governments to provide, at almost all costs, the conditions for a 'favourable business climate'.

But a Swedish-type decoupling of employment from private-sector growth also has its price. It means, in essence, that public employment and publicly financed labour-market programmes were used to fill the employment gap which arose in the private sector as a consequence of the world-wide recession. The Swedes are paying for it through a tax burden which is significantly higher than in Austria or West Germany (Table 11.3). The higher tax burden, moreover, could not be placed upon private-sector profits and investments if a loss of international competitiveness and further job losses were to be avoided. Thus, just as Swedish unions had to respect the constraints of international compe-tition in their wage settlements (Edgren *et al.*, 1973), the government had to place the rising tax burden primarily upon incomes from wages and salaries and upon consumption. As a matter of fact, corporation taxes amounted to little over 4 per cent of government revenue during the 1970s in Sweden, while their share was close to 9 per cent in West Germany (DIW, 1983b). In effect, therefore, wage- and salary-earners in Sweden have been deprived of substantial parts of their disposable incomes in order to finance 'solidaristically' the employment opportunities of all those who would not otherwise have found regular employment.

TABLE 11.3. *Taxes and social security contributions as shares of GNP*

| | Austria | | West Germany | | Sweden | |
	1970	1982	1970	1982	1970	1982
Taxes	27.5	29.3	23.9	24.8	33.2	36.3
Social Security Contributions	11.0	15.2	12.5	17.7	9.1	15.1
Total	38.5	44.5	36.4	42.5	42.3	51.4

Source: DIW (1983a, Appendix: iv).

Obviously the Swedish labour movement, for all its power, still had to respect the constraints of a capitalist economy operating in open world markets, finding no economically feasible way to shift the burdens of effective full employment policies upon the capitalist class. (Przeworski & Wallerstein, 1982a; 1982b). Ultimately, even the Swedish decoupling strategy was only able to achieve a form of 'socialism in one class'—for which, during the same period, the British Left had criticized the last Labour government and its 'social contract' strategies (Tarling & Wilkinson, 1977). It surely is a tribute to the integrative capacity of the Swedish labour movement that it so far has managed to maintain a moral consensus on the need to finance full employment opportunities, in the face of substantial conflicts of interest within the heterogeneous groups of which the statistical aggregate of wage and salary earners is composed in all modern societies.

Economic Feasibility: The Mechanics of Macroeconomic Management

Unlike Sweden, Austria and West Germany have attempted to avoid mass unemployment during the world-wide recession through policies aimed at maintaining, or stimulating, economic growth in the private sector. But while both countries have pursued roughly the same overall strategy, only Austria succeeded in maintaining full employment. Before I attempt to describe and explain policy differences between these two countries in greater detail, it seems useful to set out the basic mechanisms linking economic-policy instruments to employment performance under different conditions of the economic environment. An understanding of these basic, and essentially simple, mechanics of macroeconomic management is necessary in order to appreciate the policy options, and the constraints, defining the action space of successful full-employment strategies.

In its simplest form, the macroeconomic model of employment in the private sector can be reduced to three parameters (Barro & Grossman 1971; Malinvaud, 1980): the aggregate demand for goods and services (D), the existing capacity for producing goods and services (C), and the available supply of labour (L) (all measured either in units of—potential—production or in units of—necessary—labour input). The economy is in full-employment equilibrium if $D = C = L$.

Involuntary unemployment may then occur under two radically different conditions:

(i) if effective demand falls below the available productive capacity which could be profitably utilized at prevailing costs and prices, as well as below the available supply of labour: $D < C \geqslant L$ (demand-constrained or 'Keynesian' unemployment), or

(ii) if the supply of labour, at prevailing wages, is greater than the available capacity which could be profitably utilized at prevailing costs and prices: $D \geqslant C < L$ (capacity-constrained or 'Marxian' or 'classical' unemployment).[2]

In addition of course, both disequilibria may also occur simultaneously in different segments or in the whole economy.

In order to maintain full employment in the face of these potential disequilibria, macroeconomic policy must attempt to influence either effective demand or available capacity (disregarding here the possibility of reducing or increasing the supply of labour). For this purpose, policy makers are mainly able to employ three sets of instruments, fiscal policy, monetary policy, and (under certain institutional conditions) incomes policy (while exchange-rate policy has lost much of its discretionary potential since the destruction of the Bretton-Woods regime of fixed exchange rates). Potentially, each of these three policy instruments may be employed for expansionary or restrictive purposes, for employment creation or inflation control. Each of them will also have effects upon the demand side as well as upon the capacity (or supply side) of the economy. But these effects tend to differ in their intensity and their temporal incidence. A brief discussion seems useful.

In the present state of macroeconomic theory, the absolute and relative effectiveness of government fiscal and monetary policy is in dispute. Rational-expectations theorists take the most extreme position, holding that—in the absence of money illusion—neither fiscal nor monetary policy instruments will have an impact upon real output and, hence, upon employment. Their only effect will be upon nominal prices and wages and, hence, upon the rate of inflation (Lucas & Sargent, 1981). Monetarists, who do not completely discount the possibility of real effects, at least under conditions of idle capacity, assume that monetary policy will be more effective than fiscal policy and that, within monetary policy, the control of the money supply will have greater effect than interest-rate policy. Keynesians, on the other hand, tend to have greater confidence in the effectiveness of fiscal policy and, within monetary policy, in interest rate policy.

Apparently, empirical econometric research has not been able to resolve these differences in an unambiguous fashion (Trapp, 1976). Nevertheless, it is obvious that, to the extent that they are effective, fiscal expansion and monetary expansion work in the same direction, increasing aggregate demand for goods and services in the first round. Whether demand expansion will also lead to an increase in production and, ultimately, employment, however, seems to be much less certain.

Leaving aside possible effects upon imports and exports, the outcome seems to depend mainly upon the existence of idle capacity which could be profitably employed at present wages and prices. Under such conditions of 'Keynesian unemployment', demand expansion is indeed likely to generate additional output and employment. This much seems to be conceded even by monetarists (who would, however, question the likelihood of 'Keynesian' situations ever arising).

But what if there should be significant supply-side capacity or profitability constraints? In that case of 'classical unemployment', monetarists would expect that any further expansion of aggregate demand would only lead to price and wage increases, while Keynesians would count on higher inflation rates to reduce real wages which, in turn, should increase profitability and stimulate capacity-increasing investments (Sawyer, 1982).

On microeconomic grounds, rational-expectations theorists and monetarists appear to be more persuasive here. There may be good microeconomic reasons for assuming that wages might be 'downward-sticky' (Thurow, 1983); but why should they be upward-sticky in a systematic way? Thus, the futility of demand expansion under conditions of 'classical unemployment' (which are, on theoretical grounds, the only conditions which monetarists consider likely) seems to be inescapable.

The balance of arguments would change, however, if it were possible to treat wages as a policy variable in macroeconomic models (Malinvaud, 1980: 204; Weintraub, 1978). This is, of course, the essence of incomes policy. To admit its relevance, however, one must step outside a theoretical frame of reference, shared by monetarists and Keynesians alike, which derives macroeconomic outcomes entirely from the microeconomic adjustments of optimizing individuals and firms under conditions approaching atomistic competition (Sawyer, 1982: 62). Only if it is recognized that wages (and, to some extent, prices as well) may be the result of organized, collective action (Olson, 1982: 1983), does it become plausible to think that wages settlements might also be treated as a policy variable in the macroeconomic management of demand and capacity.

To recognize the theoretical possibility of incomes policy as an instrument of macroeconomic management does not, of course, imply its institutional feasibility in all countries and at all times. This issue will be taken up in the following section. Here, I will instead discuss the distinctive economic characteristics of incomes policy as compared to the other two instruments of macroeconomic management, monetary and fiscal policy.

Monetary expansion, by increasing the supply of money and/or lowering interest rates, will increase the availability, and lower the cost, of credit financing. If successful, demand for consumer and capital goods will expand, and the latter may also have a (delayed) effect upon capacity. Conversely, monetary restraint and increasing interest rates will encourage savings and reduce consumer and investment expenditures and, eventually, will reduce the stock of productive capacity.

Fiscal expansion, increasing public expenditure at a given level of taxation, or reducing taxes at a given level of public expenditure, is generally similar to monetary expansion in its primary effects upon demand and its secondary effects on supply. The similarity seems to be closest in the case of tax reductions which, by increasing private disposable income, may (or may not) increase demand for consumer and investment goods, while increases of public expenditure will have more direct and certain first-round effects upon demand. But fiscal expansion is also associated with a critical uncertainty: whether expenditures are increased or taxes lowered, effective fiscal expansion must increase the public-sector borrowing requirement. Depending upon the prevailing conditions of capital markets, however, public borrowing may drive up interest rates, 'crowding out' some private borrowing with countervailing impacts upon effective demand. Conversely, fiscal contraction, reducing expenditure at given levels of taxation or raising taxes at given levels of expenditure, would reduce effective demand and also the public-sector borrowing requirement.[3]

Essentially, therefore, fiscal and monetary policy (if they are effective) will have parallel impacts on the demand side and the supply side of the economy, and their primary impact seems to be upon the demand side. This has important implications. If, according to Tinbergen's famous principle, the logic of macroeconomic policy requires that at least as many separate and independent policy instruments should be available as there are economic-policy targets to be attained (Tinbergen, 1967, ch. 3), it would follow that fiscal and monetary policy measures can only be employed together to achieve one target at any one time, either inflation control, or employment stimulation, but not both at the same time. If employed at cross purposes, fiscal and monetary policy would tend to cancel out, rather than achieve different targets simultaneously.

That essentially, explains the importance of incomes policy, when it is institutionally feasible, for macroeconomic management. Compared to monetary and fiscal policy, it is an instrument which has two unique properties:

(i) it tends to affect the demand-side and the supply-side of the economy in opposite directions, and

(ii) it tends to work more strongly on the supply-side than upon the demand-side.

If it is effective, wage restraint (meaning real wage increases below the rate of productivity increases) will reduce the costs of production and, thereby, increase the profitability of additional employment and of capacity-increasing investments. Together with these positive supply-side effects, wage restraint will also reduce consumer incomes and, hence, aggregate demand—but by an amount which is smaller than the amount of wages forgone because of lower savings and reduced expenditures for imports. Conversely, real wage increases above the rate of productivity gains will have negative supply-side effects by increasing real unit-labour costs, discouraging capacity-increasing investments. They will also increase consumer income and demand for domestic products, but by a smaller amount because of increasing savings and demand for imports.

We are now able to relate these macroeconomic instruments to the problems of macroeconomic management confronting European economies during the 1970s, which are systematized in Figure 11.1. Depending upon whether the origin of the problem is to be located on the demand-side or the supply-side of the economy, one may distinguish between two types of inflation (demand-pull and cost-push) and two types of unemployment (Keynesian and classical).

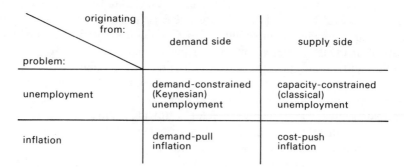

	demand side	supply side
unemployment	demand-constrained (Keynesian) unemployment	capacity-constrained (classical) unemployment
inflation	demand-pull inflation	cost-push inflation

FIG. 11.1. *Macroeconomic instruments and problems of macroeconomic management*

The simplest type of macroeconomic problem is presented by an economy fluctuating cyclically between Keynesian unemployment and demand-pull inflation. Under such conditions (which were approximated during the 1960s), the counter-cyclical management of aggregate demand, employing the instruments of monetary and fiscal policy, preferably in co-ordination, seems entirely capable of smoothing the business cycle.

If, however, the inflationary situation should include significant cost-push elements (as was true in the first half of the 1970s because of high wage settlements and, above all, because of the oil-price shock of 1973-4), fiscal and monetary demand management alone would run into trouble. The push of some factor costs could not lead to general inflation in a perfectly competitive economy (in which some other prices would have had to fall, instead). However, under conditions of oligopolistic (mark-up) pricing in large sectors of the economy, which would permit price increases when costs go up, a moderate dose of demand deflation would be unable to push down prices as long as factor costs themselves did not first go down. If they, in turn, should be downward-sticky (and if they were not, there would be no cost push) output and employment would have to be reduced by a large amount before the rate of inflation could be reduced significantly. Thus, if near-full employment was to be maintained, the government would have to switch to reflation long before inflationary expectations could be squeezed out of the economy—with the result of upwardly ratcheting rates of inflation.

If, on the other hand, demand deflation were to be pursued with the tenacity necessary to break inflationary expectations, very high levels of demand-constrained unemployment would have to be accepted as a necessary price. Worse yet, if demand deflation had to be continued for a longer period, its negative supply-side effects would also begin to matter. Existing capacity would be under-utilized, discouraging new investment. Furthermore, idle capacity would tend to disappear—some of it destroyed by bankruptcies, some of it by technological obsolescence, and some of it by 'structural' obsolescence resulting from irreversible changes in the patterns of demand. In short, a prolonged period of demand deflation would necessarily transform the character of unemployment. If it was demand-constrained (Keynesian) at the beginning, it would more and more become capacity-constrained as available productive capacity was being destroyed. As a consequence, even a radical policy-switch towards demand reflation would then be unable to eliminate unemployment. It would run into serious problems of demand-pull inflation long before full employment was again within sight (Sawyer, 1982: 129-30.)

Similarly, if unemployment is of the capacity-constrained or classical variety to begin with, the standard remedy of Keynesian macroeconomic management, demand reflation, would only push up the rate of inflation without significant increases in employment unless—as was pointed out above—nominal wages could be held back, allowing for real-wage losses in order to increase the profitability of additional employment.

Thus, in two of the four 'pure' types of macroeconomic problems, cost-push inflation and capacity-constrained unemployment, an exclusive reliance on fiscal and monetary demand management would be either ineffective or would actually make matters worse than before. The same would be true of the varieties of 'mixed' economic problems which have become increasingly prevalent during the last decade, especially combinations of demand inflation with classical unemployment or of cost-push inflation with demand-constrained unemployment (both of which are usually labelled 'stagflation') as well as of demand inflation with cost-push inflation ('price-wage spirals') and of demand-constrained unemployment with capacity-constrained unemployment.

In all these cases, demand management alone would be either ineffective or confronted with the conflicting imperatives of having to deflate and to reflate simultaneously in order to fight both inflation and unemployment.

This was the double bind of macroeconomic management during the 1970s in all countries which (like the United States) were institutionally incapable of having an effective incomes policy (or which, like West Germany, were unwilling to rely upon this capability).

Incomes policy, however, used either alone or in combination with demand management, would considerably increase the effectiveness of macroeconomic policy in most problem situations (Busch-Lüty, 1964). Because of its positive supply-side effects, wage restraint would be particularly useful in the case of cost-push inflation which it is capable of reducing without the rise in unemployment that would be associated with demand deflation. Wage restraint also appears as the most directly effective supply-side measure in the case of capacity-constrained or classical unemployment. Incomes policy could be of even greater practical importance under conditions of 'stagflation', combining demand-constrained unemployment with cost-push inflation. If wage restraint can be relied upon to control inflation, governments will be free to fight unemployment by reflating demand. In short, the availability of an effective incomes policy does increase the degrees of freedom of macroeconomic policy and, hence, its chances of success against a greater variety of the problem situations which prevailed during the 1970s (Weintraub, 1978).

It should be obvious, however, that the contribution of incomes policy to successful macroeconomic management during the 1970s would almost always have consisted in effective wage restraint, rather than wage increases. This is no accident in a decade characterized by high rates of inflation and an increasing prevalence of capacity-constrained unemployment. But it does mean that the strategy of avoiding unemployment through the successful management of capitalist growth, which Austria pursued in contrast to Sweden during the 1970s, also required a high price to be paid by the labour movement. While in Sweden that price was primarily to be paid in the form of very high taxes upon salaries, wages and consumption, the Austrian strategy presumably required the subordination of any redistributive goals of wage policy under the discipline of frequently changing, but generally restrictive, macroeconomic requirements.

Thus, there is no reason to expect that Austria was able to escape from the constraints of the capitalist economy any more than Sweden did. But, within these constraints, Austria was in fact able to maintain full employment throughout the 1970s, while West Germany, ostensibly pursuing a similar strategy, was not. I will try to show in the following section that this difference can be explained by specific institutional conditions affecting the employment of macroeconomic policy instruments in both countries.

Austria and West Germany: The Importance of Institutional Constraints

As a consequence of the oil-price shock of 1973-4 (and, again, of 1979-80) industrial countries were simultaneously confronted with two problems of economic management: they had to cope with inflationary pressures which were significantly increased by the added cost push of oil-price increases, and they had to compensate for, or to absorb, the demand gap resulting from the transfer of oil incomes to the OPEC countries. As was pointed out above, countries which could only rely upon government fiscal and monetary policy, but not upon an effective incomes policy, were faced with the unhappy choice between inflation and unemployment under these circumstances.

The institutional capability of a country to have a voluntary incomes policy seems to depend primarily upon the strength and the organizational structure of its labour unions and upon the effective locus of collective bargaining. If union organization is concentrated, with a limited number of 'encompassing' industrial unions, and if collective bargaining is centralized at the national level, the unions will tend to consider the macroeconomic consequences of wage settlements out of rational self-interest even in the absence of government guide-lines (Frey, 1966; Olson, 1982). On the other hand, if union organization is fragmented and collective bargaining decentralized, individual wage settlements are unlikely to be determined by considerations of macro-economic management. Under such circumstances, incomes policy does depend entirely upon the ability of government to either force or bribe unions to comply with guidelines which each of them will consider to be against the immediate self-interest of their members.

This, essentially, explains the difficulties encountered by British economic policy since the early 1970s. Once inflationary expectations were introduced into the economy, an extremely fragmented and decentralized collective-bargaining system would generate 'leap-frogging' wage increases adding to the inflationary momentum. At the same time, British unions were powerful enough to resist and defeat any attempt at compulsory incomes policy. Therefore, when the Labour party came to power after the oil-price shock, it aimed for a negotiated form of incomes policy in the form of a 'social contract' which would commit the unions to voluntary wage restraint in return for government commitments to full employment and an active industrial policy (Barnes & Reid, 1980). And for a while, the incomes policy of the social contract was dramatically successful. The increase of unit labour costs was reduced from 29.4 per cent in 1975 to 9.4 per cent in 1976, and the rate of inflation followed in text-book fashion moving down from 24.2 per cent in 1975 to 8.3 per cent in 1978 (Table 11.4). All the while, however, the real-income position of British workers was worsening, while the government was seemingly unable to uphold its full-employment part of the bargain (Tarling & Wilkinson, 1977). Even though employment figures were more favourable than, for instance, in Germany, by 1978 British union leadership was unable to contain rank-and-file discontent. The Labour government went down in a wave of unofficial and official strike activity which, again, pushed up unit labour costs and the rate of inflation.

When the Conservatives came to power in 1979, they renounced any hope of an effective incomes policy. Instead, the new government concentrated all its efforts upon reducing aggregate demand through monetary and fiscal retrenchment (Wagner, 1981). In this, it was eventually successful. After rising to 18 per

TABLE 11.4. *Increase in unit labour costs and in consumer prices in Austria, West Germany and the United Kingdom, 1974–82*

	Austria		West Germany		United Kingdom	
	Unit Labour Costs	Inflation	Unit Labour Costs	Inflation	Unit Labour Costs	Inflation
1974	11.4	10.0	9.5	7.3	22.7	16.0
1975	13.4	7.9	6.0	6.0	29.4	24.2
1976	5.3	6.5	1.9	4.2	9.4	16.5
1977	6.2	5.4	3.8	3.6	10.3	15.8
1978	8.9	4.3	3.5	2.8	10.1	8.3
1979	1.9	4.4	3.4	4.2	15.2	13.4
1980	4.8	6.4	6.3	5.5	21.2	18.0
1981	7.8	6.7	4.7	5.9	11.3	11.9
1982	4.5	5.4	3.5	5.3	6.5	8.6

Sources: Sachverständigenrat (1982: 21); *Aktuelle Beiträge zur Wirtschafts- und Finanzpolitik*, 34/83; OECD, *Historical Statistics 1960–1981* Paris, 1983; DIW (1983a).

cent in 1980, the rate of inflation fell to 11.9 per cent in 1981 and 8.6 per cent in 1982. Predictably, however, the successful effort to reduce inflation by a cutback of effective demand was preceded by a fall in employment from 24.8 million in 1979 to 23.1 million in 1981, and by a rise of unemployment rates from 5.3 per cent in 1979 to 11.8 per cent in 1982.

Thus, the British experience illustrates the price which a country had to pay, after the mid-1970s, if price stability was to be pursued without the support of an effective incomes policy. The point is emphasized by a comparison with the Austrian and German experience (Table 11.4). Like Britain, both countries managed to achieve a dramatic drop in unit-labour-cost increases from 1975 to 1976, after the unions had realized the seriousness of the recession. But while in Britain wage moderation broke down in 1979, it continued in Austria and Germany, even though inflation rates were again rising after 1979 as a result of the second oil-price shock. Thus, the Austrian and German governments never were under the same pressure to employ restrictive fiscal and monetary policies in order to control inflation. Instead, these instruments of government policy could have been used to reflate domestic demand without the excessive inflationary consequences which that would have entailed in Britain. But only Austria was able to maintain full employment by adopting a two-track strategy, combining wage restraint with demand reflation.

The difference between the Austrian and the German employment performance is described by Table 11.2. Austria entered the recession period with a more vigorous rate of economic growth, while Germany was hit by the oil-price shock just at the moment when stabilization policy had managed to bring the economy almost to a standstill in 1974. After that, economic growth was roughly similar in both countries: both suffered from a reduction of output in

1975 followed by a relatively vigorous recovery in 1976, slowing down in 1977-8 and accelerating again in 1979. But despite roughly similar growth rates, the labour market performance of both countries was dramatically different. While Germany lost about 5.1 per cent (or 1.36 million) of all jobs between 1973 and 1977, Austrian employment barely registered the slump of 1975 and increased altogether by 4.9 per cent between 1973 and 1977. During the upswing between 1977 and 1980, employment in both countries increased at about the same rate. Thus, the difference between continuing full employment in Austria and relatively high unemployment in Germany must find its explanation in the 1973-7 period.

Compared to Germany, the Austrian labour market of that period profited from a number of favourable circumstances. First of all, Austria entered the recession at the end of a vigorous economic boom, while in Germany the slowdown had already begun in 1974. Thus, Austrian firms, which had still suffered from labour shortages in 1974, would be more hesitant to reduce their labour force in 1975. This was particularly true of the nationalized industries which, under the moral suasion of government and the unions, maintained significantly higher employment levels than private industry did in 1975 (Nowotny, 1979). In addition, the long-term expansion of the public-service sector which had more or less come to an end in Germany by the middle 1970s, was still continuing in Austria and, finally, a statutory reduction of the standard working week from 42 to 40 hours also happened to become effective in 1974-5. These, surely, were lucky breaks, rather than well-thought-out full-employment strategies. But they did help in cushioning the impact of the recession upon the Austrian labour market.

On the other hand, however, Austria profited less than Germany did from developments on the supply side of the labour market. While both countries did reduce the number of foreign workers after 1974, the Austrian labour force still increased by 2.2 per cent between 1973 and 1977, while the supply of labour was reduced by 1.2 per cent over the same period in Germany, as a consequence of early retirement and a general demographic decline. In addition, Germany also, if half-heartedly, pursued an *active labour-market policy* along Swedish lines, while Austria did not (Wösendorfer, 1980). As a result, registered unemployment in Germany was reduced by 1.6 percentage points in 1975, while the employment effect of Austrian labour-market policy was negligible at around 0.3 per cent of the labour force throughout the recession (Table 11.2). On the whole, therefore, circumstantial factors favourable or unfavourable to either Austria or West Germany tend to cancel out without providing a compelling explanation for the persistence of full employment in Austria and high unemployment in Germany.

Among foreign observers, there seems to be general agreement that the Austrian 'employment miracle' is to be explained primarily by a more aggressive Keynesian policy of demand reflation during the recession, especially by means of an expansionary fiscal policy financed primarily through borrowing abroad

(Hankel, 1979; DIW, 1983a). Upon a closer look, however, it seems unlikely that fiscal expansion alone could explain employment differences between Austria and West Germany. The Austrian federal government, to be sure, responded to the economic crisis in classical Keynesian fashion. After 1974, its budget deficits were consistently higher, expressed as a percentage of total expenditures, than those of the German federal government. And, given the larger relative size of the federal budget in Austria (52.8 per cent of total public expenditure in 1982, as compared to 32.5 per cent in West Germany), the Austrian lead is even greater when the deficit is expressed as a share of GNP (Table 11.5).

TABLE 11.5. *Budget deficits of central government and of total government as % of GNP in Austria and West Germany, 1974–82*

	Austria		West Germany	
	Central Government	Total Government	Central Government	Total Government
1974	−1.2	1.3	−0.5	−1.3
1975	−3.8	−2.5	−3.0	−5.7
1976	−3.8	−3.8	−2.3	−3.4
1977	−3.2	−2.4	−1.6	−2.4
1978	−3.4	−2.8	−1.6	−2.5
1979	−2.8	−2.5	−1.5	−2.7
1980	−2.6	−2.0	−1.7	−3.1
1981	−2.4	−1.8	·−2.2	−4.0
1982	−3.4	−2.2	−2.0	−3.7

Source: Calculations based on data in DIW (1983a).

But the economy is affected not only by the federal budget, but by *Länder* and local budgets as well. And this was the weak spot of Austrian fiscal policy. All through the recession, the economic stimulus of deficit spending at the federal level was counteracted by budget surpluses elsewhere in the public sector (*Länder* governments, local governments, and the insurance funds). In Germany, on the other hand, the rest of the public sector, while clearly less committed to anti-cyclical spending than the federal government, still contributed significantly to the overall public deficit. Thus, while the Austrian federal government strained its budget more than the German federal government did in 1974–5, and much more in the following years, the overall public-sector deficit, expressed as a share of GNP, was more than twice as high in Germany in 1975, about the same in both countries between 1976 and 1979, and higher in Germany after that. Obviously this difference does require more study than it has received so far. It is conceivable, at any rate, that the larger size, and greater political importance, of the *Länder* in the German federal system induced them to share to some extent the federal government's political responsibility for macroeconomic management (Knott, 1981), while *Länder* governments in Austria, which are smaller in size and in political (and budgetary) significance, feel free to indulge in the type of pro-cyclical budgeting which in Germany is characteristic of local governments.

Of course, there is also the possibility that the Austrians might have been able to employ their budget deficits with greater economic efficiency than the Germans did. In particular, there are suggestions that the very generous depreciation allowance in Austrian tax law has created a compulsion to reinvest profits among tax-conscious Austrian entrepreneurs (Abele *et al.*, 1982). Compared to a more erratic German policy (which had imposed a surcharge on investments before 1974, and which attempted to encourage investments through a short-lived bonus programme in 1975), this steady subsidization of investments might explain the fact that Austria continued to have very high (though falling) GNP-shares of gross-fixed investment during the 1970s—the highest in Western Europe and much higher than in Germany (Table 11.6). As a result, Austria was able to modernize its capital stock during the recession, and to increase the productivity and international competitiveness of its industry (Hankel, 1979). Still, it seems unlikely that even a very efficient choice of fiscal-policy measures could have translated the smaller volume of fiscal impulses into so much larger employment effects in Austria as compared to West Germany.

TABLE 11.6. *Gross fixed investments as % of GNP in Austria, West Germany, and Sweden, 1973-82*

	1973	1974	1975	1976	1977	1978	1979	1980	1981	1982
Austria	28.7	28.5	26.8	26.2	27.0	25.8	24.9	25.3	25.1	23.6
West Germany	23.9	21.6	20.4	20.1	20.3	20.7	21.8	22.8	22.0	20.4
Sweden	21.8	21.5	20.9	21.1	21.2	19.5	20.0	20.3	19.8	19.4

Source: Calculations based on data in DIW (1983a).

If macroeconomic policy can explain the Austrian success at all, therefore, the explanation is more likely to be found in the area of monetary policy. Here, we indeed have significant differences (Table 11.7). Apparently, Austrian monetary policy was not entirely preoccupied with the problem of restraining the inflationary pressures of the early 1970s. Its major contribution to inflation control was a self-conscious hard-currency policy, pegging the Austrian Schilling to the German Deutschmark whose international value was moving up during most of the 1970s (Handler, 1982). By itself, however, this policy could have had disastrous consequences for domestic employment, encouraging imports and pricing Austrian exports out of the world market, unless domestic costs and prices were also brought under control. Thus, the temptation must have been very great for the Austrian Nationalbank to back up its hard-currency policy with a tightly deflationary domestic monetary policy. For a brief period, lasting from the fall of 1973 until February of 1974, the annual rate of increase of the M1-money supply was indeed close to zero. After that, however, the money supply was allowed to increase again, even though the rate of inflation had not yet reached its peak. More important, the long-standing policy of maintaining relatively stable nominal interest rates was continued throughout, with the consequence that inflation-adjusted real interest rates were even allowed to become negative in 1974. In short, at the first hint of a world-wide recession, Austrian monetary policy seems to have abandoned any measures specifically aimed at inflation control, facilitating through its cautionary monetary reflation the federal government's strategy of deficit-financed fiscal expansion and contributing a massive expansionary push of its own by allowing real interest rates to become negative.

TABLE 11.7. *Discount rates, rates of return of long-term bonds, inflation and real interest rates in Austria and West Germany, 1973–82*

	Austria				West Germany			
	Discount Rate	Return on Bonds	Inflation	R–1	D	R	I	R–1
1973	5.5	7.7	6.6	1.1	6.5	9.3	7.0	2.3
1974	6.1	9.0	10.0	–1.0	6.8	10.2	7.3	2.9
1975	6.2	9.5	7.9	1.6	4.1	8.6	6.0	2.6
1976	4.5	8.6	6.5	2.1	3.5	7.9	4.2	3.7
1977	4.8	8.3	5.4	2.9	3.4	6.3	3.6	2.7
1978	5.0	7.9	4.3	3.6	3.0	6.0	2.8	3.2
1979	3.8	7.6	4.4	3.2	4.0	7.5	4.2	3.3
1980	6.3	9.1	6.4	2.7	7.0	8.5	5.5	3.0
1981	6.8	10.2	6.7	3.5	7.5	10.2	5.9	4.3
1982	5.8	10.1[a]	5.4	4.7	7.1	8.9	5.3	3.6

[a] Calculations based on OECD data of first three quarters.

Sources: Abele *et al.* (1982); *Aktuelle Beiträge zur Wirtschafts- und Finanzpolitik* 34/1983; OECD, *Economic Survey Austria*, Paris, 1983; *Wifo-Monatsberichte* 8/1983; *Bundesbank, Monatsbericht*, Juli 1983.

But what about the need to hold down wages and prices in order to protect Austrian employment against the risks of a hard-currency policy? Apparently, this task was explicitly and entirely delegated to the institutions of social partnership (Marin, 1982; Pollan, 1982; Handler, 1982: 420). Once they had taken charge of the problem, the rate of inflation began to drop, and so did the increase in unit labour costs (Table 11.4). Thus, while it is possible to interpret Austria's hard-currency policy as an attempt to 'import stability' from Germany (as some Austrian economists are quick to suggest), it seems only fair to point out that imported stability would have had disastrous economic consequences unless it could be reproduced at home either through demand deflation or through the voluntary wage restraint and price discipline of the social partners.

In Germany, by contrast, the transition to floating exchange rates in the spring of 1973 had been the signal for a policy of massive fiscal and monetary deflation in order to break the inflationary expectations of the early 1970s. But while the federal government shifted to a course of fiscal expansion immediately after the oil-price shock, the Bundesbank continued its policy of extreme monetary restraint well into the second quarter of 1974. Even more important, the discount rate which had been pushed up to 7 per cent in the spring of 1973 was maintained at that high level until the fall of 1974, followed by small-step reductions until the summer of 1975. As a consequence, interest rates for short-term credit remained above 13 per cent and for long-term credit above 10 per cent throughout 1974, with real interest rates rising almost to 3 per cent. As a matter of fact, at the bottom of the recession in 1975 interest rates were still significantly higher than they had been during the boom period of the early 1970s.

Thus, while Austrian monetary policy was accommodating fiscal expansion, German monetary policy in 1973 and 1974 single-mindedly exploited the new freedom for deflationary action which it had gained through floating exchange rates (Schlesinger, 1977). There are suggestions in reports of the Bundesbank that the contrary directions of fiscal and monetary policy should be considered as elements of a double-track strategy, in which the government was to maintain employment while the bank was pursuing price stability. But the essential parallelism, discussed above, between both sets of instruments rendered such expectations unrealistic. As econometric studies have shown, when fiscal and monetary policy instruments are employed at cross purposes, a severly restrictive monetary policy will win out in practice over fiscal expansion (Trapp, 1976; Neumann, 1973; 1978; 1981; Andersen & Jordan, 1968). Thus, the steep rise in German unemployment in 1975 can be attributed to the continuation of a sharply deflationary monetary policy even after the onset of the world-wide recession and, in particular, to the opposition between the fiscal policy of the federal government and the monetary policy of the Bundesbank during most of 1974.

The crucial question, therefore, is why monetary policy should have been more restrictive in Germany than it was in Austria between 1973 and 1977. On the face of it, at least, the difference is not explained by differences in the price- and wage-setting performance of the social partners. As a matter of fact, inflation rates were lower in Germany than in Austria in each year after 1973, and unit-labour-cost increases were also significantly lower until 1978 (Table 11.4). In fact, macroeconomic policy in West Germany was less exposed to the pressures of wage-push inflation in the mid-1970s than in any other Western European country. Objectively, at least, the Bundesbank would seem to have been entirely free to pursue a less restrictive monetary policy without having to fear accelerating rates of inflation. But, apparently, this was not its subjective view of the world.

Reading through the qurterly reports of the Bundesbank on the state of the German economy, one definitely receives the impression that by 1973–4 the bank had come to regard wage push as the major threat to price stability, and that it was following current wage settlements with the greatest apprehension and with the expectation that they might transgress all tolerable bounds if given any chance to do so (Bundesbank *Monatsberichte*, Februar, 1974; Mai, 1974; August, 1974). There is no suggestion anywhere that there could be a reliable division of labour in which incomes policy, or voluntary wage restraint, might carry the burden of inflation control while the Bundesbank was free to allow monetary expansion in order to combat unemployment.

To interpret this policy stance, it would be necessary to describe and analyse institutional differences between Austria and West Germany in greater detail than is possible here. Nevertheless, two factors seem to be of paramount importance. First, the German Bundesbank enjoys a much greater degree of statutory and practical independence from the federal government, than does the Austrian Nationalbank. Even more important, while there are no institutional linkages at all between the Bundesbank and the German labour unions and employers' associations, half the shares of the Nationalbank corporation are held by the social partners, who are represented accordingly on its governing board. In addition, alumni of the Austrian social partnership institutions have often moved up to become top-level officers of the Nationalbank. Thus, the degree of familiarity, and the ease of communication, between decision makers responsible for monetary policy and for wage settlements is much greater in Austria than it is in Germany (Nowotny, 1982: 119-20).

Secondly, there are also significant differences in the institutional structures of collective bargaining. In principle, both countries have 'encompassing' patterns of union organization with a limited number of relatively large industrial unions with non-overlapping jurisdictions. In addition, however, the central union organization, the Österreichischer Gewerkschaftsbund (ÖGB) is more directly involved in collective bargaining decisions than its German counterpart, the DGB. In this respect, its authority is reinforced by its role as the gatekeeper to the Paritätische Kommission für Preis- und Lohnfragen (Joint Commission) whose subcommittee on wages must authorize the initiation of wage negotiations. Obviously, applications by member unions are unlikely to succeed without the support of the ÖGB, and wage claims are more likely to be successful (in a country in which strikes are extremely rare) if they are considered to be macroeconomically acceptable by the wages subcommittee of the Joint Commission (Marin, 1982, ch. 5).

The Joint Commission and its mechanisms for consensual wage and price policies had enjoyed almost a decade of institutional development and consolidation before they were put to the first serious test in the recession of 1966. The general strategy of wage moderation which was then agreed upon ushered in a long boom which came to an end only in 1974. In its later years, when the labour market had become very tight, wage settlements were by no means moderate any longer, and inflation rates were moving up. Still, these were understood as agreed-upon wage increases, justified by labour's earlier sacrifices, rather than as an uncontrollable escalation of union demands. Thus, when the seriousness of the new recession was appreciated in Austria by 1975, the expectations still prevailed that incomes policy could be relied upon to do its share, just as it had done in 1966, and that the Nationalbank was free to pursue a moderately expansionary course while the social partners would look after wages and prices (Pollan, 1982).

In Germany, wage moderation had also been a crucial factor contributing to the rapid economic recovery of the 1950s. It had resulted, however, from the enlightened self-interest of large, 'encompassing' union organizations (Olson, 1982), rather than from any 'neo-corporatist' arrangements for the negotiation of explicit incomes policies between the government and the social partners. Nevertheless, the unions had continued to demand a more formal recognition of their role in macroeconomic policy making, and when the Social Democrats joined the Grand Coalition in the fall of 1966, one of their institutional reforms was the establishment of the *Konzertierte Aktion*. Unlike the Austrian Joint Commission, however, the German concerted action never exercised any direct control over wage settlements, pretending to be no more than a high-level discussion forum at which the government, the employers' associations and the unions would compare notes on their current readings of the macroeconomic situation (Hardes, 1974).

Nevertheless, like its more developed Austrian counterpart, concerted action proved to be a spectacular success in the recession of 1967. Even though all participants refused to be formally bound by its discussions, wage settlements in 1967 and 1968 followed precisely the informal guidelines which had been proposed by government. Combined with government deficit spending, low wage settlements contributed significantly (under a regime of fixed exchange rates) to an export-led recovery which re-achieved full employment by 1969. But then things began to go wrong. The government had underestimated the strength of the boom, and union wage demands for 1969 turned out to be much too low. The resulting wage drift and a series of wildcat strikes forced union leaders to adopt a militant stance in the 1970 and 1971 wage rounds, in order to regain control over their own rank and file. In the process, government guidelines were more or less ignored (Hardes, 1974: 94-6). Together with inflationary pressures imported from abroad, these wage increases pushed up the inflation rate in 1971. When the unions returned to wage moderation in 1972, inflation continued to rise nevertheless because of speculative capital imports fuelled by the expectation of further revaluations of the DM. Thus, when inflation seemed to continue unabated, the unions again pushed for higher settlements in 1973 in order to protect the real-wage position of their members.

In the absence of any institutional machinery for effective wage controls, and without institutional arrangements in which the complicated pressures and motives behind actual wage settlements could be communicated adequately, the Bundesbank had reason to think that concerted action was now a complete failure, and that wages were out of control at least since 1970. At the same time, the government also seemed to be losing its nerve, agreeing to rather exorbiant wage increases in the public sector as late as February 1974. Not surprisingly, perhaps, the bank in its quarterly reports seemed to regard government fiscal policy with almost as much apprehension as it did union wage settlements. Perceiving itself as the lone champion in the fight for price stability, the federal bank stepped on the monetary brakes as soon as floating exchange rates, in the spring of 1973, seemed to provide the opportunity for 'stability in one country'.

In the summer of 1974, the bank also decided to switch from an essentially Keynesian counter-cyclical philosophy to an explicitly monetarist strategy—long before similar switches occured in Britain and in the United States (Schlesinger, 1977). By and large, monetary policy would now be committed to annual targets for the increase of 'central bank money' which were derived from the bank's estimates of the real growth potential of the economy. In effect, however, this switch to a monetarist strategy meant that the Bundesbank was abdicating its own responsibility for full employment. If the money supply could be limited to just the amount which was necessary and sufficient to finance inflation-free growth, it would not only achieve control over demand-pull inflation, but it would also make sure that any cost-push impulses would reduce output, rather than push up inflation rates. In fact, this implied an exact reversal of the allocation of functions between monetary and incomes policy which was practised in Austria. According to the bank's new philosophy, it was entirely up to the unions to adjust their wage settlements to previously announced targets for monetary growth in such a way that full employment could be maintained.

Thus, the Bundesbank had finally found a strategy with which it could discipline union wage demands. In this, it had the full support of the dominant opinion among professional economists in Germany. A good example is the standard textbook on economic policy by Giersch, one of the most influential members of the German Council of Economic Advisers. While admitting that an Austrian-type allocation of functions was theoretically also feasible (Giersch, 1977: 198), the subsequent analysis focuses entirely upon an allocation of functions in which incomes policy must assume responsibility for full employment while monetary policy should concentrate upon price stability (ch. 7). Following the author's logic, one of his collaborators even suggested that the unions should have to finance the deficits of the unemployment insurance fund—which seems only reasonable if one has come to believe that excessive wage settlements are the cause of current of mass unemployment (Risch, 1983).

It is, unfortunately, all too easy to point out the flaws in this line of reasoning. Obviously, wage settlements are not the only possible source of cost-push inflation, and they have in fact not been a significant cost-push factor in Germany since 1975. However, if the money supply is limited to the financing needs of inflation-free growth, any unanticipated cost-push (such as that provided by the two oil-price explosions of 1973–4, and 1979–80), will have the effect of reducing aggregate demand significantly below the real-growth potential of the economy. The result will be not only demand-constrained unemployment but also a discouragement of real investment and, thus, a reduction of the real growth potential available in the next period (Maier-Rigaud, 1982; 1983). Union wage restraint, by itself, would be entirely powerless to prevent this downward spiralling of economic activity, real investment and employment.

In fact, therefore, the monetarist strategy adopted by the Bundesbank, and the underlying assignment of roles to incomes policy and to monetary policy, left unions with a part in which they could not win full employment through wage moderation. The question is why they nevertheless continued to play the role assigned to them in the script written by the bank and its ideological supporters. The significance of the question becomes obvious if one analyses the relationship between the bank and the unions in game-theoretic terms as a Prisoners' Dilemma (von Weizsäcker, 1978: 45). If co-operative strategies for the bank and the unions are defined as monetary expansion and wage restraint, respectively, the Prisoners' Dilemma would lead one to expect a non-cooperative equilibrium in which the bank would always choose monetary restraint while the unions would always pursue aggressive wage policies. But, apparently, this was not the game that was actually played in Germany after 1974. While the bank did, indeed, pursue the non-cooperative strategy associated with a Prisoner's Dilemma view of the world, the unions have stuck to co-operative strategies throughout. There are two possible explanations for this surprising result.

First, it is likely that the unions did regard the Social-Liberal coalition government in office until 1982 at least as a 'lesser evil', and that they hesitated to add to the government's obvious political difficulties by aggressive wage conflicts. But, by itself, political loyalty is unlikely to have completely overridden economic self-interest. Thus, I am led to believe that the definition of self-interest implied in a Prisoners' Dilemma analysis is inappropriate for the German unions in the latter half of the 1970s.

Given their organizational concentration, and the macroeconomic sophistication of their headquarters staff, German union leaders would probably have considered aggressive wage policies as economically self-defeating under the conditions of the late 1970s. Instead of improving the real-wage position of their members, they would have pushed up inflation rates, leading to a further tightening of monetary policy and to higher unemployment. Thus, in a sense, German unions may have become captives of their own rationality. Finding themselves compelled by their own organizational logic to pursue strategies which they considered macroeconomically rational, they were no longer able to extract a political price for their de facto collaboration. There was no need in Germany for the government to bribe the unions into a British-style 'social contract', and there also was no need for the Bundesbank to depart from its own preferred strategy in order to save the economy from the 'worst case' of militant union strategies clashing head-on with highly restrictive stabilization policies. Thus, even though German unions have accepted greater losses in their real-wage position than unions in Austria or any other OECD country

(*Sachverständigenrat*, 1982: 21), they were not rewarded for their willingness to collaborate. Instead, low wage settlements after 1975 could be interpreted by the bank as a success of the monetary strategy which it had adopted in 1973–4, thus reinforcing its underlying monetarist philosophy. Having found a unilateral strategy which was so successful, in its own terms, the Bundesbank had no more reason to consider the desirability of an agreed allocation of functions along Austrian lines in which it might have had to trade some price stability for more employment.

To summarize: the Austrian and German experiences during the second half of the 1970s have two important lessons to teach. Austria has demonstrated that it was indeed possible, under the conditions obtaining between 1974 and 1979, to maintain full employment through economic growth if one could agree upon an allocation of macroeconomic functions in which incomes policy would provide protection against inflation while monetary and fiscal policies would, in concertation, ensure an adequate growth of aggregate demand. The German experience, on the other hand, has demonstrated, that a positive outcome does not depend only upon the institutional prerequisites for an effective incomes policy (which were absent in Britain but present in Germany). Wage restraint alone, and even in combination with an expansionary fiscal policy, was unable to ensure full employment when monetary policy was not also willing to accept its own role in an Austrian-type allocation of macroeconomic functions. In Germany, the tenuous co-ordination between monetary policy and incomes policy disintegrated under circumstances which can be explained by a lack of communication and mutual trust between the central bank and the unions. In that sense, the German case illustrates the more general proposition that neo-corporatist institutions may be extremely beneficial where they exist, but that they are always vulnerable to the entropy law of dissensus, conflict, and dis-integration (Schmitter, 1982).

The 1980s: New Challenges in Search of New Strategies

In the last section I have tried to show that the Austrian strategy could have worked for Germany and other countries if institutional conditions had only allowed for a co-ordination between fiscal policy, monetary policy and incomes policy within an overall allocation of functions in which fiscal and monetary policy would assume responsibility for full employment while incomes policy would provide protection on the inflation front. It should also be clear that the Austrian strategy (while profiting institutionally from the ease of communi-cation within a small policy-making community) did not particularly profit from the smallness of the Austrian economy, and that it definitely was not a beggar-my-neighbour strategy which, by definition, could only be played successfully by a minority of national economies. On the contrary, the Austrian reflation in the face of a world-wide recession predictably led to deficits on current account providing an economic stimulus to the rest of the world. The world economy would have been in a much better shape if more countries had followed the 'Austrian model' after the mid-1970s.

But what of the early 1980s? The new Socialist government in France, which had explicitly decided to follow the Austrian example, was forced to reverse its expansionist full-employment policy within less than two years. Of course, one might argue that France had adopted only half of the Austrian strategy, being unable to achieve inflation control through effective wage restraint, and apparently unwilling to let its currency devalue to the degree which then would have been necessary in order to limit the deficit on current account. But Austria herself is now also suffering from reduced economic growth and a rate of unemployment which is almost twice as high as it was during the 1970s. The question is, therefore, whether the Austrian strategy itself has now lost its power to maintain full employment in the face of the continuing world-wide recession.

The 1980s have indeed confronted Western Europe with new economic challenges to which even the more successful strategies of the 1970s do not provide ready answers. Unlike the first oil-price shock of 1973-4, the second one of 1979-80 was accompanied by a tightening of the over-extended international credit markets in the face of the virtual bankruptcy of large debtor countries, such as Poland, Mexico, or Brazil. At the same time, the US Federal Reserve, having recently been converted to a monetarist philosophy also switched to a tight-money policy in order to finally break the inflationary momentum of the Carter years. In addition, President Reagan's 1981 tax cut, intended as a supply-side measure, increased the federal borrowing requirement while the Fed was limiting the money supply. The results were extremely high interest rates, attracting foreign capital into the United States which, in turn, led to a continuous upward revaluation of the US dollar that further increased the attractiveness of investing in US financial markets.

For European countries, the new strength of the dollar meant greater competitiveness of exports and higher import prices. More important, however, were the difficulties following from the extremely high interest rates in the Euro-dollar and US financial markets. In order to protect their own currencies against rapid devaluation, European countries had to raise their own interest rates to comparable levels. In doing so, they were forced to contract consumer and investment credit beyond the needs of domestic stabilization, and they were creating opportunities to invest in financial assets whose real rates of return compared favourably with higher-risk real investments (Hankel, 1983). As a consequence, employment-creating new investment was squeezed out by the cost-push of high interest rates as well as by the opportunity-pull of financial markets.

If, on the other hand, a country was willing to pursue a policy of monetary reflation and lower interest rates in order to stimulate domestic investment, speculative capital would begin to leave, and its currency would begin to devalue more rapidly, with further incentives to capital exports. In the end, therefore, reflationary policies designed to stimulate domestic investment would result in accelerating capital flight. This, essentially, seems to have been the mechanism which forced the French government to reverse its expansionary course.

Under such conditions, the original Austrian strategy of combining a hard-currency policy with easy money became infeasible. As a matter of fact, Austrian interest rates had already had to follow German ones after the value of the schilling was formally tied to the DM in 1977. When interest rates began to rise internationally, therefore, Austria could not again resort to the easy-money policy which had pulled it through the 1974-5 recession. Instead, its economic performance now became entirely dependent upon the ability of its fiscal policy to counteract the cost-push and opportunity-pull of international financial markets through subsidies to domestic investment. Obviously, this is a strategy which must become either inadequate or progressively more expensive if the difference between US interest rates (compounded by the expectation of further revaluations of the US dollar) and the profitability of real investments in Austria increases. Under such conditions, exacerbated by the possibility of political tensions within a coalition government, the ability to neutralize high interest rates through investment subsidies is likely to run into fiscal constraints even in Austria. And, of course, West Germany, entering the 1980s with a much higher level of unemployment and operating under much tighter political constraints upon deficit spending, is suffering much greater losses in employment.

But what about the Swedish strategy—can it continue indefinitely in the absence of economic growth and under the threat of capital flight? Apparently, the Social Democratic government, returned to power in the fall of 1982, did not think so. Instead, it immediately devaluated the krona by a rate which was much larger than expected, in order to give Swedish exports an additional push and, at the same time, to forestall any capital exports based upon expectations of further devaluation. Furthermore, the unions were prevailed upon to absorb the rise in import prices without asking for compensatory wage increases (Matzner & Matzner, 1983). But, of course, this was an expedient which could not be repeated easily and which, at any rate, would become self-defeating if other countries were to follow suit. Thus, rather than providing a definitive solution, the devaluation of the krona by 16 per cent in October 1982 demonstrated that the Swedish strategy of pursuing full employment through publicly financed employment opportunities has also become vulnerable to the discouragement of domestic private investment caused by excessively high interest rates abroad.

Short of proposals for an internationally co-ordinated reorganization of international credit markets (Hankel, 1983), or for internationally co-ordinated strategies of reflating major currencies (McKinnon, 1983), what are the prospects for purely national full-employment strategies in the 1980s? One solution is suggested by the contrast between the behaviour of investors in Japan and in other Western countries during the 1970s. Between 1972 and 1982, the capital stock in Japan increased by 219 per cent, much more than in all Western countries. During the same period, however, returns on assets declined from

15 to 3 per cent in Japan, while continuing at pre-crisis levels in most other industrial nations. It seems, therefore, that Japanese entrepreneurs continued to invest at pre-crisis levels, disregarding deteriorating rates of return, while in Western countries real investment was cut back in order to maintain pre-crisis rates of return (DIW, 1983b). Unfortunately, however, the insensitivity of Japanese investors to declining rates of profit, and their immunity to the lure of international money markets, seem to be characteristics which other countries may envy without being able to imitate.

As a consequence, I am led to the conclusion that as long as the international economic environment does not change, national full-employment strategies during the 1980s will depend upon the possibility of solidaristic redistribution between those who are employed in productive jobs and those who are not. One form which this redistribution may take is the Swedish strategy of tax-financed increases in public-sector employment and publicly subsidized employment. The question here is whether other countries without the strong egalitarian ideology developed in Sweden since the 1930s (Huntford, 1971; Hedborg & Meidner, 1984) will have the political capability to adopt and enforce similarly high levels of taxation. If not, work-sharing through reducing the working week, the working year or the working life of those that have jobs seems to be a more attractive alternative because it will at least reward solidaristic sacrifices with an increase in leisure time. But the institutional obstacles to work-sharing strategies intended to combat unemployment are formidable enough (Offe *et al.*, 1982). It is not at all clear that countries which, in the past, have pursued full employment through economic growth will be able to switch over to work-sharing without overstraining the underlying consensus, upon which their strategic capabilities depend. But that will be another story.

Notes

1. I realize that Korpi and other 'power-resources' theorists are primarily interested in the distributive outcomes of economic and social-policy choices. But, at least in open economies with free capital movement, distributive policies may be self-defeating unless their impacts upon domestic investment and production are correctly anticipated.

2. The distinction between 'Marxian' and 'classical' unemployment depends on whether the emphasis is more upon the physical constraints of the existing capital stock (resulting from past under-accumulation) or upon the unprofitability of employing more labour (resulting from, among other things, presently prevailing high real wages) (Malinvaud, 1980: 175).

3. There has also been a hope, especially among supply-side economists in the United States, that it might be possible to target expansionary fiscal policy measures in such a way that they would stimulate the supply-side of the economy more than aggregate demand. In this train of thought, it was even expected that fiscal expansion through tax cuts might be employed as an effective instrument of inflation control. On the whole, these hopes were unrealistic. Of course, fiscal measures may be more easily targeted toward certain sectors or regions of the economy than would be possible for monetary policy. Thus, at least the first-round effects of fiscal expansion may be employed to further more selective industrial or 'structural' policy goals. But, unless supply-side effects are limited entirely to the more productive utilization of presently existing and employed capacity, any increase in output

must be associated with, or preceded by, increases of personal income and of demand for capital goods. To this extent at least, Say's Law seems inexorable: fiscal expansion cannot be effective on the supply side without also increasing aggregate demand in the economy.

12

Neo-Corporatist Industrial Relations and the Economic Crisis in West Germany

WOLFGANG STREECK

Many different things—in fact, too many—have been labelled 'neo-corporatist'. This paper will be concerned exclusively with industrial relations, conceived in a wide sense as comprising the regulation not only of wages and conditions but also of (public and quasi-public) social policy and of the institutional framework within which the parties in the labour market interact. For the purposes of the argument, an industrial relations system will be called neo-corporatist if it regulates significant aspects of the exchange between capital and labour through bargained agreements between strong, encompassing class associations at the national or industrial level, and if such joint regulation takes place under procedural and political facilitation, conditional upon its substantive outcomes, by the state (Schmitter, 1983). The subject of the paper, then, is how neo-corporatist industrial relations systems thus defined, and the large interest aggregates and bargaining compacts that are their essential and characteristic constituents, are likely to react to a lasting economic crisis that is accompanied by high unemployment.

The Changing Balance of Power and Interests: Neo-corporatist Institutions Under the Pressure of the Market

The impact of economic decline on neo-corporatist industrial relations has been a subject of speculation since the early 1970s (cf. Lehmbruch, 1979b; Panitch, 1977a; Sabel, 1981). Now that the crisis has finally arrived, we can see that its effects differ considerably from what was for long accepted as received wisdom by nearly everybody. Neo-corporatist industrial relations were widely regarded as 'fair-weather systems', depending for their stability on continuous economic growth and the associated low level of unemployment. Their critical element was believed to be the trade unions whose 'wage restraint' had to be rewarded by government commitments to an expensive social policy, and by gradually increasing real wages. This required a growing economy, and failing this pre-condition, it was almost taken for granted that unions, under the pressure of their frustrated members, would (have to) refuse to be further 'concerted' by tripartite agreements.

With hindsight, it is not difficult to see why this expectation was bound to be disappointed. For one thing, the 'incomes policy' view of neo-corporatism has always been one-sided and top-heavy, in the sense that it has essentially limited itself to the problem of demand management and distribution at national level, neglecting the central role of neo-corporatist institutions on the supply side and at the work-place. Neo-corporatist demand management, to be more than a short-lived political expedient, always needed to be supported by congenial institutions of interest accommodation at the work-place, and these tend to be conducive not just to consensus but also to high efficiency and superior productivity (Streeck, 1981b). It is not at all accidental that countries like Sweden, Austria, and West Germany, in addition to having had relatively successful national incomes policies and peaceful industrial relations in the 1970s, are also characterized by highly flexible systems of manpower use at the point of production, with few if any 'restrictive practices' and with high responsiveness to technological change (Hotz, 1982; Jacobs *et al.*, 1978). One can build a complex argument around this and we will return to the point later on; what is important in the present context is that, whatever 'compensations' may or may not be gained from 'political exchange' at the national level, high real wages and safe employment can only be sustained, over a longer term, if they are underwritten by a productive economy. To the extent that neo-corporatist institutions contribute to superior productivity, unions—especially in countries, sectors or firms that depend heavily on exports—will find it hard in a crisis to make their members abandon practices and structures of 'class co-operation' at the work-place which constitute a competitive advantage in the international job market.

The second factor that speculation about the fate of neo-corporatism in an economic crisis has overlooked, is that trade unions have other stakes in neo-corporatist bargaining than just the material benefits of favourable economic and social-policy exchanges. Organizational privileges have often been mentioned as one such additional pay-off (Streeck, 1982). However, more important for our argument is the fact that unions—and in particular those large, encompassing unions which typically take part in corporatist national bargaining—are interested in the existence of institutions of industrial (self-) government that are capable of creating and enforcing general and uniform regulation, not just of wages but also of employment conditions in the widest sense. The reasons are in part ideological and in part organizational. The idea of 'solidarity' demands that workers in economically weak regions, industries or firms should not have less employment protection, inferior training, weaker representation, harder working conditions, lower pensions, poorer access to health services etc. than workers in strong regions, industries or firms. In organizational terms, internally hetero-geneous unions that do not redistribute at least some of the bargaining power of their stronger members to their weaker ones, and that permit the forces of the market to widen the disparities between their differently privileged member groups, will sooner or later have to face their own disintegration as collective actors. Central bargaining and central agreements, and the assistance of the state and the legal system in making these 'stick' in vastly different places of work, are indispensable for trade unions trying to develop a 'capacity for strategy'.

In so far as neo-corporatist arrangements support such a capacity—and there is no doubt that they do—trade unions cannot easily afford to abandon them, even if the substance of central regulations and their actual impact may be less than fully satisfactory for them in changed economic circumstances.

How does this compare to the interests of the second partner at the bargaining table, namely, business? A central leitmotiv of the 'incomes policy' tradition of neo-corporatist theory is the more or less explicit assumption of a built-in asymmetry in neo-corporatist industrial relations (Lehmbruch, 1979b: 303). While there always was considerable discussion and disagreement over the benefits of neo-corporatist co-operation for labour, it was widely accepted that capital gained significantly and unambiguously from trade-union wage restraint. By and large, this resulted in an emerging consensus that the rewards of neo-corporatism were unequally distributed in favour of capital. If this was true, however, then there was no reason to even consider the possibility that centrifugal tendencies in established neo-corporatist systems might originate among capital. Wage restraint, after all, was something that capitalists always have use for, and it seemed difficult to imagine a situation in which capitalists might lose interest in an institutional framework that was so effectively providing them with this important commodity.

Again, at least two points were overlooked. Neo-corporatist incomes policy was, rightly or wrongly, explained as a device to make unions abstain from fully exploiting an 'excessive' amount of bargaining power—excessive in the sense that it could yield nominal wage increases higher than the increase in productivity. But not much attention was paid to the possibility that, in an economic crisis and after a 'withering away' of Keynesian economic policy, union bargaining power as such might drop back to a level that would render institutional constraints and negotiated restraint dispensable. If trade unions simply lack the clout to 'distort the market', why should employers make any, even if only symbolic, concessions to them for agreeing not to do so? Again with hindsight, it seems that from the very logic of the prevailing incomes-policy concept of neo-corporatism, one should have expected that when wage restraint is imposed on the unions by an adverse economic situation, neo-corporatism, conceived of as negotiated wage restraint, should lose much of its attraction to employers.

Of course, declining functional importance of neo-corporatist institutions for capital may not be a sufficient reason to disband them—especially since they may again become useful after the economy has recovered. On the other hand, it seems that not only do the benefits of neo-corporatism for capital decline in an economic crisis, but the costs increase at the same time. Neo-corporatist centralized bargaining typically produces comprehensive and uniform regulations of a wide range of aspects of the employment relationship. The economic burden that such regulations impose on employers may be relatively easy to bear in periods of expansion; but as soon as the economy moves into crisis, it is likely to become increasingly heavy. From the perspective of the individual employer, a crisis is a situation in which his survival depends on fast and innovative reactions to changing market conditions. But centrally negotiated regulations are by defintion insensitive to the market situation of individual firms, and it is precisely this element of (relative) institutional autonomy that makes them such an important instrument for trade unions in protecting the interests of their members.

Neo-corporatism, that is to say, produces a body of (jointly agreed) central rules and regulations that, especially under critical economic conditions, is experienced by the individual firm as rigid, inflexible, and severely constraining its adaptive responses to market contingencies. Clearly, the 'rules of the game' of neo-corporatist collective bargaining do not preclude revisions of existing regulations so as to take into account changed economic conditions. In fact, pressing for such revisions is the first and natural response of employers' associations to economic setbacks; and while it is true that neo-corporatist institutions are 'sticky'—in the sense of having a logic of their own that is different from that of the market—there is a good chance that unions, weakened by the crisis and desperate to protect the principle of centralized joint regulation as such, will agree to considerable downward flexibility of wages and conditions. In this, they may even be able to carry their members by presenting their concessions as a contribution to a reduction of unemployment. Nevertheless, renegotiation of existing agreements remains difficult, burdened with high uncertainty, and time-consuming, and it may in fact be too uncertain and too slow for firms that have to undergo rapid structural change. Moreover, even a renegotiated central agreement, with relatively favourable terms for employers, continues to impose uniform standards on firms and industrial branches that are subject to different market conditions and that are forced by the crisis to respond more closely than ever to their specific, rapidly changing environments.

It is at this point that the conflicting interests and options of capital and organized labour with regard to the further operation of neo-corporatist institutions become most clearly apparent. For centralized, encompassing trade unions, disintegration of the neo-corporatist machinery of joint regulation would destroy their strategic capacity for solidaristic interest representation aimed at protecting, as much as possible, the status of individual workers from the whims and uncertainties of the market. For employers' associations, given the decline of union bargaining power in the crisis, the same development would mean the realization of an important interest of their members—the interest in flexibility, 'de-bureaucratization', higher autonomy in dealing with the uncertainties of more competitive and volatile markets, etc. Employers therefore have an alternative, and in principle a preferred alternative, to re-negotiating existing agreements—which is to let the machinery of central negotiations fall into disuse and return the regulation of the employment relationship to the market. This places them at a strategic advantage over their trade-union adversaries for which the market becomes *less* rather than more acceptable as a regulator of working conditions when the economy declines.

It is important to emphasize that this constellation of interests does not necessarily have to result in an abrupt, wholesale withdrawal of capital from neo-corporatist bargaining. The legal and procedural safeguards that typically protect corporatist institutions are not the only factor that makes a sudden withdrawal indeed unlikely. Existing institutions always create vested interests in their further existence, if only because nobody can know for certain what will replace them. Employers' associations, as distinct from their members, un- doubtedly do have an interest in central negotiations as such. Moreover, to the extent that neo-corporatist conflict management contributes to social peace and productivity at the work-place, even their members may not be willing to do without them. Anti-corporatist responses by capital to the crisis are therefore likely to be more subtle than the formal withdrawal of union recognition at the central bargaining level, *and in fact they can be so without being less effective.*

Here again, it is useful to remind oneself of the fact that neo-corporatist industrial relations systems are multi-tier structures, and that the functional relationships and the structural linkages between their various levels constitute a central dimension of their development and evolution. Employers, in struggling against the constraints of centralized regulation, may find that they can achieve their objective relatively easily by re-setting, in line with the changed balance of power, the institutional balance between the different levels of bargained interest accommodation. All that is needed for this are constant pressures, inside and outside the various bargaining arenas, for special regulations and exemptions for individual firms and industries, and for a general delegation of bargaining issues down to the level of the individual firm. Superficially, this may not look much different from the routine renegotiation of existing agreements in the light of new economic circumstances. In fact, however, it is the opposite of corporatist 'business as usual', in that it is bound to result in a gradual erosion of the practice and principle of centralized joint regulation, making negotiations at the central level increasingly meaningless for the work-place, and making the work-place increasingly autonomous *vis-à-vis* the central level.

For unions that have accommodated to a neo-corporatist mode of operation, such a development must represent a fundamental political challenge. Not only would they be deprived of the institutional preconditions for the kind of solidar- istic, unified interest politics that they have to pursue for reasons of their organizational stability. They would also, as national, 'external' unions, lose control over the main resource they have to sell in exchange for recognition as collective actors, namely, co-operation at the work-place. From the perspective of labour organized as a class, erosion of the central bargaining level in the crisis amounts to a *decapitation* of the workplace-based structures of interest accom- modation whose functioning ceases to be controlled by, and conditional upon, bargained agreements at the central level and becomes instead secured and enforced by market pressures. In this sense, the decomposition of comprehensive bargaining aggregates by exemptions and decentralization is nothing else but the very 'return to the market' that is at the core of the neo-liberal offensive against corporatist 'rigidities'. How much the crisis has changed, and even reversed, the situation in this respect is illustrated by the fact that in Germany in the prosperity of the 1960s and 1970s, it was the radical wing of the trade union movement that pressed, under the catchword of *betriebsnahe Tarifpolitik*, for exemptions in national agreements, allowing for decentralized wage bargaining at the level of individual firms. Today, exactly the same demand is being put forward with increasing force by employers, and the very factions in the unions that once opposed centralization are now its most outspoken defenders.

If by neo-corporatism we mean a system of collective industrial self-government in which significant elements of the employment relationship are negotiated, with state facilitation, between central organizations of capital and labour, then we would indeed predict that its stability is likely to be negatively affected by an economic crisis. But to understand more profoundly the course and the underlying dynamics of corporatist institutional decay, one has to get away from preconceived notions of class interests and take into account the impact of the crisis on employing firms. If 'crisis' means a growing need for firms to pay attention to more rapidly fluctuating and increasingly specific market signals—driving up dramatically the opportunity costs of conformity to established practices and general, bureaucratic rules—then the pressure on neo-corporatist institutions will originate first and foremost not from trade unions dissatisfied with the declining material benefits of centralized bargaining, but from capital trying to restore flexibility to the individual enterprise through, among other things, deregulation of the labour market (cf. Schmitter, 1982: 277). This is not only because capital—or whoever has to make up for a firm's losses—is more sensitive to declining profits and more negatively affected by costly institutional rigidities than labour. It is also because where the market rules, capital—or management—rules, and in this sense economic weakness constitutes a source of political strength for capital in its power game with labour.

In a nutshell, then, the stability of neo-corporatist industrial relations in an economic crisis depends essentially on the capacity of trade unions to defeat business offensives for a 'return to the market', and the question becomes how strong this defence can be. Given the loss of bargaining power trade unions suffer as a result of declining demand for labour, the chances of survival of neo-corporatist structures seem, to an important extent, determined by the support unions as institutions receive from the state and the legal system. But even where such support is forthcoming, the outcome is far from certain. Trade unions trying to preserve corporatist institutions against the disintegrating impact of a crisis are faced not just with opposition from employers but also with internal opposition from their rank and file. Here, the 'labour discontent' theory of corporatist decay is indeed valid. Where it goes wrong is that it assumes that the pressures inside unions that undermine the corporatist defences will come from radicalized militants. While member revolts of this kind are always possible, they can safely be expected to remain isolated incidents in comparison with a development that represents, in many ways, their exact opposite: *the integration of workers at the level of individual enterprises in co-operative alliances with their employers.* This, too, is a response to the market, and it reflects the fact that the relative insensitivity of corporatist-industrial unions to the market is much more a product of sophisticated institution building than an expression of a fundamental dissociation of the interests of labour from the functioning of the (capitalist) economy. What the crisis does to organized labour is, in essence, to make the organizational transformation of specific economic, into general class interests much more difficult (Carrieri & Donolo, 1983). Under crisis conditions, the rule of the market asserts itself not just over the behaviour of firms but also over workers' definitions of their interests—with their interests in the economic survival of 'their' employer becoming so intense that they escape union control. Thus, even less space is left for other, more general and less market-determined interests. The emerging 'wildcat co-operation' of individual work-forces in workplace-based productivity alliances (cf. Goldthorpe, this volume, on micro-corporatism) parallels and reinforces, *inside the organization of labour itself,* the pressures from employers for a relaxation of corporatist controls over the work-place. Paradoxically, as will be shown below for the German case, such fragmentation and differentiation of class interests among workers may be facilitated by the very institutions of interest accommodation at the work-place which, in better times, provided an essential substructure of centralized joint regulation.

In sum, the prospects for neo-corporatist industrial relations to weather an economic crisis are uncertain. While economic decline does pose serious challenges to centralized class bargaining and interest accommodation, a sudden breakdown of established practices and procedures appears unlikely, given the considerable inertia of developed and long-standing institutional structures. The decay of neo-corporatism, if decay there will be, is likely to be slow and creeping, proceeding step by step over several years from one gradual change to another, until the institutional *Gestalt* may switch, and neo-corporatism may finally give way to some other mode of interest politics. Whether or not this will happen, and how far the involution of corporatist institutions will go, seems to be determined by the strength of three countervailing forces:

(i) the legal backing by the state of existing neo-corporatist structures;
(ii) the resistance of central trade unions to a 'downward' transfer of bargaining issues to the work-place; and,
(iii) the cohesion of industrial unions as collective actors in the face of the centrifugal pull of the market on their members.

In all three respects, it is the unions whose behaviour, strategy and capacity to act are decisive. Trade unions trying to defend neo-corporatist institutions have to fight a war on two fronts: against employers pressing for decentralization, and against members who are no longer willing to believe that centralized class politics can help them keep their jobs. It is only if national and sectoral unions can mobilize, from the state and with state assistance, sufficient resources to prevail on both sides, that neo-corporatist industrial relations may have a future.

The following two parts of this paper will illustrate in greater detail the external and internal pressures on trade unions trying to protect neo-corporatist institutions from the destabilizing impact of the crisis. For empirical reference, the discussion will draw on West Germany, mainly because this is the country which the author knows best. Another, less idiosyncratic reason is that, as a consequence of the legal institutionalization of work-place participation and co-operation in Germany—in the form of 'co-determination' (Adams & Rummel, 1977; Streeck, 1984)—changes in the relationship between the different levels of interest accommodation are easier to observe and to analyse in this country than in others. Given the specificities of the German case—for example, the fact that West Germany has long been, and in some respects continues to be, a 'dominant economy'—one cannot expect that the German experience will be exactly replicated elsewhere. But it should be possible from this account to identify in general terms some of the problems for which trade unions in similar conditions have to find solutions, and to compare different solutions from the perspective of their functions for the stability of centralized collective interest accommodation.

Restoring Flexibility to a Bargained Economy: the Case of ARBED Saarstahl

Since the beginning of the crisis in the late 1970s, there have been increasingly vocal complaints from both business and government in West Germany over the rigidities imposed on the economy by the central and uniform regulation of working conditions. Among the first to voice this new theme was the Council of Economic Advisors, which repeatedly expressed doubts over the wisdom of nego-tiating essentially identical agreements for weak and strong industrial sectors or firms. Similar doubts were expressed by representatives of business, especially from the ranks of small and medium-sized firms who proposed exemptions from central agreements for the *Mittelstand*, and they were echoed even by a small number of union leaders from sectors like textiles which have been especially severely affected by the crisis. In 1982, the new government succeeded in breaking up, for the first time since the early 1960s, the industry-wide bargaining unit of the civil service. Rather than, as had become established practice, auto-matically extending the wage settlement for employees in the public sector to civil servants (*Beamten*) who have no right to collective bargaining, the govern-ment increased the salaries of civil servants at a rate below that of the industrial agreement.

Otherwise, however, apart from the fact that all new trade-union projects for industry-level joint regulation have come to a standstill—for example, in the crucial area of 'protection against rationalization'—the large bargaining compacts that are characteristic of the West German industrial relations system are still basically intact. Undoubtedly, this is due to the strong support offered by the existing institutional and legal system to comprehensive, nation-wide bargaining. On the other hand, there is at least one recent example showing that, while the decomposition of 'bloc' bargaining is exceedingly difficult, it is not impossible even in the German context. The example, which is the case of ARBED Saarstahl, is instructive not least because it shows the extraordinary lengths to which the opponents of corporatist rigidities may have to go in a neo-corporatist environment in order to achieve their objectives.

The endemic crisis of the West German steel industry is a subject of wide-spread attention, and it is not necessary here to present the details. (For a recent account, see Esser *et al.*, 1983.) There has long been agreement between government, industry and union (the IG Metall) that a substantial reduction of capacity is inevitable, and that the survival of the industry will not be possible without a considerable infusion of public subsidies. No agreement exists, how-ever, on the future structure of the industry. Although the situation continued to deteriorate throughout 1983, no co-ordinated restructuring effort was under-taken owing to lack of consensus between, and within, the three parties.

The firm that is most severely affected by the crisis is ARBED Saarstahl. Formed in 1978 as a result of a government-sponsored merger (Esser *et al.*, 1983: 91), ARBED is the only remaining major steel producer in the old industrial centre of the Saarland. Although the firm was never economically viable, both the Federal and the Saarland government felt they had no choice but to keep it alive through public subsidies. Unemployment in the Saarland has always been above the national average, and past efforts to create alternative employment opportunities for redundant steel workers have failed. By 1982, ARBED had received no less than DM 2.2 billion in subsidies (Esser *et al.*, 1983: 94) without any substantial improvement in its condition.

Part of the public money was used to finance significant redundancy pay-ments. Under a 'social plan' (*Sozialplan*) negotiated, corporatist-style, between the union, the company and the government in 1978 (Esser *et al.*, 1983: 90), employment reductions at ARBED are to be accomplished basically through natural wastage and early retirement. Workers above age 55 who accept an offer of early retirement are guaranteed 90 per cent of their last take-home pay, with the employer making up the difference between this figure and unemployment insurance benefits which amount to 68 per cent. In addition, future wage increases received by the remaining work-force are to be extended to the early-retired workers. This agreement has contributed considerably to preventing social unrest and preserving social peace, and it was one of the cornerstones of the trilateral pact between capital, labour and the state that emerged, in response to the crisis of the steel industry, in the 1970s (Esser *et al.*, 1983).

A first major conflict over the terms of crisis management arose in 1982, shortly after the new Federal Government had taken office. When ARBED came in for another subsidy of DM 310 million, the Ministry of Economics asked, as a precondition for further public support, for a *Belegschaftsopfer*–a 'sacrifice' by the work-force contributing to the rescue of the firm (Esser *et al.*, 1983:

94 ff.). In particular, the work-force was to accept a reduction of its Christmas bonus—equivalent to one month's pay—by half. This would have saved the firm about DM 60 million. However, the size of the bonus is fixed by the regional industrial agreement, and the IG Metall argued that since the agreement was legally binding, the bonus could not be cut even with the assent of the work-force and its elected representative, the Works Council. It soon turned out, however, that this position was not tenable. Under pressure from its members at ARBED who were afraid of the firm going bankrupt, the union—in order to protect at least the principle of wage regulation through industrial agreement—proposed a renegotiation of the agreement to the effect that one half of the 1983 and 1984 Christmas bonuses were to be given, as an interest-free loan, to the firm. The money was to be paid back in 1985 and 1986. After an agreement to this effect was signed, the government agreed to provide the requested support.

A similar sequence of events occurred in the following year. In October 1983, the ARBED management proposed to the Federal Government a restructuring plan envisaging a reduction in the work-force from 17,200 to 12,100 by the end of 1986. The plan also asked for further subsidies amounting to a total of DM 658 million for the years from 1983 to 1985. In the ensuing negotiations, the government refused to commit itself to financial support beyond 1983 and 1984. It insisted that the proposed work-force reduction plan was fully implemented, and future subsidies were made conditional on this. It also made a number of additional demands which the management, given that the firm was only a few days short of bankruptcy, had no choice but to accept. Among other things, the members of the management board had to agree to a cut in their salaries of one quarter (they themselves had offered 17 per cent). More importantly, the government asked for another *Belegschaftsopfer*, including significant cuts in payments to redundant workers under the social plan and a commitment to a wage freeze (*Nullrunde*) in 1984. To put pressure on both management and the work-force, the government stated publicly that unless such an agreement was reached, no money would be forthcoming even if the firm had to go to the receiver.

Under the management restructuring plan, the 1984–7 employment cut was to be again effected by the early retirement of workers of age 55 and older. But since not many workers of this age group were left, early retirement was to be offered also to 'disabled' workers between 50 and 55. However, as one condition of further subsidies, the Federal Government demanded that the guaranteed income of retired workers be lowered to 82 per cent of final pay, and this was to apply not just to workers affected by the impending employment reduction but also to those (former) workers who were already receiving payments under the social plan.

Both Works Council and IG Metall refused to accept. However, their position weakened as the breakdown of the firm came closer. The decisive cabinet meeting was scheduled for 7 November; if the government declined on this occasion to pay out the first instalment of DM 84 million, the firm would have had to declare bankruptcy the following day. In the week before the cabinet meeting, the Works Council polled the workforce on the 82 per cent offer; the result was not made public. However, a few days later the IG Metall agreed to let the matter go to a conciliation committee. Literally at the last minute, the committee, with the vote of its neutral chairwoman (the President of the Saarland labour administration) and against the votes of the Works Council and the union, ruled in favour of the 82 per cent offer made by the management. A few hours later, the Federal Government agreed to pay the subsidy for 1983.

It soon turned out, however, that this was far from being the end of the matter. Formally, the conciliation committee decision applied only to the social plan for the disabled workers between 50 and 55 who were to lose their jobs in the years up to 1986. Since the existing social plan for workers between 55 and 60 was legally binding until December 1985—and thus could have been changed only by the mutual consent of the Works Council and management—this was all the committee could do. It is an open question if the Works Council was willing, in later negotiations, to bring the terms of the existing social plan into line with the new one and with the demands of the Federal Government. But whatever potential for agreement may have existed seems to have been destroyed by a parallel development on the second issue, the *Nullrunde*. This will be discussed shortly. By mid-November, unable to reopen negotiations on the old social plan and responding to continuing government pressures, the management unilaterally suspended the existing regulations and reduced payments to early-retired workers above 55 to 82 per cent. The union and the Works Council in turn announced that they would take legal action.

The second string the government had attached to its financial support was a wage freeze for ARBED workers in 1984. Wages at ARBED are settled by an industrial agreement which is negotiated between the IG Metall and the Employers Association of the Iron and Steel Industry (Arbeitgeberverband Eisen und Stahlindustrie) of which ARBED is a member. Although the steel industry is in a poor economic condition, the industrial agreement for 1984 is likely to provide for a small wage increase, probably at or slightly below the level of inflation. By the time the conciliation committee made its award, it became known that the government, in order to ensure that there would indeed be a *Nullrunde* at ARBED in 1984, had made it a condition of further subsidies that ARBED resign from membership in the employers' association, so as to be able to negotiate a wage freeze directly with the IG Metall. Four days after the cabinet meeting, ARBED informed the *Arbeitgeberverband* of its intended resignation.

It is difficult at this stage to assess the implications of this event. For a start, it is not clear whether ARBED's forced resignation will not—in just the same way, perhaps, as the cutting of the social plan—fall victim to the stickiness of the legal 'rules of the game': formally, under the constitution of the employers association, the resignation does not become effective until the end of 1984. Moreover, while the association may be able to release ARBED earlier, it may not be willing to do so. In an interview with the *Handelsblatt* on 14 November, the director of the association criticized the pressure by the government on ARBED as a 'severe interference with the solidarity of the German steel industry' which was likely to make collective bargaining more difficult: 'Breaking a weak firm away from a bargaining unit is bound to lead to a higher settlement since the union will then demand more from the actually or reputedly stronger members'. The convoy, he argued, now had to travel without its slowest ship. If the other members acted according to the same logic, firms could be torpedoed by the union one by one'.

Other comments centred on the reasons why the government had demanded ARBED's resignation, and on the consequences of this for ARBED itself. In principle, since the Saarland has a formally separate industrial agreement covering only ARBED and two other, smaller firms, a wage freeze for ARBED could have been negotiated by the employers association as well as by ARBED itself. Although in the past two decades the Saar agreement has increasingly turned into a mere replication of the Ruhrgebiet agreement, it could conceivably have been revitalized. However, the problem seems to have been that the other steel producers were unwilling to pay strike support—as they would have had to under the rules of the association—to a competitor trying to win a zero settlement while they themselves would have to accept a settlement above zero. On the other hand, as a non-member ARBED will not get strike support either. The difference may be that where there is no question of outside support, the bargaining position of the union, faced with a firm on the verge of bankruptcy, may not improve but in fact deteriorate—assuming, of course, that the union and its ARBED membership want to avoid destroying the firm.

In any case, the strongest protests against the government's attack on 'the solidarity of the German steel industry' came from the IG Metall, and had there still been a need to demonstrate the interest of industrial trade unions in strong employers' associations, this would be a perfect example. According to the vice-chairman of IG Metall (*Handelsblatt*, 21 November), the government's pressure on ARBED to resign from the association was 'a blatant infringement of the constitutional freedom of association', aimed at abolishing the principle of free collective bargaining: 'The Federal Government imposes, through conditions attached to subsidies, a wage *Diktat*. This is a clear violation of the constitutional rights of association and collective bargaining.' For the union, the ARBED case represents an attempt by the government to create a precedent for further interventions of this kind. This applied already to the imposed renegotiation of the social plan. According to a union spokesman, the renegotiation would save the company no more than DM 4 million a year, and what the government was really asking for was 'a gesture of deference' by the union. This suspicion was felt to be confirmed when the resignation from the employers' association was announced, together with the wage freeze, in 1984. It was at this point that the renegotiation of the social plan finally failed. The newly elected chairman of IG Metall voiced his opposition to the government taking future zero settlements for granted in restructuring projects. His deputy saw a strategy of the government to create 'many little ARBEDs' and stated that the union would not allow this. By mid-November, IG Metall began to mobilize its membership; among other things by distributing two million copies of a special ARBED edition of its journal.

It is not inconceivable that the present government indeed uses ARBED as an exercise ground for new strategies to undo, in response to and with the help of the crisis, the rigidities created by and inherent in a neo-corporatist system of industrial relations. That the approach chosen in 1983 did not attack the union directly, but rather took a detour through the employers' association, is indicative not just of the considerable institutional strength of German trade unions (a strength that had proved itself in 1982 when the IG Metall was able to turn the intended cut of the Christmas bonus into a repayable loan). It is also in line with the observation that the weaker pillar of neo-corporatism—weaker both in its organizational cohesion and in its commitment—is not labour but capital. It is true that in the ARBED case, the *spiritus rector* of the company's resignation from the employers' association was the government. But this was due to the fact that in the German steel industry, it has long been the government rather than private investors that pays the bills. Moreover, ARBED as a company is subject to the coal-and-steel type of codetermination, which undoubtedly limits the capacity of its management to engage, without strong outside encouragement and backing, in confrontation with the union. In other sectors, where private capital has a greater stake and where management is still more autonomous and aggressive, anti-corporatist movements could as well emerge from business directly. Even so, however, government support will be vital for what neo-liberals would undoubtedly call the restoration of flexibility to a bargained economy, just as it was vital to the growth of centralized joint regulation in the 1960s and 1970s.

The Decomposition of Class Interests: Consequences of Unemployment for Trade Union Organization

The impact of an economic crisis on trade unions is usually seen primarily in terms of a loss of bargaining power and, perhaps, of membership and financial resources. Both are direct and indirect consequences of high unemployment, and their importance lies in the fact that they weaken unions in their relations with employers and government. But crisis and unemployment have other consequences as well that affect the internal politics of trade unions, and these may in the long run be even more subversive of neo-corporatist institutions than the deterioration of unions' market power.

Unemployment changes fundamentally the structure and the functioning of the labour market. High unemployment is accompanied, and produced, not just by redundancies and dismissals but also by a sharp decline in labour recruitment. In fact, the latter may be much more significant than the former, especially in countries or industries where employment cut-backs are accomplished primarily through early retirement and natural wastage. Workers in a crisis economy know that there is a higher chance than normal for them to lose their jobs by dismissal or as a result of their employer going bankrupt; but they also know that they have no chance at all to find a new job once they have lost, or given up, their present one. It is difficult to say which of the two aspects of high unemployment has greater impact on workers' consciousness; however, given that unemployment will always be limited to some, *relatively* small, proportion of the work-force while the disappearance of employment alternatives affects nearly everybody, there is good reason to believe that it is the latter. This is borne out by, among other things, the fact that one of the most obvious effects of increasing unemployment is a decline in voluntary job-leaving and in the mobility of workers between different employers.

If it is true that a lasting crisis ties workers to their present place of employment, then this should have a profound impact on both their definition of interest and, accordingly, the policy options open to their trade unions. It has often been observed that unemployment tends to be accompanied by declining absenteeism, increased preparedness to work overtime or at higher speeds, fewer disciplinary problems, higher acceptance of managerial authority, etc. Normally, this has been interpreted as a consequence of the deteriorating power position, in relation to their employer, of individual workers faced with the disappearance of alternative employment opportunities, and there is no doubt that this indeed plays an important part. But, in some cases at least, there is also another factor present which is an increased interest of workers, in an environment dominated by firm breakdowns and the absence of job openings, in the economic competitiveness and the survival of the firm with which they are (still) employed. This interest, newly discovered in the crisis and reinforced by the dismal state of the external labour market, can lead to, and in fact demand, a hitherto unknown degree of co-operation with the employer, especially if the firm is in a critical condition in which its further existence may be at stake.

Why should such a development affect the internal stability of the comprehensive and centralized trade unions that form an integral part of neo-corporatist industrial relations systems? The reason is essentially that a solidaristic, class-based union policy presupposes a labour market with high external mobility and, as a consequence, low identification of workers with the economic fate of their present employer. Trade unions undertaking to negotiate general standards of wages and working conditions that apply to an entire industry or economy cannot exhaust the 'ability to pay' of the more prosperous enterprises, and this is why they have to fend off, in times of economic expansion, internal criticism by their more economically favoured members for being too moderate. But neither can they limit their demands to what marginal firms can offer without having to go out of operation. In fact, both the West German and the Swedish trade union movement have, in the post-war era, entertained a doctrine of wages policy under which the bankruptcy of marginal firms was seen not just as an inevitable but as an entirely desirable result of centralized collective bargaining. This was possible only under the assumption that there was a functioning external labour market that could absorb into more productive employment those workers who lost their jobs as a result of such a 'solidaristic' wages policy. The role of Swedish active labour-market policy—which was invented by the unions and instituted at their demand—was to ensure that the external labour market could indeed perform this function; to present it, as some authors do, as a political compensation for wage moderation (cf. Lehmbruch, 1979b: 306), would not go down well with the employers who were driven out of business with its assistance. On the part of the unions, such a strategy thus requires that workers in weak firms or regions do not side with their employers in order to defend their jobs, but are willing to support the demands of their union—that is, of their *class*—even if, as a consequence, they have to seek alternative employment.

Another case in which the members of industrial unions are asked to divorce their interests from those of their employer is that of strikes. For an industry-wide strike to be effective, a worker who is called upon to walk out must do so, even if he happens to have no particular grievance against his employer. He must also walk out regardless of whether this is likely to do lasting damage to his employer's competitive position or even to endanger his economic survival. That this is by no means a merely hypothetical problem is indicated by the intense inside bargaining, behind closed doors, between German national unions and (unionized) work-force representatives at individual work-places on the maximum permissible level of 'maintenance work' (*Notdienst*) during a strike. The same problem is present in the designation of targets for selective strikes, which are, for financial reasons, the most suitable strike tactic for industrial unions. Again, one would expect that the willingness of workers to inflict damage on their employer in the support of class-wide, solidaristic interests is inversely related to the degree to which their own economic fate has become, as a result of a decline of the external labour market, inseparable from that of their employer.

Identification of workers with the economic interests of their employer can take various forms. One example is 'employee bailouts', where workers in firms on the brink of bankruptcy accept substantial wage cuts, work unpaid overtime, or extend interest-free credit to their employer. In a country like the United States, this tends to be accompanied by formal collective resignation from union membership, or by a withdrawal of the bargaining mandate from the union. Developments of this kind, while they cannot be entirely precluded, are unlikely in more corporatist systems where collective agreements are more difficult to undercut and where the status of trade unions is better protected—a fact that is increasingly recognized by former critics of *Verrechtlichung* (cf. Erd, 1978). Under these conditions, enterprise-centred interests of workers tend to articulate themselves less conspicuously and without dramatic institutional discontinuities. In the West German case, they crystallize around the existing institutions of the Works Constitution which, as has been indicated, assumes new representational functions in the course of the creeping erosion of the industry-wide bargaining system. The reason why these functional changes are both difficult to observe and almost irresistible is that they represent basically an acceleration of trends that have been present for some time and that in fact started long before the crisis (Streeck 1981a). Nevertheless, the changes that are under way are fundamental in that they involve a gradual transformation of institutions which once formed an indispensable substructure of centralized joint regulation into the nuclei of an *emergent enterprise unionism*—not necessarily in a formal and official sense but, more likely, *de facto* under the cover of the existing but functionally pre-empted institutional structure.

Workers in Germany are represented at the work-place by Works Councils which are formally not trade union bodies but elements of the legally based Works Constitution. Works Councils are elected every three years by all workers regardless of union membership, and while unions can nominate candidates, they may have to compete with candidates from non-union groups. Nevertheless, the industrial unions affiliated to the Deutscher Gewerksschaftsbund (DGB) regularly win about 80 per cent of all Works Council seats. Works Council members are entitled to be released from work for the performance of their functions, and the employer has to provide them with office space and other material resources. They also have wide-ranging legal rights to 'codetermination', especially in the area of manpower use and manpower policy. But Works Councils have no right to take industrial action, and they are under a legal obligation to co-operate with the employer in the best interests of the firm.

The positive functions of the Works Constitution for industrial unionism have been analysed in detail elsewhere (Streeck, 1979). Since Works Councils, having a *de facto* monopoly on interest representation at the work-place, are elected at large, they prevent the articulation of sectional interests of fractions of the work-force—e.g. of specific craft occupations. They thus relieve the industrial union of problems of interest aggregation that otherwise might be insoluble. Furthermore, Works Councils are legally charged with supervising the implementation of industrial agreements. The prohibition on Works Councils calling strikes protects the 'strike monopoly' and, with it, the bargaining monopoly of industrial unions. Without such protection, the difficulties of external unions in keeping workers in firms with an above-average 'ability to pay' from negotiating their own agreements would seem unsurmountable. It is notable that the role of the Works Constitution, as an organizational substructure of industrial unionism, was considerably strengthened by the Works Constitution Act of 1972 which was passed at the demand of the unions.

Nevertheless, while the Works Constitution has helped unions solve a wide range of organizational problems, it also created new ones. Independent action of privileged or radicalized sections of the membership (which is referred to as 'syndicalism' in German trade union language) is effectively controlled by the Works Council system. But in addition to the conflictual type of 'syndicalism', there always was another, co-operative one—*Betriebsegoismus*; and this the Works Constitution not only fails to control but indeed encourages (Kotthoff, 1979; Miller, 1982; Tegtmeier, 1973; Teschner, 1977). The problem is not so much that Works Councils may fail to use their full legal powers; in such cases, trade unions have ways and means to intervene. More important is the case in which they do use their powers, but for objectives that differ from union policy. For example, the Works Council of a large firm may negotiate a supplementary pension plan or a co-ownership scheme—both viewed with suspicion by the union—and concede to management in exchange the introduction of a new kind of job classification or of a manpower information system that the union is trying to prevent through action at the sectoral level. The common political denominator of such bilateral agreements at enterprise level is the shared interest of management and Works Council in the economic success of 'their' enterprise— as distinguished from competing firms and the industry as a whole. In fact, given that Works Councils organize workers on the basis of their being employed with one specific employer, the identification of the collective interest they represent with the (long-term) interest of the firm seems so natural that the legal obligation to 'peaceful co-operation' appears almost unnecessary.

It was suggested as early as in the late 1970s that the Works Council system, having been so considerably strengthened in 1972 and further by the Co-determination Act of 1976, may at some stage turn into a liability, rather than an asset, for the stability of industrial unionism (Streeck, 1982: 76). But what a few years ago was visible only to a few close observers, is now becoming increasingly obvious. If one had to design an ideal institutional structure in which to accommodate the emergent, workplace-specific interests of workers in a crisis economy, this could not conceivably look much different from the present Works Constitution. With the diminishing control of central collective bargaining over the exercise of codetermination at the work-place, the last remaining criterion of decision-making and interest accommodation inside the institutions of the Works Constitution becomes the well-being of the firm. Not that labour has lost its voice; if it had, the specific kind of co-operation that is so characteristic of large German firms—and that is based on the confidence of workers that they can indeed get a share of the proceeds—would not be possible. But the voice of labour is now more than ever that of those employed, and wanting to remain employed, in a specific place of work; and it is their interest, highly particularistic from a class perspective and no longer contaminated by organizationally enforced 'solidarity', that puts to its own use the institutional instruments of work-place participation which were created in the past for other, more general purposes.

At the heart of the new *Betriebsegoismus* of Works Councils, as one would expect given the state of the external labour market, lies employment protection. But this is very widely defined, comprising both the full utilization of existing legal safeguards *and* co-operation with management in maintaining and improving the firm's competitive position. The institutional structure of the

Works Constitution permits both at the same time; while management trying to improve productivity depends, under codetermination, on the co-operation of the Works Council, the Works Council is well enough protected from sectional pressures from the labour force—and from trade-union pressure as well—to be able to co-operate and deliver its constituents. The political formula on which this kind of interest accommodation is based is closure of the internal labour market in exchange for the highest possible measure of internal flexibility, with the Works Council accepting responsibility for continuous adaptation of an essentially fixed work-force to changing technical and economic needs (Hohn, 1983). In some instances, this may involve employment cuts. But the considerable powers of Works Councils, and the strong hold they have on large firms' personnel departments under board-level codetermination (Streeck, 1984), has led to the development of manpower planning systems that often allow work-force reductions to be stretched over a relatively long period of time, so that they can be accomplished by natural wastage and early retirement.

Otherwise and in the normal case, Works Councils become the border guards and, indeed, the rulers of the internal labour market, ensuring that nobody is allowed in who might in the future threaten the employment status of those already employed. The latter may happen in two ways (Hohn, 1983; Hohn and Windolf, 1983). New recruitment may lead to an oversized work-force which may later have to be again reduced, and the larger the number of workers to be made redundant, the more difficult it is to avoid forced dismissals. Consequently, overtime is much preferred by Works Councils to new recruitment as a way of coping with additional work-loads, and work-forces thus remain small and lean. Also, the recruitment of workers who are unable or unwilling to undergo future retraining and redeployment may make it more difficult for the Works Council to provide for internal flexibility in exchange for employment security; moreover, it may negatively affect the firm's economic performance. In these areas as well as in others—for example, in the selection of workers for retraining or in the invention of payment schemes allowing for frictionless redeployment— Works Councils under codetermination have taken over essential functions of manpower management. Partly, this transfer of responsibility was a matter of legal entitlement; but it was often also a result of voluntary delegation by management itself, leaving the problem of making stable employment compatible with economic performance to those who are most strongly interested in the former while knowing that, for this very reason, they have also to be interested in the latter.

As (co-)managers of internal labour markets (Streeck, 1984), Works Councils may find central industrial agreements as 'rigid' and 'impractable' as management. But being legally charged with supervising their enforcement, they can more easily circumvent them. Since their leading members normally wield considerable power inside the union, they also can influence sectoral and national trade-union policy so that it does not get in their way. The impasse of central collective bargaining in the crisis is bound to increase their autonomy

and discretion even further. In fact, there is very little today that can prevent
Works Councils from giving precedence to internal labour market flexibility
over trade-union policy. Particularly interesting examples are found in the area
of working time. In spite of the vigorous opposition of industrial unions to part-
time work, job sharing and flexible working time according to production
requirements, Works Councils in several large firms have recently concluded
agreements with management on exactly these matters.

There is no demand on the part of business—a small number of radical outsiders excepted—for a repeal of the Works Constitution Act; and the new government has formally stated that it has no intention of repealing it. In part, this is
because any attempt to abolish the Works Constitution may end up in industrial
civil war. But it is also true that the Works Constitution, left on its own, is the
one element of neo-corporatism that business can accept. The delegation of
managerial responsibilities to a co-operative Works Council has proved an
effective instrument of preserving social peace at the point of production in a
period of intensive industrial restructuring. Moreover, the internal labour market
option favoured by Works Councils, provided that it is made viable through
bargained, binding interest accommodation, seems to be well adapted to the
new technologies and new forms of work organization necessary for survival in
tighter and more volatile markets. Here, the Japanese example looms large
in the background. If employment stability and codetermination help create a
work-force that is highly qualified, willing to undergo continuous re-training,
motivated to do quality work, prepared to accept flexible work schedules, able
to switch between different jobs with broad and frequently changing tasks,
ready to suggest improvements that increase productivity, and capable of
operating a work organization based on semi-autonomous groups—then they are
worth their price, and managerial unilateralism, combined with a reassertion of
the right to hire and fire, may well be the inferior strategy. Here again, as in the
neo-corporatism of the 1970s, but this time at the level of individual firms, a
'virtuous circle' may emerge within which an institutional system whose stability
depends on economic success sustains itself precisely by making this success
possible.

For the unions, of course, the gradual 'Japanization', if the term is permitted,
of German industrial relations in the crisis is nothing less than the most serious
organizational challenge they have ever faced. The longer the crisis lasts, the
more difficult it is to imagine that the emerging pattern of *social partnership
without corporatism* (cf. Miller, 1982: 45) inside the large, world-market
oriented enterprises can again be undone in the name of class solidarity. The
danger for national trade-union headquarters that they may degenerate into
service organizations (*ausgelagerte Stäbe*) for the powerful Works Councils of
large enterprises—providing them at their request with legal and economic advice
instead of directing their policies—has been pointed out by this author in the
past (Streeck, 1981b; 1982). Today, it is clear that this development has
progressed much faster than was expected. The preparations presently made by

IG Metall for a nation-wide strike in 1984 in support of a reduction of the standard working week to thirty-five hours and a limitation of overtime can in this perspective be interpreted as a monumental effort to reclaim, for the central bargaining level, the initiative on a wide range of issues, in particular manpower policy and manpower planning, that are presently dealt with exclusively at the enterprise level under co-determination. Heroic as this strategy is, it is more likely to fail than to succeed. Even if the union were to win significant concessions from the employers—which is extremely unlikely—it is highly questionable whether such concessions will actually be implemented at the work-place. In at least one large enterprise—which is among the largest in the Federal Republic—the Works Council is already today looking for ways to prevent a general reduction of working time from negatively affecting the competitiveness of, and thus the level of employment at, the company. One solution that is being considered is to eliminate breaks that had in the past been introduced by voluntary agreement between Works Council and management, so as to minimize the reduction of effective working time. Another is the introduction of flexible time schedules responding to changing work-loads ('guaranteed yearly working time'). A third is the continued operation of industrial robots during breaks; and there are more such proposals. There is reason to believe that the autonomy, the sophistication and the sense of separate identity of bargaining systems at the work-place have by now far exceeded the control capacity of the traditional industrial agreement.

New Lines of Cleavage

Where will all this lead? As we leave behind the 1960s and 1970s, the defenders of the grand simplicity and the elegant unity of the neo-corporatist institutional design are becoming smaller in number, and their resistance is weakening. Certainly the present, and most likely the future as well, is dominated by a growing divergence of interests that once were contained inside the big neo-corporatist aggregates. As a result, the problems facing their private governments in what we have called, elsewhere, the 'management of interest diversity' (Schmitter & Streeck, 1981), are becoming ever more difficult to resolve. It is not just business that feels tempted today to abandon the historical project of regulating a complex labour market by centralized, negotiated accommodation of interests—although business clearly has the strongest motivation to do so. Governments, especially those of a conservative political complexion, may also become impatient with the costs and the slow pace of bargained industrial restructuring. Only the unions seem to stand firm, but as we have seen, the pull of the market separating special interests from each other does not stop at their doorsteps, and national unions may increasingly find themselves fighting for a cause that their members have long begun to desert.

Inside and outside existing neo-corporatist institutions and often behind their cover, new lines of cleavage are emerging which do not look as if they will soon disappear (cf. Goldthorpe, this volume). Five such cleavages are making themselves felt with growing strength:

(i) The division between workers in weak and strong sectors. As long as there was enough slack in the economy, the negative impact on weaker industries of the central, encompassing regulation of the labour market was comparatively easy to accept. Not only were there alternative employment opportunities for workers from declining sectors. There was also the possibility of using a share of the proceeds of a growing economy to finance an orderly retreat from declining industries, buying the necessary time for socially acceptable structural adaptation. All this has changed now. The external labour market is closed; state budgets are overspent; even the strong sectors need all they can get for their own survival; and the slow and soft 'management of decline' of yesteryear has given way to the brute reality of employment cuts and bankruptcies at short notice. For workers in the weak sectors of the economy—not to mention their employers—a solidaristic trade-union policy that tries to override market forces may, in these circumstances appear rather frightening, and trade unions sticking to the time-honoured principles of class solidarity may ever more often be asked by their members in crisis-ridden sectors to be left to their own devices.

(ii) The division between workers in weak and strong firms. Solidarity demands that workers in weak firms do not permit negative precedents to be created for other workers by their employers' undercutting national agreements. But this presupposes that, in return, there can be a meaningful transfer of bargaining power from the strong to the weak. To the extent that the central bargaining level loses its significance, and adherence to the national agreement may for workers in weak firms result in lasting unemployment, this condition is no longer given, and structural differences of interest arise that are more difficult than ever to bridge by normative concepts like 'solidarity'.

(iii) The division between workers in large and small firms. Firm size has always made a difference with regard to the effectiveness of the representation of workers at the work-place. This holds in particular in the German context where the influence of Works Councils depends on nothing more than the size of the firm. To a large part, solidaristic trade-union policy in West Germany was aimed at spreading, through the instrument of the collective agreement, some of the concessions won by workers in large firms through their Works Councils to the work-force as a whole. The more the neo-corporatist institutions at the industrial and national level fall into disuse, the more this mechanism of redistribution is weakened. As the institutional structures of interest accommodation at the work-place become 'decapitated', the division intensifies between workers in large firms who continue to have a voice

in the management of their affairs, and workers in small firms which
fail to sustain effective structures of work-place representation.

(iv) The division between workers in competing production units. Labour
can organize and act as a class only if, in the perception of workers, the
political cleavage between them and capital supersedes the market
cleavage between their present firm and its competitors. Mobilizing
and sustaining collective identifications based on class rather than
firm was never easy for trade unions, but the changing structure of the
labour market in the crisis has compounded the problem. Solidaristic
trade-union strategy demands that workers stay neutral in the struggles
that their employers fight with each other in the market-place. However, if the number of jobs in an industry is declining, and the only
alternative to one's present job is unemployment, there is a considerable incentive for workers and their work-place representatives to help
their employer prevail and thereby shift the burden of unemployment
to their fellow workers who happen to work for the competition. A
related case, which has become rather frequent in West Germany, is
firms with overcapacity cancelling contracts with suppliers and
changing to in-house production, as a way of protecting their employment. Often, this is in response to demands by the Works Council—
which are made regardless of the fact that they are in contradiction to
official trade-union policy.

(v) The division between the 'ins' and the 'outs'. It has often been argued
that the segmentation of labour markets is to a significant degree
produced by trade-union intervention. But while this was always highly
plausible where unions are workplace- or craft-based, industrial unions
aspire to represent all workers equally, including those who are not
organized. As has been said, this is one reason why they find it so
difficult to resist the 'neo-corporatist temptation'. However, with the
centre of gravity of industrial relations shifting to the work-place, it is
no longer the industrial union but increasingly the Works Councils that
represent labour in the joint regulation of the conditions of employment, and this, indeed, does result in segmentation (Hohn, 1983).
But the pattern of segmentation in an emergent, 'post-corporatist'
system, being conditioned by the institutional structure from whose
decay it originates, differs from that in systems that never were
corporatist. For example, the German employment system is relatively
inflexible with regard to the introduction of unequal wages and conditions for new entrants into a given work-force; this is different
from the situation in the United States where agreements between
(work-place) union and management are becoming more widespread
under which new workers are paid only part of the wage of already-
employed workers. Also, segmentation in Germany is not caused by
declining access to training for skilled occupations; on the contrary, the

number of apprentices in large firms has been increasing in recent years, not least due to Works Council pressure. (In exchange, Works Councils have agreed that skilled workers upon completion of their apprenticeship may be employed in unskilled jobs, until the internal labour market offers an opportunity for promotion.) And while there was always some discrimination by ascriptive criteria, the main line of segmentation in German 'post-corporatism' is between those who are employed and those who are not—and cannot be, even with inferior conditions, because this would undermine the defence at work-place level of the past accomplishments of solidaristic union policy. Thus, to the extent that there is a contribution of organized labour to labour-market segmentation in West Germany, this consists primarily in the successful efforts of Works Councils to control, and in effect prevent, new recruitment (Hohn, 1983). One expression of the resulting social closure of internal labour markets—which is facilitated by the absence of formal seniority rules and job demarcations, allowing for high internal flexibility through retraining and redeployment—is the high level of overtime working in large firms. While from the perspective of the industrial union, this violates the principle of solidarity with the unemployed, for those who are in employment it is an essential pre-condition of their continued employment security.

Just as there was no 'corporatist convergence' in the 1970s, so there is un-likely to be a 'post-corporatist convergence' in the 1980s. Trying to draw out the lines of recent German developments, one may envisage that the joint regulation of the relations between capital and labour may for a long time effectively shift from the national or industrial to the enterprise level. The dominant pattern here—dominant in the sense that it prevails in the leading sectors and firms of the economy—seems to be one of close, and closed, productivity coalitions within individual production units, joining together management and a relatively secure 'fixed' work-force in a campaign for competitive success on domestic and world markets (Streeck, 1984). It is tempting to speculate what the next step may then be in the historical sequence from (centrally regulated) employ-ment contracts in an open external labour market to institutionally protected job ownership in closed industrial sub-societies. One possibility, given the forceful emergence and the sustained precedence of fixed, static interests of workers in the economic fate of 'their' enterprise, would be a gradual transform-ation of job ownership into share ownership. In fact, this would seem to be no more than the logical conclusion of the earlier evolution, much assisted by neo-corporatist collective bargaining and legislation, from *contract* to *status*, as the defining principle in the relationship between workers and their employing organizations. With the work-force acquiring a vested interest in the success of the firm comparable to that of the original shareholders, there is no reason why workers should be represented exclusively through traditional institutions of industrial relations, and not (also) directly in the shareholders' assembly. Not only would share ownership give adequate institutional expression to the specific relation of a fixed work-force to 'its' enterprise in a closed external labour market; it would also allow for considerable upward and downward flexibility of remuneration unimpeded by industrial agreements and in line with both the enterprise's ability to pay and its need to survive.

Neo-corporatism may not disappear, even though it seems to have given rise to a new enterprise constitution which, under changed economic conditions, undermines the neo-corporatist institutional pattern of industrial relations. If one was daring enough, one might venture the hypothesis that it is industrial relations as we have known it, and not neo-corporatism, that is about to wither away. With the cleavage between labour and capital as organized social classes being superseded by the new cleavages between unified sectors and consensually organized firms, as well as between privileged and unprivileged class sections, new issues like the protection and the restructuring of industrial sectors will take precedence. These may well again lend themselves to neo-corporatist forms of interest intermediation and public policy-making. On the other hand, however, the indications are that the interests and actors called forth by the new issues will be much more fragmented and specific than in the highly organized labour markets of the past. Moreover, for each of the new corporatist policy arenas—if corporatist they will be—there will also be outsiders challenging the legitimacy of state-facilitated interest accommodation between those who have been admitted as participants. If the institutional simplicity and the political comprehensiveness of neo-corporatist industrial relations was ever more than just a delusion, then with the entanglement of class politics in the economics of individual firms and sectors its days would seem numbered.

13

The End of Convergence: Corporatist and Dualist Tendencies in Modern Western Societies

JOHN H. GOLDTHORPE

Introduction

The idea of 'industrial society', in its present-day acceptation, was developed in the 1950s and 1960s by both European and American social scientists within a liberal critique of contemporary Marxism. For some of the authors in question, the aim was primarily to show how Marxist analyses of modern capitalism, as well as being often empirically inadequate, were also conceptually restrictive and misleading. *All* technologically and economically advanced societies, it was argued, whether capitalist or not, displayed essentially similar structural and processual features, which were associated with the requirements and conse-quences of large-scale industrial production: thus, the idea of 'industrial society' must be recognized as superordinate to that of 'capitalist society', and take precedence for analytical purposes (e.g. Aron, 1962, 1968). However, for other liberal authors, to achieve such a conceptual reorientation marked no more than a first step. It was then their objective to move on to the formulation of a *theory* of industrial society, of a similar character to that of the Marxist theory of the long-term dynamics of capitalism, but which would be capable of quite transcending the latter in its scope and explanatory power.

Thus, for example, in what must be reckoned as the most ambitious and influential attempt in this direction, Clark Kerr and his fellow authors of *Industrialism and Industrial Man* (1960, 1973) see themselves as following Marx in applying deductive methods to the understanding of the emerging pattern of global social development, but at the same time they directly contest the Marxist conception of how this development proceeds (cf. also Kerr, 1983). The funda-mental impulse in long-term social change is not, in their view, the contradic-tions that recurrently build up between the expanding forces of production and the property institutions of a particular epoch but, rather, the ever-present and universal exigencies of technological and economic rationality. At the level of social action, the key processes through which decisive historical change is actually brought about are not those of class mobilization and conflict, but those of élite leadership and mass response. And the ultimate dénouement which may be envisaged is not the revolutionary transition from capitalism to socialism, but the evolutionary convergence of all modern and 'modernizing' societies on one particular form of industrialism: namely, 'pluralistic industrial-ism'. This is the general model of society most consistent with the functional imperatives that a rationally operating technology and economy impose; and it is in fact the pressure of these imperatives which must be seen as forcing the development of industrial societies on to convergent lines, whatever the distinc-tive features of their historical formation or of their pre-industrial cultural traditions.

It has, moreover, to be added that both in the case of Kerr and his associates and of various other liberal authors who advanced essentially similar theories of industrialism (e.g. Parsons, 1964, 1966), a concern is also to a greater or lesser degree apparent to take over from Marxism the claim to provide—through a privileged cognitive grasp on the movement of history—an objective basis for political judgements (cf. Goldthorpe, 1971). Thus, it is characteristic of such authors that, rather than attempting to argue in any philosophical way either for or against particular political positions, they aim to justify the liberal values that they see embodied in pluralistic industrialism on functional and evolution-ary grounds derived directly from their sociology. These values, they hold, are actually revealing themselves in the course of social development as those most consistent with the 'logic' of industrialism. As experience of industrialism accumulates, it becomes evident what are the 'realistic' political possibilities; and unworkable 'utopian' conceptions—such as those which inspire socialism or communism or, for that matter, pure *laissez-faire*, individualistic capitalism—are eliminated as part of the evolutionary process. In the end, therefore, 'industrial man is seldom faced with real ideological alternatives' (Kerr *et al.*, 1960: 283): he must either accept the pluralistic industrialism that is being chosen for him by history or else face disillusionment and failure.

In view of the challenges, both intellectual and political, that are thus laid down by liberal theories of industrialism, it is in no way surprising that they should have provoked extensive controversy. Thus far, apart from attempts to display 'the ideology of the end of ideology' implicit in such theories, critics have chiefly raised empirically-based objections to the claim that a convergent pattern of development is now established among the societies of the industrial world. And of course to the extent that such objections can be sustained, doubt must then also fall on the existence, or at least on the cogency, of the functional logic which is supposed to generate convergence. In the present paper, this same line of criticism will be further pursued. It will in fact be contended that over recent decades—and even if attention is confined to the industrial societies of the West or only to those of Western Europe—clearly *divergent* tendencies in social development may be observed in a number of significant respects. How-ever, what will also be attempted is to provide some account of why this should be so and, in this way, to go beyond merely empirical objections to the con-vergence thesis—which might by now perhaps appear *vieux jeu*—to a more fundamental argument: that is, that contrary to what would be supposed by liberal theorists, the idea of capitalist society is not outmoded or rendered problematic by that of industrial society; and further, that an analysis of the course of change in modern Western societies in terms of the functional imperatives of industrialism is no substitute for one in terms of the political economy of capitalism—even though this may need to depart radically from conventional Marxist lines.

In what follows, attention will centre on claims made by exponents of the convergence thesis in three substantive areas: social stratification, the representation of interests, and industrial relations and organization. When these claims are examined, one point should become apparent: namely, that the convergence thesis was very much a product of its time—that is, of the 'long boom' of the post-war period. What the theorists of industrialism implicitly assumed, so far as the Western world was concerned, was that with the development of improved techniques of economic management, following the 'Keynesian revolution', and with the growing readiness of governments to apply such techniques, the problems of regulating capitalist, or 'mixed', economies were essentially solved; and that for the conceivable future, therefore, economic stability and dynamism would be reconciled and guaranteed. And in turn, then, it was also supposed that, within such an economic future, a virtually permanent status would attach to the post-war 'settlements' which had been arrived at in Western nations between capital and employers on the one hand and labour and its organizations on the other. For what these settlements typically involved, although in varying degree from one society to another, were assurances to labour that governments had assumed responsibility for the basic economic and social security of all citizens, and for the steady improvement of their material standards of living through sustained economic growth.

In other words, there was no place in the scenarios of convergent development that were elaborated in the 1950s and 1960s for the severely troubled phase in the economic history of the Western world which actually began in the early 1970s. And what then will subsequently be maintained is that it is through the responses that have emerged in different societies to the ending of the long boom—specifically, responses in what may be termed 'corporatist' and 'dualist' directions—that divergent tendencies in social development have been made most apparent. However, the argument to be presented is not that it was simply as the result of an unforeseen, and perhaps unforseeable, decline in the performance of Western economies that the convergence thesis was undermined. Rather, it will be held that the problems of inflation and of 'stagflation' with which these economies are now beset are ones that have to a significant extent been produced endogenously within the societies of the Western world, and through processes *which were already in train during the post-war period* but which exponents of the convergence thesis were conceptually ill-equipped to observe.

Changes in Social Stratification and their Consequences

In elaborations both of the idea of industrial society and of the thesis of the convergent development of Western nations towards the goal of pluralist industrialism, the treatment of changes in the degree and form of social stratification and of their consequences holds a quite central place. Three major arguments regarding stratification may be identified in the work of the leading theorists of industrialism which, in their essentials, can be stated as follows.[1]

(i) In the course of industrial development, social inequalities of both condition and opportunity show a general, long-run tendency to decline. Industrial development based on technological advance requires an increasingly differentiated labour force, and one with progressively higher standards of education and training. Thus, the proportion of the economically active population enjoying a relatively high level of occupational status and income steadily grows. Moreover, this expansion of higher-grade employment, together with the increased provision of education, greatly enlarges individuals' chances of social mobility; and the 'openness' of industrial society is further enhanced in that economic and technical rationality impose criteria of social selection which emphasize 'achieved' rather than 'ascribed' characteristics. Finally, equality is also promoted as in all industrial societies the state intervenes in market processes in order to establish certain minimum standards of welfare as the social rights of all citizens, complementary to their civil and political rights.

(ii) In industrial societies stratification takes on an increasingly unstructured and fluid form. It becomes difficult to identify either classes or status groups in the sense of relatively stable collectivities of individuals and families displaying characteristic life-styles and associational patterns. In particular, the former distinctiveness of the industrial working class fades away. An advanced industrial society has to be seen as essentially a 'middle-class' or, rather, as a 'middle-mass' society. The decomposition of classes and status groups results in large part from tendencies towards greater social equality and mobility, but is furthered too by the increasing cultural homogeneity which also follows from industrialism. All forms of subcultural particularism—those based on region, ethnicity etc., as well as those based on class—are broken down, on the one hand, by the need for greater geographical as well as social mobility within the labour force and, on the other, by the growing influence of mass consumption and mass communications.

(iii) In industrial nations, social stratification becomes steadily less divisive and thus, of declining importance as a basis of socio-political mobilization. It is in the context of early industrialism, and especially in the 'heroic' phase of capital accumulation, that class conflict reaches its peak. Subsequently, the effects of industrialism in reducing social inequalities and in blurring the lines of class division—and also, of course, in raising living standards generally—progressively undermine the potential for such conflict. The widening of opportunities for social mobility encourages the individualistic pursuit of interests, and this can, moreover, be effectively supplemented by collective action that is organized not on a class but, rather, on a *group* basis. Thus, action directed towards furthering the interests of those employed in a particular plant, occupation, or industry usually appears as far more relevant than attempts to uphold some wider but increasingly diffuse interest, such as that of the working class as a whole.

It will be apparent enough how the foregoing arguments stand in quite systematic counterpoint to those which—at least up to the 1960s—could be regarded as characteristic of Marxist analyses; and their critical force and success in this respect must be reckoned as considerable. However, what may also be suggested is that in being formulated in this polemical context, these arguments came to share in some of the same general weaknesses of those against which they were directed: most notably, an exaggeration of the extent, continuity and consistency of the particular trends of change they sought to emphasize and, at the same time, a one-sidedness in the view taken of their implications. These weaknesses are moreover particularly evident in judgements made on the future of the working class and of class conflict.

Thus, in the light of recent research and analysis, major qualifications could be made in the following respects.

(i) Liberal theorists often took as evidence of declining social inequality what was in fact evidence simply of a general increase in living standards and welfare. Research focused specifically on the extent of class *differentials* in life-chances—for example, in health and education—has frequently found that these have altered remarkably little over the post-war decades, and that disparities existing between the industrial working class and the rest of society have been especially resistent to change (cf. Wedderburn, ed., 1974; Rainwater, ed., 1974). Similarly, in the case of social mobility, liberal theorists quite failed to recognize that while the 'upgrading' of occupational structures produced by industrial development does indeed widen opportunities for social ascent, it has at the same time the effect of reducing the likelihood of downward movement. And the major finding of analyses that have been made of trends in national mobility rates considered *net* of all structural effects—which provides the best indicator of changes in the degree of openness—is that such rates display very considerable stability over time (Erikson *et al.*, 1983).

(ii) This combination of structural change with constancy in relative mobility chances, rather than threatening the decomposition of the working classes of Western nations, must tend in fact to increase their internal homogeneity, at least so far as the social origins and work-life experience of their members is concerned. For declining downward mobility into working-class positions—together with a decline in the influx of labour from greatly contracted agricultural sectors—means that in recent decades Western working classes have, for the first time, become predominantly self-recruiting. Although in most instances reduced somewhat in size, they do now mostly comprise a majority of members who may be reckoned as, at least, 'second generation'. And while it is true that opportunities for upward mobility out of the working class have expanded, the growing importance of education as a channel of such mobility has meant that those who break away increasingly do so at a relatively early age. Thus, the bulk of working-class membership, as it exists at any one moment, is likely to be made up of those who have—as Sorokin once put it—both a 'hereditary' and a 'life-time' affiliation (cf. Goldthorpe, 1980, 1983).

(iii) In emphasizing certain egalitarian tendencies which are indeed associated with Western industrialism, liberal theorists neglected the well-attested possibility that where social inequality is reduced in one particular respect, this may, rather than lowering the potential for social conflict, actually increase it, through bringing other forms of inequality into contention. Thus a consequence of the decay of status group structures of pre-industrial origin may be that class inequalities, for which the status hierarchy previously provided a 'traditionalistic' legitimation, become more often regarded as arbitrary and contingent rather than as part of 'the order of things', and that in turn normative restraints on what are seen as 'appropriate' rewards, entitlements and opportunities are weakened. Moreover, this process can only be encouraged as the ethos of consumerism and continuing material advancement secures wider acceptance, and as the limitations on wants and life-styles imposed by traditional communities and sub-cultures, especially those of the working class, are undermined. Likewise, the process through which in the Western world civil, political and social rights of citizenship have been extended to all members of national communities—while certainly egalitarian—has at the same time to be recognized as one which has its own dynamic and no very evident resting point (cf. Lockwood, 1974; Esping-Andersen & Korpi, this volume). Thus, in the post-war period a notable movement has been for citizenship rights to be further developed into the industrial sphere: that is, in the form of employees' 'rights in jobs'—pertaining to such matters as redundancy, dismissal, promotion etc.—and rights to participate in decision-making procedures affecting their working environment, conditions of service and employment prospects. From one point of view, these developments can be seen as entirely continuous with earlier ones in what Marshall (1950) referred to as the 'war' between citizenship and class—in setting limits, one could say, to the extent to which labour can be treated merely as a commodity. But from another point of view, this extension of citizenship rights into the actual organization of production raises new, and manifestly very divisive, issues concerning managerial prerogatives and the bases of authority and responsibility within the enterprise (Goldthorpe, 1978 and forthcoming).

To identify these aspects of change in the pattern of social stratification that are neglected or misconstrued in liberal theories of industrialism has significance not only by way of criticism of various specific claims that follow from these theories. It is also highly relevant to understanding why their proponents failed to envisage the possibility that, far from Western societies becoming increasingly better adapted to the functional requirements of industrialism, developments were taking place within them that could seriously threaten the continuation of their economic success.

In order to amplify this point, it is important to begin by noting that the liberalism which stands behind the idea of industrial society could be fairly described as a political, far more than an economic liberalism. This is most clearly indicated by the fact that while its adherents attached the highest importance to the freedom of individuals who recognize common interests to organize and to pursue these interests through all lawful means, they were remarkably unconcerned about the likely consequences of such activity for the free operation of market forces. In other words, there was little awareness of the contradictions that might arise within the pluralistic industrialism of the West between a form of polity characterized by the vigorous rivalries of organized interests and a form of economy which, though perhaps labelled 'mixed', remained essentially capitalist in its mode of operation; or, perhaps, as one commentator has suggested, the new liberals possessed 'an excessive faith in capitalism and in its ability to fly however much its wings are clipped' (Scitovsky, 1980). However, it is precisely contradictions of the kind in question which, of late, have become accepted by economists and other social scientists—of varying theoretical and ideological persuasions—as a factor of steadily increasing importance underlying the severity and persistence of the economic problems that Western nations now confront (Jay, 1976; Brittan, 1977, 1983; Scitovsky, 1978, 1980; Thurow, 1980; Schmitter, 1981; Olson, 1982, ch. 7 esp., 1983; Mueller, ed. 1983). Their analyses have in common the recognition of two crucial facts: first, that interest groups, as they operate in the economic sphere, aim primarily at strengthening their members' market position through action that is in some sense taken *against* market forces—for example, via organization, regulation, legislation etc.; and secondly, that such interest groups are concerned very largely with distributional issues of a 'zero-sum' kind, in which their members' interests can only be protected or advanced to the extent that those of other groups are threatened or damaged. Thus, as the number of interest groups and the amount of interest-group activity increase, it must be expected, on the one hand, that the market mechanisms on which the efficient functioning of a capitalist economy depends will work less freely; and, on the other, that distributional conflict within society will be heightened, which will in turn add to the difficulties of carrying through remedial economic policies.

Further, though, what has also to be recognized as highly relevant in this connection—but what the theorists of industrialism succeeded in concealing from themselves—is the interplay occurring between the 'organizational revolution' of the post-war period and the evolution of class structure and class relations within Western societies. Although it could certainly be said that in this period interests of all kinds increasingly sought and achieved organized expression, there can be little doubt that the major development was in the organization of *labour* (cf. Korpi, 1983, ch. 3 esp.). And while the theorists in question were well aware of, and indeed concerned to stress, this development, their appreciation of its significance was far from adequate. Their expectation clearly was that as labour unions 'matured'—that is, abandoned the ideological commitments to class struggle characteristic of their early years—and concentrated their efforts on pragmatic collective bargaining and pressure-group activities, they would come to form a quite integral part of pluralistic industrialism (Lester, 1958; Kerr *et al.*, 1960; Clegg, 1960; Ross & Hartman, 1960). However, the possibility that was here overlooked was that unions could, even while perhaps modifying their previous ideological positions, still effectively represent class as well as sectional interests and, moreover, that they might do so in a way that was capable of bringing about a significant shift in the balance of power in class relations. In particular, liberal theorists of industrialism failed to appreciate the importance of two developments that became increasingly apparent, even if with some significant cross-national variation, within trade unionism over the post-war period: first, the emergence of a new 'maximizing' militancy in collective bargaining, encouraged, one would suggest, by the weakening of traditional legitimations of class inequalities and traditional limitations on wants and life-styles, as well as by the rising confidence of trade-unionists in the bases of their organized power (Barkin, ed., 1975; Crouch & Pizzorno, eds. 1978; Sachs, 1979); and secondly, a growing concern shown by unions, especially through their central federations, with the direction of macroeconomic policy, which they increasingly recognized as capable of exerting a crucial influence on the bargaining strength of labour as a whole (Barbash, 1972).

In sum, then, the argument is that the functional viability of pluralistic industrialism was greatly over-estimated through a neglect of the generally damaging effects of interest-group activity on the operation of market mechanisms, and further of the particular problems created by the relatively rapid increase, in most Western societies, in the organized power of labour and in both the range and intensity of labour's demands. The most obvious outcome of these developments, apparent in fact already by the 1960s, was that Western economies became inherently inflationary. As organization increased the capacity of different groups to protect their incomes against unfavourable market forces, a strong downward rigidity of incomes and prices was created;

and in turn, then, the response to upward shifts in relative prices that might for any reason occur was not offsetting relative price decreases and consequent changes in income distributions, but rather an upward movement in the general price level.[2] In addition, though, the increased power of labour was also crucial in undermining the effectiveness of the techniques of economic management, in particular of demand management, on which liberal expectations of stable yet steadily expanding economies were in large part founded. On the one hand, it became apparent that where attempts were made to control inflation through policies that reduced aggregate demand, then, in the face of labour's growing ability to maintain wage levels, a larger proportion of the effect of such policies would come in the form of a reduction not in the rate of price increases but rather in real output or, in other words, in the form of rising unemployment. And, on the other hand, it was no less apparent that where, perhaps as the result of union pressure, attempts were made at reducing unemployment by policies aimed at expanding demand, then, again as a result of labour's increased bargaining strength, these policies were increasingly likely to have their intended effects dissipated in a further upturn in inflation.

In the course of the post-war years the indications thus steadily mounted that to view the major features of Western societies as developing on lines that would make these societies progressively more adapted to the functional requirements of modern economies was, to say the least, scarcely realistic; and indeed, as already remarked, by the early 1970s rather widespread attention was being given to the social-structural—and associated political—factors in the unprecedented emergence of persisting high rates of inflation and of unemployment as complementary rather than alternative expressions of economic disorder. However, what for present purposes is of major relevance is to recognize that, confronted by rising difficulties in controlling their economies, Western societies have not, so to speak, remained passive. The period of the long boom was itself not free of economic problems yet was in most cases sustained up to the 1970s, and it is further notable that in the subsequent stagflationary period the performance of Western economies has tended to become more disparate: modes of 'adaptation' have clearly varied (Scharpf, 1981). In what follows, the main concern will be to examine the nature of different responses to the central problems of capitalist economies that have formed in the West, and more specifically to see how and why these responses have involved significant—yet contrasting—divergencies from the model of pluralistic industrialism which, in the grand vision of liberal theorists, the West offered to the world as the ultimate evolutionary goal.

Corporatism

If it is the case that the problems currently faced by Western economies do have a major endogenous source in heightened and more equally balanced distributional dissent, at the level of both interest groups and classes, then one possible direction of response, so far as governments are concerned, would seem fairly apparent. That is, to try to bring some greater degree of order, and hence of predictability, not only into their own relations with particular organized interests, but further into the relations prevailing *among* these interests, where their aims and their strategies for pursuing these aims are, in some way or other, interdependent. It is, one may suggest, as a response of essentially this kind that one can best interpret developments in the form of interest representation which have become evident in a number of Western societies over recent decades, and which have been widely seen as indicating a return to, or renewal of, *corporatist* principles. What has been found significant in these developments is that they entail a blurring of the line of division, crucial to liberal political theory, between the state and civil society. Organizations representing private interests are accorded a role in the formation of public policy in areas that are of central concern to them, but are then required to assume a responsibility for the effective implementation of policies with which they have become associated and, in particular, for the appropriate conduct of their own memberships—being perhaps in this respect aided by the state as, for example, through various kinds of delegated powers, special privileges, subsidies etc. However, what needs to be added here is that it is not such a *Verstaatlichung* of private interests which in itself is all that novel. Rather, it is the increasing extent to which not simply bilateral, but tri- and multilateral arrangements have been attempted, in order to afford government the possibility not only of accommodating and regulating specific interests but, more importantly, of promoting the *concertation* of different interests which could otherwise be expected to compete or conflict in ways detrimental to the achievement of major governmental objectives (cf. Czada & Lehmbruch, 1981; Lehmbruch, 1983 and this volume).

Perhaps because the 'rediscovery of corporatism' was largely an achievement of political scientists, corporatist tendencies have often been treated as a response to governmental problems of effectiveness and consent of a quite general kind. Following the organizational revolution, it has been argued, the unregulated representation of interests becomes increasingly a recipe for disorder and unrest: claims are made on government of such a volume and range and are backed with such a capacity for collective action that channels of decision-making fail through 'overload' and societies are brought close to a condition of 'ungovernability'. However, on sober examination, such contentions must seem somewhat exaggerated—and often out of a rather transparent ideological distaste for 'over-participation'. In so far as Western governments have had to face recurrent crises of effectiveness and, perhaps, of consent in the recent past, these have in fact by far most frequently arisen in connection with *the management of the economy*, and in consequence of the actions of organizations representing major economic interests: that is, business and employer oganizations and trade unions. On account of the control that these organizations can exercise over the key resources of capital and labour, they must be placed in a quite different category from virtually all others in their ability to exert pressure on governments or simply to frustrate their initiatives. And in turn, it may be held, it is in the case of these organizations that corporatist developments, in the sense of governmentally guided attempts at the concertation of interests, have been most distinctive and have carried the furthest-reaching implications.

More specifically, what may be suggested is that these developments represent in effect attempts by governments, in dealing with the rising problems of macro-economic policy previously noted, to find institutional and ultimately political substitutes for the declining efficiency of market mechanisms. The most common, (though by no means the only,) objective has been to establish arrangements, formal or informal, for consultation and negotiation between government, employers' associations and union federations, in the context of which the latter may be induced to accept—and to commit their members to accepting—some form of restraint in their use of their collective bargaining strength. Such restraint has been seen as necessary, given the growing rigidity of modern economies, to allow governments to introduce expansionist policies aimed at sustaining employment without producing disastrously high rates of inflation; or, conversely, to allow them to introduce restrictionist policies aimed at curbing inflation without producing disastrously high rates of unemployment.

Two features of the logic of these corporatist arrangements would seem to be of key importance. First, the central—that is, the national—organizations of employers and unions are required to take on a representative function that must seek to transcend sectionalism. They must act in a way that will balance the differing interests that exist within their memberships, and concentrate their efforts on goals from which all can benefit. Such 'encompassing organizations', as Olson (1982) has termed them, should thus serve to absorb within themselves some of the distributional dissent arising from more narrowly constituted interest groups. Secondly, in the case of the unions at least, a basic change of *modus operandi* is implied. Unions are required to cede or under-utilize their economic power—that is, the power they can express in collective bargaining in labour markets—in exchange for the opportunity for their leaders to exercise political power or, at all events, political influence. Several commentators have indeed maintained that it is this exchange that is fundamental to the developments in relations between governments and unions which have been labelled 'corporatist', and would themselves wish rather to speak—as they would see it, less tendentiously—of the emergence of a form of 'political' or 'societal' bargaining, in which unions engage primarily with government rather than employers and which modifies, but can at the same time powerfully complement, conventional collective bargaining as a mode of action of labour movements (Korpi & Shalev, 1980; Korpi, 1983; cf. Pizzorno, 1978b, 1981).

This view has obviously something in common with that taken here—that significant corporatist tendencies should be regarded as primarily a response to problems of economic management. However, what can scarcely be neglected, and is in fact for present purposes of central relevance, is the way in which these tendencies, even if restricted largely to the economic sphere, do still entail departures from the model of pluralistic industrialism that are of a quite major kind.

To begin with, there can be little doubt that, whether understood as 'corporatism' or 'political bargaining', the pattern of interaction between government and major economic interests which would seem prevalent in several Western societies, such as those of Austria, Sweden and Norway—and which has at certain periods been attempted in a number of others, such as the Netherlands, West Germany, and Finland—is one that scarcely conforms with the model of interest representation envisaged by liberal theorists as that most appropriate to and characteristic of modern industrialism. In the view of these theorists, the complexity of the structure of an advanced industrial society must lead to the recognition by groups differently located within this structure of a great diversity of interests—economic and other—which then become represented through an equally great diversity of organizations. These bodies will compete with each other for influence over government within a kind of political market; and while this will, like other markets, be subject to governmental supervision and even, in particular cases, to regulative intervention, it is not seen as part of government's role to 'organize' the market itself. However, in those societies where corporatist tendencies have developed, an attempt to comprehend the relations prevailing between governments, employers and trade unions in terms of such a conception of 'pressure-group politics' would be obviously inadequate. For apart from it being unrealistic to suppose that the central organizations of employers and unions can be treated as interest groups like any others, it is precisely the purpose of corporatist arrangements to involve such organizations in the political process in a way that goes clearly beyond the exercise of external pressure: that is, in an acceptance of shared responsibility both for the formation of policy and for its implementation. And what then rather naturally follows from such arrangements is that governments are led to give increased attention to questions of how their 'partners' in policy-making manage their own internal affairs: in particular, to questions of how *they* form *their* policies and, more fundamentally, of how they come to *define* the interests that they exist to serve. In pluralist theory, group interests are seen as emerging directly from the positions that groups hold within the social structure, and the function of their organizations is then that of representation of a similarly direct, unmediated kind. But in corporatist practice, interests are clearly not treated simply as sociological 'givens', and the function of representative organizations is not merely to express, but actually to formulate interests, in response to pressure from both their memberships *and* from their bargaining partners, and also in the light of their leaders' own conceptions of appropriate strategies. Thus inter- and intra-organizational relations alike become of major political consequence, and fall within the legitimate sphere of governmental concern.[3]

Furthermore, interest representation in the form of corporatism, as here understood, clearly diverges from the pluralism envisaged by liberal theorists in that, far from reflecting and in turn reinforcing a process of class decomposition, it tends rather to endow class—as opposed to group—interests with a new significance. If the national representative bodies of employers and unions are to act as 'encompassing organizations', aiming to modify sectionalist demands from among their members and at the same time to win the support of the latter for a strategy of political bargaining, then it becomes necessary for their leaderships to take up a position on the obvious questions of exactly what interests will be served by this strategy and how. One possibility may be to claim that in this way distributional conflicts that are 'negative-sum' in their outcomes can be reduced, to the advantage of all parties involved. But distributive conflicts are more characteristically of a 'zero-sum' kind, and, in so far as this is so, the organizations representing 'the two sides of industry' can scarcely do other than define the interests that they seek to advance in essentially class terms.

This requirement arises most sharply in the case of the unions since, as earlier suggested, it is the nature of union activity that is most affected by participation in corporatist arrangements. The acceptance by a national union movement of restraint of any kind on processes of conventional collective bargaining must mean that certain groups of workers—that is, those with the strongest labour market positions—will yield more in the way of immediately available gains than will others. But the benefits that can be obtained as the quid pro quo for such restraint—through, say, employment, fiscal or social policy—will not only be somewhat deferred but will also tend to be of a rather generalized kind: for example, benefits that will accrue, if not to all citizens, then to all employees, all industrial workers, all persons with incomes below a certain level etc. Thus, union leaders engaging in political bargaining and wishing to retain the backing of their memberships are typically led to emphasize their concern with the interests of a broadly-defined working class, and usually on a relatively long-term view, as against interests of a more sectional and shorter-term kind. It can hardly be thought accidental that the national union movements which have the most consistent records of involvement in political bargaining—those of Austria, Sweden, and Norway—are also ones which, as well as being highly centralized, have attached a greater importance than most others to combatting sectionalism and to maintaining a sense of class solidarity and a class outlook on economic and political issues among their rank and file (Korpi, 1978; Hanisch, 1981; Marin, 1983). It is also worthy of note that in each of these countries, in which trade unionism and socialism have strong historical connections, union movements have passed through periods of ideological questioning—in particular of *marxisant* conceptions of class struggle—but that this has *not* prevented them from remaining movements of a distinctively class-oriented kind. What is thus demonstrated is the invalidity of the assumption, which theorists of industrialism seem regularly to have made, that such ideological reassessments must imply that unions have become ready to accept the limitation of their functions simply to conventional collective bargaining and pressure-group activity, as the model of pluralistic industrialism would require.

Following from this, one may then point to yet another way in which the emergence of corporatist tendencies in certain Western societies has led to a rather decisive contradiction of liberal expectations. Along with the decomposition of classes and the 'maturing' of unions, the theorists of industrialism looked forward to what might be termed the progressive depoliticization of industrial relations. This would be achieved by the development of industrial relations institutions, principally ones of collective bargaining and dispute settlement, which would in effect create the basis of a system of industrial democracy complementary to, but separate from, that of political democracy. In this way, issues of both industrial and political conflict could be contained within, so to speak, their proper spheres, and 'spill-over' effects avoided. In particular, it was believed that if industrial conflict could be institutionally insulated from political influences of the kind that stemmed from class-oriented labour movements, its volume would be substantially reduced. Indeed, some liberal theorists were prepared to anticipate, as the appropriate institutions came into being, a virtual 'withering away' of the strike (Ross & Hartman, 1960).

However, it is evident that corporatist arrangements providing for political bargaining between governments, employers' organizations and unions, represent a kind of institutional development that goes in more or less direct opposition to those envisaged and endorsed in liberal scenarios. Since such bargaining essentially involves unions in exchanging some form of restraint on their labour-market power for a voice in governmental decision-making, it clearly implies a strategy on both sides in which advantage is seen precisely in treating certain major industrial and political issues *together*, so that they can in effect provide a basis for 'general understandings' or 'package deals'. And so far as unions are concerned, the possibility must of course be presupposed that political action can be a viable, and indeed a preferred, alternative to industrial action in the pursuit of their objectives. It may, moreover, be noted that, in this form at least, the politicization of industrial relations cannot be linked with a high level of conflict. On the contrary, worker involvement in strike activity in Austria, Sweden, and Norway, and also in the Netherlands and West Germany, has fallen to particularly low levels. And while it need not be claimed that political bargaining is the only source of this relative industrial peace, their association can scarcely be thought surprising. For where union movements are following a strategy that requires them to hold their labour market power in check, they may be thought unlikely to initiate or to encourage a form of action which crucially depends upon such power.[4]

In sum, corporatist tendencies, as here understood, represent a response to growing problems of the management of modern capitalist economies which involves the deflection or redirection of the increased power of organized labour away from the labour market into the political arena (Korpi & Shalev, 1980; Korpi, 1983, ch. 8; Shalev, 1983). In this interpretation, it may be added, the fact that the countries in which such tendencies have been most sustained are ones in which social-democratic parties have played a dominant role in government is readily intelligible: union movements will be more prepared to enter into political bargaining, and will have greater confidence of eventual gains from it, where they possess close ideological as well as organizational ties with the ruling party. But one has also to recognize, in addition to these instances of relatively stable corporatist arrangements existing under social-democratic hegemony, those further cases—as, for example, the Netherlands and West Germany—in which unions have judged it to their advantage to participate in such arrangements, at certain times and to a certain extent, in clearly less favourable political circumstances; and, at the same time, cases—such as that of Britain—in which, even under Left governments, the effective involvement of unions in political bargaining has proved difficult to establish (Tarling & Wilkinson, 1977). However, what for the present is of chief concern is not the specific pre-conditions for the emergence of corporatist tendencies, but rather the way in which, where they have in fact emerged, such tendencies mark significant departures from the liberal model of pluralistic industrialism—departures which, far from representing damaging deviations from the functional requirements of the logic of industrialism, must rather be seen as resulting from attempts to counter the economically 'dysfunctional' effects of the reality of pluralism when in conjunction with capitalism.[5]

Dualism

If the foregoing analysis is accepted, then corporatist tendencies may be thought of as a response to the current problems of Western economies of an 'inclusionary' kind: the increased power of major economic interest groups—and of organized labour in particular—is offset by institutional developments designed to involve these interests in both the formation and the implementation of economic policy. As was earlier suggested, what is here implied is the granting of institutional recognition to actual power shifts as a means of compensating for their damaging effects on the functioning of market mechanisms. However, to view corporatist tendencies in this way is at the same time to become aware of the possibility of a response on quite constrasting, 'exclusionary' lines: that is, one which would entail offsetting the increased power of organized interests by the creation or expansion of collectivities of economic actors, within the sphere of production, who *lack* effective organization and indeed the basic resources and perhaps motivations from which such organization might be developed. Tendencies indicative of a response of this kind may be described as ones in the direction of *dualism*. This label would seem appropriate in that these tendencies do not necessarily imply any direct and comprehensive attack on organized interests, but only the enlargement of certain areas of the economy within which market forces and associated relations of authority and control are able to operate more freely than in others, and in fact in such a way as to compensate for the rigidities that prevail elsewhere.[6]

According to liberal theories of industrial society, such dualism should have little place within the modern world. Economic dualism of any kind is seen as characteristic only of the earlier stages of economic development; as the logic of industrialism imposes itself, economies are progressively unified and the social processes that underlie the functioning of markets and of production units become increasingly homogeneous (cf. Kerr *et al.*, 1960, ch. 10). However, in opposition to these claims two empirically-grounded arguments may be advanced: first, that during the post-war years of unprecedented growth, dualist features persisted in many Western economies—and contributed to their growth—to a far greater extent than liberal theorists were able to recognize; and secondly, that in the succeeding period of declining economic performance, a strengthening of dualist tendencies can be quite widely observed.

One major source of dualism, as here understood, in the economies of Western capitalist societies is that of migrant labour—recruited predominantly from the less developed regions of the Western world or from former colonies. Several authors—and most convincingly, perhaps, Kindleberger (1967)—have sought to show the importance of such labour in sustaining economic growth in Western European nations through, at least, to the late 1960s. Not only did migrant workers help to prevent manpower shortages which could have checked growth but, further, they represented a type of labour distinctive alike in its elasticity of supply, its responsiveness to economic incentives and its tractability in the hands of management (Piore, 1979). In the growth model proposed by Kindleberger, the availability of labour with such characteristics encourages investment, permits high profits and then in turn encourages reinvestment in a virtuous circle. Moreover, where employers can draw on migrant labour more or less at will, the bargaining position of indigenous labour is inevitably weakened, whatever its level of organization. It is notable, for example, that where liberal theorists saw in the moderation of the wage claims of West German unions in the 1950s and 1960s a prime illustration of growing 'maturity', Kindleberger would point rather to the brute facts of labour supply (1967: 34).

By the end of the 1960s, the impetus to growth given by migrant labour was clearly reduced. With the settlement of some proportion of migrants and the consequent growth of communities of migrant families, it became apparent that increasing social costs would have to be set against the economic advantages of this form of labour supply. For this reason, therefore, and also in response to rising prejudice and hostility against migrants, governments generally moved towards more restrictive immigration policies (UN, 1979; Rist, 1979). This tendency was then strengthened with the growing economic uncertainty of the early 1970s, and those economies which had drawn most heavily on migrant workers, such as the West German, French, Austrian, and Swiss, were able to extract one further advantage from them—that is, by 'exporting' some substantial part of their increasing unemployment, in pursuit of what have been called 'beggar-my-neighbour' labour-market policies (Pichelmann & Wagner, 1983). However, what must here be emphasized is that despite stricter controls on migrant workers, aimed chiefly at preventing settlement, and despite the extent of return migration, still at the present time persons of foreign birth represent from 5 to 15 per cent of the total population in most of the major countries of Western Europe and generally constitute a somewhat higher proportion of the active labour force. Moreover, these foreign workers continue to be to a large extent distinctive in the market and work relationships in which they are involved, and in ways which maintain their functional importance for Western economies in the straitened circumstances of the present as in the previous years of expansion.

This is most obviously the case with that part of the migrant work force which is in effect 'unfree' labour—that is, which consists of workers recruited for specific employers and jobs and for strictly limited periods. Labour of this kind, which can be hired, utilized and then discharged, as employers require, can clearly play an important part in counteracting the rigidities of indigenous labour markets. So too can the further number of foreign workers found in all host societies who are illegal or otherwise 'undocumented' migrants, and who are thus in a particularly poor bargaining position *vis-à-vis* employers and indeed highly vulnerable to exploitation. Furthermore, though, the remainder of the migrant work force, comprising its more permanent or settled members who are not tied to particular employments, is still typically differentiated as labour from the bulk of that drawn from native populations: *de jure* in lacking certain of the civil, political, social and industrial rights of full citizenship, and *de facto* in lacking organizational protection. It is estimated that only around a quarter of all migrant workers in Western Europe are members of trade unions, which is a particularly low proportion in view of their occupational and industrial distribution; and moreover, unions have for the most part taken an uncertain and ambivalent attitude towards migrants and have shown relatively little concern with their specific problems (Castles & Kosack, 1973; Rist, 1979). At the same time, efforts by migrant workers to form their own organizations have not been highly effective in the face of difficulties stemming from their lack of rights, their cultural diversity and their high mobility.[7]

In the context of present-day capitalist societies, one could then conclude, migrant workers serve in part as a kind of 'industrial reserve army', whose members may be mobilized and discharged in response to major economic fluctuations, but more importantly as an important component of a 'secondary' labour force in the sense of a pool of labour, permanently available in these societies, which is highly exposed to market forces and to managerial authority alike.[8] In this latter respect, the presence of migrant labour may be seen as, so to speak, the counterpart of the success of workers within the mainstream or 'primary' labour force in gaining rights and organizational strength as a defence against economic uncertainty in general and, more specifically, against the logic of capitalism that would have labour treated as the variable factor of production. Thus Piore has remarked (1979: 42) that 'at root, the migrants provide a way in which workers in the native labour force are able to escape the role to which the [capitalist] system assigns them'. But, conversely, it could as well be said that it is in so far as these latter workers *have made their escape* that the system needs to recruit labour from other sources of a kind which can help restore its flexibility.[9]

While turning to labour drawn from outside the national community is one resort open to employers confronted with persisting qualitative as much as quantitative problems of labour supply, another and somewhat more radical response can also be identified which is similarly productive of dualism. This involves—as well as perhaps the tapping of new sources of labour—the creation or encouragement by employers of forms of production and of associated work-roles and employment relations which in themselves serve to ease or to avoid labour problems.

In liberal theories of industrialism it was envisaged that, in order to meet requirements of reliability and predictability, production would increasingly be carried out according to one standard pattern: namely, that of the large-scale, bureaucratically-organized enterprise, run by a professional management team and regulating its work-force through a complex 'web of rules' that are in substantial part negotiated 'constitutionally' with union representatives (Harbison & Myers, 1959; Kerr et al., 1960; Kerr, 1983). A long-term historical shift in the direction of this pattern may perhaps be recognized, even if with a wide and persisting degree of cross-national variation. But what is now also becoming clear is not only that the dominance of the 'modern' enterprise is in many industrial societies still far from complete, but further that, in the context of present economic difficulties, there is a rather widespread tendency for other forms of production to increase rather than to diminish in importance. And what the latter tend to have in common is that they entail employment relationships which, rather than being closely rule-governed, are in large part either conditioned directly by market forces or subject to employers' *fiat*.

Thus, for example, there would now appear to be an increase in many Western economies in the extent to which large-scale enterprises hive off some part of their production under subcontract to smaller concerns. As several authors have documented, this practice has assumed major proportions in France and in Italy, two countries in which traditions of small-scale enterprise have persisted particularly strongly, and in which therefore ample opportunities for such subcontracting are available (Paci, 1979; Berger, 1981; Berger & Piore, 1980; Brusco & Sabel, 1981; Brusco, 1982). Through subcontracting, employers are of course able to give themselves some protection against fluctuations in demand, but it is further attractive as a means whereby employers can avoid the labour-market rigidities and limitations on the utilization of labour that are associated with the activities of powerful unions. Small firms can typically offer non-unionized work-forces, flexible wages and also exemption from—or dis-regard of—many restrictive features of health and safety regulations and other labour legislation. It is notable that a sharp upturn in the amount of sub-contracting occurred in France after the strike wave of May–June, 1968 and in Italy after that of the 'hot autumn' of 1969, in both of which instances the outbreak of worker militancy led to a strengthening of the unions' presence in large enterprises and to new legislation which extended workers' rights and threatened increased restraints on employers' customary powers in regard to discharges and deployment.[10]

Moreover, what is perhaps of yet wider significance is the growth of various kinds of employment which serve to enlarge another major component of the secondary labour force, namely, that of casual or marginal workers. For example, a further feature of the present-day Italian economy is the amount of 'outwork' undertaken by individuals or family groups in their own homes and also the extent of 'labour only' subcontracting, especially in the construction trades and services (Paci, 1973, 1979; Berger & Piore, 1980; Villa, 1981); and such employment—whether licit, 'black' or some shade of grey—would appear to be spreading extensively in many other Western societies (De Grazia, 1980). Again, there is evidence of a general increase in temporary work, and in some countries, notably France, this is now extensively organized by special agencies which in effect deal in labour (Berger & Piore, 1980; Michon, 1981). Finally, there has in most Western economies been a marked growth in part-time working, especially by married women. The increase in the participation rates of married women which has typically occurred in these economies over recent decades is substantially, and in some cases entirely, the result of an increase in part-time employment. And while not all those in such employment could be properly regarded as marginal workers—for example, many women in professinal occupations in the public sector—it is none the less evident that in this way the secondary labour force has often been considerably expanded.

Like the subcontracting of production, 'non-standard' employment arrangements of the kind in question have the advantage for employers of reducing risk in the face of uncertain demand, and provide work-forces which are rendered flexible by the very terms on which they are engaged. With outwork and labour-only subcontracting, the regulation of labour is of course largely left to the direct effects of economic incentives and constraints; while both temporary and part-time workers are typically excluded from at least the full range of protection and benefit afforded under legislation on redundancy, dismissal, sick and maternity leave, equal pay etc. as well as having only very low rates of union membership. It is furthermore important to recognize how opportunities for non-standard employment serve to mobilize a previously latent supply of labour from among groups who, for various reasons, would not otherwise regard themselves as being on offer—most obviously, perhaps, married women with young children but, in addition, juveniles, semi-retired persons, peasant-workers, and various others seeking 'second' jobs. For, what members of these groups have in common is that their commitment to the work they have taken on tends to be strictly limited and, in turn, their expectations of what they will be able to derive from it: typically, they have other sources of identity and satisfaction, and also perhaps of economic support. On account therefore of their location within the wider social structure, as well as of the form of their employment, such workers are unlikely to constitute a labour force in which any very strong interest in developing greater organizational power and in curtailing managerial prerogatives either exists or can easily be developed.

From the foregoing it should be fairly apparent how dualist tendencies in modern Western societies—no less than the corporatist tendencies previously considered—entail major departures from the model of pluralistic industrialism which, for liberal theorists, is the focus of convergent development. Thus, the massive influx and the substantial settlement of migrant workers was not only something which itself had no place in the scenarios constructed by these theorists, but further, the consequences that have directly followed are not readily reconciled with the conceptions of the emerging social order that they offered. Most obviously, those very attributes which make migrants an attractive source of labour supply for capitalist economies—their impermanence or, if settled, their restricted rights and lack of adequate organizational representation— are at the same time ones which serve largely to exclude them from the pluralist polity. In contrast with other groups definable within the social division of labour, they are seriously impeded in seeking to strengthen their economic position through collective action. Furthermore, though, migrant workers and their families represent an element in the populations of Western industrial societies which must stand as a rather striking exception to liberal theses of increasing equality, cultural homogeneity, and social integration. In view of the concentration of migrants in the least desirable types of work, of their degree of material deprivation, and of their low levels of social amenity and opportunity, they might seem well described as forming an 'under-class'—a class, that is, inferior to the lowest strata of their host society. However, as commentators such as Moore (1977) and Giner and Salcedo (1978) have pointed out, the main qualification to such a view must be that it tends to underestimate the extent to which migrants live apart from their host society altogether—differentiated from other groups and strata not only by the nature of the economic relations and circumstances in which they are involved but further by their language, their ethnicity, and the total meaning of their presence in the society.[11]

Those members of indigenous populations who are drawn on, together with migrant workers, in the development of secondary labour forces clearly do not share in the same situation of general 'apartness'. What, rather, is distinctive in their case—but also creates difficulties for the model of pluralistic industrialism— is their lack of integration specifically into the world of industrial work or, that is, their very role as casual or marginal labour. For the implication of this is not that they are of limited economic importance but, on the contrary, that they are of functional value to the economic system because of the fact that they *are* highly *disponible* or, in other words, because they stand largely outside, and in fact may not seek strenuously to become involved in, the 'web of rules' which, for liberal theorists, represents the characteristically modern way of regulating employment relationships. While, then, these workers are not, like migrants, effectively denied participation in the political life of their society, they are comparable with—and indeed often substitutable for—the latter (Piore, 1979, ch. 4) in that they represent labour which is largely excluded from the systems of *industrial* citizenship built up within Western nations in the course of the present century. Liberal theorists emphasized the steady upgrading of employment and the institutionalization of labour relations which they saw as following from the logic of industrialism. However, it is now evident that what they failed to anticipate was the way in which the logic of capitalism has required, as the counterpart to the evolving mainstream or primary labour force, the creation of a further body of labour that is still capable of being treated essentially as a commodity.

Alternatives for the Future

In the foregoing it has been argued that far from Western capitalist societies following convergent paths of development, focused on the model of pluralistic industrialism, the recent experience of Western European nations would suggest that the applicability of this model is in fact tending more to diminish than to widen. Moreover, it has been contended that this is so because, rather than pluralist forms of society and polity being progressively favoured as those functionally most consistent with an exigent logic of industrialism, it has become apparent that some serious incompatibility arises between pluralism and the requirements of *capitalist* industrial economies. The increasesd power of organized interests—and of organized labour in particular—which pluralism facilitates and encourages within capitalist society, results in the operation of market mechanisms being impeded or restricted to a degree which undermines the efficiency of the economy and frustrates standard techniques of macro-economic management. Growing awareness of this incompatibility has therefore led to movements away from the pluralist model which are of clearly divergent kinds: that is, ones going either in the direction of corporatism and aiming, so to speak, at the institutional transcendance of pluralism, or in the direction of dualism and aiming at the effective limitation of the provisions of pluralism in regard to a certain range of economic actors and collectivities.

In this concluding section, the aim is to extend the critique of liberal theories of industrialism so far presented in one other, highly consequential, way: that is, by showing that the contrasting responses to the difficulties of modern Western economies that are represented by corporatism and dualism can, and often do, embody 'real ideological alternatives' of the kind which, according to liberal theorists, the coming of advanced industrialism would progressively eliminate. It is by no means supposed that either corporatist or dualist tendencies may be understood simply as reflections of dominant ideological currents in the societies in which they occur. Indeed, it is clear enough from the historical record that developments in both directions have often come about as the result of what were, for the actors concerned, essentially pragmatic measures devised in the face of immediate and pressing problems, and further that such measures have been greatly influenced by the specific, historically-formed circumstances of different national societies and the possibilities for 'solutions' that these appeared to afford (cf. Berger & Piore, 1980; Marin, 1983). Moreover, it is also evident that corporatist and dualist tendencies can to some significant degree *co-exist* within the same society—as might of course be expected if both are responses to the same underlying problems. None the less, what may still be maintained is that these tendencies do carry with them ideological implications in, so to speak, an objective sense; and, further, that to the extent that these implications are made manifest, they will appear as ones which stand in strong opposition to each other. Rather more sharply, the argument may be put as follows: if one envisages an industrial society in which corporatist arrangements and practices of the kind that emerged in the 1960s and 1970s were sustained and developed over several more decades, then this would have to be seen as a very different kind of society, ideologically as well as institutionally—and indeed in its entire structure of social power and advantage—from one in which dualist features had become likewise established.

It is, first of all, worth noting that in the emergence of corporatist and dualist tendencies, a marked contrast arises over which actors take the crucial role. In the case of corporatism, this is clearly assumed by the unions and their members. Although actual proposals for corporatist arrangements are likely to come from government, this has typically been as a response to the demonstrated strength of the unions in labour markets; and whether or not unions are willing and able to participate effectively must, thus far at least, be reckoned as the major issue on which the success or failure of such arrangements has turned. Instances can be readily cited in which unions have been unable to agree even the initial terms for a 'partnership' with government (e.g. Delors, 1978); or in which corporatist arrangements have collapsed either as a result of the withdrawal of union leaders or of their inability to 'deliver' their rank and file (e.g. Akkermans & Grootings, 1978; Müller-Jentsch & Sperling, 1978). However, where unions do become firmly engaged in political bargaining with government, employers, even if disapproving, may still find it hard to avoid being drawn into participation themselves, since this is a preferable option to simply standing aside. In the case of dualism on the other hand, it is employers and their managements who are of central importance. It is they who take the lead in tapping new sources of labour supply and in developing new methods of organizing production and new forms of employment. Governments may act supportively as, for example, in facilitating migration or in modifying labour or social security legislation; but, in contrast with corporatist endeavours, the dualist response is essentially a decentralized one. In this case, it is the unions who are placed in the position of being able only to react to initiatives taken by others. Their attitudes to most manifestations of dualism have been hostile, but such hostility has not in fact been widely translated into effective counter-measures.

It can furthermore be claimed that although a corporatist basis for economic policy-making and management may be compatible with, and might even seem to be favoured by, some degree of economic dualism, the continued development of both corporatist and dualist tendencies within the same society must give rise to increasing tension between them. This is so because the general orientations in economic—and also in social—policy with which these tendencies have evident affinities are of clearly divergent kinds which, ultimately, presuppose quite different balance-of-power situations.

Thus, corporatism may be said to imply not only a highly interventionist approach by government, but further one that has a quite distinctive slant. To begin with, unions engaging in political bargaining in the context of stagflation may be expected to take as their first objective that of 'equality of sacrifice'— or, in other words, that of ensuring that governments do not deflect on to labour an excessive part of the costs involved in the adaptation of national economies to less favourable conditions. And indeed it can be shown that, over the period since the ending of the long boom, a rather strong association exists between the prevalence of corporatist arrangements and levels of employment (Schmidt, 1982a, 1982b; Cameron, this volume). It is only in the three countries earlier referred to as those where corporatism has become most securely established— Austria, Sweden, and Norway—that the goal of full employment has been kept at least within sight. Governments acting in partnership with unions have been clearly more likely than others to make positive efforts to maintain employment levels—whether through conventional demand-management undertaken in conjunction with incomes policy, through 'active' labour market and job creation policies, or through various policies aimed at sheltering the domestic labour force against external threats—including that of migrants. Moreover, the other major element in the quid pro quo that is typically sought by unions in return for labour-market restraint is a commitment by government to at least maintaining, and as far as possible expanding, social welfare provisions which have some redistributive effect. And again there are indications that this strategy has had a measure of success (Schmidt, 1982b; van Arnhem & Schotsman, 1982; Cameron, this volume). However, a continuing participation in political bargaining and exchange, with outcomes of the kind in question, is not something that unions can simply opt for. On the contrary—as earlier arguments have implied—such participation is only likely to be achieved, even if desired, in so far as national union movements possess two key attributes; first, considerable power within labour markets and, second, a high degree of cohesion and discipline based ultimately on class solidarity. For without the former, unions have nothing to bargain with at the political level, and there is little reason why governments should seek to enter into—inevitably difficult— negotiations with them; while without the second, unions will be unable to over- come the ever-present threat of sectionalism and to secure their members' acceptance of the political bargains to which they have committed them.

Dualism cannot, in the same way as corporatism, be directly linked with specific objectives in economic and social policies: as already suggested, the present extent of dualistic tendencies within modern economies has to be under- stood largely in terms of distinctive features of their historical development.

None the less, what can be claimed is that the strengthening of such tendencies—the widening of those sectors of production in which market forces and managerial authority are relatively unimpeded—accords extremely well with the policy orientations of what has of late become known as the 'new *laissez-faire*'. And what is distinctive about the latter as an approach to political economy is that, in direct contrast with that characteristic of corporatism, it involves an explicit retraction by government of responsibility for maintaining any particular level or pattern of economic activity, and an insistence that the performance of the economy is primarily dependent on those who play the key roles within markets and production units. The task of government is essentially that of providing an institutional context within which market incentives and disciplines can operate effectively and investors, entrepreneurs and employers—the actual creators of wealth—can enjoy a wide freedom of action (Keohane, 1978; Goldthorpe, forthcoming). Thus it is notable that the Thatcher regime in the UK, which may be taken as the leading exemplar of the new *laissez-faire* to date, is clearly bent on enlarging the size of the 'exposed' work-force within the economy, whether directly by such measures as removing 'fair wages' clauses from public contracts or the abolition of Wages Councils, or indirectly by paring back social welfare benefits and thus reducing the 'reserve price' of labour. At the same time a remarkable emphasis has been given to the part to be played by small businesses in restoring efficiency and prosperity to the British economy, not least through the contribution which it is believed they can make to the overcoming of labour problems (Scase & Goffee, 1980; Elliott & McCrone, 1982). It is moreover equally relevant to observe that the idea of political bargaining with unions was rejected from the first, as endowing them with a quite unwarranted power and influence outside their legitimate sphere of action; and that various legislative measures have been taken, or are planned, the chief significance of which lies in the limits they seek to impose precisely on the unions' potential to serve as a vehicle for class-oriented—rather than simply sectional—action, which might be of political effect. The most obvious example here is the outlawing of 'sympathetic' and 'political' strikes, but much of the government's expressed concern with creating greater democracy within unions would seem in fact to be directed more towards undermining what Pizzorno (1978b) has referred to as their 'capacity for strategy'.

Finally, if one looks to the future, there are good grounds for expecting that the ideological divergence implicit in corporatist and dualist tendencies will emerge still more sharply from the different issues that they will respectively place on the political agenda, and from the different socio-political cleavages and conflicts to which these issues will give rise. As several commentators have noted, while corporatist arrangements often face the threat of a collapse of labour support, they have also to be seen as subject to repeated renegotiation on account of the enlargement of the demands that unions believe that they can—and in their members' interests must—make in return for their participation (Martin, 1979; Lange, 1979; Schmitter, 1983; Goldthorpe, forthcoming). And already observable developments leave little doubt that among such new demands will be ones that imply an increasing entrenchment on basic institutional and structural features of capitalist society: for example, demands for greater public control over the extent and pattern of investment—witness the recent struggle over wage-earner funds in Sweden—or for the reorientation of various aspects of social policy on to more decisively egalitarian lines (cf. Esping-Andersen & Korpi, this volume). It may be unduly optimistic to suppose, as some authors have done (e.g. Stephens, 1979), that political bargaining via corporatist institutions—and under social-democratic hegemony—amounts in effect to a non-revolutionary mode of transition from capitalism to socialism. But, on the other hand, it would seem quite inadequate to regard corporatist tendencies in modern societies, in the manner of more orthodox Marxist writers, as reflecting no more than the latest or 'highest' form of the social control of labour under capitalism and as quite lacking in radical potential (e.g. Panitch, 1977b, 1981; Jessop, 1978). What corporatist institutions can be said to provide is a distinctive context within which the class conflicts of a capitalist society may be carried on. The eventual outcome of such conflicts will depend on the relative success of contending organizational leaderships in mobilizing and sustaining support within their constituencies; but under corporatism as here understood, labour attains a position in which it can at least make the attempt to convert its market strength into political measures designed to advance working-class interests in a wider-ranging and more permanent manner than could be achieved through action in the industrial sphere alone.[12]

In contrast, to the extent that dualist tendencies prevail, it must be questionable if such measures will be on the political agenda at all. From the standpoint of the unions, the first concern must be that of how best they can secure their labour-market power against the threats that dualism can pose. And what would in this respect seem crucial is which of two very different strategies national union movements aim to pursue: that is, whether they strive to uphold a class orientation, which must entail as far as possible opposing dualism—for example, by seeking legislation which can check employers' attempts to generate it and by regarding secondary workers, even if not union members, as still forming part of the unions' constituency; or whether, on the other hand, they in effect accept dualism and fall back on the defence of the specific sectional interests of their enrolled members, in the hope that these interests may then be as much protected as undermined by dualism through the 'shock-absorber' function that the secondary work-force performs (cf. Sengenberger, 1981).

While both these strategies have their own logic, there can be no doubt that it is the first which is by far the more difficult to implement. Thus, for example, in the course of the 1970s the Italian unions sought to use a significant increase in their labour-market strength and in their organizational unity as a basis for a new departure into political bargaining, in which their objectives were explicitly conceived in terms of broad class interests and solidarity. Their 'core' membership, comprising mainly industrial workers in the North, were to exercise restraint in pay negotiations in return for reforms in social policy and government efforts to expand and redirect investment so as to improve labour-market prospects for workers in the Mezzogiorno and also for women and young people (Regini, 1982). In the event, however, this initiative proved disappointing to the unions in that government largely failed to deliver (Lange et al., 1982; Regini, this volume); and in more recent attempts to secure a 'political exchange'—in which their own position has been weaker than before—it is notable that the unions have clearly reduced their ambitions and concentrated far more on safeguarding the employment of their core members themselves (Regini, 1984). Furthermore, what must in turn become open to question, if the ideological basis of the period of *solidarietà nazionale* is now eroding, is whether political bargaining on *any* terms will prove to be sustainable in the face of the inevitable sectionalist pressures for a return to unrestrained labour-market action, which the prevalence of dualism can only accentuate.[13] As is well brought out by several commentators on the present-day West German situation, the possibility of dispersing the costs of economic adjustment within a pool of secondary labour, rather than 'internalizing' them, is a powerfully attractive one to union movements, even where they possess some tradition of more solidaristic strategies (Sengenberger, 1981, 1983; Brandt, 1984; Streeck, this volume). What may be envisaged in the West German case, and perhaps elsewhere, it has been suggested, is the progressive 'Japanization' of the economy, in the sense of the development of extensive dualism alongside the growing involvement of members of the primary work-force in various forms of 'microcorporatism' at the level of plants and enterprises. To the extent, that national union movements do thus accommodate to dualism, there is only one long-term result that may be expected: that is—in direct contrast to the prospect of creative, if stressful, conflict afforded by political bargaining—the fundamental division and effective depoliticization of the working class, with the concomitant disappearance of any organized challenge to the capitalist order in the name of economic democracy and social equality.

In sum, what may be maintained is that over recent decades Western capitalist societies have moved in divergent directions in their responses to economic problems and further that, in consequence, they now face different sets of political choices in which 'real ideological alternatives' are in fact inherent. Which alternatives will be pursued, to what extent, and with what degree of success are questions that cannot be answered in advance and will be determined only by the future course of political action in particular nations. But what may at least be said is that there is no longer any reason for supposing, in the manner of the liberal theorists of industrialism, that either the course or the results of such action will be so constrained by the functional requirements of modern economies that 'the road ahead', whatever actors' goals may be, must lead to the one ultimate destination of pluralistic industrialism. On the contrary, it is the difficulties that have been encountered in reconciling the expression of pluralism within a capitalist society with the efficient working of the capitalist economy that have chiefly energized the corporatist and dualist departures from pluralism that are now evident. To future observers of the Western capitalist world, it may well appear that the failure of a nation to achieve decisive modifications of the pluralist model—in one direction or another—is the typical concomitant of persisting economic decline.

Notes

1. The following draws on the works by Aron, Kerr *et al.* and Parsons already cited; cf. also the more specific discussions of industrialism and stratification found in Lipset (1969) and Treiman (1970).

2. It is of particular importance to the argument being advanced here that the tendencies described were ones which progressively emerged over the post-war years—thus clearly prefiguring the 'stagflation' widely experienced in the 1970s, and in turn constituting strong evidence against the claim (cf. OECD, 1977) that the declining performance of Western economies could be largely understood in terms of an unfortunate coincidence of 'external shocks' plus policy errors. As Cagan has noted for the US (1979, ch. 1; cf. Sachs, 1980)— and the same observation could be made more generally—what was distinctive about the inflations of the post-war years was not the rate of price increases, but rather the fact that in intervening recessionary periods prices hardly declined at all—or even continued to rise. Cf. also Olson (1982: 219–20).

3. This argument obviously owes much to the critiques of the liberal pluralist model of interest representation which has been presented by authors such as Schmitter (1974, 1981, 1983), Berger (1981) and Lehmbruch (1983), at the same time as they have drawn attention to the development of new corporatist tendencies in the general sense here intended. However, it could be said that one source of the confusion attending current debates on corporatism has been a tendency of some critics of the pluralist model to exaggerate the extent to which its exponents would see government as no more than an 'inert' recipient of group pressures (cf. Martin, 1983). The issues are clarified in so far as critical emphasis is placed on the inadequacies of the pluralist model in recognizing (i) the role that governments may play in the concertation of interests; (ii) the role that organizations may play in the formulation of interests and in their 'intermediation' (Schmitter 1974) as distinct from *either* simply representing interests *or* controlling or disciplining their members; and (iii) the qualitative difference that exists between classic pressure-group politics—even where this involves some degree of 'symbiosis' between a private interest and an agency of government—and a situation in which government engages in concerted political bargaining with two or more competing or conflicting organizations, each of which has a 'capacity for strategy' (Pizzorno, 1978b) and can engage in interest intermediation.

4. It is important to note that although liberal writers—such as Ross and Hartman— themselves argued that increased possibilities for political action on the part of unions was a factor in reducing the recourse to strikes, the political action they had in mind was clearly that of unions acting as pressure groups—seeking improved labour legislation, social welfare provision etc.—while continuing to engage in free collective bargaining. What, however, may now be said—in the light of the industrial relations record of the 1960s and 1970s—is that the development of institutional arrangements facilitating this latter pattern of union behaviour, rather than the trade-off of labour-market for political-bargaining strength, need in no way be conducive to the 'withering away' of the strike. This point is one quite over-looked in Batstone's recent (1984) attempt to rehabilitate Ross and Hartman.

5. It is in this connection of interest to note Lehmbruch's (1983) critique of the thesis advanced by Almond and Powell (1966) that a linear relationship exists between the degree of 'sub-system autonomy' within a total political system and that system's problem-solving capacities. Rather, Lehmbruch suggests, the relationship may be a U-shaped one. Although the low level of sub-system autonomy found within Eastern European socialist societies can be regarded as having negative consequences, so too may the high level found in, say, the USA—while some Western European polities have been increasing their capacities by

moving towards an intermediate position of 'limited' sub-system autonomy. As Lehmbruch observes, there are very obvious affinities betwen the conception of a polity with high sub-system autonomy and the pluralist model of interest representation (cf. also Almond, 1970).

6. Dualism, no less than corporatism, is a concept which in the recent past has aroused a great deal of fervent, but often not very illuminating, debate—for valuable critical reviews see Cain (1976) and Hodson and Kaufman (1982). It must therefore be stressed that the way in which the concept is used here does *not* imply any commitment to the idea of dual— or segmented—labour markets which are identifiable either by the existence of strong barriers to mobility betwen them or (necessarily) by differing returns to labour of similar quality and productive potential. What rather is crucial is, in a phrase, the degree to which labour is commodified: or, that is, the degree to which workers' wages, conditions, work-tasks, job-security etc. are exposed to the effects of market forces and to the exercise of employers'—or their managements'—prerogatives, rather than being protected by legislation, by work-rules embodied in collective agreements (or custom and practice), or simply by a capacity for organized action. Although it is, in principle, possible for this degree of exposure or protection to vary continuously, the central argument of the paper leads to the expectation that at least a marked 'bimodality' will tend empirically to be found. There is an obvious affinity between the dualism here suggested and that implicit in Hicks's (1974) distinction between the 'fix-price' and 'flex-price' sectors of modern economics (cf. also Olson, 1983).

7. It is of interest to note that in the rather exceptional British case, in which, up to the passing of the Immigration Act of 1971, Commonwealth migrants could generally lay claim to citizenship and Irish migrants hold a special status, it was never government policy—as it often was in other Western European countries—to give positive encouragement to the inflow of migrant workers for specifically economic reasons. For an insightful comparison of the British and French cases, see Freeman (1979).

8. For arguments on the extent to which migrant workers may or may not be usefully regarded as constituting an 'industrial reserve army', cf. Rosenberg (1977) and Lever-Tracy (1983). The crucial issue is of course how far migrants may be seen as potentially sub-stitutable for, rather than as essentially complementary to, native labour.

9. This is not to deny that employers may—even in the absence of unions—accord to at least some part of their labour force conditions of employment similar to those that unions would seek to obtain. One motivation for this may be to forestall unionization; but, in addition, employers may well feel that they can thus derive real advantages by winning the goodwill and co-operativeness of certain key groups of workers. Cf. Thurow (1980, ch. 3). It may be added that in their earlier writings Kerr, Dunlop, and other American authors who subsequently became leading exponents of the theory of pluralistic industrial-ism emphasized the advantages to employers of developing 'internal' labour markets, which operated almost independently of 'external' ones; and in this way they can in fact be regarded as among the pioneers of an interest in economic dualism (cf. Cain, 1976). Yet, strangely, this idea is, as already noted, almost entirely excluded from their later work.

10. A tendency on the part of employers to 'decentralize' production in ways often involving increased subcontracting is, however, evident in many other Western industrial societies (cf. Wilkinson ed., 1981).

11. It should not, for example, be supposed that migrant workers eligible for citizenship of their host nations will generally wish to take this up—as is shown by recent experience in West Germany. It should also be added here that to the extent that migrant workers *have* engaged in collective political activity, this has—not surprisingly—been largely expressed outside the accepted channels of parliamentary democracy. An important question for the future is that of the political orientations and modes of action of the second generation (cf. Miller, 1981).

12. It is, it may be noted, the Thatcher regime in Britain which has most decisively undermined orthodox Marxist interpretations of corporatism of the kind referred to in the text. Thatcher and her ideological mentors saw far more clearly than Marxists were apparently able to do the radical potential of new corporatist tendencies based on union involvement in political bargaining and have unremittingly opposed them. Arguments

presently being advanced by some British Marxists to the effect that sooner or later a 'monetarist corporatism' must emerge are, to say the least, implausible.

13. A more positive view than that implied here is presented by Regini (1984), who emphasizes that so far at least 'il dualismo non ha trionfato' and sees the possibility in the Italian case of some long-term coexistence of dualism with union involvement in political bargaining, albeit on relatively restricted terms.

Bibliography

Abele, Hanns, Ewald Nowotny, Stefan Schleicher and Georg Winkler, eds., (1982), *Handbuch der Österreichischen Wirtschaftspolitik*, Vienna: Manzsche Verlags-und Universitätsbuchhandlung.

Åberg, R., J. Selén and H. Tham (1984), 'Ekonomiska resurser' in R. Erikson and R. Åberg, eds., *Välfärd; Förändring*, Stockholm: Prisma.

Abert, James Goodear (1969), *Economic Policy and Planning in the Netherlands, 1950–1965*, New Haven: Yale University Press.

Adams, R. J., and C. H. Rummel (1977), 'Workers' Participation in Management in West Germany: Impact on the Worker, the Enterprise and the Trade Union', *Industrial Relations Journal*, 8.

Akkermans, Tinie and Peter Grootings (1978), 'From Corporatism to Polarisation: Elements of the Development of Dutch Industrial Relations' in Crouch and Pizzorno, eds. (1978).

Alber, J. (1980), 'The Development of the West German Welfare State', European University Institute, Florence.

——— (1982), *Von Armenhaus zum Wohlfartsstaat: Analysen zur Entwicklung der Sozialversicherung in Westeuropa*, Frankfurt a.M.: Campus.

Aldrich, Howard and David Whetten (1981), 'Organisation-Sets, Action-Sets and Networks: Making the Most of Simplicity' in Paul Nystrom and William Starbuck, eds., *Handbook of Organisational Design*, Oxford: Oxford University Press.

Almond, G. A. (1970), *Political Development: Essays in Heuristic Theory*, Boston: Little Brown.

——— and G. Powell (1966), *Comparative Politics: a Developmental Approach*, Boston: Little Brown.

Anckar, Dag and Voitto Helander, eds. (1983), *Consultation and Political Culture. Essays on the case of Finland*, Helsinki: The Finnish Society of Sciences.

Andersen, L. C. and J. L. Jordan (1968), 'Monetary and Fiscal Actions: A Test of Their Relative Importance in Economic Stabilisation', *Federal Reserve Bank of St. Louis Review*, 50.

Anderson, Charles (1977), 'Political Design and The Representation of Interests', *Comparative Political Studies* 10. Reprinted in Schmitter and Lehmbruch, eds. (1979).

Armingeon, Klaus (1983), *Neo-Korporatistische Einkommenspolitik*, Frankfurt a.M.: Haag and Herchen.

van Arnhem, J. M. Corina and Geurt J. Schotsman (1982), 'Do Parties Affect the Distribution of Incomes? The Case of Advanced Capitalist Democracies' in Castles, ed. (1982).

Aron, Raymond (1962), *Dix-huit leçons sur la société industrielle*, Paris: Gallimard.

——— (1968), *Progress and Disillusion: the Dialectics of Modern Society*, London: Pall Mall.

Aukrust, Odd (1977), 'Inflation in the Open Economy: A Norwegian Model' in Lawrence B. Krause and Walter S. Salant, eds., *Worldwide Inflation: Theory and Recent Experience*, Washington: Brookings Institution.

Axelrod, Robert and William D. Hamilton (1981), 'The Evolution of Co-operation', *Science*, 211.

Baldwin, Robert E. (1982), 'The Political Economy of Protectionism' in Bhagwati, ed. (1982).

Balogh, Thomas (1982), *The Irrelevance of Conventional Economics*. London: Weidenfeld and Nicolson.

Barbash, Jack (1972), *Trade Unions and National Economic Policy*, Baltimore: Johns Hopkins Press.

Barkin, Solomon, ed. (1975), *Worker Militancy and its Consequences, 1965-75*, New York: Praeger.

Barnes, Denis and Eileen Reid (1980), *Governments and Trade Unions. The British Experience 1964-79*, London: Heinemann Educational Books.

Barro, Robert J. and Herschel I. Grossman (1971), 'A General Disequilibrium Model of Income and Employment'. *American Economic Review*, 61.

Bartholomäi, R. (1977), 'Der Volksversicherungsplan der SPD' in Bartholomäi W. Bodenbender, H. Henkel and R. Hüttel, eds., *Sozialpolitik nach 1945*, Bonn: Verlag Neu Gesellschaft.

Batstone, E. V. (1984), *Working Order: Workplace Industrial Relations over Two Decades*, Oxford: Blackwell.

Bechhofer, Frank and Brian Elliott, eds. (1981), *The Petite Bourgeoisie*, London: Macmillan.

Beer, Samuel H. (1967), *British Politics in the Collectivist Age*, New York: Knopf.

Belassa, Bela (1980), 'Structural Change in Trade in Manufactured Goods between Industrial and Developing Countries'. World Bank Staff Working Paper 396.

Bell, Daniel (1976), *The Cultural Contradictions of Capitalism*, London: Heinemann.

Ben Ami, Schlomo (1983), *Fascism from Above: The Dictatorship of Primo De Rivera in Spain, 1923-1930*, Fairlawn, N.J.: Oxford University Press.

Berchthold, K. (1967), *Österreichische Parteiprogramme 1868-1966*, Vienna: Verlag fur Geschichte und Politik.

Berger, Suzanne (1981), 'The Uses of the Traditional Sector in Italy: Why Declining Classes Survive' in Bechhofer and Elliott, eds. (1981).

— ed. (1981), *Organizing Interests in Western Europe*, Cambridge: Cambridge Univeristy Press.

— and Michael J. Piore (1980), *Dualism and Discontinuity in Industrial Societies*, Cambridge: Cambridge University Press.

Bergmann, J. and S. Tokunaga, eds. (1984), *Industrial Relations in Transition*, Tokyo: University of Tokyo Press.

Bergstrom, Villy and Jan Södersten (1979a), 'Nominal and Real Profit in Swedish Industry'. *Skandinaviska Enskilda Banken Quarterly Review*, 1-2.

— (1979b), 'Have Profits in Industry Really Declined?' *Skandinaviska Enskilda Banken Quarterly Review*, 3-4.

Bernstein, Karen (1983), 'Britain and The International Monetary Fund, 1974-1979', Ph.D. dissertation, Stanford University.

Bertmar, Lars (1979), 'Profit measurement: A chaotic picture'. *Skandinaviska Enskilda Banken Quarterly Review*, 3-4.

— Magnus Forssblad, Anders Gutenbrant, Kenth Skogsvik, Per Wärnegård and Karin Åkerman (1979), 'Löner, Lönsamhet och Soliditet i Svenska Industriföretag' in SOU, *Löntagarna och Kapitaltillväxten 3*. Stockholm.

von Beyme, Klaus (1977), *Gewerkschaften und Arbeitsbeziehungen in Kapitalistischen Ländern*, Munich: Piper.

— (1980), *Challenge to Power*, London: Sage.

Bhagwati, Jagdish (1982), 'Shifting Comparative Advantage, Protectionist Demands and Policy Response' in Bhagwati, ed. (1982).

— ed. (1982), *Import Competition and Response,* Chicago: University of Chicago Press.

Billerbeck, Ulrich (1982), 'Gesundheitspolitik und Korporatismus' in Billerbeck, Rainer Erd, Otto Jacobi and Edwin Schudlich (eds.), *Korporatismus und gesellschaftliche Interessenvertretung,* Frankfurt a.M: Campus.

BIS (Bank for International Settlements) (annual), *Annual Report,* Basle.

Björklund, Anders and Bertil Holmlund (1981), 'The Structure and Dynamics of Unemployment: Sweden and United States' in *Studies in Labor Market Behavior: Sweden and the United States,* Stockholm: IUI Conference Reports.

Blackhurst, Richard, Nicolas Mariah and Jan Tumlir (1977), *Trade Liberalisation, Protectionism and Interdependence,* Geneva: GATT Studies in International Trade, 5.

Block, Fred (1977), *The Origins of International Economic Disorder,* Berkeley: University of California Press.

Blum, Albert A., ed. (1981), *International Handbook of Industrial Relations,* Westport: Greenwood.

Bornstein, Stephen and Peter Gourevitch (1983), 'Unions in a Declining Economy: The Case of the British TUC', Department of Politics, University of Montreal.

Boston, Jonathan (1983), 'The Theory and Practice of Voluntary Incomes Policies, with Particular Reference to the British Labour Government's Social Contract 1974–1979'. University of Oxford, D.Phil thesis.

Bradford, Colin, I., Jr. (1982a), 'The Rise of the NICs as Exporters on a Global Scale' in Turner *et al.* (1982).

— — (1982b), 'The NICs and World Economic Adjustment' in Turner *et al.* (1982).

Brandt, Gerhard (1984), 'Industrial Relations in the Federal Republic of Germany under Conditions of Economic Crisis' in Bergman and Tokunaga, eds. (1984).

Branson, William H. (1980), 'Trends in United States International Trade and Investment since World War II' in Feldstein, ed. (1980).

Brittan, Samuel (1977), *The Economic Contradictions of Democracy,* London: Temple Smith.

— — (1983), *The Role and Limits of Government: Essays in Political Economy.* London: Temple Smith.

Brock, W. A. and S. P. Magee (1978), 'The Economics of Special Interest Politics: the Case of the Tariff'. *American Economic Review, Papers and Proceedings,* 68.

Bruno, Michael and Jeffrey Sachs (forthcoming), *The Economics of Worldwide Stagflation.* Cambridge, Mass.: Harvard University Press.

Brusco, Sebastiano (1982), 'The Emilian Model: Productive Decentralisation and Social Integration'. *Cambridge Journal of Economics,* 6.

— — and Charles Sabel (1981), 'Artisan Production and Economic Growth' in Wilkinson, ed. (1981).

Bundesministerium für Soziale Verwaltung (1979), *Kampf Gegen die Armut in Österreich,* Vienna.

— — (1982), *Soziale Struktur Österreichs,* Vienna.

— — (1983), *Bericht über die Soziale Lage 1982,* Vienna.

Busch-Lüty, Christiane (1964), *Gesamtwirtschaftliche Lohnpolitik: Möglichkeiten und Grenzen. Untersucht am Beispiel der Niederlande, Schwedens und Österreichs,* Basle: Kyklos.

Butt, Ronald (1969), *The Power of Parliament*, 2nd ed., London: Constable.
BWS (Beirat für Wirtschafts-und Sozialfragen) (1981), *Wohnbau*, Vienna.

Cagan, Phillip (1979), *Persistent Inflation: Historical and Policy Essays*, New York: Columbia University Press.
Cain, Glen G. (1976), 'The Challenge of Segmented Labour Market Theories to Orthodox Theory: a Survey'. *Journal of Economic Literature*, 14.
Calleo, David P. (1982), *The Imperious Economy*, Cambridge, Mass.: Harvard University Press.
Calmfors, Lars (1983), 'Stabilization Policy and Wage Formation in the Smaller European Economies'. Centre for European Studies, Brussels.
Cameron, David (1978), 'The Expansion of the Public Economy: a Comparative Analysis'. *American Political Science Review*, 72.
— — (1982), 'On the Limits of the Public Economy'. *Annals*, 459.
Carrieri, Mimmo and Carlo Donolo (1983), 'Oltre l'orizzonte neo-corporatista: Alcuni scenari sul futuro politico del sindacato'. *Stato e Mercato*, 9.
Castles, Francis G. (1978), *The Social Democratic Image of Society*, London: Routledge.
— — (1982), 'The Impact of Parties on Public Expenditure' in Castles, ed. (1982).
— — ed. (1982), *The Impact of Parties*, London: Sage.
Castles, Stephen and Godula Kosack (1973), *Immigrant Workers and Class Structures in Western Europe*, Oxford: Oxford University Press.
Cella, G. Primo (1983), 'Tipologia e determinanti della conflittualita'. Paper presented at the AISRI Congress, Riva del Garda.
Cessari, Aldo (1983), *Pluralismo, Neocorporativismo, Neocontrattualismo*, Milan: Giuffrè.
Chaloupek, G and H. Ostleitner (1982), 'Einkommensverteilung und Verteilungs-politik in Österreich' in H. Fischer, ed., *Das Politische System Österreichs*, Vienna: Europaverlag.
Choi, Kwang (1983), 'A Statistical Test of Olson's Model' in Mueller, ed. (1983).
Clegg, H. A. (1960), *A New Approach to Industrial Democracy*, Oxford: Blackwell.
Coates, David (1980), *Labour in Power? A Study of The Labour Government, 1974–1979*, London: Longman.
Cohen, Stephen (1969), *Modern Capitalist Planning: The French Model*, Cambridge, Mass.: Harvard University Press.
Conrad, Wolfgang (1981), 'Germany' in Blum, ed. (1981).
Cordova, E. (1982), '"Workers" Participation in Decisions within Enterprises: Recent Trends and Problems'. *International Labour Review*, 121.
Cowart, Andrew T. (1978), 'The Economic Policies of European Governments'. *British Journal of Political Science*, 8.
Crouch, Colin (1977), *Class Conflict and The Industrial Relations Crisis*, London: Heinemann.
— — 1980, 'Varieties of Trade Union Weakness: Organised Labour and Capital Formation in Britain, Federal Germany and Sweden'. *West European Politics*, 3.
— — 1982, *Trade Unions: The Logic of Collective Action*, London: Fontana.
Crouch, Colin, ed. (1979), *State and Economy in Contemporary Capitalism*, London: Croom Helm.
Crouch, Colin and Alessandro Pizzorno, eds. (1978), *The Resurgence of Class Conflict in Western Europe since 1968*, London: Macmillan.

Crozier, Michel (1977), 'The Governability of West European Societies'. The Noel Buxton Lecture, University of Essex.
— — M. J., S. P. Huntington and Josi Watanubi (1975), The Crisis of Democracy, New York: New York University Press.
Czada, Roland (1983), 'Konsensbedingungen und Auswirkungen neo-korporatistischer Politikentwicklung'. Journal für Sozialforschung, 23.
Czada, Roland and Gerhard Lehmbruch (1981), 'Economic Policies and Societal Consensus Mobilization', University of Konstanz.

Daalder, Hans (1966), 'The Netherlands: Opposition in a Segmented Society' in Dahl, ed. (1966).
Dahl, Robert A., ed. (1966), Political Oppositions in Western Democracies, New Haven: Yale University Press.
Dahrendorf, R. (1967), Society and Democracy in Germany, New York: Anchor.
De Grazia, Raffaele (1980), 'Clandestine Employment: a Problem of our Times' International Labour Review, 119.
Delors, Jacques (1978), 'The Decline of French Planning' in Holland, ed. (1978).
Diamant, Alfred (1982), 'Industrial Democracy in Western Europe'. Paper presented at the Annual Meeting of The American Political Science Association, Denver.
DIW (Deutsches Institut für Wirtschaftsforschung) (1983a), Budgetpolitik Österreichs im Internationalen Vergleich, Berlin.
— — (1983b), 'Kapitalrentabilität der Investitionen im internationalen Vergleich' in DIW Wochenbericht, 22.
Downs, A. (1957), An Economic Theory of Democracy, New York: Harper and Row.

Edel, Matthew (1979), 'A Note on Collective Action, Marxism and The Prisoner's Dilemma'. Journal of Economic Issues, XIII.
Edgren, Gösta, Karl-Otto Faxén, and Clas-Erik Odhner (1973), Wage Formation and the Economy, London: Allen and Unwin.
Edinger, L. (1977), Politics in Germany, Boston: Little Brown.
Einaudi, Luigi (1933), La condotta economica e gli effetti sociali della guerra italiana. Bari and New Haven: La Terza.
Ekonomisk Översikt (1982), Bilag til Regeringens Proposition angående Statsförslaget för 1983, Finansministeriet, Helsinki.
Elliot, Brian and David McCrone (1982), 'The Social World of Petty Property' in Hollowell, ed. (1982).
Elmér, A. (1960), Folkpensioneringen i Sverige, Lund: Gleerup.
Elster, Jon (1979), Ulysses and the Sirens: Studies in Rationality and Irrationality, Cambridge: Cambridge University Press.
— — (1982), 'Marxism, Functionalism and Game Theory'. Theory and Society, 11.
— — (1984), Karl Marx: a Critical Examination, Cambridge: Cambridge University Press.
Elvander, Nils (1972a), Intresseorganisationerna i dagens Sverige: Andra reviderade upplagan, Lund: Gleerup.
— — (1972b), 'The Politics of Taxation in Sweden: 1945–1970'. Scandinavian Political Studies, 7.
— — (1974), 'In search of New Relationships: Parties, Unions and Salaried Employer Associations in Sweden'. Industrial and Labor Relations Review, 28.

Elvander, Nils (1979), *Scandinavian Social Democracy: Its Strength and Weaknesses*, Stockholm: Almqvist and Wiksell.

Engelmann, Frederick C. (1966), 'Austria: The Pooling of Opposition' in Dahl, ed. (1966).

Eppel, P. and H. Lotter (1982), *Dokumentation zur Österreichischen Zeitgesichte, 1955–1980*, Vienna: Jugend und Volk.

Erd, Rainer (1978), *Verrechtlichung industrieller Konflikte: Normative Rahmbedingungen des dualen Systems der Interessenvertretung*, Frankfurt a. M.: Campus.

Erikson, Robert, John H. Goldthorpe and Lucienne Portocarero (1983), 'Intergenerational Class Mobility and the Convergence Thesis'. *British Journal of Sociology*, 34.

Esping-Andersen, Gösta (1978), 'Social Class, Social Democracy and State Policy'. *Comparative Politics*, 11.

–– (1981), 'Politics against Markets: De-commodification in Social Policy'. Paper presented at the Arne Ryde Symposium on the Economics of Social Security, Lund.

–– (1984), *The Social Democratic Road to Power*, Princeton: Princeton University Press.

Esping-Andersen, Gösta and Walter Korpi (forthcoming), 'From Poor Relief to Institutional Welfare States' in Robert Erikson *et al.*, eds., *Welfare Research and Welfare Societies*, New York: Sharpe.

Esser, J., W. Fach and W. Vaeth (1983), *Krisenregulierung*, Frankfurt a. M.: Suhrkamp.

Estor, Marita (1965), *Der Sozial-Ökonomische Rat der niederländischen Wirtschaft*, Berlin: Duncker and Humblot.

Fausto, D. (1978), *Il Sistema Italiano di Sicurezza Sociale*, Bologna: Il Mulino.

Feldman, Gerald D. (1966), *Army, Industry, and the State in Germany, 1914–1918*, Princeton, N.J.: Princeton University Press.

–– (1970), 'German Business between War and Revolution: The Origins of the Stinnes-Legien Agreement' in Gerhard A. Ritter, ed., *Entstehung und Wandel der modernen Gesellschaft, Festschrift für Hans Rosenberg*, Berlin: Walter De Gruyter.

–– (1981), 'German Interest Group Alliances in War and Inflation, 1914–1923' in Berger, ed. (1981).

Feldstein, Martin, ed. (1980), *The American Economy in Transition*, Chicago: University of Chicago Press.

Fennema, Meindert and Huibert Schijf (1978/9), 'Analysing Interlocking Directorates: Theory and Methods'. *Social Networks*, 1.

Finansplan (Sweden) (1982), *Regeringens Proposition 1982/83*.

Flanagan, Robert J., David W. Soskice and Lloyd Ulman (1983), *Unionism, Economic Stabilization and Incomes Policies: European Experience*, Washington: Brookings Institution.

Freeman, Gary P. (1979), *Immigrant Labor and Racial Conflict in Industrial Societies*, Princeton: Princeton University Press.

Freeman, Richard B. (1980), 'Unionism and the Dispersion of Wages'. *Industrial and Labor Relations Review*, 34.

Freeman, Richard B. and James L. Medoff (1979), 'New Estimates of Private Sector Unionism in the United States'. *Industrial and Labor Relations Review*, 32.

Frey, Bruno (1966), 'Lohn- und Sparpolitik als optimale Gewerkschaftsstrategien' in *Jahrbuch für Sozialwissenschaften*, 17.
Friedman, Milton (1977), 'Inflation and Unemployment'. *Journal of Political Economy*, 85.
Frohlich, Norman and J. A. Oppenheimer (1978), *Modern Political Economy*, Englewood Cliffs, N.J.: Prentice-Hall.
Fromm, E. (1966), 'The Psychological Aspects of the Guaranteed Income' in R. Theobald, ed., *The Guaranteed Income*, New York: Doubleday.

Gardner, Richard (1956), *Sterling-Dollar Diplomacy*, New York: Oxford University Press.
Garrison, Charles B. and Anne Mayhew (1983), 'The Alleged Vietnam War Origins of the Current Inflation'. *Journal of Economic Issues*, 17.
Giersch, Herbert (1977), *Konjunktur- und Wachstumspolitik in der Offenen Wirtschaft*, Wiesbaden: Gabler.
Gigliobianco, Alfredo, and Michele Salvati (1980), *Il maggio francese e l'autunno caldo italiano: la risposta di due borghesie*, Bologna: Il Mulino.
Gilpin, Robert (1975), *US Power and the Multinational Corporation: The Political Economy of Direct Foreign Investment*, New York: Basic Books.
—— 1981, *War and Change in World Politics*, Cambridge: Cambridge University Press.
Giner, Salvador and Juan Salcedo (1978), 'Migrant Workers in European Social Structures' in Giner and Margaret S. Archer, eds., *Contemporary Europe: Social Structures and Cultural Patterns*, London: Weidenfeld and Nicolson.
Golden, Miriam (1983), 'Austerity and its Opposition: the Politics of Italian Organized Labor in the 1970s', Cornell University Ph.D. dissertation.
Goldthorpe, John H. (1962), 'Social Stratification in Industrial Society' in Paul Halmos, ed., *The Development of Industrial Societies*, Keele. *Sociological Review Monographs*, 8.
—— (1971), 'Theories of Industrial Society: Reflections on the Recrudescence of Historicism and the Future of Futurology'. *Archives européennes de sociologie*, 12.
—— (1974), 'Social Inequality, and Social Integration in Modern Britain' in Wedderburn, ed. (1974).
—— (1978), 'The Current Inflation: Towards a Sociological Account' in Hirsch and Goldthorpe, eds. (1978).
—— (1983), 'Social Mobility and Class Formation: on the Renewal of a Tradition in Sociological Theory'. CASMIN-Projekt, Universität Mannheim.
—— forthcoming, 'Problems of Political Economy after the End of the Post-War Period' in Maier, ed. (forthcoming).
Goldthorpe, John H. (with Catriona Llewellyn and Clive Payne) (1980), *Social Mobility and Class Structure in Modern Britain*, Oxford: Clarendon Press.
Goodwin, Crauford (1975), *Exhortation and Controls: The Search for a Wage-Price Policy, 1945–1971*, Washington, D.C.: Brookings Institution.
Gordon, David M., Richard Edwards and Michael Reich (1982), *Segmented Work, Divided Workers,* Cambridge: Cambridge University Press.
Gourevitch, Peter Alexis (1978), 'The Second Image Reversed: the International Sources of Domestic Politics'. *International Organization*, 32.

Hager, Wolfgang (1982), 'Protectionism and Autonomy: how to preserve Free Trade in Europe'. *International Affairs*, Summer.
Hall, Peter A. (1984), 'Patterns of Economic Policy: An Organizational Approach'

in S. Bernstein, D. Held and J. Krieger (eds.), *The State in Capitalist Europe*, London: Allen and Unwin.

Handler, Heinz (1982), 'Die Österreichische Hartwährungspolitik' in Abele *et al.* (1982).

Hanisch, Ted (1981), 'Markets and Politics in Wage Determination', Institut för Samfunnsförskning, Oslo.

Hankel, Wilhelm (1979), *Prosperität in der Krise. Eine Analyse der Wirtschaftspolitik in der Energiekrise am Beispiel Österreichs: Aktive Binnenbilanz durch passive Aussenbilanz,* Vienna: Molden.

— — (1983), 'Die Finanzkrise zwischen Nord und Süd: Gründe, Lehren, Schlussfolgerungen'. Wissenschaftszentrum, Berlin.

Harbison, Frederick and Charles A. Myers (1959), *Management in the Industrial World,* New York: McGraw-Hill.

Hardach, Gerd (1977), *The First World War, 1914–1918,* Berkeley: University of California Press.

Hardes, Heinz Dieter (1974), *Einkommenspolitik in der BRD. Stabilität und Gruppeninteressen: der Fall Konzertierte Aktion,* Frankfurt a.M.: Herder and Herder.

Hardin, Russell (1971), 'Collective Action as an Agreeable Prisoner's Dilemma'. *Behavioral Science,* 16.

— — (1982), *Collective Action,* Baltimore: Johns Hopkins Press.

Harrison, Reginald (1980), *Pluralism and Corporatism: The Political Evolution of Modern Democracies,* London: Allen and Unwin.

Hauck, K. (1981), 'Von einer Existenzsicherung zur Lebensstandardversicherung' in Bundesministerium für Arbeit und Sozialordnung, *Hundert Jahre Sozialversicherung,* Bonn: Bundesarbeitsblatt.

Hawley, Ellis (1966), *The New Deal and the Problem of Monopoly,* Princeton: Princeton University Press.

Headey, Bruce (1970), 'Trade Unions and National Wages Policies'. *Journal of Politics,* 32.

Heclo, H. (1974), *Modern Social Politics in Britain and Sweden,* New Haven: Yale University Press.

Hedborg, Anna and Rudolf Meidner (1984), *Modell Schweden: Konzept, Methoden und Erfahrungen einer Wohlfahrtsgesellschaft,* Frankfurt a.M.: Campus.

Heimann, E. (1980), *Soziale Theorie des Kapitalismus,* Frankfurt a.M.: Suhrkamp.

Hibbs, Douglas A., Jr. (1976), 'Industrial Conflict in Advanced Industrial Societies'. *American Political Science Review,* 70.

— — (1977), 'Political Parties and Macroeconomic Policy'. *American Political Science Review,* 71.

— — (1978), 'On the Political Economy of Long-Run Trends in Strike Activity'. *British Journal of Political Science,* 8.

— — (1979), 'Communication'. *American Political Science Review,* 73.

Hicks, J. R. (1964), *The Theory of Wages,* 2nd ed., London: Macmillan.

— — (1974), *The Crisis in Keynesian Economics,* Oxford: Blackwell.

Hill, T. K. (1979), *Profits and Rates of Return,* Paris: OECD.

Hirsch, Fred (1976), *Social Limits to Growth,* Cambridge, Mass., Harvard University Press.

— — (1978), 'The Ideological Underlay of Inflation' in Hirsch and Goldthorpe, eds. (1978).

— — and Michael Doyle (1977), 'Politicization in the World Economy: Necessary Conditions for an International Economic Order' in Hirsch, Doyle and Edward L. Morse, eds., *Alternatives to Monetary Disorder,* New York: McGraw Hill.

Hirsch, Fred and John H. Goldthorpe, eds. (1978), *The Political Economy of Inflation*, London: Martin Robertson.

Hirschman, Albert O. (1945), *National Power and The Structure of Foreign Trade*, Berkeley: University of California Press.

— — (1970), *Exit, Voice and Loyalty: Responses to Decline in Firms Organisations and States*, Cambridge, Mass.: Harvard University Press.

— — (1981), 'The Social and Political Matrix of Inflation: Elaborations on The Latin American Experience' in *Essays in Trespassing: Economics to Politics and Beyond*, Cambridge: Cambridge University Press.

Hockerts, H. (1981), 'German postwar social policies against the background of the Beveridge Plan' in W. J. Mommsen, ed., *The Emergence of the Welfare State in Britain and Germany*, London: Croom Helm.

Hodson, Randy and Robert L. Kaufman (1982), 'Economic Dualism: a Critical Review'. *American Sociological Review*, 47.

Hofmeister, H. (1981), 'Landesbericht Österreich' in P. A. Kohler and H. F. Zacher, eds., *Ein Jahrhundert Sozialversicherung in der Bundesrepublik Deutschland, Frankreich, Grossbritannien, Österreich und der Schweiz*, Berlin: Duncker & Humblot.

Hofstadter, Douglas R. (1983), 'Metamagical Themes', *Scientific American*, 248.

Hohn, H.-W. (1983), 'Interne Arbeitsmarkte und betriebliche Mitbestimmung: Tendenzen der sozialen Schliessung im "dualen" System der Interessenvertretung', Wissenschaftszentrum, Berlin.

— — and P. Windolf (1983), 'Selektion und Qualifikation: Die betriebliche Personalauswahl in der Krise'. Wissenschaftszentrum, Berlin.

Holland, Stuart, ed. (1978), *Beyond Capitalist Planning*, Oxford: Blackwell.

Hollowell, Peter, ed. (1982), *Property and Social Relations*, London: Heinemann.

Horowitz, Daniel L. (1963), *The Italian Labor Movement*, Cambridge, Mass., Harvard University Press.

Hotz, B. (1982), 'Productivity Differences and Industrial Relations Structures: Engineering Companies in the United Kingdom and the Federal Republic of Germany'. *Labour and Society*, 7.

Huntford, Roland (1971), *The New Totalitarians*, London: Penguin.

Hyman, Richard and Ian Brough (1975), *Social Values and Industrial Relations*, Oxford: Blackwell.

Hymer, Stephen (1972), 'The Internationalization of Capital'. *Journal of Economic Issues*, 6.

ILO (annual), *Yearbook of Labour Statistics*, Geneva.

Immergut, E. (1984), 'Between State and Market: The Case of Sickness Pay' in M. Rein and L. Rainwater, eds., *The Public-Private Interplay in Social Protection*, New York: Sharpe.

Ingelhart, R. (1977), *The Silent Revolution*, Princeton: Princeton University Press.

International Energy Agency (1982), *World Energy Outlook*, Paris: OECD.

International Monetary Fund (annual), *World Economic Outlook*, Washington D.C.

Jacobs, E., S. Orwell, P. Paterson and F. Weltz (1978), *The Approach to Industrial Change in Britain and Germany*, London: Anglo-German Foundation for the Study of Industrial Society.

Jay, Peter (1976), *A General Hypothesis of Employment, Inflation and Politics*, London: Institute of Economic Affairs.

Jessop, Bob (1977), 'Recent Theories of the Capitalist State'. *Cambridge Journal of Economics*, 1.
— — (1978), 'Capitalism and Democracy: the Best Possible Political Shell?' in Littlejohn *et al.*, eds. (1978).
Jocteau, Gian Carlo (1978), *La Magistratura e i conflitti di lavoro durante il fascismo 1926-1934*, Milan: Feltrinelli.
Johannesson, Jan (1979), 'Swedish Labour Market Policy During the 1960s and the 1970s', Wissenschaftszentrum, Berlin.
— — (1981), 'On the Composition of Swedish Labour Market Policy'. EFA, Stockholm.
Johansen, L. N. and O. P. Kristensen (1978), 'Corporatist Traits in Denmark, 1946-76', University of Arhus.
Johansson, Sten (1982), 'When is the Time Ripe?' *Political Power and Social Theory*, 3.
Johnston, T. L. (1962), *Collective Bargaining in Sweden*, Cambridge, Mass. Harvard University Press.
Jungen, E. (1931), *Socialpolitik och Socialism,* Stockholm: Tiden.

Kalecki, M. (1972), 'Political Aspects of Full Employment' in E. K. Hunt and J. G. Schwartz, eds., *A Critique of Economic Theory*, London: Penguin.
Karisch, Artur (1965), *Staat Parteien und Verbände in Österreichs Wirtschaftsordnung*, Vienna: Jupiter Verlag.
Katzenstein, Peter J. (1976), 'International Relations and Domestic Structures: Foreign Economic Policies of Advanced Industrial States'. *International Organisation*, 30.
— — (1983), 'The Small European States in The International Economy: Economic Dependence and Corporatist Politics' in J. Ruggie, ed., *The Antinomies of Interdependence*, New York: Columbia University Press.
— — (1984), *Corporatism and Change: Switzerland, Austria and The Politics of Industry*, Ithaca: Cornell University Press.
Katzenstein, Peter J. ed. (1978), *Between Power and Plenty: Foreign Economic Policies of Advanced Industrial States*, Madison: University of Wisconsin Press.
Kautsky, K. (1971), *The Class Struggle*, New York: Norton.
Keeler, John T. S. (1981), 'Corporatism and Official Union Hegemony: the case of French Agricultural Syndicalism' in Berger, ed. (1981).
Keohane, Robert O. (1978), 'Economics, Inflation and the Role of the State: Political Implications of the McCracken Report'. *World Politics*, 31.
— — (1979), 'U.S. Foreign Economic Policy toward other Advanced Capitalist States: The Struggle to Make Others Adjust' in Kenneth Oye, Donald Rothchild and Robert J. Lieber (eds.), *Eagle Entangled: U.S. Foreign Policy in a Complex World*, New York: Longman.
— — (1984), *After Hegemony: Cooperation and Discord in the World Political Economy*, Princeton: Princeton University Press.
— — (1985), 'The International Politics of the Great Inflation' in Lindberg and Maier, eds. (1985).
Kerr, Clark (1957), 'Collective Bargaining in Postwar Germany' in Sturmthal, ed. (1957).
— — (1983), *The Future of Industrial Societies*, Cambridge, Mass., Harvard University Press.
— — John T. Dunlop, Frederick H. Harbison and Charles A. Myers, (1960), (1973), *Industrialism and Industrial Man*, Cambridge, Mass., Harvard University Press, 2nd ed., London: Penguin.

Kindleberger, Charles P. (1967), *Europe's Postwar Growth: the Role of Labour Supply*, Cambridge, Mass., Harvard University Press.
— — (1974), *The World in Depression*, Berkeley: University of California Press.
Kirschen, E. S. and associates (1964), *Economic Policy in Our Time*, Amsterdam: North Holland.
Klose, Alfred (1970), *Ein Weg zur Sozialpartnerschaft: Das Österreichische Modell*, Vienna: Verlag fur Geschichte und Politik.
Knott, Jack H. (1981), *Managing the German Economy, Budgetary Politics in a Federal State*, Lexington, Mass., Heath.
Kolko, Gabriel (1968), *The Politics of War: The World and United States Foreign Policy, 1943-1945*, New York: Vintage Books.
Konjunkturläget (1983), *Reviderad Nationalbudget (April)*, Stockholm: Ekonomidepartementet och Konjunkturinstitutet.
Korpi, Walter (1978), *The Working Class in Welfare Capitalism: Work, Unions and Politics in Sweden*, London: Routledge.
— — (1980), 'Social Policy and Distributional Conflict in the Capitalist Democracies. A Preliminary Comparative Framework'. *West European Politics*. 3.
— — (1983), *The Democratic Class Struggle*, London: Routledge.
Korpi, Walter and Michael Shalev (1979), 'Strikes, Industrial Relations and Class Conflict in Capitalist Societies'. *British Journal of Sociology*, 30.
— — (1980), 'Strikes, Power and Politics in the Western Nations, 1900-1976'. *Political Power and Social Theory*, 1.
Kotthoff, H. (1979), 'Zum Verhältnis von Betriebsrat und Gewerkschaft: Ergebnisse einer empirischen Untersuchung' in J. Bergmann, ed., *Beiträge zur Soziologie der Gewerkschaften*, Frankfurt a.M.: Suhrkamp.
Kriesi, Hanspeter (1980), *Entscheidungsstrukturen und Entscheidungsprozesse in der Schweizer Politik*, Frankfurt a.M.: Campus.
— — (1982), 'The Structure of the Swiss Political System' in Lehmbruch and Schmitter, eds. (1982).
Krugman, Paul (1982), 'Trade in Differentiated Products and The Political Economy of Trade Liberalisation' in Bhagwati, ed. (1982).
Kuusi, P. (1964), *Social Policy for the Sixties*, Helsinki: Finnish Association for Social Policy.
Kvavik, Robert B. (1974), 'Interest Groups in a "Cooptive" Political System: The Case of Norway' in Martin O. Heisler ed., *Politics in Europe*, New York: McKay.
— — (1976), *Interest Groups in Norwegian Politics*, Oslo: Universitetsforlaget.

Lancaster, Kelvin (1973), 'The Dynamic Inefficiency of Capitalism'. *Journal of Political Economy*, 81.
Lang, Werner (1978), *Kooperative Gewerkschaften und Einkommenspolitik: Das Beispiel Osterreichs*, Frankfurt a.M.: Peter Lang.
Lange, Peter (1979), 'Sindacati, partiti, stato e liberal-corporativismo'. *Il Mulino*, 28.
Lange, Peter (1981), 'Consenting to Restraint'. Paper presented to The Annual Meeting of The American Political Science Association, New York.
— — (1983), 'Politiche die redditi e democrazia sindacale in Europa occidentale'. *Stato e Mercato*, 9.
— — (1984), *Union Democracy and Liberal Corporatism: Exit, Voice and Wage Regulation in Post-War Europe*, Ithaca: Cornell University Western Societies Program Monograph.
— — and Geoffrey Garrett (1983), 'Organizational and Political Determinants of

Economic Performance, 1974-1980'. Paper presented at the IV Conference of Europeanists, Washington, D.C.

—— George Ross and Maurizio Vannicelli (1982), *Unions, Change and Crisis: French and Italian Union Strategy and the Political Economy, 1945-1980*, London: Allen and Unwin.

Langer, E. (1982), *Wohnbauförderung und Wohnbaufinanzierung in Österreich*, Vienna: Bundeswirtschaftskammer.

Lauman, E. O. ed. (1970), *Social Stratification: Research and Theory for the 1970s*, Indianapolis: Bobbs Merrill.

Laver, Michael (1981), *The Politics of Private Desires*, New York: Penguin.

Lefranc, Georges (1967), *Le mouvement syndical sous la Troisième République*, Paris: Presses Universitaires de France.

—— (1969), *Le mouvement syndical de la libération aux événements de mai-juin 1968*, Paris: Presses Universitaires de France.

Lehmbruch, Gerhard (1977), 'Liberal Corporatism and Party Government'. *Comparative Political Studies*, 10. Reprinted in Schmitter and Lehmbruch, eds. (1979).

—— (1979a), 'Consociational Democracy, Class Conflict and the New Corporatism' in Schmitter and Lehmbruch, eds. (1979).

—— (1979b), 'Concluding Remarks: Problems for Future Research on Corporatist Intermediation and Policy Making' in Schmitter and Lehmbruch, eds. (1979).

—— (1982), 'Introduction: Neo-corporatism in Comparative Perspective' in Lehmbruch and Schmitter, eds. (1982).

—— (1983), 'Interest Intermediation in Capitalist and Socialist Systems'. *International Political Science Review*, 4.

—— (1984), *Österreichs sozialpartnerschaftliches System im internationalen Vergleich*, Vienna: Beirat für Wirtschafts-und Sozialfragen.

—— and Phillipe Schmitter, eds. (1982), *Patterns of Corporatist Policy-Making*, Beverly Hills: Sage.

Lensberg, Terje (1982), 'Kapitalavkastningsrater i norsk industri fra 1970-1978'. *Sosialøkonomen*, 36.

Lenski, G. (1966), *Power and Privilege: A Theory of Social Stratification*, New York: McGraw Hill.

Lester, Richard A. (1958), *As Unions Mature*, Princeton: Princeton University Press.

Lever-Tracy, Constance (1983), 'Immigrant Workers and Post-War Capitalism: In Reserve or Core Troops in the Front Line?'. *Politics and Society*, 12.

Lewin, Leif (1980), *Governing Trade Unions in Sweden*, Cambridge: Harvard University Press.

Lieberman, S. (1977), *The Growth of European Mixed Economies, 1945-1970*, New York: Wiley.

Lijphart, Arend (1968, 2nd. ed. 1975), *The Politics of Accommodation: Pluralism and Democracy in The Netherlands*, Berkeley: University of Carolina Press.

Lindbeck, Assar (1980), *Work Disincentives in the Welfare State*, Stockholm: Institute for International Economic Studies.

—— (1983), 'Interpreting Income Distribution in a Welfare State. The Case of Sweden'. *European Economic Review*, 21.

—— ed. (1979), *Inflation and Employment in Open Economies*, Amsterdam: North Holland.

Lindberg, Leon and Charles Maier, eds. |(1985), *The Politics of Inflation and Economic Stagnation*, Washington D.C.: Brookings Institution.

Lipset, S. M. (1969), *Revolution and Counter Revolution,* London: Heinemann.
— — and Stein Rokkan (1967), *Party Systems and Voter Alignments,* New York: Free Press.
Littlejohn, Gary, Barry Smart, John Wakeford and Nira Yuval-Davis, eds. (1978), *Power and the State,* London: Croom Helm.
Lockwood, David (1974), 'For T. H. Marshall'. *Sociology,* 8.
Loewenberg, G. (1978), 'The Development of the German Party System' in K. Cerny, ed., *Germany at the Polls,* Washington D.C.: American Enterprise Institute.
Lorwin, Val, R. (1954), *The French Labour Movement,* Cambridge, Mass.: Harvard University Press.
— — (1966), 'Belgium: Religion, Class, and Language in National Politics' in Dahl, ed. (1966).
Lucas, R. E. and Thomas J. Sargent (1981), *Rational Expectations and Econometric Practices,* Minneapolis: University of Minnesota Press.
Lyttelton, Adrian (1973), *The Seizure of Power: Fascism in Italy, 1919–1929,* London: Weidenfeld & Nicolson.

McConnell, Grant (1966), *Private Power and American Democracy,* New York: Knopf.
McKeown, Timothy (1982), 'The Rise and Decline of The Open Trading System of The Nineteenth Century', Ph.D. dissertation: Stanford University.
McKinnon, Ronald I. (1983), 'Why US Monetary Policy Should be Internationalised', Stanford University.
Maddison, A. (1982), *Phases of Capitalist Development,* Oxford: Oxford University Press.
Magee, Stephen P. (1982), 'Comment on Baldwin' in Bhagwati, ed. (1982).
Mai, Gunter (1983), 'Die Nationalsozialistische Betriebszellen-Organisation: Zum Verhältnis von Arbeiterschaft und Nationalsozialismus.' *Vierteljahrshefte fur Zeitgeschichte,* 4.
Maier, Charles S. (1975), *Recasting Bourgeois Europe: Stabilization in France, Germany, and Italy in the Decade after World War I,* Princeton: Princeton University Press.
— — (1978), 'The Politics of Productivity: Foundations of American Economic Policy after World War II' in Katzenstein, ed. (1978).
— — (1981), 'Fictitious Bonds of Wealth and Law: On The Theory and Practice of Interest Representation' in Berger, ed. (1981).
Maier, Charles S., ed. (forthcoming), *The Changing Boundaries of the Political,* Cambridge: Cambridge University Press.
Maier-Rigaud, Gerhard (1982), 'Die Fiktion vom Produktionspotential'. *Wirtschaftsdienst,* VII.
— — (1983), 'Der Zins, das Potential und der Aufschwung'. *Wirtschaftsdienst,* I.
Malinvaud, Edmond (1980), 'Macro-economic Rationing of Employment' in Malinvaud and J. P. Fitoussi, eds., *Unemployment in Western Countries,* London: Macmillan.
Marks, Gary W. (1983), 'Neocorporatism, Incomes Policy and Socialist Participation in Government'. Paper presented at the Annual Meeting of the American Political Science Association, Chicago.
Marin, Bernd (1981), 'Cooperative Interest Politics: Organizing Principles of Technocorporatism'. Vienna: Institut für Konfliktforschung.
— — (1982), *Die Paritätische Kommission: Aufgeklärter Technokorporatismus in Österreich,* Vienna: Internationale Publikationen.
— — (1983), 'Organizing Interests by Interest Organizations: Associational Pre-

requisites of Cooperation in Austria'. *International Political Science Review*, 4.

Marshall, T. H. (1950), *Citizenship and Social Class*. Cambridge: Cambridge University Press.

Martin, Andrew (1975), 'Labour Movement Parties and Inflation: Contrasting Responses in Britain and Sweden'. *Polity*, 7.

— — (1979), 'The Dynamics of Change in a Keynesian Political Economy: the Swedish Case and its Implications' in Crouch, ed. (1979).

— — (1985), 'Distributive Conflict, Inflation and Investment: The Swedish Case' in Lindberg and Maier, eds. (1985).

Martin, Penny Gill (1974), 'Strategic Opportunities and Limitations: The Norwegian Labour Party and the Trade Unions'. *Industrial and Labour Relations Review*, 28.

Martin, Ross M. (1983), 'Pluralism and the New Corporatism'. *Political Studies*, 31.

Marx, Karl (1852, 1963), *The Eighteenth Brumaire of Louis Bonaparte*, New York: International.

Mason, Timothy W. (1977), *Sozialpolitik im Dritten Reich. Arbeiterklasse und Volksgemeinschaft*, Opladen: Westdeutscher Verlag.

Matzner, Monika and Egon Matzner (1983), 'Wie Schweden die Krise bekampfen will'. *Die Zukunft*, 1.

Maull, Hans (1980), *Europe and World Energy*, London: Butterworth.

Meade, J. (1982), *Wage Fixing*, London: Allen and Unwin.

Medley, R. (1981), 'Monetary Stability and Industrial Adaptation in West Germany' in Joint Economic Committee, *Monetary Policy, Selective Credit Policy and Industrial Policy in France, Britain, West Germany and Sweden*, Washington, D.C.: United States Congress.

Meidner, Rudolf (with Anna Hedborg and Gunnar Fond) (1978), *Employee Investment Funds*, London: Allen and Unwin.

Messner, J. (1964), *Die Soziale Frage im Blickfeld der Irrwege von Gestern, die Sozialkämpfe von Heute, die Weltenscheidungen von Morgen*, Innsbruck: Tyrolia Verlag.

Meynaud, Jean (1963), *Les Organisations Professionelles en Suisse*, Lausanne: Payot.

Michon, François (1981), 'Dualism and the French Labour Market: Business Strategy, Non-standard Job Forms and Secondary Jobs', in Wilkinson, ed. (1981).

Middlemas, Keith (1979), *Politics in Industrial Society: The Experience of the British System Since 1911*, London: André Deutsch.

Miliband, Ralph (1961), *Parliamentary Socialism*, London: Allen and Unwin.

— — (1977), *Marxism and Politics*, Oxford: Oxford University Press.

Miller, D. (1982), 'Social Partnership and the Determinants of Workplace Independence in West Germany'. *British Journal of Industrial Relations*, 20.

Miller, Mark J. (1981), *Foreign Workers in Western Europe*, New York: Praeger.

Minkin, Lewis (1974), 'The British Labour Party and The Trade Unions: Crisis and Compact'. *Industrial and Labour Relations Review*, 28.

Misslbeck, Johannes (1983), *Der Österreichische Gewerkschaftsbund: Analyse einer korporatistischen Gewerkschaft*, Frankfurt a.M.: Wisslit Verlag.

Moore, Robert (1977), 'Migrants and the Class Structure of Western Europe' in Scase, ed. (1977).

Mueller, Dennis C., ed. (1983), *The Political Economy of Growth*, New Haven: Yale University Press.

Müller-Jentsch, Walter and Hans Joachim Sperling (1978), 'Economic Development, Labour Conflicts and the Industrial Relations System in West Germany' in Crouch and Pizzorno, eds. (1978).
Muhr, Gerd (1977), 'Sozialpolitik der Nachkriegszeit-Betrachtungen aus der Sicht des DGB' in Bartholomäi *et al.*, eds. (1977).
Mutti, Antonio (1982), 'Lo scambio politico nelle relazioni industriali'. *Stato e Mercato*, 9.

Nasjonalbudsjettet (1983), *Nasjonalbudsjettet 1984*, Oslo: Storting melding, 1. Finans-og tolldepartmentet.
Nedelmann, Birgitta and Kurt G. Meier (1977), 'Theories of Contemporary Corporatism: Static or Dynamic?'. *Comparative Political Studies*, 10. Reprinted in Schmitter and Lehmbruch, eds. (1979).
Neumann, Manfred J. M. (1973), 'Zur relativen Bedeutung fiskalpolitischer und monetärer Impulse. Evidenz vom Konjunkturzyklus 1967–1971'. *WSI-Mitteilungen*, 1.
— — (1978), 'The Impulse-theoretic Explanation of Changing Inflation and Output Growth: Evidence from Germany' in K. Brunner and A. H. Meltzer, eds. *The Problem of Inflation*, Amsterdam: North Holland.
— — (1981), 'Der Beitrag der Geldpolitik zur Konjunkturellen Entwicklung in der Bundesrepublik Deutschland 1973–1980'. *Kyklos*, 34.
Nocken, Ulrich (1981), 'Korporatistische Theorien und Strukturen in der deutschen Geschichte des 19. und frühen 20. Jahrhunderts' in Ulrich von Alemann, ed., *Neokorporatismus*, Frankfurt a.M.: Campus.
Nowotny, Ewald (1979), 'Verstaatliche und Private Industrie in der Rezession—Gemeinsamkeiten und Unterschiede'. *Wirtschaft- und Sozialpolitische Zeitschrift des Instituts für Sozial- und Wirtschaftswissenschaft*, 3.
— — (1982), 'Institutionen und Entscheidungsstrukturen in der Österreichischen Wirtschaftspolitik' in Abele *et al.* eds. (1982).

Offe, Claus (1981), 'The Attribution of Public Status to Interest Groups: Observations on The West German Case' in Berger, ed. (1981).
— — and Helmut Wiesenthal (1980), 'Two Logics of Collective Action: Theoretical Notes on Social Class and Organisational Form'. *Political Power and Social Theory* 1.
— —, K. Hinricks, and H. Wiesenthal, eds. (1982), *Arbeitszeitpolitik: Formen und Folgen einer Neuverteilung der Arbeitszeit*, Frankfurt a.M.: Campus.
Olsen, Johan P. (1983), *Organized Democracy: Political Institutions in a Welfare State–The Case of Norway*, Oslo: Universtetsforlaget.
Olson, Mancur (1965), *The Logic of Collective Action*, Cambridge Mass., Harvard University Press.
Olson, Mancur (1982), *The Rise and Decline of Nations*, New Haven: Yale University Press.
— — (1983), 'Beyond Keynesianism and Monetarism', Wissenschaftszentrum, Berlin.
OECD (Organisation for Economic Cooperation and Development) (1977), *Towards Full Employment and Price Stability*, Paris.
— — (1979), *The Impact of the Newly Industrializing Countries on Production and Trade in Manufactures*, Paris.
— — (1980), *Review of Integrated Social Policy in Austria*, Paris.
— — (1982a), *Economic Survey: Denmark*, Paris.
— — (1982b), *Economic Survey: Sweden*, Paris.

OECD (1982c), *Employment in The Public Sector*, Paris.
— — (1983a), *Economic Survey: Denmark*, Paris.
— — (1983b), *Economic Outlook 33*, Paris.
Ostry, Sylvia, John Llewellyn and Lee Samuelson (1982), 'The Cost of OPEC II'. *OECD Observer*, 115.
Oualid, William and Charles Picquenard (1928), *Salaries et tariffes, conventions collectives et grèves. La politique du Ministere de l'Armement*, New Haven: Yale University Press.

Paci, Massimo (1973), *Mercato del lavoro e classi sociali in Italia*, Bologna: Il Mulino.
— — (1979), 'Class Structure in Italian Society', *Archives européennes de sociologie*, 20.
Panitch, Leo (1976), *Social Democracy and Industrial Militancy: The Labour Party, the Trade Unions and Incomes Policy, 1945–1974*, Cambridge: Cambridge University Press.
— — (1977a) 'The Development of Corporatism in Liberal Democracies'. *Comparative Political Studies*, 10. Reprinted in Schmitter and Lehmbruch, eds. (1979).
— — (1977b), 'Profits and Politics: Labour and the Crisis of British Corporatism' *Politics and Society*, 7.
— — (1980), 'Recent Theorizations of Corporatism: Reflections on a Growth Industry'. *British Journal of Sociology*, 31.
— — (1981), 'Trade Unions and the Capitalist State', *New Left Review*, 125.
Parsons, Talcott (1959), '"Voting" and the Equilibrium of the American Political System' in E. Burdick and A. Brodbeck, eds., *American Voting Behavior*, Glencoe: Free Press.
— — (1964), 'Evolutionary Universals in Society', *American Sociological Review*, 29.
— — (1966), *Societies: Evolutionary and Comparative Perspectives*, Englewood Cliffs: Prentice Hall.
Pelinka, Anton (1980), *Gewerkschaften im Parteienstaat. Ein Vergleich Zwischen dem Deutschen und dem Österreichischen Gewerkschaftsbund*, Berlin: Duncker and Humblot.
Pempel, T. J. and Ki'ichi Tsunekawa (1979), 'Corporatism without Labour? The Japanese Anomaly' in Schmitter and Lehmbruch, eds. (1979).
Perulli, Paolo (1982), 'Negoziato, politico e negoziato contrattuale (1975–1982)', *Problemi del socialismo*, XXIII.
Phelps Brown, Henry (1975), 'A Non-Monetarist View of the Pay Explosion', *Three Banks Review*, 105.
— — (1977), *The Inequality of Pay*, Oxford: Oxford University Press.
Phillips, A. W. (1958), 'The Relation Between Unemployment and the Rate of Change of Money Wage Rates in the United Kingdom, 1861–1957'. *Economica*, XXV.
Pichelmann, Karl and Michael Wagner (1983), 'Full Employment at All Costs: Trends in Employment and Labour-Market Policy in Austria 1975–1983', Vienna: Institut für Höhere Studien.
Pimlott, Ben (1977), *Labour and the Left in the 1930s*, Cambridge: Cambridge University Press.
Piore, Michael (1979), *Birds of Passage: Migrant Labour and Industrial Societies*, Cambridge: Cambridge University Press.
Piore, Michael, ed. (1979), *Inflation and Unemployment: Institutionalist and Structuralist Views*, White Plains, N.Y.: Sharpe.

Pizzorno, Alessandro (1978a), 'Le due logiche dell' azione di classe' in Pizzorno, E. Reyneri, M. Regini and I. Regalia, *Lotte operaie e sindacato: il ciclo 1968-72 in Italia*, Bologna: Il Mulino.

—— (1978b), 'Political Exchange and Collective Identity in Industrial Conflict' in Crouch and Pizzorno, eds. (1978).

—— (1980), *I soggetti del pluralismo*, Bologna: Il Mulino.

—— (1981), 'Interests and Parties in Pluralism' in Berger, ed. (1981).

—— (1983), 'Sulla razionalita della scelta democratica'. *Stato e Mercato*, 7.

Polanyi, Karl (1944), *The Great Transformation*, Boston: Beacon Press.

Pollan, Wolfgang (1982), 'Lohnpolitik und Einkommensverteilung' in Abele *et al.*, eds. (1982).

Pontryagin, L. S., V. G. Boltynaskii, R. V. Gamkrelidze and E. F. Mishchenko (1964), *The Mathematical Theory of Optimal Processes*, Oxford: Pergamon.

Preller, L. (1949), *Sozialpolitik in der Weimarer Republik*, Stuttgart: Mittelbach Verlag.

Procacci, Giovanna, ed. (1983), *Stato e classe operaia in Italia durante la Prima Guerra Mondiale*, Milan: Franco Angeli.

Przeworski, Adam and Michael Wallerstein (1982a), 'The Structure of Class Conflict in Democratic Capitalist Societies'. *American Political Sciencce Review*, 76.

—— (1982b), 'Democratic Capitalism at the Crossroads'. *Democracy*, July.

Putz, Theodor, ed. (1966), *Verbände und Wirtschaftspolitik in Österreich*, Berlin: Duncker and Humblot.

Rainwater, Lee, ed. (1974), *Inequality and Justice*, Chicago: Aldine.

Rasmussen, E. (1933), 'Socialdemokratiets Stilling til det Sociale Sporgsmaal, 1890-1901' in P. Engelstoft and H. Jensen, eds. *Maend og Meninger i Dansk Socialpolitik 1866-1901*, Copenhagen: Nordisk Forlag.

Regalia, Ida (1984), 'Le politiche del lavoro' in U. Ascoli, ed., *Welfare State all' italiana*, Bari: Laterza.

Regini, Marino (1979), 'Labour Unions, Industrial Action and Politics' in P. Lange and S. Tarrow, eds., *Italy in Transition*. London: Cass.

—— (1981), 'Sindacati e stato nell 'Europa occidentale'. *Democrazia e diritto*, XXI.

—— (1982), 'Changing Relationships Between Labour and the State in Italy: Towards a Neo-Corporatist System?' in Lehmbruch and Schmitter, eds. (1982).

—— (1983), 'The Crisis of Representation in Class-Oriented Unions: Some Reflections Based on The Italian Case' in S. Clegg, G. Dow and P. Boreham, eds., *The State, Class and The Recession*, London: Croom Helm.

—— (1984), 'I tentativi italiani di patto sociale a cavallo degli anni ottanta'. *Il Mulino*, 33.

—— and Gloria Regonini (1981), 'La politica delle pensioni in Italia: il ruolo del movimento sindacale'. *Giornale di diritto del lavoro e di relazioni industriali*, III.

Riemer, Jeremiah M. (1982), 'Alterations in the Design of Model Germany: Critical Innovations in the Policy Machinery for Economic Steering' in Andrei S. Markovits, ed., *The Political Economy of West Germany: Modell Deutschland*, New York: Praeger.

Rimlinger, G. (1971), *Welfare and Industrialization in Europe, America and Russia*, New York: Wiley.

—— (1983), 'Capitalism and Human Rights', *Daedelus*, Fall.

Risch, Bodo (1983), 'Ein Vorschlag für eine beschäftigungswirksame Neurege-
lung der Arbeitslosenversicherung'. *Wirtschaftsdienst*, V.
Rist, Ray C. (1979), 'Migration and Marginality: Guestworkers in Germany and
France'. *Daedalus*, Spring.
Rokkan, Stein (1966), 'Norway: Numerical Democracy and Corporate Pluralism'
in Dahl, ed. (1966).
Rose, Richard (1980), *Do Parties Make a Difference?*, London: Chatham House.
Rosenberg, Sam (1977), 'The Marxian Reserve Army of Labor and the Dual
Labour Market'. *Politics and Society*, 7.
Ross, Arthur M. and Paul T. Hartman (1960), *Changing Patterns of Industrial
Conflict*, New York: Wiley.
Ruggie, John Gerard (1982), 'International Regimes, Transactions and Change:
Embedded Liberalism in The Postwar Economic Order'. *International
Organisation*, 36.
Rustow, Dankwart (1955), *The Politics of Compromise: A Study of Parties and
Cabinet Government in Sweden*, Princeton: Princeton University Press.

Sabel, Charles F. (1981), 'The Internal Politics of Trade Unions' in Berger, ed.
(1981).
Sachs, Jeffrey D. (1979), 'Wages, Profits and Macroeconomic Adjustment: A
Comparative Study' *Brookings Papers on Economic Activity*.
— — (1980), 'The Changing Cyclical Behaviour of Wages and Prices 1890–1976'.
American Economic Review, 70.
— — (1983), 'Real Wages and Unemployment in the OECD Countries', *Brookings
Papers on Economic Activity*.
— — (1984), 'Labour Markets and Comparative Macro-economic Performance' in
Sachs and Michael Bruno, *A Study in Stagflation*.
Sachverständigenrat (1982), *Sachverständigenrat zur Begutachtung der gesamst-
wirtschaftlichen Entwicklung: Gegen Pessimismus*, Stuttgart/Mainz: Kohl-
hammer.
Salant, Walter S. (1977), 'International Transmission of Inflation' in Laurence
B. Krause and Salant, eds., *Worldwide Inflation: Theory and Recent Ex-
perience* Washington: Brookings Institution.
Salvati, Michele (1981), 'Ciclo politico e onde lunghe. Note su Kalecki e Phelps
Brown', *Stato e Mercato*, 1.
— — (1982), 'Strutture politiche ed esiti economici'. *Stato e Mercato*, 4.
Samuelson, Paul A. (1980), 'The Public Role in the Modern American Economy',
in Martin Feldstein ed., *The American Economy in Transition*, Chicago:
University of Chicago Press.
Sassoon, Donald (1982), 'Contratto sociale e stato sociale: Sindacato e sistema
politico nell' esperienza britannica'. *Problemi del socialismo*, XXIII.
Sawyer, Malcolm C. (1976), *Income Distribution in OECD Countries*, Paris:
OECD.
— — (1982), *Macro-Economics in Question: The Keynesian-Monetarist Ortho-
doxies and The Kaleckian Alternative*, Brighton: Wheatsheaf Books.
Scase, Richard, ed. (1977), *Industrial Society: Class, Cleavage and Control*,
London: Allen and Unwin.
— — and Robert Goffee (1980), *The Real World of the Small Business Owner*,
London: Croom Helm.
Schain, Martin A. (1980), 'Corporatism and Industrial Relations in France'
in G. Cerny and Schain, eds., *French Politics and Public Policy*, London:
Frances Pinter.

Scharpf, Fritz W. (1981), 'The Political Economy of Inflation and Unemployment in Western Europe: an Outline', Berlin: Wissenschaftszentrum.
—— (1983), 'Zur Bedeutung institutioneller Forschungsansätze' in Scharpf and M. Brockman eds., *Institutionelle Bedingungen der Arbeitsmarkt-und Beschäftigungspolitik,*/Frankfurt a.M.: Campus.
Schlesinger, Helmut (1977), 'Recent Developments in West German Monetary Policy' in S. F. Frowen, A. S. Courakis and M. H. Miller, eds., *Monetary Policy and Economic Activity in West Germany*, London: Surrey University Press.
Schmid, Günther (1982), 'Arbeitsmarktpolitik in Schweden und in der Bundesrepublik' in F. W. Scharpf *et al.*, eds., *Aktive Arbeitsmarktpolitik Erfahrungen und neue Wege*, Frankfurt a.M.: Campus.
Schmidt, Manfred G. (1982a), 'Does Corporatism Matter? Economic Crisis, Politics and Rates of Unemployment in Capitalist Democracies in the 1970s' in Lehmbruch and Schmitter, eds. (1982).
—— (1982b), 'The Role of the Parties in Shaping Macroeconomic Policy' in Castles, ed. (1982).
—— (1983), 'The Welfare State and The Economy in Periods of Economic Crisis: a Comparative Study of Twenty-Three OECD Nations'. *European Journal of Political Research*. 11.
Schmitter, Philippe, C. (1974), 'Still the Century of Corporatism?' *Review of Politics*, 36. Reprinted in Schmitter and Lehmbruch, eds. (1979).
—— (1977), 'Modes of Interest Intermediation and Models of Societal Change in Western Europe'. *Comparative Political Studies*, 10. Reprinted in Schmitter and Lehmbruch, eds. (1979).
—— (1981), 'Interest Intermediation and Regime Governability in Contemporary Western Europe and North America' in Berger, ed. (1981).
—— (1982), 'Reflections on Where the Theory of Neo-Corporatism Has Gone and Where the Preaxis of Neo-Corporatism May be Going' in Lehmbruch and Schmitter, eds. (1982).
—— (1983), '"Neo-Corporatism", "Consensus", "Governability" and "Democracy" in the Management of Crisis in Contemporary Advanced Industrial/ Capitalist Societies', Florence: European University Institute.
—— and Wolfgang Streeck (1981), 'The Organisation of Business Interests', Wissenschaftszentrum, Berlin.
—— and Gerhard Lehmbruch, eds. (1979), *Trends Toward Corporatist Intermediation*, Beverly Hills: Sage
Schorske, Carl E. (1955), *German Social Democracy, 1905-1917*, New York: Harper and Row.
Schott, Kerry (1984), *Policy, Power and Order: the Persistence of Economic Problems in Capitalist Economies*, New Haven: Yale University Press.
Schregle, Johannes (1976), 'Workers' Participation in Decisions Within Undertakings'. *International Labour Review*, 115.
Schumpeter, Joseph (.1943), *Capitalism, Socialism, and Democracy*, London: Allen and Unwin.
Schwerin, Don S. (1980a), 'The Limits of Organization as a Response to Wage-Price Problems' in Richard Rose, ed. *Challenge to Governance*, London: Sage.
—— (1980b), 'Norwegian and Danish incomes policies and European monetary integration'. *West European Politics*, 3.
—— (1981), *Corporatism and Protest: Organizational Politics in The Norwegian Trade Unions*, Kent, Ohio: Kent Popular Press.

Schwerin, Don S. (1982), 'Incomes policy in Norway: Second-best corporate institutions.' *Polity*, 14.

Scitovsky, Tibor (1978), 'Market Power and Inflation'. *Economica*, 45.

— — (1980), 'Can Capitalism Survive?—An Old Question in a New Setting'. *American Economic Review*, 70.

Scott, Maurice (with Robert A. Laslett) (1978), *Can We Get Back to Full Employment?* London: Macmillan.

Sen, A. K. (1974), 'Choice Orderings and Morality' in S. Korner, ed., *Practical Reason*, New Haven: Yale University Press.

— — (1977), 'Rational Fools: A Critique of the Behavioral Foundations of Economic Theory'. *Philosophy and Public Affairs*, 6.

Sengenberger, Werner (1981), 'Labour Market Segmentation and the Business Cycle' in Wilkinson, ed. (1981).

— — (1983), 'The Gradual Re-activation of the Labour Reserve Army Mechanism', Munich: Institut für Sozialwissenschaftliche Forschung.

Shalev, Michael (1978), 'Strikers and The State: A Comment'. *British Journal of Political Science*, 8.

— — (1983), 'Strikes and the Crisis: Industrial Conflict and Unemployment in the Western Nations'. *Economic and Industrial Democracy*, 4.

Shell, Kurt L. (1962), *The Transformation of Austrian Socialism*, New York: University Publishers.

Shonfield, Andrew (1965), *Modern Capitalism*, Oxford: Oxford University Press.

Shorter, Edward and Charles Tilly (1974), *Strikes in France 1830–1968*, Cambridge: Cambridge University Press.

Skocpol, T. and J. Ikenberry (1983), 'The Political Formation of the American Welfare State in Historical and Comparative Perspective'. *Comparative Social Research*, 6.

Solow, Robert M. (1979), 'Alternative Approaches to Macroeconomic Theory: a Partial View', *Canadian Journal of Economics*, 12.

Sontheimer, K. (1977), *Handbuch des Politischen Systems der Bundesrepublik*, Munich: Piper.

Spånt, R. (1976), 'Den Svenska inkomstfördelningens utveckling'. *Studia Oeconomica Uppsaliensia*, 4.

SPD (Sozialdemokratische Partei Deutschlands) (1957), *Sozialplan für Deutschland*, Berlin and Hanover: Dietz.

Stafford, F. (1981), 'Unemployment and Labor Market Policy in Sweden and The United States' in *Studies in Labor Market Behavior: Sweden and the United States*, Stockholm: IUI Conference Reports.

SOU (Statens Offentliga Utredningar) 1980, *Langtidsutredningen*. Stockholm: SOU.

— — 1982a, *En Effektivare Kreditpolitik*, Stockholm: SOU.

— — 1982b, *Tillväxt eller Stagnation?* Stockholm: SOU.

Stein, Leslie (1981), 'The Growth and Implications of LDC Manufactured Exports to Advanced Countries'. *Kyklos*, 34.

Stephens, John D. (1979), *The Transition from Capitalism to Socialism*, London: Macmillan.

Streeck, Wolfgang (1979), 'Gewerkschaftsorganisation und industrielle Beziehungen' in J. Matthes, ed., *Sozialer Wandel in Westeuropa*, Frankfurt a.M.: Campus.

— — (1981a) *Gewerkschaftliche Organisationsprobleme in der sozialstaatlichen Demokratie*, Koenigstein: Athenaeum.

Streeck, Wolfgang (1981b), 'Qualitative Demands and the Neo-Corporatist Manageability of Industrial Relations: Trade Unions and Industrial Relations in West Germany at the Beginning of the Eighties'. *British Journal of Industrial Relations*, 14.
—— (1982), 'Organizational Consequences of Corporatist Cooperation in West German Labor Unions' in Lehmbruch and Schmitter, eds. (1982).
—— (1984), 'Co-Determination: The Fourth Decade', *International Yearbook of Organizational Democracy*, II.
Sturmthal, Adolf, ed. (1957), *Contemporary Collective Bargaining in Seven Countries*, Ithaca: Cornell University Press.
—— (1983), *Left of Center: European Labor Since World War II*, Urbana, Ill.: University of Illinois Press.

Talos, E. (1981), *Staatliche Sozialpolitik in Österreich. Rekonstruktion und Analyse*, Vienna: Verlag für Gesellschaftskritik.
Tarling, Roger and Frank Wilkinson (1977), 'The Social Contract: Post-War Incomes Policies and their Inflationary Impact'. *Cambridge Journal of Economics*, 1.
Taylor, Michael (1976), *Anarchy and Cooperation*, New York: Wiley.
Tegtmeier, W. (1973), *Wirkungen der Mitbestimmung der Arbeitnehmer*, Göttingen: Vandenhoeck und Ruprecht.
Tennstedt, F. (1976), 'Sozialgeschichte der Sozialversicherung' in M. Blohmke *et al.* eds. *Handbuch der Sozialmedizin*, Stuttgart: Ferdinand Enke.
Teschner, E. (1977), *Lohnpolitik im Betrieb*, Frankfurt a.M.: Campus.
Thomson, Andrew W. J. (1981), 'Industrial Relations in Britain during the Period of Recession' in Ezio Tarantelli and Gerhard Wilke, eds., *The Management of of Industrial Conflict in the Recession of the 1970s*, Florence: Le Monnier.
Thurow, Lester C. (1980), *The Zero-Sum Society*, New York: Basic Books.
—— (1983), *Dangerous Currents: The State of Economics*, New York: Random House.
Tinbergen, Jan (1967), *Economic Policy: Principles and Design*, 4th ed., Amsterdam: North Holland.
Titmuss, R. M. (1974), *Social Policy*, London: Allen & Unwin.
Trapp, Peter (1976), *Geldmenge, Ausgaben und Preisanstieg in der Bundesrepublik Deutschland*, Tubingen: J. C. B. Mohr.
Traxler, F. (1982), *Evolution gewerkschaftlicher Interessenvertretung: Entwicklungslogik und Organisationsdynamik gewerkschaftlichen Handelns am Beispiel Österreich*, Vienna and Frankfurt: Braumuller and Campus.
Treiman, Donald (1970), 'Industrialization and Social Stratification' in Lauman, ed. (1970).
Tufte, Edward R. (1978), *Political Control of The Economy*, Princeton: Princeton University Press.
Turner, Louis and Neil McMullen, eds., (1982), *The Newly Industrializing Countries: Trade and Adjustment*, London: Allen and Unwin.
Turone, Sergio (1973), *Storia del Sindacato in Italia*, Bari: Laterza.

United Nations (1979), *Labour Supply and Migration in Europe: Demographic Dimensions 1950–1975 and Prospects*, New York: United Nations.
Uusitalo, Hannu (1983), 'Incomes Policy in Finland: Economic and Social Effects in a Comparative Perspective'. *Scandinavian Political Studies*, 6.

Verreydt, Eric and Jean Waelbroeck (1982), 'European Community Protection

Against Manufactured Imports from Developing Countries: a Case Study in The Political Economy of Protection' in Bhagwati, ed. (1982).

Villa, Paola (1981), 'Labour Market Segmentation and the Construction Industry in Italy' in Wilkinson, ed. (1981).

Vissa Ekonomisk-Politiska Åtgärder (1982), *Vissa ekonomiska-politiska Åtgärder m.m.* Regeringens Proposition.

Visser, Jelle (1983), 'The Unification and Centralisation of the Trade Union Movement: a Comparison of Ten Countries'. Paper presented at the Summer School of the European University Institute, Florence.

Wagner, Michael (1981), 'Massenarbeitslosigkeit bei niedrigem Wirtschaftswachstum: Die Erfahrungen Grossbritanniens'. *Journal für Sozialforschung*, 1.

Wallich, H. (1955), *Mainsprings of the German Revival*, New Haven: Yale University Press.

Walterskirschen, E. (1979), 'Die Entwicklung der Lohnunterschiede in Österreich'. WIFO *Monatsberichte*, 1.

Weber, Arnold R., and Daniel J. B. Mitchell (1978), *The Pay Board's Progress. Wage Controls in Phase II*, Washington, D.C.: Brookings Institution.

Wedderburn, Dorothy, ed. (1974), *Poverty, Inequality and Class Structure*, Cambridge: Cambridge University Press.

Weintraub, Sidney (1978), *Capitalism's Inflation and Unemployment Crisis*, Reading, Mass., Addison-Wesley.

von Weizsäcker, Carl-Christian (1978), 'Das Problem der Vollbeschäftigung heute', *Zeitschrift für Wirtschafts- und Sozialwissenschaften*, 98.

Wiesenthal, Helmut (1981), *Die Konzertierte Aktion im Gesundheitswesen*, Frankfurt a.M.: Campus.

Wigforss, E. (1932), *Har vi råd att arbeta?* Stockholm: Tiden.

Wilensky, Harold L. (1975), *The Welfare State and Equality: the Roots of Public Expenditures*, Berkeley, Cal.: University of California Press.

—— (1976), *The 'New Corporatism'. Centralisation and The Welfare State*, Beverly Hills: Sage.

—— (1981a) 'Democratic Corporatism, Consensus and Social Policy: Reflections on Changing Values and the "Crisis" of the Welfare State' in OECD, *The Welfare State in Crisis: An Account of The Conference on Social Policies in the 1980s*, Paris: OECD.

—— (1981b), 'Leftism, Catholicism, and Democratic Corporatism: The Role of Political Parties in Recent Welfare State Development' in P. Flora and A. J. Heidenheimer, ed., *The Development of Welfare States in Europe and America*, New Brunswick: Transaction Books.

Wilkinson, Frank, ed. (1981), *The Dynamics of Labour Market Segmentation*, London: Academic Press.

Windmuller, John P. (1957), 'Post-War Wage Determination in the Netherlands'. *Annals*, 310.

—— 1969, *Labor Relations in The Netherlands*, Ithaca: Cornell University Press.

—— (1981), 'Concentration Trends in Union Structure: An International Comparison', *Industrial and Labor Relations Review*, 35.

Winkler, Jack (1974), 'Corporatism', *Archives européennes de sociologie*, 15.

Woolcock, Stephen (1982), 'Adjustment in Western Europe' in Turner *et al.* (1982).

Wösendorfer, Johann (1980), *Arbeitsmarktpolitik: Beurteilungskriterien für das Arbeitsmarktförderungsgesetz*, Linz: Österreichisches Institut für Arbeitsmarktpolitik.

Zetterberg, H. (1983), 'The Victory of Reason—Max Weber Revisited' in Göran
    Cigén, Anders Lindblad und Rune Åberg eds., *Sociologi i brytningstid*, Umeå:
    Umeå Universitet.
Zinn, K. G. (1978), 'The Social Market in Crisis' in S. Holland, ed., *Beyond
    Capitalist Planning*, Oxford: Blackwell.
Zöllner, F. (1982), 'Germany' in P. Kohler and H. F. Zacher, eds., *A Century
    of Social Insurance*, Berlin: Duncker and Humblot.
Zysman, John (1983), *Government, Markets and Growth: Financial Systems and
    The Politics of Industrial Change*, Ithaca: Cornell University Press.

Index